The Searchers

ANDY BECKETT

The Searchers

Five Rebels, Their Dream of a Different Britain, and Their Many Enemies

ALLEN LANE
an imprint of
PENGUIN BOOKS

ALLEN LANE

UK | USA | Canada | Ireland | Australia
India | New Zealand | South Africa

Allen Lane is part of the Penguin Random House group of companies
whose addresses can be found at global.penguinrandomhouse.com.

Penguin
Random House
UK

First published by Allen Lane 2024
001

Copyright © Andy Beckett, 2024

The moral right of the author has been asserted

Set in 10.5/14pt Sabon LT Std
Typeset by Jouve (UK), Milton Keynes
Printed and bound in Great Britain by Clays Ltd, Elcograf S.p.A.

The authorized representative in the EEA is Penguin Random House Ireland,
Morrison Chambers, 32 Nassau Street, Dublin D02 YH68

A CIP catalogue record for this book is available from the British Library

ISBN: 978–0–241–39422–9

www.greenpenguin.co.uk

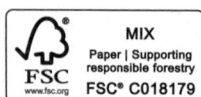

For Sara

Contents

CONTENTS

Introduction: Five Heretics

On 28 April 1983, Tony and Cherie Blair picked up a Labour politician in their car from his home in west London. The Blairs were still in their twenties, bright young barristers both trying to become Labour MPs. The politician, who was twice their age, and a friend of Cherie's father, the actor Tony Booth, had agreed to speak alongside Cherie at a rally. She had been chosen as the Labour candidate for Thanet North, a new constituency in Kent.

Although it was her first candidacy, her expectations were not that high. Thanet North consisted of a strip of coastal towns in the far east of the county, running from Herne Bay to Margate, with lots of retirees who usually voted Tory. The local Labour party was small and quiet. Nationally, the Tories were well ahead of Labour in the polls, as Margaret Thatcher's government basked in its recent victory in the Falklands, and the prime minister was expected to call a general election at any moment. The best result that Cherie could realistically hope for was a respectable second place: the traditional first step towards contesting an easier seat next time. As the impatient young Blairs endured the slow, two-and-a-half-hour drive from west London to east Kent, they hoped that their passenger would help bring about both those outcomes.

He was a former cabinet minister, and for a long time had been considered a possible Labour leader and prime minister. But his rise in the party had recently stalled. 'I am very, very depressed,' he had recorded in his diary a few weeks before the Thanet trip. 'I feel . . . a sense of isolation . . . uncertain about the future.' His relationship with some of the ambitious newcomers to the party, such as the Blairs, was an increasingly uneasy one, as they gradually moved away from his political ideas, which from the early 1970s to the early 80s had shaped many of Labour's policies. Now only more basic political forces, such as party camaraderie, his and Cherie's mutual need for public attention, and the requirement to unite against the Conservatives before the election, held the carload of Labour partisans together.

They arrived in Margate. The evening rally was to take place in its old town hall, a modestly sized Georgian building a few streets back from the seafront. Margate was well past its peak: a tired resort increasingly avoided by British holidaymakers, who since the 1960s had been going abroad in large and growing numbers. Yet few local people seemed to blame the Conservatives for failing to reverse the town's decline. The local Tory majority had increased at the previous general election in 1979. The rally for Cherie Blair had the potential to be a dispiriting occasion.

But it did not turn out like that. The room booked for the event, which had a small stage, soon filled up. Other rooms in the town hall were unlocked. They filled with people too. Later arrivals had to stand on the stairs. A speaker system had to be rigged up to broadcast the speeches through the building.

The rally finally began. Cherie spoke first. Then came her father, a sitcom star known onscreen and in real life for his blunt socialism and roguish persona. Yet it was the politician from west London who made the biggest impression. He was the person most of the audience had come to hear.

'I had never heard him speak before that night,' Tony Blair wrote in his memoirs, a quarter of a century later. He went on:

> I sat enraptured, absolutely captivated and inspired. I thought: If only I could speak like that. What impressed me was not so much the content – actually I didn't agree with a lot of it – but the power of it, the ability to use words to move people, not simply to persuade . . .
>
> First, there was his utter confidence. From the outset, the audience were relaxed and able to listen, because they knew the speaker was in control. When he began and he looked around at them, there was . . . no uncertainty, no negative energy. It wasn't the absence of nerves. It was the presence of self-belief. He held them, easily and naturally.
>
> Second, he used humour. If someone can make you laugh, you are already in their power . . . Third, there was a thread that ran

throughout the speech ... an argument. Sometimes there was digression and the thread was momentarily obscured, but always he returned and the thread was visible once more.

Fourth, the argument was built, not plonked down. Although introduced broadly at the beginning, it was not glimpsed fully until layer upon layer of supporting words built up to it and finally the argument was brought forth. Suddenly all the words were connected ... and the argument was out there, and you thought only the wilfully obdurate could not see its force and agree with it.

The rally felt like a triumph. In the car back to London afterwards, the Blairs and the politician talked and argued: about the future of the Labour party, about socialism, about the relationship between leftwing politics and religion. When they pulled up outside the politician's house, in the early hours, they were still talking. He introduced the Blairs to his wife. And then they finally parted.

'For days, weeks' after hearing the politician's speech in Margate, Blair wrote, 'I sat going over it in my mind. Probably to him it was one of half a dozen he did that week and was nothing special, but for me it was a revelation.' Shortly after he was elected Labour leader eleven years later, in 1994, Blair had a brief correspondence with the politician, and mentioned the Margate rally. 'I've always regarded your speech for Cherie,' Blair wrote, 'as the finest statement for socialism I've ever heard.'

Yet it did not help Cherie much, if at all. At the 1983 general election, she came third: far behind not just the Conservatives but also the new Social Democratic Party, which had been created by Labour MPs precisely because they could no longer stand being in the same party as the politician who had spoken alongside her in Margate. She did not stand for parliament again.

Tony Blair had a better experience at the 1983 election. He was elected for the much more winnable seat of Sedgefield, in what was then one of Labour's northern English heartlands. Over the next 24 years, as an MP, shadow minister, party leader and then prime minister, he abandoned almost every element of the socialist faith that he had heard so mesmerically articulated in Margate. Summing up that encounter with the politician in his memoirs, Blair wrote, 'I spotted the fundamental weakness in his position: he was in love with his role as idealist, as standard-bearer, as the man of principle . . . He was the preacher, not the general. And battles aren't won by preachers.'

The politician that Blair found both so flawed and so inspiring was Tony Benn. When he died in 2014, at the age of 89, it was widely said that a national treasure had been lost. Yet for the most important part of his career, during the 1970s and 80s, no politician except Thatcher so divided British opinion.

Like her, Benn was a radical and a disruptor. Like her, he believed that the way the country had been run by Labour and the Conservatives during the postwar era, a period many considered to be one of welcome stability and prosperity, was actually a dead end. Thatcher and Benn both tried for over a decade to convert their parties to a new way of thinking. To an extent, they succeeded. But then they were brutally pushed aside by party colleagues who found their ideas too dogmatic – only for those ideas to resurface in the 2010s, and retain a following and a relevance right up to the present day.

As British capitalism and the British state prove less and less able to provide most of us with decent 21st-century lives, so the critique of both systems which Benn made during the 1970s and 80s – that they were inefficient, over-centralised and constantly produced injustices – seems more and more prescient. And yet he never saw much of his alternative vision enacted. While Thatcherism was relentlessly implemented by her governments and those of her Tory successors, the kind of society he advocated through the once-famous, now increasingly forgotten creed of Bennism – a society where citizens dominated politicians and corporations, rather than vice versa – remains tantalisingly unrealised.

Or at least, it may seem so if you are on the radical left. If you are a rightwinger, a centrist, or even someone on the centre-left, then Bennism, and its direct descendant, Corbynism, may well be something very different: a dangerous form of extremism. Discredited but never quite dead, as far as its many enemies are concerned this mutation of socialism can never be buried deep enough.

Benn's journey into radicalism began in a more hopeful time, the 1960s. And so did those of four other, younger Labour politicians, who over the next half century would variously be his disciples, pro-tégés, collaborators, rivals and successors: Ken Livingstone, John McDonnell, Diane Abbott, and Jeremy Corbyn himself.

The four took ideas from Benn, but also from other dissident sources, many of which were outside the often narrow world of Labour politics, such as anarchism, anti-racism, Marxism, pacifism and identity politics. The four helped create a new left in Britain. And it flourished in environments where socialism was expected to strug-gle: the materialistic, booming London of the 1980s and 2000s, and the sour Brexit Britain of the 2010s.

The four also developed their own close and complicated relation-ships with each other. There were ideological and personal feuds, periods of coolness and jostling for prominence, times of intense camaraderie, diverging levels of success, and constantly shifting align-ments. Yet whatever the precise state of their relationships at any given moment, in their minds and in the minds of others, the four were often a group, and sometimes something tighter: a cell, or a sect.

Partly, this was down to their personalities. Like Benn, all four were stubborn, and more attached to their principles than most politicians. They were simultaneously outspoken and secretive, individualistic and looking for kindred spirits. They were suspicious of authority and mainstream opinion. Their politics sought to maximise both equality and freedom – rather than choose between them, as the left and right had traditionally done. They believed, probably correctly, that this new politics had a very wide potential appeal. Yet they were also com-fortable with, and sometimes even relished, being in a minority. Unlike most of their parliamentary peers, they could cope with being unpopu-lar or ignored, at least outside their constituencies, for a very long time.

In Britain more than in many comparable democracies, left-of-centre politicians generate suspicion and hostility: from most of the press and from other powerful interests, such as the City of London. This is hardly surprising. Since the 1970s, Britain has become one of the most unequal wealthy countries in the world. Anyone seeking to reverse that trend threatens, or is believed to threaten, the beneficiaries of almost half a century of fundamental economic and social change, from billionaire financiers to buy-to-let landlords. Even Labour politicians who promise to leave much of this landscape unaltered, as Blair did, are on constant probation, their words and deeds scrutinised for the smallest leftwing deviations. As for Labour figures who do want to transform the country, as Benn and Corbyn did – even if their stated plans would, at least at first, only make Britain more like fairer capitalist societies such as Sweden or Germany or Japan – such politicians are frequently portrayed as fanatical, mad or illegitimate, whatever their actual electoral mandates. In effect, they are treated as heretics, to be suppressed before their ideas undermine the true faith. The five politicians in this book have at times been regarded with fear, contempt, or hatred, or all three at once. They have been threatened with violence, or physically attacked. The strength of these reactions, repeated for over half a century, tells us much about Britain beyond the left.

Heretics often lead erratic lives. Moments of great excitement and promise, when converting large numbers of people seems possible, are interspersed with long stretches on the margins. So it was for Benn and his four disciples. He and they had periods when a great breakthrough seemed close at hand. Sometimes it even happened. But more often their lives were about working on regardless, finding ways not to worry about futility, and waiting for better days. How they survived in the political and psychological wilderness where they spent much of their adult lives is the untold story of British politics in modern times.

The five of them had different strengths and weaknesses. Benn was endlessly eloquent, but his cabinet colleagues did not trust him. Livingstone could always see several steps ahead, but could rarely resist controversy. Abbott, the first black woman ever elected to parliament, had a self-sufficiency so fierce that it could isolate her completely. McDonnell had an intensity that both attracted and repelled. And Corbyn had an integrity and an ability to get on with people that helped him rise furthest, to the treacherous summit of Labour politics, but which left him least equipped to cope there.

It would probably be a mistake, however, to assume that Labour's defeat in 2019, and the marginalisation of Corbyn and his comrades since, is the end of this story. One of the most important features of their movement was its attentiveness to social, economic and cultural trends, to how Britons were actually living. Many British politicians lack this curiosity, being more interested in Westminster and what the media is saying about it. Yet in our unstable age, the issues that the Corbyn leadership focused on have not gone away; they have intensified. The yearning of younger voters for a government and an economy which benefits rather than exploits or ignores them, for example, remains a potentially enormous political force. According to the respected *Financial Times* data journalist John Burn-Murdoch, 'The dramatic breakdown of upward social mobility ... has hit young Britons much harder than their contemporaries elsewhere in the developed world.' The almost unprecedented increase in support for Labour under Corbyn at the 2017 election, including almost two-thirds of voters under 35 – a rare dominance of the younger electorate repeated in 2019 – is an event which the left's enemies have been tellingly determined to discount as a fluke, or to avoid discussing altogether.

The political solutions offered as alternatives to the left feel increasingly thin. The ever more closed country and rampant free markets of modern Conservatism; the modest reforms and retro patriotism of Labour centrism: both seem less and less suited to a world of profiteering corporations, collapsing mass living standards and accelerating climate change.

Two of the most unusual and important features of the new left which the characters in this book largely created were that it was forward-looking and open-ended. Especially in Britain, a country where Conservatism and a harsh capitalism have so long held sway, socialism can be intensely nostalgic and preservationist. Past struggles must be commemorated. What is left of a previous, better society must be protected. There is nothing wrong with these impulses, and at times the politicians in this book acted on them. But remembering and saving mid-20th-century socialism was not their main preoccupation. They were searching for something beyond it.

I began to become aware of this search long before I decided to write a book about it. I first lived in Abbott's constituency in north-east London as a young journalist in 1994. Three years later, I moved to Corbyn's seat, immediately to the west, and lived there on and off until 2004. That year, I moved back to Abbott's constituency and have lived there ever since.

These are places where politics is unusually important. Election turnouts are high, despite their predictable, Labour-dominated outcomes. Conversations in the pub often turn to politics. Protests are part of everyday life for many well-off and poor residents alike. If you write about politics, as I have since the early 1990s, it is hard, even off-duty, not to hear gossip, opinions and conspiracy theories about Corbyn and Abbott: their latest plans, their latest blunders and triumphs, the state of their health.

For two decades before Corbyn suddenly seized the Labour leadership, much of my attention was on more significant figures, in conventional Westminster terms. But I gradually came to understand that he and Abbott were unusual politicians. They intensely divided or unified people, they enraged or inspired. The Labour party is often cautious and not always compelling. But Corbyn and Abbott, I realised, were part of a bolder tradition – a tradition which is often misunderstood or misrepresented, deliberately and otherwise, and which needs to be explained.

This book is not intended to be a conventional group biography of its five main characters. Much that happened in their personal lives is not included. Nor is this book meant to be a comprehensive history of the British left, or the Labour party, or the Corbyn leadership, which took much of its energy from social and political movements which feature in this volume but are not its focus. There are plenty of books on all those subjects already.

Instead, this is the story of a group of political explorers and of a series of interlocking political journeys which are rarely considered as a whole. Often, these people are absent altogether from books about British politics since the 1970s, which tend to be dominated, still, by the assumptions of Thatcherism and New Labour and their political descendants.

This book is about its protagonists' flaws and failures as much as their successes. And it is about where the political project they started – but which has always drawn in other people: activists, intellectuals, trade unionists, younger Labour MPs, the simply curious – might go next. Already, this project has been much more influential on modern Britain than the electoral history of the left might suggest. How people in this country think about race, sexuality and minorities in general; how state and private sector institutions and political parties deal with diversity; how our cities came to be associated with multicultural vibrancy rather than postwar menace and decay; and how personal ethics and protest came to rival and sometimes supersede Westminster politics: all these huge changes since the 70s have been personified and driven by the people this book depicts.

And the fact of that influence opens up big questions about the nature of politics. What exactly does it encompass? How many of its most important developments happen in Westminster, and how many elsewhere? And across the great spectrum of political activity, what exactly is a victory, and what is a defeat? The ongoing culture wars, many of them over issues which these five radicals were among the first British politicians to raise, suggest that success and failure in politics are rarely total and almost always temporary. To adapt the answer the Chinese premier Zhou Enlai gave in 1972, when asked about the impact of the famous French student revolts four years earlier – revolts which were formative for all this book's subjects – what the precise importance is of these five epic political lives, it is too early to say.

Beyond that lurks another question. What is it like to live a life dominated by politics? Endless meetings, briefings, organising, alliance-building, vote-chasing, disappointments and betrayals; but also secrets, beliefs, power, ideas, camaraderie, rebellions and sweet victories. Without people addicted to some or all of these, democracy, or any other system for the unavoidable task of distributing society's resources, could not exist.

I hope this book will be read by people who profoundly disagree with its protagonists, as well as people who admire them, and people who think they did not go nearly far enough. Their careers also shine a light on those of more conventionally successful politicians, such as Blair and Thatcher, by revealing some of the questions that these supposedly fearless leaders avoided asking about the kind of country Britain could be.

Large parts of the careers of these five politicians took place in times when the left was whiter and more male than it is now, and this book reflects that. But even within those limits, and the many other barriers and forces which frustrated them, weakened them, and regularly threatened them with oblivion, the lives of the searchers revealed something important. Another politics is possible.

PART ONE

Radicalisation

I

Benn's Epiphany

In the spring of 1968 Tony Benn was restless. He had just turned 43. He had been a Labour MP for over 14 years and a minister for almost four. He was increasingly talked about by journalists as a future prime minister. For most politicians, that would have been a highly satisfactory career so far. But Benn was different.

His father, William Wedgwood Benn, later Viscount Stansgate, had been a Labour minister too. William Benn had also been a devotee of an early British self-help book, *How to Live on 24 Hours a Day*. Under its influence, he kept a time chart: a detailed account of how he spent each day, with no time set aside for meals or socialising, and he required his son, during his childhood, to do the same. Tony Benn revered his father, and even after William Benn died in 1960 continued to follow some of his advice on how to live. As a minister in the late 1960s, the younger Benn often worked until two or three in the morning. He sometimes neglected to eat. A gauntness tightened his lively, boyish face.

His ministerial office was on the 11th floor of Millbank Tower, an isolated finger of glass in central London, which overlooked the heavy brick-and-stone maze of the rest of Westminster, a few minutes' walk to the north. Both the tower and Benn's department, the Ministry of Technology, or Mintech for short, were only a few years old: expressions of the country's ambitions to modernise itself under Harold Wilson, who had been prime minister since 1964. Wilson had defeated a Conservative government widely seen as old-fashioned and tired. His successful election manifesto had promised 'a major national effort' to upgrade British industry, which a new ministry – Mintech – would 'guide and stimulate'. After the first minister of technology proved inadequate in Wilson's view, he put Benn in charge.

Wilson saw Benn as an able administrator, a communicator of rare talent, and sometimes as his heir apparent. Benn had been a BBC radio producer before becoming an MP, and an informal television coach to more senior Labour figures. He understood this new media world much better than most of his party colleagues. And the media – or most of it – liked him. He was constantly invited on to radio and TV shows. And he posed for newspaper photographers as well as he spoke: with a twinkly ease that seemed both charmingly upper-class and informally modern. He would be snapped striding down the steps of his handsome white house in west London, ministerial papers tucked purposefully under his arm, sometimes with his equally photogenic American wife Caroline and their four children appealingly arrayed around him. Or he would be shown seated at his desk at Mintech: pen in hand, an intense look in his eyes, surrounded by electrical gadgets, for which he was an early enthusiast. When one young business journalist came to the 11th floor to interview him, her tape recorder, then a new technology, malfunctioned halfway through. The minister asked her for the recorder, and they both sat on the floor of the office for 20 minutes while he fixed it.

But fixing British industry was much harder. After a century of underinvestment by companies, and growing foreign competition, by the late 1960s the whole country was scattered with ageing or obsolete factories. In some regions, such as the west of Scotland, these were already closing en masse. At first, Benn sought to persuade companies to innovate their way out of the crisis, by investing in new processes and equipment. He tried to make inspiring speeches to British and international business bodies. 'Technology serves a higher purpose than mere production,' he told the European Organisation for Quality Control in 1967. 'It offers us hope for the future. It is the light at the end of the long, dark tunnel of poverty through which most of mankind has been journeying throughout the whole of human history.'

Benn could be a mesmeric public speaker. His voice was modest in size, and sounded older than his age, almost grandfatherly, yet was also unusually clear and penetrating. His long sentences flowed, from one perfectly weighted clause to the next, with an establishment smoothness, but also sometimes a more unusual intensity: a conviction that felt religious. For generations, the Benn family worldview had been shaped by nonconformist Christianity. As minister of technology – only a mid-ranking cabinet position – Tony Benn sometimes gave the impression that Mintech could be Britain's salvation.

His ministry also tried more bureaucratic measures. It encouraged struggling manufacturers to seek economies of scale by merging with each other into giant, state-subsidised conglomerates such as Upper Clydeside Shipbuilders and British Leyland. Meanwhile Mintech performed mergers and acquisitions of its own within Whitehall, absorbing other government functions and institutions such as the Ministry of Aviation. Benn's department became involved in everything from promoting the use of computers to nuclear power; from buying missiles for the Royal Air Force to helping oversee the development of the overambitious Anglo-French supersonic passenger jet Concorde. In 1966, the *Observer* described 'Benn's empire' as 'the biggest state-directed complex of scientific and industrial power in Europe'.

Yet having more and more responsibilities, and making decisions that required an overview of all sorts of specialist knowledge, quickly began to feel overwhelming. 'Mintech is becoming a bit too much for me,' Benn recorded in his diary, only a few months into the job. He had a recurring nightmare about having to discuss Concorde in person with Charles de Gaulle, the grand French president, without having first read the relevant papers.

And in the real world, however late into the night Benn stayed in his office, reading and annotating in his impatient, scratchy handwriting the endless briefings from the Mintech civil servants – whom he sometimes found intimidating, as they were often much older and more experienced Whitehall operators than he was – the great industrial revival he was seeking did not materialise. Instead of investing in factories, British business increasingly preferred to focus on financial services. The number of employees in finance almost doubled during the 1950s and 60s. Yet the country's growth rate did not. In 1968, it was no stronger or more consistent than it had been when Wilson was elected four years earlier.

Benn's frustrations at Mintech fed a suspicion among some of his supposed ministerial comrades that he was a limited talent. Wilson's government was full of self-consciously clever politicians, such as Roy Jenkins, Denis Healey, Richard Crossman and Wilson himself. A skilled practitioner of divide and rule, Wilson did not discourage them from ganging up on each other. Benn's relative youth, slick personal presentation and popularity with the media invited jealousy. Meanwhile, his relative lack of interest in intellectual matters – he was in too much of a hurry to read many books – invited condescension. The fact that he had studied philosophy, politics and economics at Oxford did not impress a cabinet of Oxford graduates. Crossman, who had taught there, wrote in his sometimes bitchy diary: 'The real problem about Wedgy' – he had inherited his father's middle name – 'is that his presentation is brilliant but what he says is normally second-rate . . .'

The 1960s Benn was like Tony Blair in his early days as a shadow minister: precocious, energetic, charismatic, high-profile, clearly going places; but seen by some colleagues and commentators as both too bland and too calculating. When Labour had experienced vicious battles between its left and right during the previous decade, Benn had 'stood in the middle ground', as he admitted later. 'I didn't burn any bridges.' Partly because of this careful positioning, and partly because they correctly sensed that, for all his charm, he was in many ways a political loner, not a team player, his fellow ministers did not entirely trust him.

His own political positions were an ambiguous mixture. He had voted for the Labour rightwinger Hugh Gaitskell as party leader in 1955. He had supported Wilson's legislation in early 1968 to restrict Commonwealth immigration. He did not publicly oppose the American war in Vietnam. At Mintech, he had sought to update British capitalism, not change the balances of power within it – let alone replace it. In these and other ways, from his election as an MP in 1950 until 1968, he was a typically cautious mainstream Labour politician: focused on parliament and incremental government reforms as the way to change society, rather than working with wider social movements and pushing through transformative laws; and looking to go with public opinion (assumed to be conservative), rather than lead it. He was seen as a politician of the centre-left, not the left.

Yet there were also signs in his record of more radical impulses. Benn was an early British opponent of apartheid and supporter of anti-colonial liberation struggles. In 1963, he had backed a successful multiracial boycott of buses in Bristol, the starkly divided city where he had his constituency, after the local bus company refused to hire non-white crews. He had also criticised the British nuclear deterrent for being largely outside the control of parliament. He was a founder member of the Hydrogen Bomb National Committee, a precursor to the Campaign for Nuclear Disarmament.

Most high-profile of all, between 1960 and 1963 Benn had fought a dogged and resourceful campaign to renounce the peerage which he had inherited on his father's death, which under existing law terminated his right to be a member of parliament. With a combination of populist stunts – winning a by-election in his constituency despite being barred from the Commons – and discreet negotiations with the right people in Westminster, he had persuaded the then Conservative government to alter the law. 'You have changed the constitution of this country by your own power!' he told a crowd of his celebrating supporters in Bristol. By invoking democracy – the right of voters to elect whoever they wished – and by deploying his particular, establishment-trained personality, he had successfully challenged one of the fundamental rules of British politics. His potential to lead further rebellions was clear.

But for the rest of the 1960s he did not. A year after his victory, he took his first ministerial job, as Postmaster General. Two years after that, he moved to Mintech. His anti-peerage campaign and his radical moments as a backbencher receded, and were replaced in the public mind – and his – by his work as a minister. Did this constitute a worthwhile political existence? By 1968, he was less and less sure that it did. 'There is no doubt that in the years up to 1968,' he wrote later, 'I was just a career politician.'

By 1968 he was also losing faith in Wilson. The energising new premier elected four years earlier, and re-elected with a hugely increased majority in 1966 – a premier whom Benn had initially admired – had by 1968 become almost becalmed: his plans for the economy making little progress, his attention increasingly distracted by plots to remove him from the party leadership and Downing Street.

Voters noticed the government's drift. In early May 1968, Labour did so badly in local elections that in London, usually one of its citadels, the party lost control of 17 of the 20 boroughs it had previously held. It was Labour's worst result in a significant set of elections since the early 1930s.

During the spring of 1968, Benn decided he would start approaching politics differently. On weekdays, he would be as good a minister as he could. But at the weekend, and whenever else his diary permitted, he would look for people and situations that would make him think differently.

On 24 May 1968, a fortnight after Labour's local election disaster, a paragraph appeared in *The Times* about a small uprising near Benn's constituency. The previous day, a few dozen students and lecturers from Bristol University had occupied a satellite building close to campus. They announced that they were setting up a new educational institution: the Free University of Bristol.

'We want to provide people with a platform to air grievances about the way our [official] university is run,' one of the occupation's organisers, a 21-year-old drama student, told the newspaper. More ambitiously, the Free University planned to offer an entirely new curriculum. Teaching would be open to anyone.

The building the students had taken over was a large, airy new block on a prominent corner site, usually the Bristol University student union, which had meeting rooms and its own auditorium. A programme of public lectures and seminars was quickly drawn up, and teaching started. Within a few days, the Free University had 500 participants, a quarter as many as attended its official counterpart. On the second day, the Bristol University authorities told the occupiers that they would have to vacate their building by the end of the evening, as the next day was a Saturday, and the student union was closed at weekends. The Free University called a mass meeting. The participants voted overwhelmingly to stay.

The Free University continued into June. Benn became intrigued. On the 14th, a Friday, usually the one weekday he spent in his constituency, he left the tight terraced streets of Bristol South East and drove a mile west across the city centre to the student union building.

Despite being a longstanding local MP and one of the best-known politicians in the country, he hoped that he could spend some time at the Free University without being recognised. Usually a rather formal and old-fashioned dresser, a wearer of boxy suits and waistcoats that with his smoothed-down and side-parted hair made him look like a politician of the 1940s, on this occasion he took off his jacket, loosened his shirt collar, and put on his reading glasses. The students were half his age, hairier, and in skinnier clothes: polo necks and drainpipe trousers; but they were sufficiently absorbed in the Free University experiment, and joined by enough other Bristolians of varying ages milling around, for Benn to believe that his presence barely registered. 'Nobody took the slightest notice of me,' he wrote with satisfaction afterwards.

He found where the teaching sessions were taking place, sat down quietly in the audience, and watched and listened. Unusually for a politician, Benn was a genuinely good listener: interested in other people's lives and ideas most of the time, rather than in how appearing to be interested in these things might benefit him. And on this day, as on most days, the Free University rushed through a range of topics that was broader than the content of the average ministerial meeting. 'The first session was on the subject of Revolution,' he remembered, 'the second was on Black Power, and the third on Vietnam.' The proceedings were informal, discursive. 'I thought they asked a lot of important questions.' Later that day, after he had finished his visit to the Free University, Benn had a more personal revelation. 'I realised all of a sudden that for three and a half or four years I have done absolutely no basic thinking about politics.'

That would now change.

What Benn encountered in Bristol that Friday was a tiny part of an event so large and resonant that for decades afterwards it would be known just by an abbreviation of its date: '68. It was a revolt against the existing order – educational, social, psychological, sexual, racial, economic, political, geopolitical, technological – and an attempt to create a new one. The revolt spread from country to country, in democracies and dictatorships, in Soviet and American satellite states, in eastern and western Europe, in South America and Asia: in France,

Germany, Italy, Britain, Spain, Portugal, Czechoslovakia, Poland, Yugoslavia, Pakistan, Japan, Mexico, Brazil and the United States.

Sometimes, the individual outbreaks were brief, lasting just a few hours or days. And sometimes they persisted for months, flaring up, subsiding, then flaring again. Some involved a few hundred people, others involved millions. There were huge marches and demonstrations, mass meetings and occupations, strikes and solidarity campaigns, revolutionary cells and action committees, rebel newspapers and manifestos, collective yearnings and personal epiphanies, sudden coalitions and a few supportive politicians, improvised barricades and cobbles dug up as missiles, street battles with soldiers and the police. During 1968, it often felt 'as if a gigantic demonstration of revolutionary theorems, for so many years guarded in small groups and little-read pamphlets, was being laid on by history,' as David Widgery, an English radical leftist and '68 participant, wrote a few years later. The revolt was a huge release of political energies that in many countries had no other outlet: despite the dramatic rise in the cultural and social status of teenagers during the 1950s and 60s, the voting age in most democracies, including Britain, was still 21 in 1968.

Some of the most spectacular images of the uprisings – students seizing the prettiest parts of Paris, anti-Soviet protesters waving flags from commandeered trucks in Prague – were broadcast around the world. After a decade of rapid growth in consumer electronics, 200 million households had televisions, about a fifth of the global population. It was the first time a revolutionary year had had such an audience. This visibility helped spread and intensify the rebellion, as did a growing awareness among the participants that they were involved in historic events. 'In the rest of this century, the meaning of May 1968 will be worked out and revealed,' wrote Tom Nairn, a young Scottish political theorist, in an essay he composed while taking part in an occupation of Hornsey School of Art in north London.

The ideas and goals of the '68ers, as they would call themselves for decades afterwards, were many and various, and sometimes the product of local contexts, but they had common features: a rejection of authority; a hostility to state bureaucracy; a disillusionment with both the Soviet Union and the United States; a horror of war, and the Vietnam War in particular; an enthusiasm for individual liberty; a belief that politics and public life generally should not be top-down, but participatory; a new interest in the politics of identity; a faith in social movements; a readiness to form coalitions; and a contempt for the compromises and tribalism of the traditional political parties.

Above all, the '68ers believed – sometimes just for days, while they were part of an uprising, but sometimes for much longer – that revolutionary change was suddenly possible. 'I'll never forget the extraordinary sight of power wobbling like a nervous jelly in those weeks,' wrote the '68er and feminist historian Sheila Rowbotham in her memoir *Promise of a Dream: Remembering the Sixties*. She was referring specifically to the days in May and June when the usually commanding, politically experienced de Gaulle seemed at a loss as to how to deal with the French students and the insurrectionary alliance they formed with industrial workers, shop workers and small farmers – an alliance that organised such a wave of strikes and occupations that France seemed on the verge of revolution. But that year Rowbotham also felt that a wider overthrow of the status quo was under way: '[The] sequence of events during 1968 led my generation to believe we were moving in the same direction as history.' As the front page of *Black Dwarf*, a radical newspaper first published in London on 1 June, put it in that inaugural edition: 'We Shall Fight, We Will Win, Paris London Rome Berlin'. The words were spelled out in huge red and black capitals above the dramatic silhouette of a human pyramid of protesters, standing and sitting triumphantly with their flags on top of one of the stone lions in Trafalgar Square in central London. The image echoed famous photographs of victorious Russian and American soldiers in the Second World War. The implication was that a victory of similar magnitude was within reach. Three decades later, the former editor of *Black Dwarf* and composer of that first front page headline, Tariq Ali, co-wrote a book to celebrate 1968's 30th anniversary. He summed up what he felt the year had been about: 'an attempt to create a new world'.

Ken Livingstone watched it all on television in a semi in south London. He was in his early twenties and still living with his parents. They were working-class Conservatives, party members so firm in their pro-business opinions that they refused to buy a television until the creation of ITV ended the BBC's state-backed monopoly. In order to become property owners as fast as possible they had both done several jobs at once: Livingstone's mother as a cinema usher, bakery assistant and clerk at a catalogue-shopping business; his father as a window cleaner and a scenery shifter at a theatre. The house they bought was plain but bigger than it looked, two deep storeys on a quiet street in the neat suburb of West Norwood. The family were close. Livingstone – slight, self-sufficient, a bit of a loner – was a late developer by his own estimation. He did not leave home until he was approaching 30.

But there was also a less conventional side to the family. Ken's mother had been a circus and music hall dancer in her youth, and his father had been in the merchant navy: they had travelled widely and acquired a liberal outlook on race and sexuality. Their son, after drifting through school, spent five months in 1966 and 1967 hitchhiking with a friend through Africa. The pair had encountered remnants of empires and anti-colonial liberation movements, lingering racial divisions and anti-British locals. In Nigeria, they found the aftermath of a civil war massacre, so recent there was still blood on the pavements and walls.

Africa accelerated the development of Livingstone's interest in politics, which he had been slowly acquiring since the late 1950s: first from following the disasters of Conservative governments such as the Suez crisis and the Profumo scandal; then through teenage enthusiasm for the charismatic reformers of the early 1960s – President John F. Kennedy, the liberalising Pope John XXIII, and the young Harold Wilson; and then through darker realisations about the nature of nuclear weapons, the Cold War, and the war in Vietnam. Livingstone was also influenced by people he met in his first proper job, as an apprentice technician at a cancer research unit, which he had applied for after acquiring a mostly self-taught interest in science. The other technicians were all Labour voters, and it was the first time Livingstone had been in a strongly leftwing environment. His parents were thrilled that he was going up in the world, as they had. But at the dining table in West Norwood most evenings, Livingstone and his father would have a political row. Livingstone discovered how much he liked arguments: questioning the status quo, saying the unsayable.

usually a strong Labour area, and control of the council had passed to the Conservatives. Livingstone was the first new Labour member in Norwood for at least a year. The chair of the meeting said: 'Make sure he doesn't get away.'

Within four months, Livingstone had been elected to the constituency's executive committee, general management committee, and local government committee, which was drawing up Labour's Lambeth manifesto for the next borough elections. He was also nominated unopposed as the Norwood party's membership secretary. 'This was a new world,' he wrote, 'and I was consumed with an exhilarating round of committee meetings, canvassing and fund-raising and arguments . . .' A prodigious appetite for the seemingly small stuff of local Labour politics – along with a keen awareness of how this work could lead to bigger things – quickly became his trademark. He also demonstrated a confidence to stray outside his brief, and to say provocative things. His first speech to the General Management committee – his first real political speech – attacked the Wilson government for having the wrong policies on the economy, trade unions and defence. Livingstone shook so much as he was speaking, he had to lean against a wall. But Norwood's Labour pensioners loved it. Livingstone was on his way.

2

Jamaican Imports

In 1968 John McDonnell was still a teenager. While millions marched and protested, he was at school losing interest in his A-levels. Or he was at his summer job, on a burger production line in a factory owned by the frozen food giant Birds Eye. The factory was in Great Yarmouth, then a busy Norfolk fishing port and coastal resort, which occupies a watery spit of land at the easternmost edge of England. McDonnell was into girls, football and the Beatles, like a lot of the town's other 17-year-olds.

But he had already lived more than most of them. He had spent his early childhood somewhere very different: in Liverpool, in a slum street near the waterfront. His father, from a family of Irish immigrants, was a docker, with a hook on his belt for handling bales of cargo. His mother was a cleaner. The city had been heavily bombed in the war, and McDonnell and his friends played football in the rubble. The postwar welfare state made life better for the McDonnells. Their street was demolished and they moved to a council house close by. But the postwar economy was less hospitable. Liverpool was on the wrong side of the country for Britain's growing trade with Europe. Work in the docks began to dry up.

In 1958, when McDonnell was seven, the family moved to Great Yarmouth, partly because his mother had grown up there. His father became a bus driver, while his mother worked at the local branch of British Home Stores, behind the biscuit counter. Money was still tight. After school, McDonnell and his brother would go to the quayside, which ran all down the western side of town, and pick up any herrings that the unloading fishermen had dropped. Their mother brought home free broken biscuits from work.

Three faiths sustained the family. The first was hard work. McDonnell passed the eleven-plus and went to Great Yarmouth Grammar School, an ancient local institution where teachers' reports noted his diligence and also a stubborn, outspoken side that at times made him 'incompatible with authority'. The second faith was trade unionism. The McDonnells talked a lot about politics at home. His father had been a trade unionist in Liverpool, and in Great Yarmouth he became the eastern counties branch secretary of the huge Transport and General Workers' Union. Unlike growing numbers of people in mid-20th-century Britain, the McDonnells did not believe that individual self-reliance and loyalty to the collective were incompatible.

Their third belief system was Catholicism. In Liverpool and then Great Yarmouth, its routines ran unquestioned through the family schedule. McDonnell became an altar boy, and by his early teens his faith was strong enough for him to feel a vocation. In 1963 he got a grant from the church and left Great Yarmouth for a fee-paying Catholic boarding school, St Joseph's College, near Ipswich, 50 miles to the south. There he began training for the priesthood.

It was a heady time to be a Catholic with leftwing opinions. Since his accession five years earlier, Pope John XXIII had 'let in some fresh air' to the church, as he put it, by transforming its approach to the outside world. He visited prisons and spoke to inmates in everyday language. He acted as an intermediary between Italy's centre-right Christian Democrats and centre-left Socialists, and between the East and West during Cold War crises over Cuba and Berlin. Most boldly of all, in April 1963 he issued *Pacem in terris* ('Peace on Earth'), the first papal encyclical addressed to both Catholics and non-Catholics. It was an ambitious, often politically radical document, declaring that everyone had 'the right to a decent standard of living'; that 'collaboration' was the basis of civilisation; that discrimination against ethnic minorities was 'a flagrant violation of justice'; and that 'nuclear weapons must be banned'. For the teenage McDonnell, like the teenage Ken Livingstone, six years his senior, Pope John was an inspiration, and a sign that the world was getting better.

But St Joseph's quickly showed McDonnell that that was not always the case. The school stood behind thick hedges on a hilltop in the Ipswich suburbs. Its grounds were extensive, some of its buildings were handsome, including a 19th-century mansion, and it was run by a prestigious international order, the De La Salle Brothers, which had been founded to educate poor children almost three hundred years earlier. Yet St Joseph's in the 1960s could be a grim place: like a tough, boys-only private school, but with an additional religious austerity. There were cold dormitories, Saturday morning lessons and endless rugby. Each week, pupils' marks in every subject were collated and announced publicly, and the lowest scorers were caned. Violence from some of the Brothers – McDonnell later called it 'sado-Christianity' – was a constant threat. Pupils were even slippered for each item they retrieved from lost property. They were ordered to leave the letters they wrote home in unsealed envelopes.

McDonnell lasted four years, from the age of 12 to 16. Pope John died while he was there; and so, gradually, did his desire to be a priest. He realised he did not want a life of prayer and celibacy. And he began to believe that the potential for social change he had seen in Christianity was more present in the other McDonnell family faith, leftwing politics. In 1967 he left St Joseph's and went back to Great Yarmouth.

For the next year, he drifted through sixth form at the grammar school while also working in burger bars, cafés, a bingo hall and the Birds Eye factory. One of the calls at the bingo hall was 'Wilson's den: number ten', so entrenched in power did the Labour leader seem. But school and seasonal or menial work in a town that offered little else was no longer enough. Instead of doing the final year of his A-levels, he left school at 17, left home, and headed back north.

He took a job in a mattress factory near Burnley in Lancashire, then a job in a local plant that made televisions. Like the Liverpool docks and Great Yarmouth, the small manufacturing towns of north Lancashire were not a part of England with great long-term prospects as the 1960s turned into the 1970s and foreign factories offered steadily more competition. But McDonnell was a resourceful young man who was used to moving around and hungry for new experiences, for anything that might give his life a new pattern and meaning. His Catholic faith, and indeed his belief in God, were slowly evaporating. In 1971, at the age of 20, he got married. His wife, who worked in childcare and had managerial ambitions, said he should do his A-levels again, and finish them this time, so he would have a chance of going to university and getting better jobs. He agreed. During 1972, he made televisions on the day shift or the night shift according to the factory schedule, and in between took A-level evening classes at Burnley Technical College, in sociology, history and politics. He studied with renewed focus and completed the two-year courses in 12 months. In 1973 he joined the Labour party.

The following year, his wife got a job in London, as the live-in manager of a residential home for children in care. It was in Hayes, a faded suburb out near Heathrow airport with plenty of cheap housing. Nearby, McDonnell found a part-time undergraduate course that he liked: politics and government at Brunel University. Seemingly everyone in his year wanted to be a politician or a union leader. Despite all his wanderings, McDonnell was still only in his early twenties: there was plenty of time to try to become either. A new vocation was forming.

Jeremy Corbyn also wandered through the late 1960s and early 70s. But his self-discoveries often happened in warmer places.

As 1968 began, he was 18 and living in Jamaica. His stay there had been arranged by Voluntary Service Overseas (VSO), a British charity which sent young Britons to teach in poorer countries. The charity had been founded during the final years of the British empire, and when Corbyn joined its programme in 1967 it still had an imperial flavour. He and the other volunteers were school leavers or graduates, not trained teachers, and they were often despatched to former British colonies, where they each worked for two years in return for free accommodation and pocket money. They were expected to be good ambassadors for Britain, and their behaviour was lightly monitored by the Foreign Office. In Jamaica, which had become independent from Britain just five years before Corbyn got there, the volunteers were expected to attend pep talks and the Christmas party at the British High Commission in the capital, Kingston. After their character-building adventures abroad, VSO expected some of its alumni to go on to greater things back in Britain, to become business leaders or senior politicians.

But Corbyn was a little different. He did not go to the High

Commission's Christmas party. He did not mix that much with the two dozen other VSO volunteers in Kingston. He was an earnest, self-contained young man with a dry sense of humour he often kept well hidden. He had never been to a poor country before, and he tried to absorb as much as he could about Jamaica and Kingston, and the complicated webs of race and class and colonialism that still entwined them. He spent a lot of time walking and taking buses round the city, watching and listening. What he learned would be formative.

The school he worked at, Kingston College, only taught him so much. It was a little like St Joseph's in Ipswich: prestigious, founded by the church (though Anglican rather than Catholic), with an emphasis on competitiveness and sport and a pompous, public school-style Latin motto which translated as 'The Brave May Fall But Never Yield'. Corbyn was asked to teach the geography of the Caribbean, which was almost completely unfamiliar to him, to large classes of cheeky boys who were only a few years younger and who claimed they found it hard to understand his accent. Pale and slight, with a tendency to redden dramatically when provoked, he only just maintained his authority: usually by staying one chapter ahead of the class in the textbook, and slyly telling any pupil who caught up with him that they were rushing ahead too much and not giving the others a fair chance. During break times, he watchfully explored the school's grounds, shirtsleeves neatly rolled up, a camera hanging from one shoulder, squinting in the hard sun. Until he grew a beard, a few months into his stay, he looked very young.

Kingston in the late 1960s was a very divided city, with villas on breezy, shaded hillsides looking down on hot dusty flatlands which contained some of the Caribbean's worst slums. Two of them, Tivoli Gardens and Trenchtown, were close to the school. One of the flats Corbyn lived in was not far from Trenchtown. 'I would hear gunfire every night,' he told me. The city was becoming more violent, as long-established gangs vied to control a growing drug trade, and also became increasingly involved in post-independence politics, which was polarising between the socialist People's National Party and the conservative Jamaica Labour Party. Corbyn's own political views were already leftwing, but until now had been mainly about Britain. He was unsettled and fascinated by Jamaica's turbulence, and by his own country's responsibility for so much of it as the former colonial power.

In 1968 Walter Rodney, a prominent black activist and historian from Guyana, was teaching in Kingston at the University of the West Indies. Rodney wrote and lectured about slavery and colonialism with a withering clarity that made the connection between those historical movements and the unequal modern world impossible to deny. One of his books, *How Europe Underdeveloped Africa*, published in 1972, would shape Corbyn's thinking for decades to come.

It presented Western imperialism, past and present, as crucial to capitalism, and to the whole 20th-century world order. In this and other books, Rodney took ideas from Karl Marx, third-world revolutionaries and the Black Power movement in the United States. He made the study and understanding of history seem intensely political, even dangerous to the status quo. During 1968, he increasingly took his message off campus and into the slums of Kingston, speaking to impromptu crowds about the oppressive hierarchies of supposedly free and equal independent Jamaica. The rightwing Labour government, aware of all the uprisings elsewhere in the world, 'panicked', as Corbyn later put it. When Rodney left the country to speak at a black writers' conference in Canada that October, the Jamaican government banned him from returning. Days of rioting followed, with dozens of buses overturned and set on fire, shops gutted, and locals who were considered 'enemies of the people', as Rodney later put it, 'spat upon, dragged out of their cars and beaten'.

Corbyn witnessed some of the disorder. One evening after school, some of his pupils escorted him home, he told me, because they were 'worried about me being attacked as an unwelcome British person on the streets'. He blamed the government for the riots. While not supporting political violence, he quickly became fascinated by Rodney's ideas and the reactions they provoked. He wrote a long article about the whole controversy, and speculatively posted it to the *New Statesman* in London. The magazine rejected it. But the riots and the article awakened his interest in liberation movements, and he began going to Kingston's one black history bookshop. He also made small attempts to help alleviate the city's inequalities. He volunteered at a rehabilitation centre for polio sufferers. He took city children camping and climbing in the cooler Blue Mountains above Kingston. And he worked as a lighting technician in the Barn Theatre, a recently opened venue that was the first in Jamaica to put on plays by Caribbean writers. Barely competent, he lasted for one production.

By 1969, his VSO commitment was over. But after what he saw as his 'awakening' in Jamaica, he did not head straight back to Britain. Having never been on a plane before flying to Kingston, he had now decided to travel on his own through South America. In one of the countries at its furthest tip a revolution was coming that would make Walter Rodney's rebellion look minor.

The adventure-seeking Corbyn of the late 1960s and early 70s was a product of both confidence and frustration. His parents were middle-class leftists, an electrical engineer and a maths teacher, who had met at a meeting for British supporters of the Republican side in the Spanish Civil War. They were both Londoners. When Oswald Mosley's British Union of Fascists tried to parade through the then heavily Jewish East End in 1936, with the police clearing a route for them, Corbyn's mother was part of the crowd of leftwing protesters that famously fought both the fascists and the police and successfully blocked the march.

Work took his parents away from the capital. From the 1940s onwards they brought up four boys in a succession of comfortable country properties in the west of England. Jeremy was the youngest. Their most permanent home was Yew Tree Manor in Shropshire, which they bought in 1956. A pretty seven-bedroom house off a busy road, with a few dozen yards of driveway, an outbuilding, and an acre of land, it was not quite the palatial country seat that the Conservative press would later present it as; but for a leftwing family it was quite grand. The Corbyns changed its name to the less lordly Yew Tree House.

The family lived more like middle-class bohemians than aristocrats. Books were everywhere, and hobbies were encouraged. The boys played polo on the lawn, on bicycles, and scattered the property with home-made contraptions such as wooden go-karts. But Jeremy was a little more introverted than his brothers. While his older sibling Piers asked their father endless scientific questions, Jeremy preferred to disappear into the countryside to go fishing, or to read at home, a habit his mother encouraged. He liked adventure and travel books, and looking at maps and atlases: visions of other worlds. When he wanted to read, he was not easy to dissuade. From a young age, it was clear that he was going to follow his own path, and did not mind whether or not others came along.

This approach to life was harder to keep up away from home. Like a lot of leftwing families in postwar Britain, the Corbyns did not let their egalitarian politics restrict their educational choices. The boys were sent to private primary schools, then to a grand old local institution, Adams' Grammar School in Newport, a prosperous nearby country town. Like McDonnell at St Joseph's, Corbyn did not enjoy it. The school was strict: pupils could be beaten for wearing their uniform cap at the wrong angle. While political debate was encouraged, and the library even had a subscription to the socialist newspaper the *Morning Star*, which Corbyn began to read regularly, it was clear where the school's politics really lay. Some teachers and pupils took part in local hunts, and the school had a military cadet force. In 1964, to mark the general election, the school held its own party contest. Piers stood for the Communists, and Jeremy for Labour. The many Tory pupils tried to shout Jeremy down. He was not intimidated. But he won a total of two votes.

He got into more arguments with classmates by joining the League Against Cruel Sports. He refused to serve in the school cadet force, and instead joined the Campaign for Nuclear Disarmament. He also signalled his distance from the school in smaller ways, for example by wearing odd socks, in blatant contravention of the uniform code. The prefects, who were allowed to beat pupils, discovered that summoning Corbyn to their study did not deter him. He broke rules that he did not respect with a quiet but unyielding defiance.

The school's teaching did not inspire him. He was more interested in what he learned from the *Morning Star* and his books at home. In his mid-teens, he moved on from escapist titles to realistic ones: political novels such as *Things Fall Apart*, Chinua Achebe's terse, bleak 1958 fable about colonialism's destructive impact on Nigeria; and polemical histories such as Cecil Woodham-Smith's 1962 study of the Irish famine, *The Great Hunger*. The books Corbyn was drawn to combined brutal material about the consequences of British imperialism – rats ate the bodies of Irish famine victims, Woodham-Smith recorded – with direct, often didactic prose styles. To Corbyn at the time, and for long afterwards, these books seemed to explain the world.

In 1966, at the age of 16, he became a member of the Labour party's Young Socialists. Unlike Piers, and an increasing number of other young Britons, he thought the party was the only vehicle that could deliver desirable political change. Labour were in government, after all. Yet they had only a tiny majority of four, and little chance of pushing through significant reforms; so in 1966 Wilson called an early general election to try to strengthen his position. The Corbyns' constituency, a mixture of rural Tory areas and Labour-supporting towns such as industrial Telford, had been narrowly held by the Conservatives for 15 years. In 1966 it was a Labour target.

Instead of concentrating on his A-levels, Corbyn obtained a duplicating machine, a kind of mechanical predecessor to the photocopier, so that he could print party leaflets. He installed it in his bedroom – to his parents it was just another family contraption – and started cranking the handle. If he stayed up all night, he discovered, he could turn out a couple of thousand leaflets. He and his new friends from the Young Socialists then distributed them while out canvassing.

Their Labour constituency candidate lost by a tantalising 846 votes. But Wilson increased his majority to 98. And Corbyn had his first inkling of how addictive politics can be. That other career avenues might not be open to him he began to appreciate when he got the results of his A-levels: two Es. On his last day at school, the headmaster told him, 'You'll never make anything of your life.'

With his grades too poor for university, applying to VSO offered Corbyn another way out of Shropshire. In late 1967, he flew to Jamaica.

A decade and a half earlier, Diane Abbott's parents had come the other way. Both of them had emigrated to England from Smithville, a straggling village in the wooded hills of central Jamaica, separated from Kingston by miles of winding roads. Smithville had a history of self-reliance: its residents traditionally lived off their own land rather than working on the island's sugar plantations. That gave them a certain self-assurance.

Abbott's parents, not yet married, moved separately to England in the early 1950s, her mother to become an NHS nurse, her father to find factory work. They married in London in 1951, and their daughter was born two years later. For the first five years of her life, they lived in north Paddington, then a crowded quarter of Caribbean and Irish immigrants who shared the elegant but run-down houses. The Abbotts bought a three-storey terrace. Council housing was hard for immigrants to access, and despite being Labour voters, the Abbotts saw the opportunities in owning property. They rented out two floors to other families to help pay the mortgage.

As immigration and the tensions around it grew during the late 1950s, the area became a target for racists. In 1958, the year of major anti-immigrant riots in nearby Notting Hill, the Abbotts' road was visited by a white mob who hammered on the doors of the houses to see who lived inside. Diane and her frightened mother were at home. An Irish tenant of theirs answered the door to protect them. Seeing a white man, the racists walked on. Diane was four at the time, but she remembered the Irishman's intervention to her biographers Robin Bunce and Samara Linton over 60 years later.

Shortly after the incident, the Abbotts moved out of Paddington to somewhere that seemed calmer, the trim suburban town of Harrow, eight miles to the north. Although it was absorbed into London in 1965, Harrow's roomy Edwardian houses, smart private and state schools, mostly Conservative MPs and almost entirely white population made it feel more like the home counties. Abbott's father instigated the move, as a risky piece of upward mobility. Their friends and family were all back in inner London. Diane and her brother Hugh, who was two years younger, went to a Harrow primary school which had one other black pupil.

Diane was precocious. Every morning before primary school, while her mother was putting Diane's hair into plaits in front of a mirror, they would listen to the BBC's eight o'clock news on the radio. Diane became fascinated by the drama of world events, especially in politics. She would imagine how she would deal with them if she was prime minister, or secretary-general of the United Nations. Then she would walk past the mock-Tudor houses to school.

Her work there would often be considered good enough to be put up on the classroom wall, or read aloud to the other pupils. She acquired a conviction, which she never lost, that she could excel at any written task she put her mind to. Yet at the same time, some of the teachers and pupils made her feel that she did not quite belong, singling her out for attention, treating her as alien. Even her white best friend did not invite her home. Diane was becoming interested in power: in what it might feel like to have it, and what might be done with it. But people with power over her were beginning to show her that her opportunities would not be as limitless as she thought.

In 1965, she got into Harrow County School for Girls, a grammar as correct and sure of itself as its name suggested. Again, she was a rare black pupil in a wary white world. Her first English teacher refused to accept that 'a chubby black girl with pebble lenses', as Abbott later described her 12-year-old self, could have written the first essay that Abbott handed in, and accused her of copying it. To avoid being accused again, she dumbed down her English essays for the rest of the year.

But gradually her abilities were recognised. In a reference for university, her headmistress wrote: 'She has a quick mind and unusual independence of judgement, though the tenacity of her personality, not to say stubbornness at times, occasionally has led her to persevere in somewhat idiosyncratic views . . .'

At the school debating society and in the school magazine, Abbott supported the women's liberation movement and questioned the post-war welfare state, on the grounds that it was well-meaning but too intrusive. She acquired a reputation for being opinionated, and for being tough enough to cope with the consequences. One of her English set texts was the 19th-century novel *Vanity Fair*, and she became fascinated by its anti-heroine Becky Sharp, for her independence, fearlessness and ruthless social climbing, and for her ability to reinvent herself and recover from disasters.

When Abbott was 15, her parents' marriage fell apart. Her mother left to live in Yorkshire. Abbott and her brother and father moved out of Harrow to live in other, less prestigious London suburbs: first Edgware, then Queensbury. As well as studying for her O-levels and then her A-levels, Abbott did all the cooking and cleaning, feminism not being a concept her father recognised. Eventually, like her mother,

Abbott found him impossible to live with. For the final stages of her A-levels, she moved out to live with friends.

Her experience of the upheavals of the late 1960s was different from that of Jeremy Corbyn, John McDonnell, Ken Livingstone and Tony Benn. She watched them from a less secure vantage point. The first formative political event of her 1968 was not the student revolt in Paris in May, but Enoch Powell's 'rivers of blood' speech a month earlier. The already high-profile Conservative MP, then shadow defence minister, delivered his inflammatory diatribe about the dangers of immigration on a Saturday. When Abbott went to school the following Monday, 'Everything seemed different,' she told her biographers. 'You felt a little scared . . . that something had happened which carried a hint of menace, towards you personally.'

Like Paddington when she had lived there, Harrow temporarily became a focus for racists, despite its tiny number of immigrants. Its two Conservative MPs publicly supported Powell's position on immigration (the town's Labour MP did not). Later in the year, the two Tories openly argued that black and Asian Britons should be repatriated, encouraged by the state to return to the countries where they or their families had originated, as if Britain's empire and postwar appeals for immigrant workers had never happened. Over the summer, Harrow was visited by the far-right Racial Preservation Society and the Union Movement, which Oswald Mosley led as a successor organisation to his British Union of Fascists. While the Racial Preservation Society just distributed leaflets, the Union Movement campaigned in a council by-election, knocking on doors.

But the other political shift that Abbott felt in 1968 was hopeful rather than ominous. In October, at the Olympics in Mexico City, the African American athletes Tommie Smith and John Carlos won gold and bronze respectively in the 200 metres. As they stood on the winners' podium and the American national anthem played, they gave Black Power salutes, fists raised. It was Abbott's first sight of the Black Power movement, and she was stirred and inspired. Soon afterwards she began reading *Race Today*, a new magazine published in London which took an increasingly critical view of British race relations and which passed on ideas, news and contacts to the country's emerging network of Black Power and anti-racism activists.

An important part of this network were new black bookshops, which were opening in multiracial parts of London where the rents were cheap enough, such as the scruffy inner suburb of Finsbury Park. These shops stocked an international selection of previously hard-to-find works by black novelists and poets, as well as black histories, polemics, flyers and pamphlets. The shops validated their customers as well as informing them: they demonstrated that black Britain had a distinct culture and needs, and also that it was part of a much wider black diaspora. Abbott began regularly travelling in from outer London to visit New Beacon Books in Finsbury Park. About the subjects that Harrow County School for Girls would not touch, she would teach herself.

Yet by her late teens she had also begun to work out that, if she was going to pursue her interest in politics and power further, she would need to go where much of that power still was: the exclusive institutions that still dominated postwar England despite the country's slowly growing egalitarianism. Blotting out the turmoil at home, Abbott took four A-levels and got good enough grades to apply to an elite university. She chose Cambridge.

The teacher at Harrow County who supervised Oxbridge applications tried to dissuade her – 'I don't think you're up to it' – but that only made Abbott more determined. As state-educated applicants were required to at the time, she stayed on at her school for an extra term to prepare for the entrance exams and interviews, and tried to put the teacher's lack of faith in her out of her mind. She applied to study history, mainly because at Cambridge the subject included a lot of political content for students who wanted it. For her choice of college, she followed her school's strong advice – her ability to push back against authority was not limitless – and selected Newnham, a relatively modest and modern one, founded a century earlier to help equalise opportunities for women at the university. After her interview, one of her interrogators wrote: 'This girl a definite possibility'.

3

Politics for a New Society

In September 1970, two years after his epiphany at the Free University of Bristol, Tony Benn published a slim pamphlet which went on sale for five shillings. It was put out by the venerable centre-left think tank the Fabian Society, and from its red cover to its cautious title, *The New Politics: A Socialist Reconnaissance*, it looked like a pretty standard work by a Labour politician. But it was not. It was an attempt to describe a new world – to a large extent, the world we still live in today – and how the left might be able to dominate it.

Benn had been thinking hard since the heady months of 1968. As a busy minister, and a person more naturally drawn to activity than reflection, it did not come easily to him at first. But his family, which was at least as important to him as politics, helped him to become more exploratory. His teenage son Stephen protested against the Vietnam War. His teenage daughter Melissa became a feminist in the early 1970s. And his wife Caroline was a leftwing activist and author whose ideas about how to make Britain more equal, such as by the mass introduction of comprehensive schools, were often bolder than those of her husband's cabinet colleagues. Always candid and yet discreet – she did not give interviews – she was usually his most important advisor.

Thanks to his family, his encounters with the counterculture, his frustrations at Mintech and the period's generally disorientating rush of events, during the late 1960s and early 70s Benn underwent what he later called a 'radicalisation'. He began to move away from the Labour mainstream, and away from the mainstream of British politics altogether, into a new political role that he would find more fulfilling, and that others would see as highly dangerous.

His transformation was accelerated by a reduction in his own power and responsibilities. In June 1970, the government he had served so prominently was unexpectedly defeated in a general election. Voters rejected Harold Wilson's charismatic but ultimately underwhelming leadership – rather as Benn was in the process of doing – and opted instead for a more earnest Conservative premier, Edward Heath. Freed from his endless ministerial duties, Benn was able to develop more fully a set of bold themes which since 1968 he had been sketching out in occasional speeches.

These speeches were controversial: Wilson privately warned Benn that one of them 'had caused a lot of trouble', and less deft Labour figures than Wilson sometimes publicly criticised the speeches for weeks afterwards. But Benn was undeterred. The speeches further raised his profile, abroad as well as at home. In 1968, *Newsweek* magazine described him as 'the only European statesman who has so far made a public attempt to apply the lessons of the new French revolution'. Such praise was useful, and possibly a little intoxicating, for a politician who was beginning to consider trying for the Labour leadership, with Wilson's tenure seemingly nearing its end. But a more important motive for Benn's radicalisation was that he thought the times demanded it, that the compromising Labour politics of Wilson and much of the party were out of date. So during the summer of 1970 Benn poured all his new insights into his pamphlet.

After an opening page that was mostly uncharacteristic, throat-clearing rhetoric – a sign of nerves, perhaps, in someone usually so fluent – Benn introduced much of his argument in two short paragraphs:

> . . . Fewer people now really believe that the problems of our society can be solved simply by voting for a Government every four or five years. More people want to do more for themselves, and believe they are capable of doing so, if the conditions could only be created that would make this possible.
>
> If the Labour party could see in this rising tide of opinion a new expression of grass roots socialism, then it might renew itself and move nearer to the time when it is seen as the natural Government of a more fully self-governing society . . .

For a member of parliament, very recently a minister, who was a rising and increasingly important figure in a party which had spent much of its history arguing that the whole point of government was to provide things for citizens, the first paragraph sounded like heresy. Benn's bald statement of the limits of British parliamentary democracy, and his emphasis on self-reliance and the government's duty to foster it, felt like the prelude to a renunciation – to one of the journeys from left to right that politicians were beginning to make in Britain and the United States, as the limits of postwar social democracy became apparent during the 1970s.

But then the second paragraph did something different. With its claim that the rise of self-reliance was actually 'a new expression of grass roots socialism', which could make Labour stronger, Benn's argument swerved away from any obvious, right-leaning conclusions and into fresher, more radical territory. The decline of deference, the struggles of the centralised postwar state in trying to solve Britain's problems, even the growth of individualism: all these powerful ongoing trends did not mean that the left was doomed, he argued. On the contrary, they created huge new opportunities, if the left could change enough to take them.

The previous year, the voting age in the UK had been lowered from 21 to 18 by the Wilson government. There had been a protracted argument in the cabinet, with some ministers warning that teenagers were too wild or impressionable to have the vote, while others insisted that voting would channel their energies into orderly democratic politics and away from 1968-style rebellions. Some ministers argued that being able to vote was simply a right that everyone aged 18 or over should have. Benn was one of the most forceful and idealistic pro-youth voices. According to the minister and diarist Richard Crossman, 'Wedgy Benn made it clear he wouldn't stay a member of the Cabinet unless the eighteen-year-olds got justice.'

Like the first Wilson administration's numerous other social reforms, such as decriminalising homosexuality, relaxing the laws covering abortion and divorce, and outlawing the most blatant forms of racial discrimination, lowering the voting age would have long-term consequences, at least as long-term as Wilson's failure to modernise the economy, which quickly came to dominate how his first government was regarded. From 1970, when the new voting age came into force, the young mattered politically much more than before, and Benn understood this more quickly than most British politicians. In his pamphlet, he wrote that Labour ought to prioritise attracting their support.

More pioneering still, his pamphlet also explored the social and political consequences of changes in technology. Drawing on his Mintech experience and his love of gadgets, he attributed much of the flux of the late 1960s and early 70s to the increase of automation, 'information flow' and 'the growth of machine capability'. He was well aware that the postwar revolution in computing was gathering pace. At Mintech he had initiated the merger of the main British computer companies into a state-supported conglomerate, International Computers Limited, which was intended to compete with foreign computer giants such as IBM. Yet while technological advances were leading to the creation of bigger and bigger corporations, his pamphlet continued, 'Technology also releases forces that simultaneously permit and encourage decentralisation, diversity and the fuller development of human personality.'

Like prophetic counterculture thinkers such as the American hippie entrepreneur Stewart Brand, but decades before most British politicians, Benn saw that new technologies were helping to create what he called a 'new citizen'. This person, Benn wrote, 'dislikes being ordered around by anyone'. Instead, new citizens were part of 'the do-it-yourself society that is now being born' across the West. Yet these people were not pure individualists, he argued. Rather, they were a new, less biddable kind of collectivist:

> banding together with others of like mind . . . [into] pressure groups or action groups . . . community associations, amenity groups, shop-stewards movements, consumer societies, educational campaigns, organisations to help the old, the homeless, the sick, the poor or under-developed societies, militant communal organisations, student power, noise abatement societies . . .

Such groups were 'often seen as more attractive, relevant and effective by new citizens than working through the party system'. And they were producing 'a new style of political leadership', which was 'committed to a cause rather than the search for elected authority'.

The idea that getting elected was not the only worthwhile goal of politics was an appealing one to Benn, his party having recently lost a general election; and it would become more so over the next few decades, as he and his political descendants developed public personas and policies that were hard to sell to much of the electorate. More positively, he also saw the new politics of protest as a way for the left to expand its electoral appeal, through alliances between his party and outside activists and movements:

> The relationship that develops between this new [single] issue politics and the political parties, especially the Labour Party, is of crucial importance. Some groups will be working for causes hostile to our own objectives. But the majority, being the expression of human values against oppression by authority and the system of centralised power would be natural allies if only we can discover the right sort of relationship with them. We must not mistake their criticism for hostility, nor resent the fact that those who work in them have chosen such a role in preference to work exclusively within the Party. Each side has its own part to play in the process of socialist construction . . .

In essence, Benn wanted his habitually tribal party to open up, to realise that its efforts to change Britain from Westminster and Whitehall – Labour's usual top-down approach – would be much more effective if they were combined with the efforts of allies outside parliament who were 'achieving change from below'.

He appreciated that these social and protest movements would make demanding allies. Besides being intensely focused on their own goals, they disliked 'bureaucracy' and 'secrecy in decision-making', as he put it – again, hallmarks of past Labour governments. The difference between reaching a consensus in, say, a roomful of student activists, which might involve a few off-the-cuff speeches and a show of hands, and doing the same in a huge ministry, with all the necessary paperwork and meetings, was enormous. But really Labour had no choice, he argued, but to start trying to combine these two ways of doing politics. 'The demand for more popular power,' he wrote, 'is building up.'

One of the places this was most obvious was in factories. During the 1960s, the general decline of British deference had not stopped at the factory gates. Instead it had begun to radicalise trade unionism. The relatively placid unions of the previous three decades, which had been top-down organisations dominated by London-based leaders, largely content to grow their memberships and maintain mutually beneficial relationships with both Labour and Tory governments, became more restive in the rebellious years around 1968. A substantial and growing minority of union members and shop stewards, their elected representatives in individual workplaces, started to want more than gradual improvements in pay and conditions, negotiated and then enacted by others. They also wanted a say in how their workplaces were run – or even to run them themselves. In Britain during the 60s and 70s this potentially transformative idea was sometimes known by the benign-sounding phrase 'industrial democracy', and sometimes by a more provocative one: 'workers' control'.

In 1968, an Institute for Workers' Control (IWC) was set up in Nottingham to refine and lobby for the concept. One of its co-founders was Ken Coates, an energising former coalminer who had become an activist for multiple leftwing causes which emphasised bottom-up participation rather than top-down hierarchies, and building coalitions rather than being sectarian. In the late 60s and throughout the 70s, Coates relentlessly promoted the IWC's ideas, with conferences, informal gatherings of leftwing activists and trade unionists, and conversations with any Labour politician he could interest. As Benn became radicalised, the two men recognised they had shared political preoccupations. They began talking for hours on the phone.

One of their favourite topics was Yugoslavia. Since the early 1950s, the one-party eastern European state had fascinated many Western leftists by diverging from Soviet-style communism and pursuing its own, more liberal version, fundamental to which was a version of workers' control. Instead of factories being told what to do by central government, as in the Soviet Union – or by corporate headquarters, as in the West – in Yugoslavia all economic enterprises with over 30 employees were largely controlled by workers' councils, elected every two years. Investment was provided by the state, as was a national economic strategy; and the state had to be handed just over half of each enterprise's profits. Otherwise, the workers' councils were free to manage: setting prices for what their factory produced, deciding the levels of its employees' wages and benefits, and choosing which other factories it would do business with. All these enterprises then competed with each other, almost as they did in the capitalist West. Officially, the system was known as 'socialist self-management', but excited observers outside Yugoslavia sometimes called it a 'socialist market economy', or 'a new workers' capitalism'.

It was not perfect. Workers who lacked social confidence or simply did not have the time did not get involved in the councils. The management of factories sometimes became dominated by cliques, which could lead to corruption. And as in any competitive economic system, some enterprises performed better than others, and that polarised and ultimately helped to fragment an already divided country. Yet during the postwar years the break-up of Yugoslavia in the 1990s was still decades away. The economy grew fast, and new industries modernised the lives of millions of former rural labourers. Yugoslavia seemed to offer a model to people dissatisfied with the economic status quo, in the East and the West. In 1971, Benn visited the country. 'Three most interesting days,' he recorded in his diary. 'Their self-management . . . we should study.'

In his pamphlet the year before, he had written about workers' control enthusiastically and at length. To reassure readers who might think the concept too foreign or revolutionary, he had cleverly compared the concept to British democracy. Advocates of workers' control in Britain, he said, wanted essentially 'the same relationship' between employers and employees as had long ago been established in British politics, when 'the universal adult franchise brought about full political democracy, or what it might be more helpful to re-name "voters' control"'.

He extended the comparison:

There is no more reason why industrial power at plant or office level should be exclusively linked to ownership of shares, than that political power should have been exclusively linked to the ownership of land and other property as it was in Britain until the 'voters' control' movement won its battle.

Nor, and this is the important point, is there any reason why the new demands should be any more revolutionary, in the sense of paving the way for violence, than were the old demands. It is true that some of the advocates of workers' control are believers in the violent overthrow of the existing order. But then so were some of the advocates of the wider franchise. In the event, by one of those characteristically skilful and long drawn out withdrawals in the face of the inevitable which is the genius of the British ... that has given us 300 years free of violent revolution – the powers that be ... granted the demands [for political democracy] in full.

This passage was the new, radical Benn at his most seductive: proposing a fundamental shift in the balance of power in Britain, yet making it sound like patriotic common sense. His tone was not grand or fanatical, but calm, informal, conversational, even witty – gently mocking those who defended the status quo. His breadth of historical reference was persuasive. And his argument seemed logical.

In fact, there were gaps in it. The pamphlet said little about the people who wielded great power over many businesses without necessarily owning shares in them – the senior management – other than to suggest that the workers and their more immediate managers should join forces and persuade those in company headquarters to devolve power. This sounded optimistic, especially as Benn also proposed that workers should have the ability to 'hire and fire' their immediate managers. Would it really be so easy for workers and bosses to agree 'a common solution', as he put it, 'to the problem of how human satisfaction can be found in work'? The state of industrial relations in Britain in the early 1970s, with strikes at their highest level for half a century, suggested otherwise.

And yet, in a more worldly passage of the pamphlet, Benn argued that it was precisely this acrimony that made workers' control essential. Employees currently had 'enormous negative power' – the power to strike – but little or no 'constructive power' such as 'the power to plan their own work'. Under a system of workers' control, he argued, employees would be more involved in their businesses and therefore have more of an incentive to make a success of them. There would be 'real gains in self-respect, self-fulfilment, improved working conditions, better management and productivity'.

However, he ended with a warning:

[Workers' control] will prove to be no more, and no less, a panacea for industrial workers than parliamentary democracy has been for the electors. With real power will come real responsibility for dealing with some of the outer realities of our competitive world, including the inescapable market mechanisms ... which will set severe limits on the freedom the new power will bring ... There will almost certainly be failures. [But] these could hardly be worse than ... those experienced by many thousands of workers who became redundant every year under the owner-imposed management of today.

The Benn of 1970, increasingly thinking of himself, and being thought of, as a potential prime minister, was beginning to propose a very different Britain. But the case he was making for it was still quite pragmatic, and accepted that checks would remain on what could be achieved, such as 'the inescapable market mechanisms' of global capitalism. As the decade went on, he would become more aware, but also less accepting, of such limits.

The rest of the pamphlet carried hints that his radicalisation had only just begun. In two dozen pages it sketched his evolving thoughts on almost as many topics, including economics, international relations, education, and how to restore 'human dignity' to Britain's racial minorities. The latter section in particular was startlingly ambitious, especially for someone who until recently had seemed to be just another keen young minister. In it Benn criticised 'the traditional socialist concern with money' as the main 'measure of inequality'. While this emphasis was understandable, he said, it caused the left to neglect other 'problems of power'. One of these was the treatment of racial and other minorities by government and the dominant social groups. To end this discrimination, he called for the left 'actively to encourage diversity ... so that each feels proud of his or her individual identity'. He argued:

Unless everyone adopts the philosophy associated with the phrase 'Black is Beautiful' by which is meant 'I am proud of what I am and want to develop within the best tradition of my own culture', we shall progressively ... dehumanise people ...

47

In effect, Benn was saying that the left should embrace identity politics: the idea that who an individual is – racially or sexually, for
example – is a profoundly political matter, and should be a basis for
how they are treated by government and society. Not only was Benn
making this argument as an upper-class, heterosexual white man, the
kind of Briton who stood to lose the most privilege relative to others
if the country treated its diverse citizens more equally, he was also
making this argument long before identity politics became a recognised concept. The first use of the phrase, it is generally agreed, would
not be for another seven years, in a 1977 manifesto produced by the
Combahee River Collective, a pioneering group of black socialist
feminist lesbians in Boston, Massachusetts.

Benn's pamphlet also pointed towards another area of huge future
contention. In a section near the end titled 'beyond parliamentary
democracy', he argued that greater participation by the public was
needed in British politics. This ought to include 'some direct decision-
making', he continued, such as 'holding nationwide referenda on
specific issues'. He cited one controversy which was increasingly pre-
occupying him:

> We have to face the fact that a demand for a referendum has begun to
> emerge over the Common Market issue where there are such sharp dif-
> ferences of opinion within each party that it would not be possible to
> decide the issue at a general election . . .

In 1970 Britain had not yet joined the Common Market, as the EEC
was often known then. That would come three years later. And Benn
was not yet opposed to British membership. During the late 1960s
and early 70s he supported it, because he believed that the sheer size
of the EEC would partially protect its members against the ever more
global powers of corporations. 'If we have to have some sort of organisation to control international companies,' he recorded in his diary in
April 1970, 'the Common Market is probably the right one.'

But behind his qualified enthusiasm he was also becoming convinced that for Britain to join, especially in an era of 'popular power',
would require more of a democratic mandate than a parliamentary
majority. Otherwise, he wrote, the dissatisfaction of 'those who were

opposed to entry' could be such that 'something like a breakdown' in British democracy 'might occur'. A vague outline of the British wars over Europe to come was forming in his political imagination.

Yet in 1970 he did not spend too much time worrying about the future. He believed that politics was opening up for him, and for many other Britons. A new left seemed possible, that would be more expansive and attuned to modern life than the old one. A new left that, like the '68ers, prioritised freedom and participation as much as equality. In one of his pamphlet's key sentences, Benn set out how this change should begin to come about. 'It must be a prime objective of socialists,' he wrote, 'to work for the redistribution of political power.'

Perhaps because he did not read many books, Benn's pamphlet presented his ideas as novel, without reference to other politicians or to political thinkers, except for a fleeting mention of Karl Marx. And indeed Benn's argument for bottom-up rather than top-down socialism was an unusual one for a member of Britain's postwar governing elite to be making. Since 1945 Labour had generally believed that the House of Commons and Whitehall were where leftwing policies such as nationalisation should be conceived and honed before being rolled out across the country. Enlightened and able reformers, like Benn at Mintech, would lead Britain into a better future. Or so the theory went.

However, alongside this approach existed another, more marginal but more democratic Labour tradition. It predated Benn's radicalisation, and 1968, by at least half a century. And it sometimes drew ideas and inspiration from non-Labour sources such as anarchism, the most egalitarian early phases of the 1917 Russian Revolution, and the early 19th-century Welsh utopian socialist Robert Owen, who founded two short-lived communities in England and the United States which replaced the market economy with workers' cooperatives and property held in common.

The strand of Labour politics influenced by these radicals was ambitious, even revolutionary. Two of its main theorists were R. H. Tawney and G. D. H. Cole, both leftwing historians at Oxford University. During the early 1920s they each produced a provocative, readable book arguing that workers should manage themselves, rather than submit to employers or shareholders – or to the state, as more orthodox Labour figures in favour of nationalisation envisaged. In economic life, exactly as in politics, Tawney wrote, 'Men should not be ruled by an authority which they cannot control'. Unlike the 'socialist self-management' introduced in Yugoslavia three decades later, Tawney and Cole wanted the democratic workplace to be an extension of political democracy. And this empowerment of the workers was intended to be only the first step in a larger transformation. 'The real aim,' wrote Cole in 1920, should be 'wresting bit by bit from the hands of the possessing classes the economic power which they now exercise', in order ultimately to 'make possible an equitable distribution of the national income and a reasonable reorganisation of Society as a whole'.

Yet Cole was vague about how this overturning of the traditional order would happen. 'He who wishes revolution to succeed should hasten towards it slowly,' he wrote cryptically. 'The thing to aim at . . . is . . . the consolidation of all [leftwing] forces . . . with a view to making the "revolution" . . . as little as possible like a civil war.'

For the next four decades, both he and Tawney had prolific academic careers, and intermittent influence over Labour. Cole was largely responsible for his student Harold Wilson joining the party. But amid all this activity their radical 1920s ideas were gradually forgotten. Cole died in 1959, and Tawney three years later. When Benn took up their search for a version of socialism that would make Britain more democratic as well as more equal – what Cole called a 'self-governing' society – he did so with the winds of 1968 behind him. But in the top echelons of the Labour party, he was alone.

Yet away from Britain, on the other side of the world, there was a country where the dream of democratic socialism seemed much closer to realisation. In September 1970, the same month that Benn published his pamphlet, a presidential election took place in Chile. The winner, by a narrow 1.3 per cent of the vote, was Salvador Allende of the Socialist Party.

Unlike Benn, he was not an obviously charismatic politician. Sixty-two years old, stout and bespectacled, with a modest voice that he struggled to raise when he addressed rallies, Allende had been standing for the presidency at every election for almost 20 years. Until his victory he used to joke that his epitaph would be 'Here lies the next president of Chile'. He came from a prestigious family of doctors and free-masons, a tradition he continued, and as a young man had even spent a year in the army. Up to 1970 it was possible to see him as a token leftwinger: a respectable dissenting figure whose dogged but never decisive presence in Chilean politics enabled the country to present itself as one of South America's few genuinely diverse democracies.

But Allende's sensible exterior concealed more adventurous impulses. His interest in politics had started when he was a teenager in Val-paraiso, a rackety old port on Chile's Pacific coast. His family's house happened to be opposite a workshop used by an Italian immigrant shoemaker, Juan De Marchi. De Marchi was an anarchist, and had been an activist in Chile and Argentina for decades. Now in his early sixties, he and the 14-year-old Allende became friends. After school, they played chess and talked about Chilean and foreign politics. De Marchi became Allende's informal tutor, lending him political books, guiding him through their more theoretical passages, and intro-ducing his protégé, as Allende put it later, 'to the straightforward generosity of the average worker'.

Although a decade later, in 1933, Allende became one of the co-founders of the Socialist Party of Chile, some of anarchism's preoccupation with liberty stayed with him. In his first public speech as president he declared, 'The road to socialism lies through democ-racy, pluralism and freedom.' Cannily exploiting his isolated country's sense of exceptionalism, he called his government's guiding philoso-phy 'the Chilean road to socialism'. His administration aggressively nationalised businesses and redistributed wealth, but also protected free speech and parliamentary democracy. Seemingly answering G. D. H. Cole's call for a socialist revolution without civil war, Allende said he wanted a 'peaceful evolution from the old society to the new'. Unlike in the Soviet bloc, Yugoslavia, or Cuba, Allende's Chile had no secret police or other authoritarian machinery.

Even the rightwing press in Britain were intrigued. 'An astonishing experiment [is] taking place in Chile,' reported the *Daily Mail* on the first anniversary of Allende's election. To the paper's visiting reporter, one of hundreds from around the world, Chilean socialism seemed both effective and vibrant, even hedonistic, with average wages up '36 per cent' in a year, young women in the capital Santiago 'wearing hot pants', and restaurants 'crammed with people eating the local sea-food, washed down with one of Chile's excellent wines'. If the Chilean experiment survived, the *Mail* concluded, 'The implications will be immense' for the many Western countries, including Britain, which had long believed they had to choose between radical leftwing gov-ernment and democracy. Labour sent its shadow minister for overseas development, Judith Hart, a future ally of Tony Benn from the left of the party, to have a look at what was happening in Chile and to meet Allende. 'It is unique, this democratic revolution,' she wrote after-wards. 'There are no patterns to follow: it is new ground all the way.'

One much younger Labour party member was already well aware of that. After leaving Jamaica, travelling across the Caribbean on a cargo boat, and then down through South America by hitchhiking, Jeremy Corbyn arrived in Chile in early 1969, not long before his 20th birthday. He became one of the first Britons to witness what was stirring there.

Allende's latest campaign for the presidency had not yet formally started, but a feeling of anticipation was already building. In the pre-vious two elections, in 1958 and 1964, he had dramatically increased his share of the vote to almost 40 per cent, as the candidate for a suc-cession of broad but volatile coalitions of leftwing and centre-left parties, ranging from the Communists to the Christian Democrats. In 1969 the coalition renamed itself Popular Unity. During the 60s a protest movement had also emerged from Chilean folk music, with popular and photogenic singer-songwriters such as Victor Jara attack-ing the country's social divisions and backing Allende. And Chile's large indigenous population, the Mapuche, who had been stripped of their land by the government during the 19th century, were increas-ingly organising politically and moving leftwards, hoping that an Allende government would return their territory.

Corbyn knew a little about all this before he arrived, having learned about Popular Unity as he was travelling, from South American news-papers and the BBC World Service. Chile was surrounded by countries with military governments, so Allende's much more liberal approach was attracting attention across the continent. The fact that his coalition included communists and politicians from the radical left did not trouble Corbyn, despite his own loyalties to the more centrist Labour party. He had already encountered and worked with communists in Britain, as a young CND activist.

On May Day 1969, in Chile as elsewhere a key day in the left's calendar, Popular Unity mounted a giant march and rally in Santiago. Corbyn joined the march:

> I noticed something very different to any experience I'd had before. A political march that was fun, that was a celebration, that [had] music, enjoyment, optimism, hope . . . Salvador Allende was doing this incredible tour around Chile . . . [to] weld together the folk tradition, the song tradition, the artistic tradition, the intellectual tradition with a quite bureaucratic political tradition . . . The May Day march was full of hopeful talk of the left coming together to elect a president who would lead the transformation of Chile.

In Santiago, Corbyn stayed in a shared flat with other visiting leftists and political observers from outside Chile. As the impact of '68 seemed to be fading in Europe, people were looking for new causes. One of Corbyn's flatmates was a member of the British Trotskyist group, the International Socialists, sworn enemies of Communist parties everywhere, and suspicious of Allende for including one in his coalition. This flatmate's view, Corbyn told me, was that Allende was a 'depressing constitutionalist': not confrontational enough.

Exploring Santiago, Corbyn was amazed by the wealth of the city's elite eastern suburbs, which rose in a maze of private driveways and hillside golf courses towards the nearby Andes. Those suburbs contained few Allende supporters, unlike the universities of the crowded city centre and the shanty towns straggling out to the west.

Corbyn left Santiago to learn more about the Chilean situation. On the coast, he went to a leftwing folk festival in the usually escapist casino resort of Vina del Mar. It was held on the beach, even though it was winter, and the weather was 'bloody cold', he remembered. But the excited audience was large, young and diverse, including some Mapuche, and he was captivated by the social realism and militancy of the performers.

He travelled all over the country, from the copper mining city of Antofagasta in the desert north, where he noticed that the workers were unionised and well-paid, to the port of Puerto Montt in the damp south, which was 'miserable, grey and very angry'. Armed police had recently killed ten people there who had squatted unoccupied farmland owned by an absentee landlord. To Corbyn, the countryside seemed 'totally feudal', with huge estates worked by generations of landless labourers. The towns and cities were more modern, European-seeming, but still starkly divided, and tense with discontent. 'You could see that the basis for Popular Unity was there,' Corbyn said.

He became more and more inspired by Allende's promises to end Chile's social, economic and racial disparities, and to do so democratically, through a fresh, inclusive approach to leftwing government. Almost half a century later, when Corbyn unexpectedly became the frontrunner for the Labour leadership, and started to make big promises about changing Britain, he was asked by the *New Statesman* which historical figure he most identified with. 'Probably Salvador Allende,' he said.

4

The Young Turks

Corbyn did not have enough money to see Allende elected. In mid-1970, with his funds exhausted after two years abroad, he returned to England. He moved back in with his parents in Shropshire, with no idea what he was going to do next. He was even more obsessed by politics than when he had left for Jamaica, but political activism was not a way of making a living. And with his two Es at A-level and no university degree, his career options were limited. Shropshire is one of England's most rural counties, with few big towns and no cities. He found a job at a farm, looking after pigs.

The experience turned him into a vegetarian. More upset than he expected to be at the animals he looked after going off to slaughter, he did not stay at the farm long. Shortly afterwards, he made a career decision. He would use his curiosity about how societies worked and become a journalist. Following the usual path for aspiring reporters then, he started at his local paper, the *Newport and Market Drayton Advertiser*. During the day he cycled with his notebook between weddings, funerals and minor crime scenes, back and forth along the country lanes. At home in the early mornings and the evenings, he scoured the national newspapers for news of Chile.

It was not hard to find. Throughout its existence, the Allende government interested the British press to an extent that is hard to imagine now, when regular coverage of such faraway, relatively small countries has almost vanished. The interest in Chile was partly because the country had historic links with Britain: economic, military and political ones going back almost 200 years, which during the 19th century had been so intricate that both British writers and Chilean politicians then called Chile 'the England of the Pacific'. To British journalists,

Allende also seemed a familiar sort of politician: pragmatic, understated, committed to parliamentary democracy – not one of the grandiose authoritarians often found in the rest of South America. In 1971, when his policies were still widely seen as a success, the *Daily Telegraph* compared his 'quiet revolution' to the postwar Labour government of Clement Attlee.

Meanwhile, for leftwing Britons the Allende experiment was a source of hope, and an escape. In the early 1970s Britain had a Conservative government. Yet as in Chile, the political situation still seemed full of potential for the left. The stiff Tory prime minister Edward Heath was struggling with waves of strikes, trade unions were growing and radicalising, and more campuses were being influenced by leftwing students and ideas than in 1968. The revolt of that year was not over; it had spread. As the British counterculture magazine *Frendz* put it in 1972: 'If flower power has gone to seed then germination must soon begin. And what King Weeds they'll be.'

Stuck in Shropshire, Corbyn found it hard to join in. He resumed his membership of the Young Socialists, but with the next general election not due until possibly as late as 1975, there was no immediate prospect of any exciting campaign work to help Labour finally capture his local seat. He also discovered that while he had been away the Young Socialists had been taken over by the Militant Tendency, a small but rapidly growing Trotskyist sect which infiltrated Labour party organisations in order to increase its political leverage. Militant was revolutionary, but also quite conservative on non-economic issues, dismissing causes which Corbyn supported such as nuclear disarmament as 'trendy' distractions, and against forming genuinely cooperative alliances with other leftwing groups. In May 1972, when Corbyn went to the Young Socialists' annual conference at the Lincolnshire seaside town of Skegness, he found not a Chilean-style carnival of the left but a more dour gathering, where the national committee was controlled by Militant and resolutions moved by delegates loyal to Militant passed with monotonous regularity. Like the other genuine Labour leftwingers present, Corbyn had the disorientating experience of being treated by the Militant delegates as a rightwinger.

But at Skegness he also met two people who would help open up a new world for him. Among the beleaguered Labour leftwingers were a young couple, Valerie and Keith Veness. Keith was blunt but warm, Valerie a bit more steely, and they were dedicated constituency activists. Yet they were not the kind of activists who just did what the party told them. They wanted to change Labour: from the gradualist, broadly centre-left body which Wilson was currently leading in opposition, into a bolder, more radical, more modern party – a party not very different from the one that Tony Benn was beginning to envisage. The Venesses did their activism in the area of the country where such a transformation had the best chance of getting under way: inner London.

Ken Livingstone was already at work for the left in the south of the city, in Lambeth. The Venesses operated in the north, in Islington. Over the weekend of the Skegness conference, Valerie and Keith quickly took a liking to Corbyn, finding him bright and committed. He liked their frankness and political experience. Keith suggested that he come to London and join the cause. After Labour's defeats in the 1968 local elections and 1970 general election, its membership in the capital had plunged. In London, Keith said, Labour was 'an empty shell' – a shell that could be filled.

In the early 1970s, London and its politics were very different from how they are now. The city's population had been shrinking for three decades. There was still damage and trauma from the bombings of the Second World War. The docks were closing, too small to adapt to the postwar invention of the shipping container. Made less viable by factories in cheaper locations abroad, more than half the city's manufacturing jobs disappeared between 1961 and 1981. London's ageing transport system was starved of investment by cash-strapped governments. Meanwhile, Londoners moved out to the home counties and the postwar new towns, as Whitehall tried to make the capital less dominant economically and the electrification of railway lines across south-east England made commuting more practical. London in the 70s was in some ways still the city it had always been – huge, atmospheric, historic – but its best days seemed to be behind it.

And yet, in cities, decline and recovery are often intertwined. The tattier and emptier inner London became, the more affordable its still handsome Georgian and Victorian housing stock was for a new kind of homebuyer. In postwar Britain, the middle class was growing and changing: professions such as social work and advertising were expanding, more women were working, and tastes were becoming more cosmopolitan. Instead of moving to the suburbs, as bourgeois Londoners had done for much of the 19th and 20th centuries, abandoning or ignoring the inner-city housing originally built for them, some of this new, less formal middle class moved back into the inner city, nearer to work and childcare, and to the novel foods and culture brought by postwar immigrants, who had chosen inner London as the only place they could afford. The first boroughs to be reoccupied by the middle class were ones with good transport links, such as Islington, Camden, and Lambeth; a few years later the process spread to more cut-off boroughs such as Hackney and Haringey. In 1964 the pioneering Anglo-German urbanist Ruth Glass gave this process a name: 'gentrification'.

Many of London's gentrifiers, while acquisitive about property and consumer pleasures, were left of centre in their politics, or became so, as the inner city's mix of people and environments made the capital's poverty and decaying infrastructure hard to ignore. By the 1968 local elections, there were not enough of these new leftists to offset the decline in Labour's traditional working-class London vote, some of whom were simply fed up with the Wilson government, and some of whom had left the capital for housing estates in the new towns. But by the early 1970s, the left's metamorphosis in the capital had progressed further. With the Conservatives now unpopular because of the Heath government's struggles, in 1971 Labour recaptured most of the London councils it had lost three years earlier, including Islington and Lambeth. And as a celebratory article in the *New Statesman* explained, London's leftwing incomers became more than just a new bloc of voters.

'Young Turks of the Town Halls' portrayed Islington and Lambeth as promising territories for the left: 'a vast acreage of council housing, large numbers of black immigrants and important areas of middle-class colonisation', where some gentrifiers were already activists, of a non-party sort, in 'aggressive Action Groups' and 'anxious amenity societies'. Inner London was also home to the country's greatest concentration of new social and political movements: squatters, feminists, environmentalists, Black Power groups, the Gay Liberation Front. In this politically febrile environment, some of the middle-class incomers had quickly moved from being Labour voters to Labour members to Labour councillors. Of the latter, many were 'political virgins' – had never stood for office before – and had

> an appropriately virginal combination of innocence and ambition ... They were very young, especially for politicians: average age around 30 ... [Their] slogan is 'Do it now!' [Council] rents have been frozen; Lambeth worked out within days a copybook agreement with the powerful London squatters group; Islington declared war on the private townhouse developer ...

Previously, Labour councillors in London, as elsewhere, had often been middle-aged or elderly men from the right of the party, working-class social conservatives often elected by voters like themselves, and governing in a studiedly respectable manner, with little feel or sympathy for the new urban activists of the 1960s and 1970s. But now that London municipal style was giving way to another. The Labour councillors' rooms in Lambeth Town Hall, reported the *New Statesman*, now 'resembled a frenetic newspaper office in a thirties film – all shirtsleeves and urgency'. Like Tony Benn, the new councillors wanted what the magazine called 'a democratic opening up' of the state's 'thought processes to the public'. The fact that such a liberated, probably fractious form of local government had never been tried in Britain before did not seem to matter to the new councillors: 'They see themselves as the first example of a new kind of political animal.'

The author of the 'Young Turks' article was a London Labour councillor and journalist called Illtyd Harrington. He was a decade older and much more politically experienced than his subjects, having been a councillor since the late 1950s. But he shared some of their disregard for the status quo. A roguish, outspoken leftwinger, he had lived openly with his partner since long before homosexuality was decriminalised. During the 1960s he had been rejected as a Labour parliamentary candidate because of his support for radical non-party bodies such as CND. In the party's new, more socially liberal London councillors he saw a welcome change coming. 'The youthful meritocracy who have seized power in parts of London may well have long political lives ahead of them,' he wrote. '[They] already see themselves as the fulcrum of political power in the party ...' And he envisaged a more high-profile role for them still: 'Here are the men who will run [London], in the teeth of any Prime Minister.'

One of the new Lambeth councillors was Ken Livingstone. He was not mentioned in the *New Statesman* article, either because Harrington had not come across him, or because he did not completely fit the picture the article painted. Although he shared much of their political outlook, Livingstone was hardly a leftwing gentrifier: he was a working-class inner London native who lived with his parents. At first, he lacked the social and political confidence of the posher Lambeth council candidates. 'As an awkward twenty-five-year-old,' he wrote later, 'I found it embarrassing knocking on doors in the 1971 borough elections and pleading, "Vote for me."'

The idea that he should stand, barely two years after becoming a party member, had come from a local Labour agent called Eddie Lopez. The son of a Spanish Civil War refugee, Lopez was a driven and persuasive activist who was determined to make the council both more leftwing and more dynamic. 'He would have us [the party members] stuffing envelopes until four or five in the morning,' wrote Livingstone. The two men became friends as well as comrades, partly because they liked the same music. They would listen to the florid British rock band Cream on huge headphones in Lopez's living room. Cream were a supergroup, a trio of already famous musicians whose egos you could hear in their thundering, competitive solos. The band's short life, from 1966 to 1968, said something about how the decade's preoccupations with both individualism and collectivism were not always reconcilable.

Livingstone's successful election campaign also had help from a more traditional but less likely source. His Tory father, while still voting Conservative in a neighbouring ward, drove Labour supporters to polling stations in his van to help his son. Livingstone's father was in his mid-fifties, finally working less hard, and beginning to think about retirement. As an elected politician now, Livingstone had other audiences for his opinions. Their relationship mellowed.

Livingstone entered local government with very high expectations –
expectations that may seem baffling if you think municipal politics is
minor and grey. 'In local government,' he told his biographer John
Carvel, 'you had a chance to involve people in the running of their
lives, to break up the concentrations of power.' It was a very 1968
rationale for becoming a politician. And it never left him.

This enthusiasm was not naive. Livingstone read about politics
constantly: not works of theory, but biographies of both rightwing
and leftwing figures, studies of voting behaviour, history books, official reports, council agendas. He saw politics as an ever-shifting
battleground, where effective politicians, without ditching their
underlying ideology, always had to be watching for changes in the
rules of engagement and the balance of forces, and how those changes
could be exploited.

During the 1960s London's borough councils, until then relatively
small and weak bodies, had acquired more powers, such as managing
social services. Livingstone understood these adjustments to the
system, and their political implications. He also understood the new
political forces that were appearing outside the system, and how they
could become Labour's allies and also reinvigorate the party. During
the late 60s and early 70s, pupils in Lambeth became involved in the
Schools Action Union (SAU), an increasingly militant movement for
liberalising education which was inspired by the university occupations of 1968. Many of SAU's south London activists were from
private and grammar schools, but their privilege did not bother Livingstone, who was a fan of the anarchic British film *If*, released in late
1968, about a violent rebellion at a boarding school. He and Lopez let
the school activists hold meetings at Labour's Lambeth offices, and
urged Labour-supporting school governors not to expel them for
going on strike. Some of the activists joined the local Labour party,
and two became Lambeth councillors. One of the two, Paul Moore,
then worked with Livingstone in London government on and off for
the next 30 years. Livingstone often thought about politics in cold,
transactional terms: 'People worked with you on issues,' he said in
2013. 'There are no permanent alliances.' But he also saw the value of
having a small circle of longstanding collaborators, to draw on when
required.

In Lambeth, he also worked closely with another social movement: the squatters. Like most inner London boroughs, Lambeth had whole streets of empty houses, a consequence of the city's dwindling population, the construction of new council estates and the sheer cost of modernising dilapidated, sometimes bomb-damaged Victorian terraces. If the houses were still habitable, they were often occupied by squatters, usually young people with a countercultural outlook who could not or would not pay rent. Often, councils were hostile towards these hairy interlopers, and deliberately damaged the houses to prevent squats being established, tearing out their toilets and punching holes in their roofs.

Even before he became a councillor, Livingstone saw this stance as intolerant and wasteful in a city which, despite depopulation, still did not have enough cheap housing. Before the 1971 elections he met the squatters, and experts from the anti-homelessness charity Shelter, and together they came up with a plan for the squatting groups to form a housing association, the Family Squatting Association: it would be given the use of the empty properties until the council either refurbished or demolished them. Once Livingstone had been elected – quite possibly with some of their votes – he met the squatters again, accompanied by council officials, and the arrangement was quickly formalised. This was the 'copybook agreement' cited by Harrington in the *New Statesman*. Within two years, over 300 people were living in the previously abandoned properties.

Livingstone was exhilarated by his early experiences as a councillor:

> It was intoxicating to be at what seemed the centre of events. We were pushing ahead with our schemes. We had honoured our pledge that pensioners travel free on London Transport buses. We introduced . . . free contraception for anyone who lived or worked in the borough. When Mrs Thatcher (then Education Secretary) made it illegal for Education Authorities to give children free milk, Lambeth – which was not an education authority – stepped in to continue paying for the service.

Successful political stunts; defiance of central government; ingenuity at finding ways round Westminster restrictions; provocative social liberalism; and attentiveness to traditional public services such as transport – many of the ingredients of what would become the Livingstone recipe for local government were already being stirred together during his time at Lambeth. Not all the initiatives were his: he was only a junior councillor and the vice-chair of housing. But he was involved in Lambeth's politics and government on multiple, interconnected levels. With the local left's other activists and councillors, he pushed for Labour's election manifestos for the borough to be more radical. He helped game the party's candidate selection process to maximise the likely number of leftwing councillors. And after each election he then plotted to strengthen their influence in the town hall. This was 'a vicious struggle', he wrote, 'in which I was an enthusiastic participant'.

There was little in his life to get in the way of politics. He had few personal responsibilities. His home was provided by his parents. In 1970, he left his work as a lab technician for a three-year course at an undemanding teacher training college, which he attended as little as possible and where he did the absolute minimum required to pass. He was a much more familiar figure at Lambeth Town Hall: slight, young-looking, wispily bearded, his hairstyles getting gradually longer until they curled down to the collars of his open-necked shirts. He dressed casually, and spoke in a nasal south London drone, but his narrow eyes were busy, flicking between watchfulness, amusement, and mischief. His future seemed wide open.

Then his father suddenly died at the age of 56. Having only recently grown close to him, Livingstone was devastated. 'I assumed the pain would lessen,' he wrote long afterwards, 'but it was twenty years before it began to fade.' His mother stayed in London for one more year, until 1972. Then she sold the family home and moved to Lincolnshire.

Livingstone focused even more on politics. Partly, it was to avoid thinking about his father, and partly it was a new awareness of his own mortality. Livingstone's own health was good, but he would worry about it from now on. Meanwhile, he worked with greater urgency: 'Dad's early death taught me not to play safe. I would take risks.'

There were a few Lambeth council officers who were open-minded, even excited, about finding new solutions to the borough's entrenched problems. One was Harry Simpson, the director of housing. He wanted Lambeth to have more council homes, and their tenants to have a say in the running of their estates; and also to stop his department's unofficial practice of letting new properties to 'whites only', as a pencilled note on their documents traditionally put it. On all these issues, he and Livingstone agreed. Simpson became his mentor, giving him books and reports on housing to read, and encouraging him to come to the housing department and badger officers with questions (which they did not always welcome). Livingstone had a huge appetite for the detail of government, which co-existed with a distrust of the state which came from his interest in anarchism and in the revolts of 1968. These qualities would make him a highly effective local politician, but also an erratic one.

Yet a combination of political change and obstructive officers undermined many of his schemes. In 1973, two years after he had been elected, the council leadership and the position of housing chair were both captured by councillors from the Labour right. However energetically the left plotted, the right plotted too, and the left ultimately did not have the numbers to control the council.

The same year, Simpson left his job as housing director. The programme offering empty properties to squatters was halted. Meanwhile, housing officials and councillors who liked the old, more hierarchical way of doing things reduced the ways in which council tenants and neighbourhood groups could inform or influence the workings of the town hall, partly dismantling a more participatory system that Livingstone had helped set up. In August, he tried to use the media to shame the traditionalists, telling a local paper, the *South London Press*, that he would resign as vice-chair of housing if Lambeth did not quickly fulfil a commitment to move tenants of three run-down blocks into better homes. The council bureaucracy called his bluff: in December, with the transfer of tenants still yet to happen, he stepped down. His first taste of power was over.

Fourteen years later, in 1987, he published a memoir of his political career so far, *If Voting Changed Anything, They'd Abolish It*. The title was an adaptation of a quote attributed to the early anarchist Emma Goldman. The first chapter was called 'Lambeth Lessons'. It did not contain much self-criticism – Livingstone would leave that for his retirement – but if you read between the lines, there was some useful advice for the Labour left. To get power and hold on to it, and to do significant things with it, the left needed to form coalitions rather than pursue ideological purity. At the same time, the left needed to master a less inclusive politics: to know how to weaponise voting procedures, pack committees, mount internal coups. And finally, it needed to understand what it was up against: not just the Conservatives, and much of the state, but also Labour rightwingers, who would be at least as aggressive and strategic as the left – and, if all else failed, would sometimes be prepared to abandon Labour altogether. Many of those who opposed him on Lambeth council during the 1970s, Livingstone noted, defected a few years later to the Social Democratic Party.

Only a very streetwise socialism could survive in such a hostile environment. After Lambeth, Livingstone's life would be devoted to practising it.

Corbyn moved to this troubled but politically alive London in 1972. What he had heard about leftwing life in the city from the Venesses had made Shropshire feel even more of a backwater. He resigned from his job at the *Newport and Market Drayton Advertiser* and successfully applied to one of the few further education institutions in the capital open to someone with such bad A-levels.

The Polytechnic of North London was in an angular, still optimistic-feeling 1960s tower and an outcrop of older buildings on the otherwise low-rise, congested Holloway Road in northern Islington. The poly's origins were in a Victorian scheme to provide vocational courses for the borough's 'poorer classes', but middle-class students had long attended it, and Corbyn's chosen subject seemed a good fit with his interests: trade union studies. He moved into a flat nearby and began exploring the area, a lattice of terraced streets increasingly inhabited by immigrants from Ireland, southern Europe, the Caribbean and the Middle East. With its bustle and traffic jams, tropical fruit stands and squeezed-in car repair yards, it was a little like Kingston, Jamaica. He loved it.

He also explored leftwing London. On a speculative visit to the offices of the socialist newspaper *Tribune*, he ran into Valerie Veness, who was working there unknown to him. She and her husband Keith were also busy as activists in the constituency where Corbyn was living, Islington North, where they were part of a leftwing faction that was trying to replace, or 'deselect' in the party jargon, its Labour MP Michael O'Halloran.

O'Halloran was from the right of the party, an Irish immigrant of conservative social views, including opposition to abortion, which alienated the liberal-left gentrifiers who made up an increasingly large minority of Labour's local supporters. The Venesses hoped that Corbyn would join their campaign against him. But Corbyn was not rooted enough in Islington yet. Finding his studies at the poly no more compelling than his lessons at school, he abandoned his course after a few months. No longer needing to live in Islington, he found a cheaper flat in Haringey, a similar, less central borough immediately to the north. He stayed in touch with the Venesses, occasionally helping them in their long war against O'Halloran. But until the early 1980s he followed a different path.

Looking for work, he came across an ad for a research assistant at the National Union of Tailors and Garment Workers (NUTGW). Once the tenth-biggest union in the country, by the time it hired Corbyn it was a declining organisation, shrinking with the British garment manufacturing trade as much of the work disappeared to factories overseas. The union had long represented Jewish tailors in the East End, and some of its officials were veteran Jewish leftists, full of tales and attitude. It was an institution still partly rooted in the early and mid-20th-century decades when many British Jews were socialists or communists. Other trade unionists nicknamed the NUTGW the 'National Union of Jewish Stalinists'.

Corbyn worked in the union's offices in Charles Square in Hoxton, a handsome Georgian building hemmed in by blocks of council flats, on the traffic-dominated edge of east London. In its basement were old records written in Hebrew, from a Jewish union which the NUTGW had once taken over.

Corbyn's job included scouring the newspapers for stories relevant to the union, often about changes in manufacturing technology and about new foreign imports. In effect, he was 'monitoring the decline of our own industry', as he saw it. He also took part in negotiations with employers, and helped represent the union at meetings of the wages council, a government body which regulated pay levels. He was not a smart dresser, despite the fact that the union had members who worked for Savile Row tailors. After a meeting at one of them, Kilgour, French and Stanbury, he was told, 'Bring in a bolt of cloth, and we'll run you up a suit. You're not representing the trade very well.' He declined the offer. He saw it as corruption.

While working at the union, he also began to climb the ladder of Labour politics. As in Islington and right across inner London, in Haringey a struggle was under way for control of the local party between generally more conservative older members and leftwing incomers. Corbyn sided with the latter. Yet, in keeping with his low-key, outwardly mild personality, his approach was to avoid confrontation wherever possible, and instead try to strengthen Labour and the left's position by being more diligent than anyone else. He chaired the local Young Socialists. He handed out application forms to potential Labour members. He organised demonstrations and jumble sales to raise funds for the party. He went on early-morning pickets, and canvassed in elections. He became the party's agent for the local constituency of Hornsey. In 1974, he was elected as a Haringey councillor.

Corbyn did not particularly stand out as a debater or an orator. His voice was small, and sounded strained when he raised it. But he became a ubiquitous and locally powerful figure. Away from work, his look was vaguely countercultural: heavy beard, green army surplus jacket, grease on his clothes from his motorcycle. In the Irish pubs near the local Labour headquarters where the party's activists socialised, and then in their flats afterwards, he drank judiciously, joined in with Irish republican songs, discussed the coming collapse of capitalism, and handed out party leaflets to be distributed the following morning. He helped turn Hornsey into one of the largest constituency Labour parties in the country, despite the fact that the seat had a Tory MP.

There was not much time in his life for anything else. At home in his small studio flat, he mostly slept, rarely cleaned or cooked, and sometimes ate baked beans cold, straight from the can. During 1973 he had started going out with another Haringey Labour activist, Jane

Chapman, a postgraduate student at the London School of Economics. She was elected to the council at the same time as him, but was more conventionally ambitious, wanting to become an MP, whereas at this stage he saw his political role as less public. Like Livingstone and many of their rising generation of municipal radicals, Corbyn did not see the House of Commons of the early 1970s, with all its stuffy rituals and seemingly ineffectual pragmatists such as Heath and Wilson, as the place where the most worthwhile politics happened.

Two days after being elected as councillors, Corbyn and Chapman got married. They moved to a bigger flat in Haringey, a ground floor one with a garden, where they kept chickens. But he continued to be mostly elsewhere, spending evenings at political meetings, or photocopying at the party offices, or faithfully attending social events put on by the immigrant communities in his council ward. His political circle widened. He got to know the activist Tariq Ali, who was living nearby, and Bernie Grant, an outspoken local trade unionist originally from British Guiana. Ali's principal allegiance was to the International Marxist Group, a turbulent Trotskyist sect, while Grant's was to advancing the rights of immigrants and racial minorities. While Corbyn was faithful to Labour, he was not party-political in his choice of comrades and allies. This openness to new causes would give him a political career that outstripped his modest conventional abilities.

One of the main inspirations for Corbyn's capacious politics was Allende's coalition government in faraway Santiago. But by 1973 this was in trouble. What was going wrong in Chile, and where those problems led, would haunt the left and raise questions about how it could govern, in any democracy, for decades to come.

The Allende administration's popularity peaked in 1971, during its first months in office. At local elections across the country it won 49.7 per cent of the total vote – an increase of over a third compared to the share of the vote with which it had won power. During this initial phase, the economy grew fast, the fruits of this growth were distributed much more widely than ever before, and the government pushed through huge nationalisations and increases in welfare benefits, while remaining scrupulously democratic. Chile did seem to be turning peacefully into a new, fairer society.

But during 1972 and 1973 the atmosphere and reality of life under Allende darkened. The opposition parties decided that the best way to challenge his government was to call it illegitimate, and to obstruct its plans through constitutional loopholes. In response, his coalition, which had always been quarrelsome, began to divide more seriously between committed democrats and those who wanted 'the Chilean road to socialism' to become more authoritarian. Allende had to devote increasing amounts of energy to defending Chilean democracy and holding the government together.

Meanwhile, drawbacks to some of his policies began to emerge. All the increased spending by the state and previously badly off Chileans produced soaring inflation, which began to wipe out the financial gains many ordinary people had made since Allende's election. The government's nationalisation and land reform programmes also created problems. While justified as solutions to an extremely unequal economy, they prompted factory occupations by workers and land seizures by rural labourers, with or without official approval. These led in turn to shortages of some foods and goods, and a rising sense of disorder. The expectations generated by the election of a radical leftwing government proved increasingly difficult for that government to control.

Allende accumulated enemies. The US government was influenced by American corporations with interests in Chile, some of which were being nationalised. From Washington's Cold War perspective, the election of a socialist government was also a dangerous precedent. So the US mounted an economic blockade of Chile, and successfully pressured international institutions such as the World Bank to do the same. Meanwhile, many wealthy and middle-class Chileans, believing, often correctly, that their economic and social dominance was threatened, protested on the streets and organised unprecedented strikes against the Allende regime. Less prosperous self-employed people also stopped work, from dentists to truck drivers, encouraged by opposition politicians and Chile's rightwing newspapers to believe that the government was hostile to all private business. Some of the strikes received covert American financial backing.

This strengthening counter-revolution would be seen around the world, by the right and left alike, as a model for how an elected leftwing government could be subverted. It gained its final, crucial momentum when it won the backing of conservative members of the Chilean military. Fiercely anti-communist, and increasingly appalled by Allende's upsetting of the status quo, they worried that his government was becoming more popular despite all the disorder. At congressional elections in March 1973, the anti-Allende movement won 44 per cent of the vote – substantially up on the 36 per cent with which it had been elected in 1970, and probably more than enough for the left to win the next presidential election unless the opposition parties collaborated very effectively. Many poor and left-leaning Chileans remained loyal to Allende, partly because of tangible gains from his presidency, and partly because of his public persona, which began to take on a martyred quality as he became more besieged. During the middle months of 1973, with encouragement from some of the opposition parties, the rightwingers in the military began to make their move. They marginalised those senior officers who were still loyal to Allende as the elected head of state, and prepared a coup.

For Corbyn, the volatile life of the Allende presidency was a completely gripping and resonant story, despite all his other political interests. When he read the newspapers every day for the tailors' union, he cut out and kept articles on Chile, from the pro-Allende reports and comment pieces of the leftwing *Morning Star* to the more neutral work of the *Financial Times*'s authoritative Santiago correspondent, Hugh O'Shaughnessy. The Allende government and its mounting troubles were endlessly discussed by the British left: in print, in the pub, at protests and at political conferences that were supposed to be about other causes. As in Chile, British leftists argued about whether Allende's attachment to liberal democracy, despite his opponents' more and more obvious willingness to abandon it, would be his undoing or his salvation. Corbyn was a democrat. But he also realised by 1973 that the Allende regime was 'under pressure'.

The coup began at dawn on 11 September. Like 1968, it was one of the first insurrections to be broadcast on worldwide television. Viewers saw jets bombing the presidential palace, books being burned by soldiers, frightened-looking leftists rounded up in a Santiago stadium; and, a few days later, a new ruling junta, including the general soon to be dictator of Chile. Augusto Pinochet sat very upright in one of the army's Germanic uniforms, arms implacably folded, sunglasses only partly obscuring cold eyes. Allende, who had worn thick-rimmed, avuncular spectacles, was found shot dead in the palace. The junta said he had committed suicide. His supporters said he had been assassinated.

Corbyn spent much of the day of the coup, and the following night, at the union office, on the phone to a friend and fellow leftist who worked at the news agency Reuters, who read him updates about what was happening in Chile. In a few factories occupied by workers, and in university and office buildings, armed government personnel and supporters were fighting on, despite their doomed prospects and Allende's death. 'It was horrifying,' Corbyn remembered. 'You felt this sense of helplessness, and anger.'

The following day, he and other Allende supporters in London decided to mount a protest. From Corbyn's workplace and other union offices across the city they set up a telephone tree – a widening network of callers – and put the word out that anyone angry about the coup should converge on the Chilean embassy.

The embassy was on a side street in Marylebone, in an elegant but usually rather inscrutable four-storey townhouse, one of many such buildings in the area, much of which was given over to private medical clinics. Corbyn and a couple of hundred comrades, including Tony Benn, gathered on the narrow pavement outside the embassy, a few feet from its front door. They held hastily made placards and banners, and chanted. They were unsure what, if anything, would happen next.

Then a man climbed out of a window on the top floor. The window opened on to a narrow ledge, about a foot deep, which was partially protected by a low balustrade. The man stood on the ledge, silhouetted against the sky, looking down at them, and waving. He was middle-aged, almost bald, with a smooth, rather urbane face. 'We thought, "Arrogant sod,"' Corbyn remembered. '"These people have just killed the president and taken over the government. Who are they to be waving at us?"' Then Corbyn and some of the protesters realised that the man was the Chilean ambassador, Alvaro Bunster, who had been appointed by Allende two years earlier. Still looking down at the demonstration, the ambassador bent one of his arms and raised a fist.

Forty years later, just after the anniversary of the coup, Corbyn spoke publicly about what the Allende government still meant to him. His audience was small: a few dozen members of the Sussex branch of the Labour Representation Committee (LRC), a group set up by John McDonnell and others in 2004 to revive the left of the party. After a decade of trying and apparently failing in its mission, the LRC was now in decline, with only a few hundred members, often elderly, scattered across the country. Corbyn's capture of the Labour leadership was still two years away, and still an unthinkable eventuality.

Yet at the meeting he was among trusted comrades, so he spoke with a fluency and an openness which he rarely showed in less friendly contexts. Wearing a casual open-necked shirt, the sort of shirt he might have worn on his Chilean travels in the 1960s, he began with some good jokes about how MI5 would be eavesdropping on the meeting. But his 20-minute talk quickly grew in intensity. It became about his time in Chile, about the rise and fall of Allende, about what happened to the leftists that managed to flee Chile after the coup, and what these refugees in turn contributed to the left in Britain; and also about the wider political changes around the world that the Allende and Pinochet regimes inspired, from Thatcherism to the leftwing Latin American governments of the 2000s.

As Corbyn spoke, the dim, wood-panelled room swirled with politics, economics, personal stories, broader history, so that everyday life and political activism, and the past and the present, seemed endlessly connected. Sometimes, he spoke with anger: 'Pinochet ... no words bad enough to describe him'; 'Allende ... in my view, murdered'. And sometimes Corbyn spread a chill through the audience. Pinochet, he said, had launched 'a pogrom of the left. Every single one of us in this room would have been rounded up.'

Finally, he returned to the Allende government. 'We can all learn lessons from it,' he said, 'about real pressures, real power, and real attacks on those of us that dream – not dream, strive – to achieve a world based on social justice.' The words could have sounded pious and vague – sometimes a weakness of his rhetoric. But on this occasion, they did not.

For several days after the coup, Bunster stayed in the embassy. He was unsure whether Britain's Conservative government, which did not condemn the coup, would grant him asylum. He also wanted to use the embassy as a platform for resistance. He refused to acknowledge Chile's new military government, and issued a statement contradicting the official line on Allende's fate. 'If he is dead,' wrote Bunster, 'he has been killed.' He also ordered the embassy staff not to let the new ambassador appointed by the junta on to the premises.

Eventually, Bunster and seven of his subordinates left the building and sought asylum in the UK. A couple of weeks later, in late September, he addressed the Labour party conference: the first foreigner to do so since Dolores Ibarruri, a celebrated anti-fascist in the Spanish Civil War. 'Bunster . . . has been looked after with embarrassing kindness by particularly Wedgwood Benn,' wrote Henry Hankey, director of the Americas section of the Foreign Office, in an internal memo. 'We have bent over backwards to ensure he was given all suitable courtesies, if only in order to prevent him from representing to his Labour friends that we had failed to do so.'

The connection between the British left and the Chilean left was now firmly established. The fear that the former might suffer the same fate as the latter, should it challenge too many powerful interests in Britain, was stitched into this relationship, a dark strand of anxiety.

PART TWO

Into Power

5

Workers' Control

In March 1974 Tony Benn was given a new job. It did not sound particularly promising. He became secretary of state for industry, at a time when British industry was entering its worst slump since the Great Depression of the 1930s. It was a hastily established ministry, part of a new Labour government without a majority. At the election a month earlier, the party had got 227,000 fewer votes than the Conservatives, but had won more seats: enough to return to power as a minority government.

Benn's former hero Harold Wilson was still prime minister, but Wilson's energies were dimming. Increasingly, those energies were devoted to influencing who might succeed him. Wilson's own politics were becoming more cautious, yet in his wily way he liked to keep his options open. The Department of Industry could be a place for Benn to prove himself, while also solving some of the government's most pressing and difficult problems. Or it could be a trap: the place where he and his increasingly radical ideas would be found out.

To Benn, the sheer difficulty of the post was a sign of what an opportunity it was. He entered the ministry with a confidence that his new ideas could rescue British industry, and even British society as a whole, which never completely left him while he was there. 'I shall win over the [company] managers and the small businessmen,' he declared in his diary in April 1974, 'and I shall get the nationalised industries to welcome [my policies]; I shall isolate the big Tory [supporting] companies, then show them how much money they have been getting from the government [in subsidies], and if they don't want it . . .' The following April, after his first year at the ministry had not gone according to plan, he recorded in his diary nevertheless, 'I have got a marvellous job.'

The department was a descendant of the Ministry of Technology created by Wilson and run by Benn in the 1960s. The fact that the earlier ministry had failed in many of its objectives, and had been abolished by the Conservatives in the early 1970s, had not dissuaded the two Labour politicians from trying again. In Britain, as in many countries during these ambitious postwar decades, reshaping the state was assumed to be a necessary first step towards reshaping society.

As Mintech had been, Benn's new department was ambiguously sited, in a prominent new building but away from the heart of Whitehall: towards the far end of Victoria Street, the grey canyon of offices which leads to the railway station. The ministry building was a long modular block that looked like an irregular stack of hundreds of glass-sided boxes. Compared to much of Whitehall, it looked flexible, informal, open. When Benn moved into his office, he had a painting commemorating the British empire, which had been hanging behind the desk, taken down. Instead, he hung a trade union banner, which showed a male and female worker shaking hands, above the words, 'United to Obtain the Just Reward of Our Labour'. He also had a map of the United Kingdom put up, but upside down, so that the poorer north had more prominence. These were reminders to see the country differently and to serve other interests than those usually prioritised by British governments. In his first month, Benn told the chairman of Rolls-Royce, Sir Kenneth Keith, that he would only see him for a meeting after first seeing the company's shop stewards.

Benn believed that his job was to transform the power structures as well as the performance of British industry: partly because of his strengthening commitment to egalitarian economic ideas such as workers' control; and partly because he believed that Labour's recent election manifesto committed him to doing so. In frank, almost confrontational language rarely found in Labour manifestos, it promised to 'bring about a fundamental and irreversible shift in the balance of power and wealth in favour of working people'. Alongside this appeal to the working class was a populist message to the whole nation: 'The British people, both as workers and consumers, must have more control over the powerful private forces that at present dominate our economic life.' That 'the British people' included many citizens who benefited from, or even led, these 'powerful private forces' was not acknowledged.

One of the main tools Labour promised to use for this limitless-sounding project – in essence, an attempt to democratise the economy – would be 'a new Industry Act'. Some of what it would do was an extension of existing government practice. There would be 'direct aid' for troubled companies from public funds, a common practice during the economically fragile 1970s, with both Conservative and Labour governments desperate to limit bankruptcies. And in return for this help, the state would 'reserve the right to take a share of the ownership of the company'. Following another postwar cross-party orthodoxy, there would be further nationalisations: 'We shall also take shipbuilding, ship-repairing and marine engineering, ports, the manufacture of airframes and aero-engines into public ownership.'

But then the manifesto said something much bolder and more divisive:

'We shall not confine the extension of the public sector to the loss-making and subsidised industries', that is, the usual candidates for nationalisation. 'We shall also take over profitable sections [of companies] or individual firms in those industries where a public holding is essential to enable the government to control prices, stimulate investment, encourage exports, create employment, protect workers and consumers from the activities of irresponsible multinational companies, and to plan the national economy in the national interest.'

These hugely expanded powers – 'the national interest' could be almost limitlessly defined – would first be applied to 'sections' of manufacturing and transport industries such as 'pharmaceuticals, road haulage, construction, machine tools'. But there was a strong suggestion that the powers might be extended further, into white-collar enterprises with cultural prestige and strong connections to the rightwing press that the British state usually left alone: 'Our decision in the field of banking, insurance and building societies is still under consideration.'

In all these businesses, whether nationalised, part-nationalised or subsidised, Labour promised to 'make power ... genuinely accountable to the workers and the community at large'. In the nationalised industries, for example, which by the 1970s were becoming notorious for their remote, top-down management and slow customer service,

'We shall take steps to make the management . . . more responsible to the workers . . . and more responsive to their consumers' needs.'

The manifesto left much unexplained. What 'steps' would a Labour government take to reform the nationalised industries? How, exactly, would it 'plan the national economy in the national interest'? How would it avoid repeating the failures of such planning in many countries, from the Soviet Union to Britain itself? And did businesses being 'accountable' to their workers mean workers' control? The phrase did not appear in the manifesto.

The whole document was only ten pages long: the shortest Labour election manifesto for almost 40 years. Was it just a sketch and a fantasy, indulgently permitted by a declining Labour leader? According to a later account by his close advisor Bernard Donoughue, Wilson had been expecting to lose the election, as Labour were behind in the polls, and then disappear to a 'secret hideaway in the country', presumably to lick his wounds before resigning as party leader.

Or, on the contrary, was the manifesto actually something much more serious: a blueprint for a new Britain? Benn certainly thought so. His thinking permeated the document. He had spent much of his time out of government trying to push Labour's policies in the same leftward direction as his own developing ideas. As party chairman during 1971 and 1972, he made frequent speeches to the Labour membership, which was already moving to the left, radicalised by battles with Edward Heath's Conservative government, by foreign causes such as Chile, and by the general post-1968 political ferment. During the early 1970s Benn also published his own policy papers; spoke at the raucous, often televised conferences held by the party and the unions; and began playing a major part in Labour's elaborate policy-drafting process. In 1974, he was elected chairman of the party's powerful home policy committee, which did much of the development of Labour's election manifestos. He would hold the position for the next eight years. In pamphlets and policy documents, private rooms and public halls, he argued that the manifestos should be more democratically produced, more leftwing, and much more faithfully followed by Labour ministers. Applying his ideas about mass participation in political and economic power structures to the party itself, he argued that its members, rather than its leader and MPs, should decide most of what Labour did. Like his support for workers' control, this stance set Benn against powerful people.

But his sense of boldness and his public profile continued to grow. He was alert to any events that might help his causes. In 1971 Upper Clyde Shipbuilders had gone into receivership. This was a state-subsidised Scottish conglomerate which Benn, as minister of technology, had helped create in the 1960s to protect several shipyards which were struggling against foreign competition. When the Heath government refused to rescue it, the workers occupied the yards. Rather than just protest, they carried on working, hoping to demonstrate, by completing the company's existing orders, that there was still a future for the yards and their skills. It was a kind of workers' control, with young shop stewards, some of them Communist Party members, replacing the usual managers.

Benn rushed up to Scotland and joined a march in support, which grew into the biggest Scottish demonstration since the Second World War. He walked through the centre of Glasgow at the head of the march, still in the dark suit and shiny shoes he wore as a shadow minister, flanked by the communist shop stewards and surrounded by photographers. His body language was a little stiff and self-conscious, but his eyes were alight. He addressed a huge rally for the shipyard workers on Glasgow Green. 'We are seeing the birth pangs of industrial democracy,' he said. 'Give responsibility to ordinary people, and take away the privilege from a minority who have dominated this country.' A smoke bomb was thrown at the stage, and landed gushing at his feet. He had to pause while it was kicked off the stage. But he quickly regained his composure. 'Good luck comrades,' he said. 'And thanks for inviting me.'

A few months later, the Conservative government agreed to save the shipyards. It was hard to say exactly how important Benn's intervention had been. The campaign in support of the workers had become so large and broad that it included a donation of £5,000 from John Lennon. But Benn had demonstrated an ability to present disruptive, egalitarian ideas in an attention-getting way, with class-war bluntness softened by privileged eloquence and charm. It was a potent combination, and a provocative one.

The other provocative thing that Benn brought to the Department of Industry was the thinking of Stuart Holland. Holland was a combative young economist who had been a prime ministerial advisor to Wilson during the 1960s. Like Benn, Holland had become disillusioned by Wilson's diminishing boldness, and left Downing Street for academia. By the early 1970s, he was teaching at Sussex University, then a new campus which was becoming a centre for radical economists.

At Sussex Holland began exploring what he saw as the failings of both contemporary capitalism and state economic planning. Whether in Britain, the United States, or the Soviet Union, major economies were either too loose and anarchic and/or too centralised and rigid, he believed. Neither approach was capable, he wrote in 1972, of properly 'mobilising' a society's 'economic resources' for the 'attainment of higher economic and welfare aims'.

Part of the answer, he argued, was to learn from one of western Europe's most successful postwar economies, which received relatively little attention in Britain. In Italy, both rapid national growth and the reduction of poverty in the historically poor south had been achieved, he said, by the application of a clear but novel principle: 'The state itself should become an entrepreneur.' Rather than just lend to companies, it should manage them, 'in order to ensure that ventures which are viable over a longer period than that acceptable to private investors . . . are undertaken.'

The Italian state body at the centre of this miraculous-sounding process was the Institute for Industrial Reconstruction (IRI). It had a history which did not fit into conventional political categories: set up by Benito Mussolini's Fascist government in the 1930s, the IRI had then flourished under a succession of unstable postwar coalition governments, usually made up of centre-left Socialists and centre-right Christian Democrats. In Britain, the book that Holland published in 1972 about the IRI, *The State As Entrepreneur*, initially interested intellectually curious Europhile figures from the right of the Labour party, such as Roy Jenkins, rather than leftwingers such as Benn.

But then Holland's thinking developed in a more explicitly anti-capitalist direction. In *The Socialist Challenge*, written mostly before Labour returned to office but not published until 1975, he declared that the job of a leftwing government was to 'transform' – in other words, remove – 'the injustice, inequality and inefficiency of modern capitalism'. The way to do this, he argued, was to combine Yugoslavianstyle management by workers with 'a strategic planning framework' maintained by the state, including a British version of the IRI. This framework would be agreed through 'bargaining' between 'worker representatives, worker-elected [company] management and the government' – or, in short, by 'bringing the workers into Whitehall'.

It was a vision of a very different state and economy, likely to horrify the business establishment and the many economically conservative civil servants, and likely to appeal hugely to Benn and the Labour left. The latter process started first. Thanks to his Downing Street experiences with Wilson, Holland understood how the Labour party worked. During the early 1970s, he successfully fed his ideas into its policy committees, into its February 1974 election manifesto, and into Benn's hungry mind. When Benn became secretary of state for industry, he asked Holland to join a working group of his most trusted advisors. Its job was to draft the first version of Labour's promised industry bill. Benn believed that his job would then be to sell this challenging document to his colleagues in the cabinet.

He would also have to win over his own department. Sir Antony Part had already been a civil servant for 37 years when he became permanent secretary, the most senior non-ministerial figure at the Department of Industry. He was almost a decade older than Benn, and nearing retirement. With his smoothed-back black hair like a Dickensian undertaker, his extensive repertoire of small nods and smiles, and his narrow eyes, he had seen nine governments come and go. He had survived their Whitehall reorganisations. He had realised that some of these had happened, as he put it with a hint of contempt in his memoirs, 'for political reasons'. The creation of the industry department was such a change, he believed. Yet he also believed in his own fairmindedness: that he was no more sceptical about Labour governments than Conservative ones. All economic ministers and civil servants, he thought, should 'stay close to the realities of industry and commerce'. Those 'realities' would not tolerate policies which were too radical.

Benn was already suspicious of civil servants when he arrived at Industry. Ten years before, in his first ministerial job, overseeing the Post Office, he had opened a filing cabinet beside his desk and found nothing inside. The filing cabinet 'was just for show', he concluded. 'Decisions had always been taken elsewhere.' He tried to run the Post Office more actively, proposing for example that the Queen's head should no longer appear on stamps. But there was resistance: he believed some of his civil servants were undermining him, in collaboration with others in 10 Downing Street. The Queen's head stayed on stamps, reduced in size.

One of the first things Benn did as industry secretary was to have copies of Labour's election manifesto circulated to civil servants. Yet at his first meeting with Part, the permanent secretary began by saying: 'I presume, secretary of state, that you do not intend to implement the industrial strategy in Labour's programme.' In his memoirs, published 16 years later, Part described the strategy both as too superficial, 'papering over the cracks' in the British economy, and too ambitious, 'unlikely to make sense in practice' or to lead to 'effective cooperation' between government and business. Even a decade and a half on, it seemed that he still could not decide which aspect of Benn and Holland's blueprint displeased him most. Yet there was also a brief passage where he set out his attitude to Benn's policies, as it was in the mid-1970s, more clearly:

> In 1974 the [industry] department's most important job was to help Mr Benn implement the proposals in the manifesto in so far as they were approved by the Prime Minister and the Cabinet as realistic in the circumstances in which the government took office.

In this one sentence, with its steely formality and air of propriety, its friendly-seeming first half and icy second half, its sly bureaucratic switches between precision and vagueness, its references to higher authorities outside the department, and its comma-free relentlessness, Part's treatment of Benn during the 1970s was perfectly encapsulated. They would often meet in Benn's office after breakfast. Part described what followed as 'verbal boxing matches'. He would begin by telling Benn that he and other civil servants in the department had misgivings about one of Benn's proposals – that workers should have a say in how companies were managed, for example – because they considered it too bold, and therefore unrealistic. Benn would respond with polite exasperation. Given the Labour manifesto's promise of 'a fundamental and irreversible shift in the balance of power and wealth', he would say, what exactly did Part and his colleagues expect?

The meeting would usually break up without agreement or rancour. Part and Benn were not people who often lost their tempers in public. But sometimes a version of the permanent secretary's doubts about his minister would appear, attributed to anonymous Whitehall sources, on the front pages of rightwing newspapers. These doubts about Benn were also conveyed, via discreet chains of civil servants, to Harold Wilson and the cabinet's numerous other Benn sceptics, such as the chancellor Denis Healey, and from them anonymously to the newspapers again. A mocking term for Benn's proposals began to circulate in Whitehall and in the press, implying that they were not bold or necessary reforms but personal obsessions, eccentricities – a damaging charge in a country that liked to tell itself that it valued compromise and moderation. The word was 'Bennery'.

At first, he was not that bothered. He thought that bigger things were going his way. He believed that British capitalism was in a vulnerable state, politically as well as economically, and therefore much more amenable than usual to plans for its reform. The Heath government had fallen largely because it had been defeated, twice, by the National Union of Mineworkers, which had called successful and highly disruptive strikes in 1972 and 1974. The assertiveness and size of union memberships were growing. Meanwhile the profits and share prices of many British companies were falling. Between mid-1972 and the end of 1974, the main FTSE share index dropped by almost three-quarters. Anxiety about the future of British capitalism – that it was being terminally damaged by the unions, by old-fashioned management, by obsolete factories, by foreign competition – spread through the business press and the murmering London members' clubs where senior executives gathered.

Among those whom Benn considered more thoughtful businessmen, he sensed a readiness to change. He called it 'a new realism'. He was particularly encouraged by a meeting with an executive from Smiths Industries, a long-established and ever-evolving British manufacturing conglomerate which made everything from ceramics to electronics. 'Don't worry, we've got no problem with planning agreements [with the Wilson government],' the executive told him. 'We've worked with MITI [the Ministry of International Trade and Industry] in Japan, you know.' In the mid-1970s, the Japanese government's reputation for successfully intervening in industry was reaching its postwar zenith. Across Asia as well as western Europe, the idea that the state should shape the economy for social as well as economic ends was not seen by business executives as outrageous.

But Benn was more interested in meeting workers than their bosses. He increasingly revered 'ordinary people', as he had put it at the rally for the shipyard workers in Glasgow. And he believed that a revolution in how industrial employees thought about their jobs was getting under way. Inspired by the worker management of Upper Clyde Shipbuilders, and by Labour's proposals for employees to have a significant say in the running of businesses, groups of shop stewards beyond Glasgow, from the shipyards of the north-east of England to the aircraft and car factories of the west Midlands, were beginning to draw up ambitious plans for reshaping their companies, from their product ranges to their internal hierarchies.

The most ambitious scheme came from a coalition of activists from different unions who all worked for Lucas Aerospace, a sprawling British company which made complex components for military and civilian aircraft. During the early 1970s, faced with increased competition, technological change and economic turbulence, the company sought to reduce its workforce by almost a third. Shop stewards scattered across the country in more than a dozen Lucas factories formed what they called a combine committee to resist the cuts. They failed; but the experience of cooperation was energising, and the committee kept meeting and discussing how the company's future could be different. When Labour returned to power, the committee decided to lobby the government to nationalise their company, not just to protect jobs but also to reform Lucas, so that it was more open to ideas from its workers, and manufactured more 'socially useful products': products that were designed for neither military nor purely commercial uses. In November 1974, after months of discussion in the Lucas factories, a delegation from the committee came to see Benn.

Thirty-four trade unionists squeezed into his office. Some of Benn's civil servants, who thought their minister's meetings should be one-on-ones with company bosses and union leaders, were horrified by the gathering's inclusive and informal flavour. The meeting went on for two and a half hours. As the workers put the case for their employer to be nationalised, and sketched out the possibilities for Lucas that might then open up, Benn realised he was listening to 'a complete shadow administration' for the company. 'I found myself completely in sympathy with them,' he recorded in his diary. It was 'one of the most inspiring meetings I have ever attended'.

Unfortunately for everyone present, Benn did not have the authority to nationalise Lucas. Such a decision would have to be made by the cabinet, and that was unlikely to happen, given how many other ministers already had misgivings about his industrial strategy. But Benn proposed an imaginative alternative: the committee should devise its own corporate plan for Lucas, including examples of socially useful products. That document could then form the core of a planning agreement between the company and Benn's department.

The shop stewards agreed. Over the next 14 months, they gathered suggestions and blueprints for new products from the Lucas workforce, many of whom were highly skilled but had never been asked for ideas before. Mike Cooley, a Lucas engineer and influential member of the combine committee, argued that many of the company's employees – and by implication, British workers in general – had 'tacit knowledge', an expertise which exceeded their usually narrowly defined jobs. At Lucas, the committee used this previously untapped resource, and edited the ideas which emerged from it into a 50-page document.

Especially for the many people in the 1970s who thought of British workers as lazy and stuck in their ways, the Lucas Plan was a startling document. It envisaged the company manufacturing wind turbines and solar panels, heat pumps for houses and hybrid power systems for vehicles, portable kidney machines and more controllable artificial limbs: many of the key technologies of the next century. The plan also promised to preserve jobs and make them more interesting by giving workers more complex tasks and greater responsibility. Decades later, this combination of economic self-interest and environmentalism, sometimes known as the green industrial revolution or the green new deal, would become the great hope of governments across the world, from the United States to the European Union, for escaping the climate emergency. At Lucas in the mid-1970s, Benn's faith in 'ordinary people' seemed vividly justified.

It also extended to less promising businesses. In December 1974, he announced an inquiry into what could be done about British Leyland, the notoriously strike-prone and inefficient British car-making conglomerate, which was close to bankruptcy. The inquiry was led by an establishment figure, Sir Donald Ryder, who had been appointed by Wilson as chairman of the National Enterprise Board, a body created to oversee and bring order to Benn's industrial experiments. However, in parallel with this relatively conventional inquiry, Benn also commissioned a more radical one, led by trade unionists. One of those involved in it was Jeremy Corbyn.

Corbyn had first met Benn four years earlier, at a fringe event during the 1970 Labour party conference. The party had recently lost power, and Benn was billed to speak about his experiences in government. Not many people turned up to hear him, perhaps 30 at the most, including Corbyn. But Benn was at his most candid and compelling. He spoke for 45 minutes. 'He said, "You all think you elect a government that has national power,"' Corbyn remembered, '"and obviously it has. But all these global corporations, which we [Labour] are now facilitating, they're the ones who have real power."'

Corbyn's father had worked for English Electric, a long-established manufacturing business which in 1968 had been taken over by the General Electric Company (GEC), a huge and acquisitive conglomerate which aggressively cut costs as it expanded. The takeover and GEC's subsequent treatment of English Electric made his father 'very angry', Corbyn told me. So Benn's speech particularly resonated with him. He regarded Benn as 'moving towards the left', and went to see him speak many times over the next few years. The two men began to get to know each other.

In 1973, Corbyn had left the tailors' union and become a researcher for the much larger Amalgamated Union of Engineering Workers (AUEW), which was expanding rather than declining and had thousands of members at British Leyland. The AUEW was a leftwing union, sympathetic to Benn, and when he became industry secretary he often spoke to its leaders about workers' control and other elements of his industrial strategy. For accurate information about workers' conditions and desires, Benn often trusted the research departments of unions more than civil servants. He also knew he needed allies. Even among the unions, there was opposition to the slightly amorphous concept of workers' control. Some union leaders saw it as a threat to their role, potentially making their members more active and less deferential, while some union activists saw it as a trap: they feared that workers would be landed with extra responsibilities, and lose the ability or the will to use traditional weapons of class warfare such as strikes.

Corbyn sometimes thought Benn was too optimistic about how quickly Britain's class-bound economy could be transformed. But he was persuaded by Benn's argument that the economy was being held back by a lack of investment and an excessive interest in short-term profit, and that the solution was more worker and state involvement. Benn came to see the AUEW about British Leyland. 'We had a meeting,' Corbyn remembered. 'Tony Benn, myself, Tony Banks [later a leftwing Labour MP] and some other people. Benn said, "The civil service don't know what I'm talking about." He asked us to set up a working group and write a report about the future of British Leyland and the car industry. I was one of the co-writers. We talked to the Institute for Workers' Control and lots of other people, and produced a plan for a democratic structure for a publicly owned car industry. We put the report to a conference of industry shop stewards in Digbeth in Birmingham, and there was widespread support for it.' Even at cranky old British Leyland, a new way of running the economy seemed close at hand.

In some circumstances, Benn was prepared to give workers even more agency. During the Heath government, Upper Clyde Shipbuilders had not been the only business occupied by its workers. There were over a hundred other sit-ins and work-ins. One was at a motorcycle factory in Meriden, a medieval village in the west Midlands which for centuries had claimed to be the geographical centre of England. Sleek Triumph motorbikes had been built at this symbolically potent location ever since the bombing of Triumph's original factory in nearby Coventry during the Second World War. Marlon Brando rode a Triumph in the 1953 film *The Wild One*, and the machines had remained highly popular in the United States until their market dominance was suddenly ended by cheaper, more technologically advanced Japanese bikes during the early 1970s. In September 1973, Triumph's owners announced the Meriden factory's closure. Its employees immediately took over the complex, set up a 24-hour picket at the gates to protect its production equipment and its stock of 2,000 finished motorcycles, and announced their intention to keep working as a cooperative.

The occupation survived the winter. Yet the workers did not have the funds to keep the production line running. Without a way to pay these operating costs and also invest in new models, the proposed cooperative would never happen. Benn understood this. Within weeks of becoming industry secretary, he met some of the Meriden workers in his office. A plan was devised for the government to sustain the cooperative with a one-off grant and a long-term loan. But it took almost another year to get the scheme past Benn's sceptical civil servants. Part thought it was 'novel and difficult'. The Meriden workers had to live off unemployment benefit. Their picket continued in the cold.

In March 1975 the cooperative was finally established. Instead of the usual managers, it had elected leaders. Every worker was paid £50 a week, the average wage in the factory's pre-coop days, regardless of their position or level of skill. There were no foremen or supervisors and few formal meetings. 'Every man his own inspector' became one of the factory's principles. Any difficult issues were to be dealt with by an elected 'grievance committee'. The six hundred worker-owners were to get an equal share of any profits. Capitalism and socialism, collectivism and individualism – on a modest scale, the cooperative hoped to reconcile them all.

The government kept a close eye on how the experiment was going. Meriden had to send the Industry Department monthly progress reports, and obtain consent for any major changes in how it operated, such as wage increases. And then there were Benn's visits. Sometimes, he arrived at the factory unannounced, in the middle of the night, on his way by car from his Bristol constituency back to his home in west London. On one 2am visit, Benn found some of the workers 'still busy designing the left-hand gear shift' for a motorcycle. At Meriden, he believed, 'The spirit . . . sustained them.'

But was this new spirit of collaboration and egalitarianism something that might help save the British economy, one of the most hierarchical in the Western world? Or were Benn's reforms something else: a fundamental threat to business itself?

6

Stop Benn!

The first big press attacks on Benn and his economic plans began even before Labour had been elected. The day before the February 1974 election, the famous rightwing novelist Kingsley Amis, who had once been a communist, described Benn as 'the most dangerous man in Britain' in the *London Evening Standard*.

Once Benn was at the Industry Department and outlining his policies, the rage and anxiety about him in the rightwing press became more continuous. In May, the *Daily Express* warned that he wanted to impose an Allende-style government on Britain. In July, the *Daily Mail* said that Benn wanted to destroy British democracy.

He responded to the *Mail* article by offering to explain his plans to the paper's senior staff over lunch. They agreed. During the meal he tried to make his policy proposals sound as unthreatening as possible. 'We have to make adjustments in our society from time to time,' he told them. 'The change I am proposing is no more dramatic than the New Deal, or 1945 . . .' But his attempt to associate his reforms with those of Franklin Roosevelt and Clement Attlee was in some ways naive. In the 1970s both these long-departed, left-of-centre premiers were revered, even by some on the right, yet as active politicians they had both suffered plenty of assaults from the Conservative press. One *Express* headline during the 1945 election, summarising a speech by the Tory leader Winston Churchill, was 'Gestapo in Britain if Socialists Win'.

Because Benn had been a radio producer, and then Labour's television guru during the 1960s, he felt he knew the media. But this was only partly true. He understood its more modern side, broadcasting, which was required by law to be relatively even-handed. Yet the unregulated and ancient emnity of the rightwing press towards the left, and the highly personal attacks through which it was expressed, while hardly a total surprise to him, retained the capacity to shock and depress him. In 1974, this wearing-down process was only just beginning.

To a lesser but growing extent, Wilson shared the tabloid view that Benn was dangerous. As the leader of a vulnerable minority government, and as a prime minister who was always at least as focused on the electoral cycle as on changing the country, Wilson intended to call another election and win a majority as soon as possible: probably within months, in the autumn of 1974. In the meantime, he did not want any of his ministers promoting policies which might dissuade Conservative voters from switching to Labour. He worried that Benn's near revolutionary proposals for British industry exactly fitted that description. So over the spring and summer Wilson began to take control of them.

First, he ordered that the draft of the industry bill produced by Benn's working group be sent to him for further refinement, before it was presented to the cabinet. Wilson considered himself an authority on economics. He had been a celebrated student and tutor of the subject at Oxford. But then he had watched his 1960s government's ambitious plans for reforming the economy, which Benn had helped oversee, largely fail in practice. Presented in 1974 with the equally ambitious, and more politically contentious, economic blueprint from Benn's working group, Wilson reacted like a severe don demolishing a poor essay from a once-promising student. He found the group's plans for transforming industry 'sloppy and half-baked' and 'polemical, indeed menacing, in tone', as he wrote in his memoir of his mid-1970s government, *Final Term*. The minimal, downbeat tone of the book's title was an accurate indication of his mood as prime minister then. Approaching 60, Wilson wanted his last few years in Downing Street to be as calm as possible. Benn was promising the opposite.

During the summer of 1974 Wilson created a special committee of ministers, with himself as chairman, to rewrite the industry bill. The actual redrafting was done by Downing Street officials and the employment secretary, Michael Foot. He was seen as a leftwinger, but was less bold and independent than Benn on economic issues. Foot did not tell Benn about his involvement. Benn's alienation from even parts of the Labour left was beginning.

The rewriting was efficiently done. Whitehall could move as fast when restoring the status quo as it could move slowly when instructed to disturb it. 'The section on planning agreements [between companies and the government] was cut down to size,' wrote Wilson with satisfaction. The agreements would now be voluntary rather than compulsory. 'The role and powers of the NEB [National Enterprise Board] were strictly defined.' Its ability to nationalise companies was reduced, as was its budget.

In August, when parliament and therefore many of Benn's allies were on holiday, the watered-down document was finally presented to the cabinet. To his surprise, Benn, who had not been fully aware of Wilson's manoeuvres, found himself having to defend even the few radical proposals which remained in the draft, against calls for their removal from two of the cabinet's most forceful rightwingers, Denis Healey and the foreign secretary Jim Callaghan. Benn won that battle; but he failed to persuade the rest of the cabinet to reinstate any of the earlier cuts to the document. His isolation during these supposedly private discussions was then described in detail to the press by anonymous sources.

Over the rest of 1974 and into early 1975, the industry document was further diluted by parliamentary committees, with Labour MPs who supported Benn's original proposals sometimes outvoted by an alliance between government ministers, Liberals and Conservatives. Not for the last time, the centre and the centre-left sided with the right to thwart the left. As early as October 1974, the junior industry minister Eric Heffer, a less optimistic leftwinger than Benn, decided that the document was 'toothless' and threatened to resign. Benn persuaded Heffer, and himself, that there were still things in the draft worth them trying to push through parliament. Privately, they asked other leftwing MPs to add amendments to the industry bill which would restore some of its initial boldness.

But for all his manoeuvring, Benn was basically trapped. He could not talk publicly about what had happened to his reforms without attacking his own party leader, and then having to resign as a minister.

He did not want to do that. It would, he believed, weaken the left further, undermine a fragile Labour government, and possibly end his own prospects of further advancement.

Yet as long as he remained in the high-profile Industry Department, and remained associated with a plan to dramatically level out Britain's unequal economy – however much that plan, behind the scenes, was being watered down – Benn was an object of suspicion in the press, in business circles, and in Westminster and Whitehall. Heffer wrote later: 'Harold [Wilson] became convinced that we were a pocket of "loony leftists". Joe Haines [Wilson's powerful press secretary] constantly fed stories about the department to Fleet Street. Tony Benn was portrayed [by the press] as a "commissar". We were "Soviet agents . . ."'

Sometimes Benn's entrapment was almost literal. His press enemies did not just rely on briefings against him from his government colleagues. They also conducted their own anti-Benn operations. One of the main targets was his home in west London.

The house was quite public, with long Georgian windows looking on to a typically small and sparse city front garden, and then a busy road, Holland Park Avenue: one of the main western routes in and out of central London. When the newspapers had been friendlier towards him in the 1960s, the visibility of the tall, white house had been an advantage. It acted as a stage set for his much-photographed family and his brisk ministerial comings and goings. But now the house was used against him. Shot from the right angle, with the much bigger houses elsewhere on the avenue outside the frame, it could be made to look grand, rather than shown to be a typical three-storey London terrace with a basement – the sort of home that middle-class and even many working-class families lived in, at least until the property booms of the 1980s and afterwards. Thanks to its address, 12 Holland Park Avenue, the house could also be described by journalists as being in Holland Park, one of the city's wealthiest areas, when it was actually much closer to Notting Hill Gate, the scruffiest, most traffic-blighted part of Notting Hill, which in the 1970s was a mixed neighbourhood of immigrants, middle-class bohemians and squatters rather than the bankers' enclave it is today.

The Benns' house did have an elegant painted facade, but inside it was plain, functional, even shabby, like a Whitehall office or a rectory. The Benns did not believe in spending money on domestic luxuries. Benn himself was teetotal, and spent much of his time at home in a large basement office among piles of paper, political mementoes and filing cabinets. The house was full of unopened bottles of alcohol the family had been given. When they entertained, they were good company, and generous, but it was obvious that they usually lived differently. Barbara Castle wrote after one dinner: 'Caroline is clearly no cordon bleu cook . . . I suspect she and Wedgie normally get by on mugs of tea and bread and cheese.'

Regardless, journalists looked constantly for evidence of privilege, hypocrisy and anything else damaging going on in the Benn family. Sometimes they watched the house from parked cars. Sometimes they rented a flat across the road and used long-lens cameras. Sometimes they simply stood in the Benns' front garden. Sometimes they even swore at the younger, teenage Benn children as they passed, hoping to get a reaction. Or they followed them as they walked to school.

Appropriately, the children attended one of the most controversial comprehensives in the country, Holland Park School. It had been built in the 1950s on a hilltop in the plushest part of Holland Park, where there were mansions with huge gardens and education was assumed to be private. From the start, there were objections that the new school, one of the first comprehensives, would damage the local trees and bird life, and lower the social tone. Many pupils did come from less wealthy families; but when more prosperous parents with egalitarian views, such as the Benns, began sending their children to the school as well, it began to fascinate the rightwing press, which regarded the school as an indulgent and probably reckless educational experiment, and called it 'the socialist Eton'. In 1970, the school's reputation became more provocative still when it abolished streaming and academic prizes. The same year, Caroline Benn, who had been a leading advocate of comprehensive education since the early 1960s, became the chair of governors. The Benns were increasingly living their politics: a dangerous move in a country where most of the press and many voters assumed that leftwingers from privileged backgrounds either did not really mean it, deep down; or, if their socialism was genuine, that they were class traitors.

Benn and his family did have one way to escape the press. Fifty miles from London, on the thinly populated Dengie Peninsula in Essex, his grandfather had had a big cream house built 75 years earlier. It was down a private road and screened by trees, with a garden which ran right down to the high tide mark of a river estuary. Stansgate House was the Benns' second home, and rightwing newspapers portrayed it as an aristocratic country seat. In reality, like their London house, it was less lavish than was claimed. Its boxy design had been selected from a Victorian catalogue and built out of prefabricated sections. It had eight bedrooms, but the children slept in bunk beds and there was no central heating, despite lots of draughty windows and a sometimes icy wind off the estuary. Benn loved the house anyway, its privacy and watery vistas and extra time for family, and he savoured stays there throughout the year, as his diary shows. But especially in the pre-internet age, an ambitious ministerial career could not be sustained for long from rural Essex. London, with its opportunities and dangers, always dragged him back.

He had been getting occasional death threats for years. But as he moved leftwards during the 1970s they became much more frequent – frequent enough to worry him. Sometimes, to widen their effect, the threats to him were sent to Caroline. On 16 May 1975, for example, as the press frenzy about his industry bill reached a climax, she received a letter from the 'Defenders of Private Enterprise', who described themselves as a group of Liverpool businessmen. 'Madam,' the letter began, 'we regret that your husband is going to be killed and that you will be a widow, but it is in the public interest.' Twenty thousand pounds had been raised, the letter continued, to hire an American assassin.

That plot never materialised, as far as the Benns could tell. But the death threats continued, along with other unsettling happenings. There were unexplained bangs on their front door in the middle of the night. Their rubbish was stolen, so repeatedly that their youngest son Joshua, who had inherited his father's love of gadgets, rigged up an electronic sensor and hid it under the dustbins so that they could see what time it happened. The Benns were told several times by journalists that one of their children had been taken to hospital, when no such thing had occurred. Other false rumours were spread about Benn himself. One was even printed in partial form by the *New Statesman* in June 1977. There was an 'awful story' involving Benn, said the magazine, simultaneously dismissing it and disseminating it further, which came 'complete with circumstantial detail and an attribution to the Metropolitan Police', and involved 'the violent death of a rabbit'. The implication seemed to be that Benn practised bestiality.

The innuendo, intimidation and harassment made him anxious and suspicious. He began to assume that his home telephone was bugged. He also began to assume that some of those responsible worked for the state.

These notions were not completely far-fetched. During the mid-1970s, Wilson also believed he was being bugged by MI5, right in his office at 10 Downing Street. Wilson was an increasingly paranoid politician by then, and so, to a lesser extent, was Benn. But as the former MI5 officer Peter Wright described in his famous 1987 memoir *Spycatcher*, during the late 1960s and early 1970s there was 'a decisive shift inside MI5 towards domestic concerns'. These 'concerns' were political: 'The growth of student militancy in the 1960s . . . industrial militancy in the early 1970s . . . the miners' strike in 1972 . . . [all] had a profound effect' on the secret service. 'Intelligence on domestic subversion became the overriding priority.'

'Subversion' was a usefully broad term. It could be applied to anyone seeking to upset the status quo. But thanks to the Cold War, and the conservative politics of many MI5 officers, it was usually applied to the left, and to the Labour party in particular. The idea that the party might be significantly infiltrated or influenced by Eastern bloc agents – however unlikely that was, given Labour's often stridently anti-Soviet foreign policy – spread through the British intelligence services and the rightwing think tanks and newspapers which helped feed and reflect their thinking. How strongly this idea was held is open to question, but at the least it was a way to damage Labour's credibility. According to a 1989 book by the respected leftwing investigative reporter Paul Foot about British intelligence during the 1970s and 1980s, domestic and foreign journalists who were considered open to the notion of Labour's subversion by the Soviets 'would be taken confidentially on one side', and shown what was presented to them as a secret internal document written by leftwing conspirators. Among other claims about senior Labour figures – including some even on the right of the party – the document said that Benn had 'links with Czech intelligence'. 'The essence of . . . revolutionary strategy,' the document went on, 'is to combine the struggle for reforms' – essentially Benn's approach in government – 'with the struggle for revolution.'

Foot concluded that the document was a forgery, part of a smear campaign. But in the sometimes feverish and politically charged world of British intelligence then, the boundaries between fake allegations against the left and genuine beliefs about the left were not always clear. Whether MI5 considered Benn a subversive or not, his appointment as industry minister, Foot wrote, 'greatly excited and infuriated the prejudices of the "ultras" in the intelligence services'. Benn's stable family life and financial probity, they concluded, meant that the only way to undermine him was through his politics.

Meanwhile, the limits to the methods that British intelligence would consider using against domestic subversives appeared to be loosening. After the coup in Chile, the Pinochet dictatorship collaborated with other authoritarian South American governments and the United States to create Operation Condor, a clandestine organisation which coordinated the kidnapping, torture and assassination of over 50,000 leftwingers across South America during the 1970s and 1980s. In 2019, a declassified CIA document revealed that 'Representatives of West German, French and British intelligence services had visited the Condor organization secretariat in Buenos Aires during the month of September 1977 in order to discuss methods for [the] establishment of an anti-subversion organization similar to Condor.' The visitors to the Condor secretariat, the document continued, told their hosts that 'The terrorist/subversive threat had reached such dangerous levels in Europe that they believed it best if they pooled their intelligence resources in a cooperative organization such as Condor.' It seems likely that the intelligence agencies of these liberal European democracies were more interested in Condor's bureaucratic efficiency than in its practice of throwing leftists out of helicopters. But the document did not say.

During 1974 and 1975, as Benn was gradually surrounded by obstructive or actively hostile forces, and as his plans for British industry were steadily dismantled, his moods became even more mercurial than usual: alternately upbeat, defiant, depressed and frantic.

In September 1974, just after the first anniversary of the coup in Chile, he listed some of his actual or potential enemies in his diary: 'The CIA spent $4m undermining the Allende government . . . One has to keep an eye out for the role of British intelligence here at home . . . One would be foolish to underestimate the extent to which American business is secretly mobilising in order to defeat the Labour government . . .'

In her diary that November, Barbara Castle described him as 'wild-eyed'. Castle claimed Caroline had recently told her: 'He never eats.' In cabinet meetings, Benn's contributions became ever more intense: miniature speeches that were compelling but cumulatively wearying. 'He has got himself launched so strongly on a tide of challenging everything and everyone,' wrote Castle, 'that all he can do is shoot the rapids.' No modest talent herself, one of the earliest and most able female ministers, Castle often found Benn's analyses in cabinet of what was wrong with British industry or the British state 'scintillating'. 'His capacity for vivid and telling words is immense,' she wrote in March 1975. 'Even Harold [Wilson] nodded as Wedgie declaimed . . .' When Benn's arguments were disputed by one of the cabinet's many equally confident centre-left figures, such as Healey or Wilson himself, Benn would shoot straight back, sometimes wittily, seemingly quite fearless.

But Castle and other ministers felt he lacked other crucial political qualities. In the cabinet or shadow cabinet, when he was not talking, he could seem aloof. 'Wedgie sits very pontifically these days,' she wrote in January 1974, 'looking as though he has access to some secret and superior wisdom.' While others were speaking he took lots of notes as well. Castle, being a diarist, correctly suspected that he was keeping a diary. Other ministers suspected, again correctly, that Benn was also beginning to see himself as different from them: as primarily the cabinet representative of the increasingly leftwing Labour membership, of the new, bottom-up trade unionism, and of the post-1968 social movements – in other words, as a Labour politician who put the left outside parliament first. According to party tradition, senior MPs were not supposed to do that.

Most of Benn's cabinet colleagues also felt that his radical proposals were far too optimistic. 'I mistrust Wedgie,' Castle wrote in May 1975. 'He never spells out that . . . the choices facing this country are by definition grim for everybody.'

During 1974 and 1975 the sense of economic and political crisis that had been building in Britain ever since the mid-1960s, when the relative stability of the postwar years ended, began to turn to panic. Not among the population at large, who were still enjoying high rates of employment and little poverty by 20th-century standards, but among many of the people who ran big business or governed the country from Westminster and Whitehall. In August 1975, a senior civil servant called Ronald McIntosh ran into another experienced Whitehall fixer, Sir Leonard Neal, and asked him how he was. 'Like everyone else,' said Neal. 'Waiting for the collapse.'

During this period, there did seem to be evidence that Britain's inevitable and until then relatively gentle decline from the world's leading imperial power to just another medium-sized European country was accelerating uncontrollably. That August, inflation reached almost 27 per cent – a modern British record, and the sort of rate associated in Britain with doomed democracies such as the Weimar Republic which preceded the Nazis. In fact, Weimar inflation was many times worse, but like Germany in the 1920s and 1930s, Britain was polarising in response to its problems, and considering more confrontational political options. Thatcherism was one: Margaret Thatcher usurped Heath as Conservative leader in February 1975.

Labour managed to stay in power through these feverish months, but only just. In October 1974 Wilson called another general election – it was the first year with two since 1910 – hoping to turn his minority government into one with a secure majority. Yet Labour won a majority of just three. Wilson carried on as prime minister, his physical and mental energy noticeably fading. He spent increasing amounts of time away from Downing Street, at his doctor's house in the north London suburbs, having one-to-one conversations of unknown content. Meanwhile, his cabinet of clever but often inexperienced ministers, such as the chancellor Healey, struggled to get to grips with all the problems they had inherited from Heath's overwhelmed administration.

In this context, Benn's plans for industry were seen by other ministers as far too ambitious, a political luxury. Yet Benn thought the crisis made them even more of a necessity. 'If we can't give people money,' he said in his diary in December 1974, 'we can give them power . . . Erode the power of private management.'

Two months later, the industry bill was finally debated at length in the House of Commons. Benn introduced it with great enthusiasm and expansive justifications, as if none of its watering down by Wilson and his lieutenants over the preceding months had actually happened. 'This Bill,' said Benn,

> based on policies . . . clearly set out in our manifestos, contains . . . far-reaching democratic socialist reforms affecting the relations between the community, management and workers, and is designed to deal direct with the problems of manufacturing industry that lie at the heart of Britain's present . . . economic weakness.

Riskily, given his and his party's many recent years in government, he put some of the blame for this economic weakness on the entire post-war ruling class:

> Over the last 30 years, under governments of both parties, the country has failed to obtain the level of industrial investment it needs to be effective.

Equally riskily, he said that the industry bill was not just about addressing failure, but about creating a different kind of economy:

> The argument is not about [whether to have] a [government] managed economy but about the much more important question, 'In whose interests is it to be managed?'

To achieve this simultaneous rescue and reordering, Benn said his proposed legislation had three, more concrete goals: to provide 'a new and important source of public investment' by the government taking large shareholdings in major companies; 'to inject both the national interest . . . and the interests of working people into the strategic decisions made by [these] industrial firms'; and 'to extend industrial democracy in [these] firms to make them more accountable . . . towards working people'.

These reverent references to 'working people' studded the speech. In a typical passage of Benn oratory, with precise adjectival clauses building smoothly and rhythmically to a peak of outrage, he argued that

> It is no use blaming working people or the unions if they have to work in ancient factories with obsolete equipment producing old-fashioned goods at uneconomic prices and earning low wages as well. Working people not only are not responsible for the weakness of British industry. They have hitherto been denied the tools . . . that they needed to put it right.

He did acknowledge that in many companies 'managers have suffered, too': from stingy, power-hoarding owners, who 'denied' them 'the essential information they needed to learn, in time, what might be wrong with the firms for which they worked and how their performance could be improved'. But when he talked about 'the people' or 'our people' in his speech – as in, 'release the wasted energies of our people' – the phrase had a populist and proletarian flavour. This was a speech that could be made not just in the Commons, but to a great crowd of trade unionists, in a factory or on the street.

Occasionally, his sense of conviction and mission stiffened his words into grandiose, almost nationalistic rhetoric. 'The British people will come increasingly to see the Bill,' he promised, 'as an instrument that they can use to put this country once again in the forefront of the world's industrial nations.' At these moments, the growing number of people on the right and in the centre of British politics who saw Benn as a potential demagogue did not seem quite so over-dramatic.

Yet much more often he was crisply, even wittily dismissive of the industry bill's critics: its Conservative ones in the debate, and by implication its Labour ones as well. 'What are the arguments against this Bill?' he asked rhetorically. 'One is that . . . there is to be too much power for the Government and the Secretary of State at the expense of Parliament. That criticism is made by a party that transferred more power to the [European] Commission in Brussels without any accountability whatsoever to the House of Commons.'

He moved on to the charge that the bill would give workers too much power: 'It cannot be true that this is a Mussolini nightmare and a Trotskyist nightmare at one and the same time.' In the next sentence, he switched from derision to emollience. The bill, he said, was merely 'seeking to get the relationship between Government, management and workers into a better balance'.

Then he switched back to derision: 'It is argued that the Bill destroys the mixed economy. But even the [proposed] Planning Agreements . . . are designed for at most 100 to 150 firms out of hundreds of thousands.' He was happy for the economy to remain a mix of state-owned, partially state-owned, state-subsidised and wholly private businesses. 'However, we do not accept the definition of a mixed economy that leaves the public sector permanently loss making . . . and the private sector permanently profitable by public subsidy.'

The Commons was used to displays of contempt for opponents. But Benn's passages of aggressive rhetoric were different: never personal attacks, rarely made up of just acidic phrases, but also containing bits of pithy analysis about what was wrong with Britain, and what he would do about it.

Finally, he tried to appeal to the left. 'Another criticism [of the bill] is that this is a socialist measure,' he said. He paused. 'It is.' Being frank about the egalitarian nature of his plans, he believed, would excite even his most cautious Labour comrades at least a little, and beyond them the working class as a whole. Labour was supposed to be an egalitarian party, after all. And after thirty postwar years of redistributive governments and rising social mobility, Britain was a country that, for all its tensions and problems, was more equal than ever before.

However, just as his sweeping Commons defence of the industry bill did not acknowledge that the proposed legislation was much less potent than the original version, so his speech also failed to acknowledge that by the mid-1970s Britain might have become as equal as it wanted to be – or, even, more equal than it wanted to be. Six days before the debate, Margaret Thatcher was elected as Conservative leader, in large part because she was known to be less accepting of the postwar status quo than her predecessors.

Yet to Benn in 1975, and for the next decade, the growing number of forces mobilised against him was not a deterrent. He believed it was a sign that he was on to something politically: that he was about to unlock a mass politics which truly threatened the elite. He was an optimist. That was his great strength, and his great weakness.

During early 1975, alongside his struggle to democratise the economy, Benn took on another extremely difficult cause: persuading the United Kingdom to leave the EEC. The country had only joined two years earlier, in one of the few completed and relatively popular moves of Heath's premiership. Benn himself had been publicly opposed to EEC membership for even less time, since mid-1974.

Before then, his view on the issue, like that of a lot of Labour and Conservative politicians, had jumped around for decades between enthusiasm, agnosticism and scepticism. In their defence, the EEC was then a new and relatively unformed organisation. For any politician who wanted to reform postwar Britain, it was not that easy to tell whether joining the EEC would be a crucial step, a distraction or a dead end.

What made up Benn's mind, finally, was his understanding of the ways in which EEC membership would affect British democracy, both the traditional parliamentary kind and the new industrial version he hoped to nurture. Membership came with a political price: in return for closer economic cooperation, and therefore greater freedom, peace and prosperity for their citizens, at least in theory, EEC countries gave up some of their ability to govern themselves, by becoming subject to European laws. Not only could these laws sometimes supersede the laws made by national governments, the EEC's law-making bodies could outlast these governments.

For Benn, increasingly preoccupied with maximising democracy, which to him often meant democracy practised as locally as possible, the EEC's undemocratic aspects became intolerable. At the same time, his dealings with Brussels as industry minister made him increasingly aware of the EEC's conventionally pro-business side: the limits it placed on how much member governments could shape or soften capitalism, for example by giving state aid to struggling but valued industries.

The fact that the governments of other EEC members such as Italy and France still managed to intervene extensively in their economies, and that his advisor Stuart Holland was strongly pro-European, partly for that reason, made no difference to the direction of Benn's thinking. In his diaries, then in cabinet meetings and finally in public speeches, his warnings about the EEC became dramatic, sometimes hyperbolic. British democracy, he wrote, 'was being strangled by entry into the Common Market'. 'Britain will be governed by a European coalition that we cannot change, dedicated to a capitalist or market economy theology.' EEC membership would mean 'the reversal of hundreds of years of history which have progressively widened the power of the people'.

Even when he had been in favour of membership, Benn had eventually decided by the beginning of the 1970s that the issues involved were so profound and divisive, with both Labour and the Conservatives badly split, that the whole question should be decided by a referendum. The fact that the UK had never held one before made him keener still, given his conviction that its democracy needed to be modernised and extended.

After many months of half-hidden battles inside Labour's policy-making labyrinth, with Benn playing a big part as both arm-twister and high-minded advocate, the party included a commitment to a referendum in its February 1974 election manifesto. In early 1975, shortly after Labour had strengthened, albeit a little, its weak hold on power at the October 1974 election, the commitment was honoured. Like the appointment of Benn as industry minister, it was a typically sly Wilson move. What looked like a concession to a troublesome and ambitious subordinate by a weakening prime minister was actually, as at the Industry Department, a way of letting Benn make his case in public – a case that Wilson knew would be intensely controversial, and opposed by powerful forces.

Another clever aspect of the decision was to keep the referendum campaign short, so that the implications of EEC membership could not be fully explored. For a few weeks in April and May 1975, with the public partly distracted by other issues such as the surging inflation rate, Benn tried to give momentum to a No campaign which had many squabbling factions but little funding and only three full-time staff. Among Benn's uncomfortable new comrades were Tory nationalists, libertarians, the SNP and Plaid Cymru, and the racist former Conservative politician Enoch Powell, with whom Benn refused to share any platform. There was some significant support from the left: from powerful trade union leaders such as Jack Jones, the majority of the parliamentary Labour party, and half a dozen cabinet ministers. But there was not enough coordination of all these headstrong forces, largely because the anti-EEC left and right were so suspicious of each other. They knew that as soon as the referendum was over, the usual left–right hostilities of the polarised 1970s would resume.

Benn privately considered the leave coalition 'an awful rag-bag'. Although he was one of its best speakers, at his own insistence he spent most of the campaign addressing leftwing audiences. His speeches combined his now familiar arguments about the EEC's threat to British democracy with new warnings about the damage membership was supposedly doing to the economy by making it easier for foreign goods to flood in, undercutting British businesses, and for investment to flow out, starving those same businesses of funds. With populist flair, at a rally in Bristol he described Britain's EEC membership as a deal done by 'the rich and powerful' to protect their own interests from the problems of capitalism, while condemning the British working class to 'a colonial relationship with the Common Market'. Deploying his authority as industry minister, he claimed that because of EEC membership half a million British jobs had already been lost.

Barbara Castle, a fellow No campaigner but sometimes a sceptical Benn-watcher, wrote in her diary that he was 'on the top of his oratorical form'. The response to him at rallies was 'only just short of idolatry'. Rather than regard this as a personal endorsement, Benn characteristically saw it as a broader political force, 'a great tide of opinion' which 'cannot be held back'. His confidence about the result of the referendum grew. A few days before the vote he told the *Glasgow Herald* that 'all the evidence' indicated 'a massive No vote'.

Yet away from his rallies, a blander but much better-resourced campaign in favour of EEC membership was under way. 'Cars, aeroplanes, helicopters, film units, stage equipment, photocopiers ... simply appeared at a flick of [the] fingers,' recalled the Liberal MP David Steel, one of the Yes campaign's immense array of centrist politicians, celebrities and businessmen. Every national newspaper except the *Morning Star* supported Yes. So did Thatcher, Wilson and Heath. To most of the British establishment, unusually rattled by all the decade's economic and political crises, as Benn had spotted, EEC membership was both a possible solution to Britain's apparent decline, and a promising experiment that needed to be given more time.

Much of the public agreed. The referendum result on 5 June was 67.2 per cent for Yes and 32.8 per cent for No. It was widely seen as a huge defeat for Benn personally. His advocacy of a referendum and his prominence in the campaign, which probably pushed many people who thought of themselves as moderates and disliked his radicalism into voting Yes, certainly left him vulnerable. In fact, Wilson was already making moves to further undermine him. During the campaign, the prime minister had been horrified by how much television coverage Benn was getting. Worried that his plan to expose him to greater scrutiny might be misfiring, in April Wilson gave an anonymous interview to a *Daily Telegraph* journalist and suggested that Benn would soon be moved from the Industry Department and demoted.

For the rest of the spring, that prospect was relentlessly talked up by the rightwing press. Even more than usual with speculation about an apparently doomed minister, the stories had a gleeful edge: 'Bye, Bye Benn' read a typical headline. Meanwhile, the briefing continued against him and his industry bill from anonymous civil servants and ministers, and from named sources in the City of London and the employers' organisation the Confederation of British Industry (CBI). In late May, Wilson himself openly joined the anti-Benn witch-hunt. 'He dreams about the future,' said the prime minister during a TV interview, 'but what he says isn't government policy.' Even before this lethal intervention, Benn recorded furiously in his diary that 'Wilson' – he usually referred to him as Harold – 'has destroyed my credibility as a minister.'

For four days after the referendum result, there were journalists almost constantly outside the Benns' London house. On the afternoon of the fourth day, Benn was told that the prime minister wanted to see him at 6pm. Without any pleasantries, Wilson told Benn that he wanted to move him from the Department of Industry to the Department of Energy, and that he had two hours to decide whether he wanted the new job. Benn refused to be rushed. He said that he wanted to speak to Caroline, and sleep on things, before making up his mind.

That evening Caroline was in a governors' meeting at Holland Park School. Their teenage daughter Melissa rushed up the hill from their house to tell her about the situation. When Caroline was pulled out of the meeting, her first thought was that her husband had been assassinated.

For the rest of the evening and for much of the next day, Benn consulted his wife and a range of other advisors and allies. Some said he should resign from the cabinet, as a protest and so that he could speak more freely. Others said that he should spare the fragile government a damaging resignation, take the energy job, and do what he could for the left from inside Whitehall. Wilson summoned him again. The two men argued. Benn accused Wilson of downgrading him and Labour's manifesto commitment to transform industry because of pressure from the City and the media. Wilson did not fully deny the charges. Nor did he change his mind about demoting Benn. Benn said that he would take the energy job. Then he walked out of the prime minister's office and slammed the door.

7

Seeding the Capital

While Benn was on his way out of the establishment, Diane Abbott was trying to find a way in. In 1973 she began her history degree at Cambridge. Although her women-only college, Newnham, was relatively progressive, having been co-founded by the Victorian feminist Millicent Fawcett, Abbott was only the second black student in its century-long history. Much of the university was even more alien. In her final year, Abbott went to a ball at another college, wearing an evening dress and lots of jewellery. As soon as she walked through the college gates, someone rushed up to her. 'Oh good,' they said, 'you must have come to do the washing up.'

As at grammar school, Abbott grew a thicker skin and got what she could out of the institution. For the optional parts of her degree, she focused on the United States, so that she could learn more about the history of racism and race. Courses on the British dimensions of those topics were not offered. She read eagerly, wrote slightly florid essays, and was not intimidated by the one-on-one sessions with academics, known as supervisions, on which Cambridge undergraduate teaching was based. One supervisor's report said that she had 'a talent for challenging everyone and everything in sight'.

At Cambridge, as at other British universities, and in Britain generally, it was quite a good time to be a rebel. The long aftershocks of 1968 were shaking up even conservative institutions. For several years before Abbott arrived at Cambridge, there had been student protests demanding, among many other things, that elected undergraduates be added to the boards that supervised the university faculties. In 1974 the history department finally agreed, and the following year the first elections took place. Abbott stood. It was her electoral debut. She won comfortably.

The faculty board she joined was a committee where white male historians discussed large and small departmental matters with the added intensity of people who studied political battles for a living. Abbott, who wore large glasses that dominated her round face and made her look younger than other undergraduates, adopted her own sly persona, 'asking outrageous questions in a little-girl voice', as a note of the proceedings recorded. Away from the committee, her voice became larger and more confident: very clear in its diction, even rather posh and commanding. It would become one of her trademarks in public life. But it was not how working-class black Britons were expected to speak at all. Eventually, it became one of the reasons why so many people wanted to see her downfall.

In private, she was quieter and more self-doubting. She spent quite a lot of time on her own, sitting by the gas fire in her college room, losing herself in books and eating toast. She was not politically active at Cambridge, except for a period in a women's group, which she saw as too middle-class, with its other members treating a working-class woman who had joined from outside the university like a 'laboratory specimen'. But she began to see herself as a feminist, a socialist and an anti-racist, and read accordingly, roaming beyond her course texts into the inflammatory and inspiring works of the era's many writer-activists: Germaine Greer, Angela Davis, Stokely Carmichael.

In 1976 Abbott left Cambridge with a 2:2, a disappointing degree for a clever student. Yet her three years at the university had given her an establishment veneer and a sense of what she wanted to do next: to use her determined intelligence to work for social change, while having some political adventures along the way. She applied for the civil service, specifically the Home Office, because it was the one government department that was beginning to take racism seriously. At the final interview, which was chaired by the renowned philosopher and public servant Mary Warnock, Warnock asked Abbott why she wanted to join the civil service. Abbott replied: 'Because I want power.'

As well as being assessed by the Home Office, her application was examined by Special Branch, the part of the Metropolitan Police responsible for national security. The process was known as 'positive vetting', a classic Whitehall euphemism for a procedure which, in an era of rising official anxiety about radical infiltration, was being applied to a wide range of would-be government employees. Special Branch questioned whether the Home Office was the right place for Abbott, since she was so 'lively' – an even drier euphemism for being forthright and political. But the Home Office liked her enough to override these doubts. She was hired as a graduate trainee.

Under the Labour home secretary Roy Jenkins, by reputation a social liberal, the Home Office was shedding some of its traditional authoritarianism and incuriosity about social disadvantage. A few months after Abbott joined the department, parliament passed the 1976 Race Relations Act, a wide-ranging piece of legislation with a lot of Home Office input, which outlawed racial discrimination in employment, education and commerce, and established the Commission for Racial Equality. In theory, it was a major step forward for ethnic minority Britons. But in reality its provisions often proved easy for racists to evade. Likewise, the supposedly liberal Jenkins still presided over a policing and prison system which was particularly brutal towards black men.

Partly for that reason, Abbott chose to work in the part of the Home Office overseeing prisons. Yet her hopes of helping to reform the overcrowded and secretive compounds were frustrated by more experienced, less idealistic colleagues, and by a rightward shift in the government, which saw public spending cut and Jenkins replaced as home secretary by the more authoritarian Merlyn Rees. Moreover, by the late 1970s the next general election was nearing and the Labour government was well behind in the opinion polls. It seemed increasingly obvious to her that prisons policy was about to become more illiberal still, under a Conservative party which was rising in popularity in part by promising voters that crime would be reduced by more punitive policies. In early 1979, a few months before the Tories returned to power, Abbott left the Home Office. She went to work for one of its strongest critics, the National Council for Civil Liberties (NCCL), now Liberty.

The pressure group was widening its work, from campaigning against state encroachments on individual freedoms to also standing up for the rights of the disadvantaged, such as ethnic minority Britons. Abbott was hired as its first race relations officer. Her brief was loose: to 'maintain contact with minority groups', the community and activist bodies, which for the first time were being set up in numbers in multiracial parts of Britain. She also organised conferences and workshops, researched the neglected history of British ethnic minorities, and convinced the NCCL of the value of 'ethnic record keeping', as a way of measuring and combatting institutional racism.

Monitoring the racial make-up of institutions is common practice today, but in late 1970s Britain it was a new and uncomfortable concept for white-dominated bodies, especially liberal ones such as the NCCL, which believed that racism happened on the streets, in the form of attacks by racists, rather than more subtly inside organisations staffed by supposedly well-meaning people. But Abbott, for all her smooth Cambridge diction, was not interested in saying comfortable things. At a time when there were no prominent British ethnic minority politicians, her combination of outspokenness and polish began to attract attention. She dressed strikingly, at least by the usually plain standards of the pressure group world, in smart white polo necks and big earrings, like a cross between a businesswoman and a slick Afro-American activist. 'Because I was smartly turned out, the NCCL didn't think I was leftwing enough,' she told me. 'But black women are always smartly turned out. [The activist] Angela Davis was always smartly turned out.' Abbott frequently changed her hairstyle, and could charm, when she wanted to, with warm eyes and a big, photogenic smile. In early 1979, she got her first significant press attention: a profile in the *London Evening Standard*.

Meanwhile she took her first steps towards a political career. The previous year, while still working in Whitehall, she had joined the Labour party. Like Ken Livingstone, she did so relatively late, in her mid-twenties, and when the party was at a low ebb electorally. Since civil servants were supposed to be politically neutral, she had to ask permission from her department head. He agreed. For the time being, the institutions of British education and politics were prepared to make room for her. In 1978, her first year in the party, she was selected as a youth delegate for the Labour party conference at Blackpool.

The conference took place in the Winter Gardens, an enormous Victorian complex near the seafront. A century of storms off the Irish Sea, and of people tramping in and out for business or pleasure, had left the ornate buildings a little worn. In the Empress Ballroom, where the conference was held, drifting clouds of cigarette smoke from the delegates sometimes obscured the arched and moulded ceiling, and made the speakers onstage appear to be shouting through fog.

Yet Abbott enjoyed Labour's gatherings there so much that she said the Winter Gardens was her favourite building. At her first conference, she was thrilled to see the party's national reach reflected in the delegates: miners from the north of England, factory workers from the Midlands, local councillors from the West Country, and young activists from the London left. One of the latter was Jeremy Corbyn.

'I was walking along the seafront,' she told me, 'and Jeremy was going in the opposite direction.' She was with Livingstone, whom she already knew a little because he was active in her constituency. Livingstone also knew Corbyn, through the interconnected workings of the still relatively small London left. A more experienced politician and networker than Corbyn or Abbott, Livingstone greeted him on the seafront and made the introductions.

Corbyn was 29, still slight and pale, with thick wavy hair that reached his shoulders. He wore an unfashionable wide-lapelled brown jacket that slightly swamped him. But he had a confidence, after over a decade in Labour politics, and he and Abbott soon discovered that they had shared interests.

In the main conference hall, Corbyn made a speech during a debate about one of her favourite topics, the government's increasingly authoritarian approach to policing. He strode purposefully, even impatiently, up to the stage, jacket flapping, holding his notes in one hand. At the podium, he seemed at ease, looking around the huge ballroom as he spoke, pausing a few times for effect. His voice may have lacked volume, and rhythm, yet he had intensity. By the end of the speech he was almost shouting, and his eyes were bulging, but his argument had force and clarity. 'If this government can find time and money, apparently, to appease the police,' he said, 'how is it that they have not found the time to do anything to bring about democratic control of the police?'

Corbyn's attack on his own party's record in government was pithy and newsworthy enough to be shown on the BBC's *Nine O'Clock News*. The newsreader described him as 'a militant young delegate', and noted that the home secretary had been forced to reply to the points Corbyn and other leftwing delegates had raised. After a decade and a half as a local activist, Corbyn had got a fleeting taste of a different kind of power.

Since being elected as a Haringey councillor four years earlier, he had become a familiar and steadily more influential figure in London Labour politics. From early each morning, he would be in perpetual motion between party meetings, demonstrations, council votes and committees, and conversations with the locally needy – and with people he simply got talking to in the street. He was often running late, but he seemed tireless. And he was a good listener: when he was doing politics, his own status and interests seemed not to matter to him.

His causes multiplied. He helped arrange housing in Haringey for leftwing refugees from Chile. Inspired by Tony Benn, he put down a motion at a council meeting opposing British membership of the EEC. He helped commission new community centres for the borough's immigrants. He joined a high-profile mass picket supporting Asian workers sacked by an exploitative photo-processing company, Grunwick. Standing up for ethnic minorities, at a time when their interests were often neglected by Labour, became one of his priorities.

In 1977 the racist National Front, rapidly gaining support as British politics became more confrontational and moved to the right, had organised a Saturday afternoon march through Wood Green, a busy shopping area in Haringey, as part of a strategy of intimidatingly occupying public space in multicultural places. The police refused a request from the council to ban the march. So Corbyn and others organised a counter-demonstration. It included everyone from local churchmen and Conservative councillors to leftwingers of all stripes, Rastafarians, white rockabillies and black teenagers. Some of the bolder counter-demonstrators pelted the outnumbered National Front marchers with rotten fruit, bottles and smoke bombs. Instead of being a show of strength by the far right, the afternoon became a humiliation, and was quickly mythologised as the Battle of Wood Green by the London left. Shortly afterwards, Corbyn was interviewed by a local paper, the *Hornsey Journal*. 'It must be clear from

Saturday,' he said, 'that there is the widest possible opposition to these modern day fascists. How much longer must it be before fascism is banned from our streets?' As he would again in his anti-police speech at the Labour conference the following year, he was beginning to sound like a national politician.

Meanwhile he worked more quietly to shift Haringey's Labour council, which had a centrist majority, further to the left. In person, his political style remained unaggressive. He presented himself as 'everyone's mate and not a faction-fighter', as his fellow leftist Keith Veness put it. But Corbyn was relentless in proposing leftwing motions to the council and attempting to isolate or bypass centrist councillors. The left did not get control of the Labour group on the council, but it influenced the borough's overall approach, which was to set the local rates, a precursor to the council tax, at a high level, and then spend freely on the most disadvantaged. And when the council's approach was judged by voters at the 1978 local elections, Labour gained votes from the Conservatives – the opposite of most results elsewhere.

The one big setback for Corbyn during these years of promise was at home. Although his wife Jane was also still a leftwing Haringey councillor, and sometimes his close political collaborator, her dedication to socialism was less total. Politics tired her, and she was also tired of Corbyn's constant absences and his lack of interest in domestic tasks, in having a social life outside politics, or in enjoying the city as a couple. They drifted apart.

When Abbott met Corbyn at the Labour party conference in September 1978, he and Chapman were not yet divorced; that would happen the following year. But Corbyn and Abbott quickly discovered that they had a lot in common: outspokenness, a loner quality, a suspicion of authority, a belief that socialism should include the defence of civil liberties and minorities; and a fascination with Jamaica, which she had recently visited for the first time. They started a relationship soon afterwards.

Politically, Livingstone was several steps ahead of them. By September 1978 he had left Lambeth council, and had embarked on a new phase of his political career, a phase during which he sought power in so many different ways simultaneously that he seemed almost manic. He became a councillor in the London Borough of Camden. It was run by a Labour authority which was more prestigious and better funded than Lambeth's. Camden drew much of its income from, and provided services for, a significant proportion of north London's middle-class liberals.

At the same time, Livingstone got himself selected as the Labour parliamentary candidate for the most high-status part of the borough: Hampstead, then a constituency of comfortably-off businessmen, bohemians, intellectuals and pockets of working-class residents, Abbott among them, which had a temptingly tiny Conservative majority. And finally, he also got elected to the Greater London Council, first representing his home turf of Norwood in south London, then switching to the Hackney North constituency in the east of the capital.

Livingstone was able to do all these things concurrently partly because he was a young man with no children, but also because they happened at different times. The GLC met during the day, while borough council meetings were in the evenings, and parliamentary canvassing could mostly be done at weekends. And there was logic as well as impatience to his manoeuvring. During the second half of the 1970s, London politics, even more than politics nationally, was in flux, with support for Labour and the Conservatives frequently surging and receding and shifting from place to place, as many voters kept changing their minds about which party had the best ideas for reviving the run-down capital. In addition, winning power as a politician of the Labour left – let alone exercising it effectively – remained a difficult path. So it made sense to hedge your bets by trying several routes simultaneously. With his background in scientific research, Livingstone had more interest in data and trends than many politicians, and followed London's voting patterns closely. He switched his GLC seat from Norwood to Hackney North, for example, because he was convinced that when they were next contested Labour would lose the former and hold the latter, which he had identified as a more reliably leftwing area. He was right.

By the late 1970s Livingstone was well known across the London Labour party as a talented but slippery operator. His early 70s beard had been replaced by a slim, almost caddish moustache. He had a taste for safari jackets, perhaps because of his travels in Africa. Unlike Corbyn, whose messy dress and air of outraged earnestness still had a hippie whiff about them, Livingstone seemed more modern and streetwise – an idealist prepared to use extremely pragmatic methods. When he first arrived at the GLC, as part of a Labour landslide that captured the council in 1973, the party's leadership there regarded him from the start as 'a troublesome little bastard', as he wrote proudly afterwards.

He spent much of the decade proving this assessment correct. When the GLC administration to which he belonged announced spending cuts – contrary to its election pledges – he rebelled in as provocative a way as possible. The GLC leader Reg Goodwin had argued that pressure from the Labour government, which was short of money as the British economy ran into trouble in the mid-1970s, made cuts by the GLC unavoidable. So Livingstone rang one of the government departments supposedly demanding cuts in London, and discovered that the department actually wanted the GLC to borrow more rather than reduce spending. He then confronted Goodwin with this information at a meeting of Labour's GLC members. 'As I was effectively calling the Leader a liar to his face in front of the whole [Labour] Group,' Livingstone wrote later, 'the atmosphere was difficult to say the least.'

The much more senior and experienced Goodwin ultimately won the battle, and most of the cuts were pushed through. But Livingstone's argument that they would prove politically disastrous was vindicated at the next GLC elections, in 1977. The Goodwin administration was ejected by voters, along with almost half of Labour's GLC members. Livingstone, protected in the leftwing stronghold of Hackney North, survived the cull. He was now well placed to advance further on the GLC whenever the elderly Goodwin stood down.

Meanwhile, Livingstone mounted his parallel campaign to get into the Commons. For three years he trawled for votes across Hampstead, from the mansions on its hilltop to the Irish pubs of flatter, poorer Kilburn, where there were republican songs and closing-time collections for the IRA. Abbott helped out, keen to see how a parliamentary campaign worked at first hand. Left-leaning local celebrities, such as the guitarist John Williams and the novelist Margaret Drabble, also assisted with canvassing.

Livingstone's deadpan charm worked with some voters, but there were challenges. At his first Hampstead dinner party, a bouquet garni of inedible herbs was left in his food. He tried to eat it, then had to explain he had never encountered such cooking in more proletarian Lambeth. Talking to Irish immigrants in Kilburn, meanwhile, he realised how little he knew about the history of Ireland and Britain's hugely intrusive role in it. He went away and read up on the subject, developed a strong sympathy for republicanism, and saw that it could be a useful electoral weapon in some London contexts. That such sympathies could also be a liability in the often anti-Irish world of British national politics and newspapers he appreciated less clearly.

His opponent in Hampstead was Geoffrey Finsberg, a Tory veteran who had been the MP since 1970. Finsberg was vain: he had his first, tiny parliamentary majority, 474, as his car number plate. But he was a good administrator, and had been involved in Hampstead politics for decades. Livingstone was an incomer. He also generated endless controversies. A non-driver and early Labour supporter of environmental causes, he became involved in a heated campaign against a plan to build a motorway through residential and green space in nearby Archway. In 1977 he lost a court action against a planning inspector, whom he claimed had hit him in the mouth. The same year, he said that if he became an MP he would do everything he could to equalise the age of sexual consent for lesbians and gay men. Again, his stance was pioneering and progressive. But for a parliamentary candidate needing to win over Conservative voters, it was a risk.

His approach as a Camden councillor was similar. As in Lambeth, he concentrated on the key issue of housing, but this time as chair rather than vice-chair of the housing committee. With populist flair, he opened up its meetings to comments from the public and even gave out his phone number to the borough's council tenants. He froze the latter's rents, and bypassed the housing department's senior officials by rarely meeting them. Instead, he set up his own office inside the department and dealt directly with more junior staff. When the department missed a deadline for producing a report, he composed his own and persuaded the committee to approve it.

His ability to win people over with clever speeches, and also to manoeuvre more covertly in the hazy areas of council business where precedent was weak, gave his initial months at Camden a great impact. But the costs soon mounted up. Tenants phoned him in the middle of the night. His workload grew out of control. Some of his fellow Labour councillors came to think that he was less interested in housing than personal publicity.

This was unfair: he was interested in both. But his iconoclastic style did damage to more than just the council bureaucracy. For decades, Camden had been building innovative public housing: spacious estates, low-rise rather than high-rise, with intricate and varied designs which acknowledged the desire for homes to feel individual. In 1978 he ordered a public inquiry into the construction of one of the estates, Alexandra Road, a great curving spine of flats with slopes of balconies like hanging gardens, which had recently been finished only after years of delays and bust budgets. Livingstone believed that the housing budget was better spent buying up and refurbishing Camden's many semi-derelict terraced houses. In a time of austerity, that was a reasonable argument. But the public inquiry, which lasted for three years, effectively froze and then ended Camden's house-building programme, and inadvertently contributed to the rightwing counter-revolution against council housing in general.

Livingstone became embroiled in other serious rows about public money. His support for keeping council rents as low as possible, while also significantly raising the wages of Camden's lowest-paid staff, who went on strike for higher pay during the winter of 1978–9, helped put the borough's whole budget under strain. As a consequence, the district auditor, a Whitehall official who oversaw local government and had very wide powers, wrote to Livingstone and other Camden Labour councillors, threatening them personally with huge fines and bans from holding office if the council did not change its policies. The controversy was not resolved until 1982, when the High Court ruled in the councillors' favour. But by then Livingstone's reputation was set. He was a politician who always sailed close to the wind.

At the 1979 election, Hampstead's voters decided that they did not want him. Livingstone increased Labour's vote by a few hundred, a better performance than the party managed in most of north London, but it was not enough. Finsberg increased his vote by more, and won with an enlarged majority of 3,681. With Livingstone's path to parliament blocked, at least for now, and his position in Camden weakening, he was left with just one promising political arena, the GLC. There he could test his theory that local government could make the most direct difference to people's lives, and to the distribution of power. It was an experiment he would carry out with relish.

But it was obviously not an experiment he could perform on his own. Even more than a borough council, the GLC was run by a mass of committees which no council leader, however charismatic and powerful, could completely control. If Livingstone became leader – and by 1980, when the discredited Goodwin resigned as head of the GLC's Labour group, Livingstone believed that he could – he would need other disruptors to act as his lieutenants.

The man who would become the most important of these spent much of the 1970s like Livingstone: trying to remove a long-serving, less radical MP from parliament. But in his case the methods employed were less democratic and more sectarian than those of Livingstone's campaign against Finsberg. The man who would become Livingstone's closest GLC comrade believed that politics should be conducted like war.

John McDonnell's worldview was partly formed by what he later called the 'the fundamental Marxist writers . . . Marx, Lenin and Trotsky'. Yet McDonnell's perspective of power, how it was distributed in society, and how the left could get more of it, came from a less well-known source: the Italian politician and theorist Antonio Gramsci.

Gramsci died prematurely in 1937, at the age of 46, his health ruined by over a decade in prison as a leftwing dissident in Mussolini's Italy. So original and politically dangerous did the dictatorship consider Gramsci's thinking that at the trial which sent him to jail the government prosecutor simply argued: 'We must stop this brain from functioning.' Yet while incarcerated Gramsci continued to think and write prolifically. The results were smuggled out of prison and first published in Italy in 1948, after the fall of the dictatorship, as *Quaderni del carcere* (the *Prison Notebooks*). In Britain, often suspicious of foreign theorists, the notebooks were not translated and published until the 1970s. But the delay meant that they appeared just as the British left, in the wake of 1968 and the failures of the Wilson government, was looking around for new ideas. As a mature student then, studying politics and government, with a leftwing background and the large intellectual appetite of an autodidact, McDonnell was typical of the British readers who belatedly discovered Gramsci, who became one of his favourite writers.

The *Prison Notebooks* covered an intoxicating range of subjects far beyond the concerns of traditional Marxism, from the psychology of folklore and factory production lines to how political belief systems were reinforced by popular culture. And Gramsci wrote in a pithy, sometimes gnomic style which could make working out what he really meant a kind of intellectual addiction. One of his ideas which appealed most to leftists such as McDonnell, who were struggling to understand why socialism had not made more headway against capitalism in the West, and also trying to work out what the left should do about this impasse, was summed up by two Gramscian phrases: the 'war of manoeuvre' and the 'war of position'.

A 'war of manoeuvre' was a revolution which overthrew the state. In Western democracies, Gramsci argued, the state was too strong to be toppled like that, because unlike in Russia in 1917 it was willingly supported by many citizens and interest groups in wider society. 'The State was just a forward trench' protecting the status quo, he wrote, and 'behind it stood a succession of sturdy fortresses and emplacements', such as pro-capitalist newspapers and university departments which taught students to value the individual above the collective. Together with the state and business, such institutions and patterns of thought made up the capitalist 'hegemony', Gramsci's favoured term for a political ascendancy.

To create a different, socialist hegemony, he argued that a 'war of position' was required: the incremental takeover of institutions, the creation of new ones, and the influencing of how people thought, so that the left ultimately became dominant without ever launching a frontal attack on the establishment. This approach was similar to G. D. H. Cole's 1920 vision of the left 'wresting bit by bit from the hands of the possessing classes the economic power', which later influenced Tony Benn, and also to the German activist and '68er Rudi Dutschke's call for a 'long march through the institutions' – the strategy which greatly influenced Ken Livingstone, though he misattributed it to the French '68er Daniel Cohn-Bendit. Yet in practice, this kind of politics could be less dramatic than Gramsci's sweeping military metaphors suggested. It required activists who were patient and relentless.

McDonnell joined the constituency Labour party in Hayes shortly after moving to the west London suburb with his wife in 1974, at the age of 23. The parliamentary seat, which also included the former village of Harlington, next to Heathrow airport, was a flat expanse of semi-detached houses and industrial estates, airport warehouses and arterial roads with traffic thundering in and out of central London. George Orwell, who briefly lived and worked as a schoolteacher in Hayes in the 1930s, called it 'one of the most god-forsaken places I have ever struck'. But his dislike of suburbia blinded him to the fact that Hayes offered relatively cheap homes and lots of jobs. During the mid-20th century people moved to the area from depressed parts of Wales, northern England and Ireland. Incomers from across Africa and Asia followed.

When McDonnell arrived in Hayes as another of these migrants, the local MP was Neville Sandelson: a practising barrister on the right of the Labour party. He was from a wealthy background. While at private school at Westminster, he claimed to have bloodied Tony Benn's nose in a boxing match. Sandelson smoked expensive cigars, supported EEC membership, and did not live in the constituency, preferring posher Ascot in Berkshire. An MP more likely to alienate the seat's generally leftwing Labour membership – often trade unionists who worked in local factories – was hard to imagine.

During the early 1970s, they had begun to mobilise to have him replaced. But Sandelson was popular with the constituency's more centrist voters: small businessmen and working-class people who were becoming property owners for the first time. Since first being elected in 1971, he had increased Labour's longstanding local majority to an impregnable-seeming 10,000. He also had the support of senior party figures such as Michael Foot and Jim Callaghan. Sandelson seemed untouchable.

Then came McDonnell. His politics degree was a sandwich course, with six months of work experience for every six months of teaching. He used the practical part to study the Hayes and Harlington constituency party, and to help change it. The local members were a promising mix: industrial activists, sometimes with Communist Party connections; community activists campaigning to get residents better access to housing and legal services; environmentalists concerned with the impact of Heathrow; and people of all ages who simply wanted to learn more about leftwing politics in theory and practice. There was a reading group which McDonnell joined, studying Marx in a member's kitchen. Some in the local party were aware of the in some ways similar Labour revival which was simultaneously happening in inner London boroughs such as Lambeth and Islington. But the Hayes new left was more locally focused, and considered itself more down to earth and proletarian. 'It wasn't that central London left,' McDonnell told me. 'We always looked upon them as a sort of bourgeois left.'

He was good at getting on with people and at organising things, and he rose quickly in the local party. He edited its newsletter, turning it from a basic information sheet into a well-written pamphlet. He became constituency vice-president, and served as the party's education officer, arranging for major figures from the left, including Tony Benn, to speak to members in the constituency. 'We had a natural affinity and support for Tony Benn,' McDonnell said. 'We were nourished by what was going on nationally.'

Like Benn and the inner London new left, McDonnell and some of his Hayes comrades wanted to widen Labour politics, and worked with community organisations which were not affiliated to the party. Some of these groups had been set up by locals with south Asian backgrounds to fight back against racism, which in the 1970s and 80s was particularly vicious in formerly white-dominated areas of suburban west London such as Hayes and neighbouring Southall. 'The National Front would turn up in numbers,' McDonnell remembered. 'Sometimes, you weren't safe on the streets.' In response, the Hayes Labour party took a proactive approach to local social tensions, such as those over the area's large stretches of council housing, which were affected first by big rent rises under a cash-strapped Labour council and then sell-offs under its Conservative successor. 'If it moved in the community, we were there. If we could get to an issue before the National Front, they couldn't exploit it.' The constituency party was helping to develop a new, practical, potentially very popular form of anti-racism.

With McDonnell's arrival, parts of the Hayes Labour party also intensified the campaign against Sandelson. 'I quite liked the guy,' McDonnell told me, disarmingly. 'I got on quite well with him. I was one of his ward agents . . . But he didn't fit the constituency.' McDonnell proposed a motion in his ward urging Sandelson to retire. The MP, who was only in his early fifties, came to the debate. He wrote afterwards: 'McDonnell . . . tried to suggest that I was a bad MP. He is shrewd enough to know (and has done his homework) that only by establishing that . . . does he stand any chance of ousting me.' The motion was passed. But one ward's dissatisfaction was not enough to remove an MP. A few months later, in 1976, McDonnell and a delegation of Hayes trade unionists came to see Sandelson at the Commons. Sandelson alleged afterwards that they made 'threats' against him, and 'demanded that I attack the [Labour] government's policies' – an unlikely, possibly suicidal strategy for an MP who shared the government's centre-left outlook.

Sandelson refused. He began talking to newspapers which were hostile to the Labour left. 'Politics Student the "Brains" Behind Campaign Against MP,' announced the front page of *The Times* in November 1976. The story included a description of McDonnell as 'an educated young Messiah', from an unnamed supporter of the anti-Sandelson campaign, and also suggested that the Hayes left was motivated by 'Trotskyism' rather than loyalty to the Labour party. There was some truth in this. The infamously dogmatic and expansionist leftwing sect Militant was active in the constituency, and had gained some recruits in the local Labour party. McDonnell was one of them. 'I joined Militant for a short period,' he told me. 'For about eighteen months in the mid-70s. There were good comrades amongst its activists. But I don't think I sold enough papers to stay in.' Selling the group's newspaper on street corners and outside factories was a key duty for its activists. 'And also . . . there was a difference of view over Ireland.' McDonnell supported Irish republicanism, while Militant saw it as insufficiently leftwing and working class.

But such distinctions were lost on a national press increasingly preoccupied by the campaign against Sandelson. In January 1977 the

Observer interviewed him. He said the campaign was part of a much wider one to purge centrist Labour MPs. It was a claim frequently made across the country during the 70s and early 80s. But the evidence that the campaign was as large and organised as alleged was never conclusive.

In 1977 a motion to remove Sandelson was put to a committee representing the whole Hayes party. He survived by a single vote. McDonnell and his comrades resumed their work against him. Finally, in the run-up to the 1979 general election, they persuaded the Hayes party to agree to select a new parliamentary candidate. But Labour's national executive overruled the decision. When the election came, McDonnell temporarily suspended hostilities with Sandelson, in order to get out the Labour vote in his role as ward agent. Sandelson was re-elected. But his majority was reduced by two-thirds. Hayes was now a marginal seat.

After the election, McDonnell and the other dissenters continued to shift the constituency party leftwards, putting down motions, filling its committees. In November 1979, Sandelson described them to the *Observer* as 'Communists and Trotskyists', who had 'infiltrated the party'. McDonnell, finally allowed by the press to speak for himself, responded that 'he [Sandelson] can't understand the grassroots trade union activist, and he has invented this myth about Trotskyists and Communists as an excuse'. All the left wanted in Hayes, McDonnell went on mildly, was 'a strong-minded activist who can act as a focus for our campaigns'.

The blandness of the statement, its lack of a partisan edge, was not an accident. One of Gramsci's key political insights was that successful ideologies no longer appeared ideological, but as 'common sense'. In Hayes and beyond, when addressing potentially hostile audiences, McDonnell would be careful to play down his radicalism.

In 1980, the anti-Sandelson activists suggested to the Labour leader, now the more leftwing Michael Foot, that Sandelson could be removed from the constituency without a loss of face if he were made a member of the House of Lords. There was widespread support for the plan, including from Sandelson himself, but it was not followed through. Instead, the MP made a cleaner break with his parliamentary party: in 1981 he defected to the SDP. At the next general election, in 1983, he stood for the new party in Hayes. He came third, and divided the anti-Conservative vote almost precisely down the middle. Hayes became a Tory seat, and remained so for the next 14 years.

McDonnell stayed in the constituency. He helped his wife with her work, looking after a dozen children in the residential home she managed. He finished his politics degree at Brunel, and then did a masters in the same subject, taking evening classes at Birkbeck College in central London. For paid work, he applied to be a manager at the Co-op retail group. His intentions were political as well as practical: 'My ambition was to transform the Co-op. I was going to demonstrate how cooperation worked. I was going to knock the hell out of Marks & Spencer.' But his intensity put off the interviewers. 'I just used to overwhelm them with all my plans. I couldn't get a job with them.'

Instead, he decided to make a career in the trade union movement. He took a job as a researcher at the central London offices of the National Union of Mineworkers, and then at the nearby headquarters of the Trades Union Congress. Meanwhile in Hayes, he kept up his Labour work, and volunteered for tenants' organisations and law centres. He sometimes shrewdly presented himself as a community activist, without a strong party affiliation, let alone an ideology. His long march through the institutions had begun.

8

Fine Margins

Persistence is one of the left's qualities that its enemies like least. A stubborn refusal to accept any defeat as final; a sentimental reverence for past struggles; an ineradicable belief that at some point in the future, always just out of reach, the left will be vindicated – these interlocking habits can be baffling, enraging, even frightening to non-believers. In Britain, as elsewhere, the left has had few electoral successes and many failures. People on the right, as well as impatient journalists, and voters who expect politics to move quickly and have clear endings and beginnings, have long wondered: why doesn't the left just give up?

In May 1976 Tony Benn provided part of an answer. He was speaking at an unlikely venue, a church of buttery old stone in the prosperous tourist town of Burford, which stood in a safe Conservative seat on the edge of the Cotswolds. It was almost a year after his sacking as industry minister. Combined with his defeat in the EEC referendum, the sacking 'brought to an abrupt end ... the brief "Benn era"', the respected political scientist Anthony King concluded.

Yet in Burford Benn talked about his political work in less personal, more expansive terms. 'Politics,' he said, 'is really about education ... It is about teaching more than management. It is about ideas and values and not only about Acts of Parliament, political institutions and ministerial office.' In Britain's long journey towards becoming a truly democratic society, he suggested, the job of leftwing politicians was to sustain and promote egalitarian 'ideas and values' that empowered people, rather than simply to seek office so that socialism could be imposed from Whitehall.

If you accepted this argument, then even the left's briefest and most beleaguered periods in office, even its most disastrous election campaigns, had a political value. They raised the profile of what Benn habitually called 'the issues' – by which he usually meant the imbalances of power in society – and gave the left a platform to say what it would do about them, and to encourage the public to join its campaigns. Whether leftwing politicians who managed to win office were actually able to carry out their promises in the face of opposition from establishment forces such as the civil service was not always the most important consideration. What mattered just as much, and sometimes more, was the continuing life of the socialist movement: its mass participatory experiences, its handing down of beliefs from generation to generation, its constant promise of a better world.

In the church in Burford, and in many of his speeches and writings from the mid-1970s onwards, Benn presented an idealistic, almost spiritual vision of leftwing politics. Yet it coexisted in his thoughts and actions with a more earthbound one, which had more in common with the mindset of Ken Livingstone, Diane Abbott and John McDonnell. This was about maximising the power of the left, and satisfying personal ambition, however hard Benn tried to persuade himself that the latter did not drive him.

A few weeks before the Burford speech, he stood for the Labour leadership. His old boss and nemesis Harold Wilson had unexpectedly resigned as party leader and prime minister shortly after his 60th birthday. Wilson's precise motives were always enigmatic, but he had undeniably been worn down by leading a succession of squabbling, half-fulfilled, often beleaguered governments. Yet this did not dissuade six of his clever and self-confident cabinet ministers from wanting to succeed him. Besides Benn, there was the employment secretary Michael Foot, who was widely regarded as a leftwinger, when actually his socialism was quite selective; and, from the right of the party, the chancellor Denis Healey, home secretary Roy Jenkins, environment secretary Anthony Crosland, and foreign secretary Jim Callaghan.

The ideological imbalance made it obvious that the parliamentary party was out of step with the Labour membership, which had become more leftwing, because of 1968, more militant trade unionism and the radicalisation of the inner cities. But the winner was to be chosen by

MPs alone. It was not a system likely to suit Benn, who was admired rather than trusted by his parliamentary comrades. The more centrist ones thought he was too radical, while some leftwing MPs thought his radicalism had been too quickly acquired.

In the first round of voting, Benn beat Healey and Crosland, both major Labour figures much more favoured by the press, but that was the limit of his success. He got 37 votes, little more than a tenth of the total, and withdrew from the contest. The eventual winner was Callaghan, a cunning, plainly spoken, deceptively low-key social conservative who was in many ways the opposite kind of politician to Benn. Callaghan quickly became a popular prime minister. Anthony King's assessment that the 'Benn era' was probably over seemed even more plausible.

The report which Corbyn and the AUEW had written for Benn about making the management and structures of the car industry more egalitarian disappeared with Benn's industry job. Instead, British Leyland was gradually turned into a more conventional company, with weakened trade unions, by an aggressive South African chief executive, Michael Edwardes. By the late 1970s, the peak of worker power in Britain seemed to have passed.

But Benn kept going regardless. The Department of Energy to which Wilson had demoted him, and where Callaghan kept him on as secretary of state, was seen by many of Benn's allies and enemies as a backwater. Only two years old, it was not one of the prestigious ministries like the Home Office or the Treasury, but an offshoot of the Industry Department from which Benn had just been fired. The energy ministry had been set up in a hurry by the Conservatives to deal with the price rises and shortages caused by the 1973 oil crisis – a crisis which had now passed – and also to oversee the new flow of oil to Britain from the North Sea. The latter operation was potentially of huge significance, requiring a whole new industry, which might help reverse the country's industrial decline, and also make the economy more self-sufficient. But Benn was not allowed to take too much credit for this rare national good news story. When the first oil came ashore, at a ceremony in Aberdeen in November 1975, it was Wilson, then still prime minister, who made a celebratory speech to the assembled dignitaries.

Benn's main responsibility was the trickier and less glamorous one of preventing the giant companies which were discovering and exploiting the new oilfields from pocketing all the gains. With his suspicion of multinational corporations, he was well-suited to the task. Benn and his department negotiated dozens of complex agreements between the companies and the state-owned British National Oil Corporation (BNOC), licensing the companies to explore for oil, extract it and pump it ashore. During his time as energy secretary, the contribution of North Sea oil revenues to the government's income more than trebled.

The new industry also needed new technology, from tiny underwater cameras to enormous semi-submerged oil rigs, in order to operate in waters that were much deeper and more stormy than oil companies had previously experienced. Between 1976 and 1979, a quarter of the UK's entire manufacturing investment was North Sea-related. Given that Benn loved new gadgets, and had long believed that British businesses did not invest enough, being energy secretary was more satisfying for him than his enemies hoped it would be.

Yet there were limits to what he could achieve. When he proposed that the state take a bigger role in the North Sea by requiring the oil companies to work as contractors for BNOC, the companies threatened to scale back their operations. Most of Benn's cabinet colleagues believed them, and the plan was abandoned. Similarly, when he suggested in 1978 that the government's oil revenues be used to set up a sovereign wealth fund, as Norway was already doing, the cabinet again said no. Benn's scheme was a shrewd one: 30 years later, the accountants PriceWaterhouseCoopers calculated that had it been implemented, the UK would have ended up with one of the largest sovereign wealth funds in the world. But as at the Department of Industry, Benn's lack of cabinet allies and the belief that his proposals were too bold for a struggling Labour government with a tiny majority doomed his far-sighted ideas. As he sometimes said of his party, he was in office but not in power.

As energy minister, alongside his renewed interest in modern technology, he also began to exhibit a more old-fashioned, even nostalgic side to his political character. He decorated his Whitehall office with miners' lamps. In some ways, this was just good politics: the state-owned coal industry was one of his responsibilities, and the National Union of Mineworkers (NUM) was arguably the most powerful union in the country, having fatally damaged the Heath government by its strikes in 1972 and 1974. But British coalmining was also in long-term decline. Output had peaked in the Edwardian era – before Benn was born. His growing reverence for the miners suggested a new aspect to his politics, an interest in defending things rather than expanding into new areas of social and economic life, as he had urged the left to do since 1968. And sometimes this new, more conservative Benn was behind the times. When he offered the NUM a veto over pit closures, the union declined it. It did not want to be blamed for opposing any closures which turned out to be justified.

Benn's emerging nostalgic side did not stop him from wanting to learn about new social movements, however. The veteran leftwing activist Hilary Wainwright told me: 'He would ring up me and [the feminist historian] Sheila Rowbotham and say, "Can you come to supper? I want to talk to you about feminism."' As with a lot of men in the 1970s and since, his interest in feminism had a limited impact on his own domestic arrangements. Caroline continued to do so much more housework than him, despite being almost as busy with work as he was, that Melissa made leaflets that read, 'End sexism in the Benn household', and handed them out to her siblings and parents.

Caroline also found gaps in her husband's politics, and helped fill them. For Christmas 1976, he recorded in his diary, she

> gave each of us a copy of The Communist Manifesto in our stockings . . . I read it yesterday, never having read it before . . . [Its] analysis of feudal society, the role of the church and religion, the class struggle, the impact of technology . . . the internationalisation of trade . . . all these things [were] set out absolutely clearly by 1848 by Marx and Engels. It is a most astonishing thing and I feel so ignorant that at the age of 51 as a socialist politician in Britain I should never had read that basic text . . .

Unusually for a middle-aged man, and especially for someone who had been an MP for a quarter of a century, Benn's political worldview was still not fixed, contrary to the increasingly common press caricature of him as a dogmatic extremist. Curious by nature, and more and more aware that he was not very well read, during the 1970s he underwent a second radicalisation, which followed and yet also overlapped with his first in the wake of 1968. Whereas the first had partly been prompted by observing modern political happenings, such as the Free University in Bristol, at first hand, the second was more intellectual: driven by belated discoveries while reading about Britain's past, and by tantalising possibilities for the left which these seemed to suggest.

In Britain during the 1970s, there was a revival of interest in the English Civil War of the 1640s. The war, and all the political experiments that grew from it, such as a profusion of radical sects and the replacement of the monarchy by a republic, was an episode which the many historians and politicians who believed that England was a fundamentally stable and peaceful country usually neglected, or portrayed as an aberration with no contemporary relevance. But in the turbulent 70s the Civil War suddenly seemed less distant.

In the 1970 film *Cromwell*, nominated for two Oscars, Richard Harris portrayed the leader of the English republic as a domineering but prescient figure, 'fighting for the liberty of the common people'. In 1975, the more low-budget but austerely beautiful cult film *Winstanley* told the story of a pioneering Civil War commune, briefly established in woodland on St George's Hill in Surrey, led by Gerrard Winstanley, the leader of a republican faction known as the Diggers. They occupied unused private land and used it to grow crops, distributing the produce among themselves and to anyone who would join their collective. Local landowners responded to this threat to rural capitalism by hiring armed men to destroy the commune.

The parallels with the factory occupations and workers' cooperatives of the 1970s were not hard to draw. Making such connections became academically respectable, even fashionable, thanks largely to Christopher Hill, an authority on the Civil War and prominent Oxford university historian who wrote vivid, panoramic books informed by Marxism but with popular appeal. In a 1970 volume on Cromwell, and another in 1972 about the Diggers and other iconoclastic Civil War groups, *The World Turned Upside Down: Radical Ideas During the English Revolution*, Hill conjured up and made topical an almost forgotten world.

'The Diggers have something to say to 20th century socialists,' he wrote. He pointed out that they held 'communal property' and practised 'economic democracy'. Along with slightly less radical but larger Civil War movements such as the Levellers, who wanted to greatly extend English democracy, religious freedom and equality before the law, the Diggers, Hill argued, 'foresaw and worked for – not our modern world, but something far nobler, something yet to be achieved – the upside-down world'. Long before the more celebrated revolutions in the United States, France and Russia, these English rebels tried to end ancient imbalances of power. In a 1649 pamphlet, Winstanley declared:

> The great Creator . . . made the earth to be a Common Treasury . . . Not one word was spoken . . . that one branch of mankind should rule over another . . . And the reason is this, every single . . . Male and Female is a perfect creature . . . his [own] Teacher and Ruler . . .

Without the religiousness and with more modern language, it could have been an anarchist or libertarian socialist pamphlet from 1968 or the fiery years afterwards. Winstanley's reverence for the individual, distrust of all authority, and view of the world's resources as 'a Common Treasury', to be equally drawn on by all: these ideas were still intoxicating over 300 years on.

Benn already knew a little about the English Civil War and its huge but buried political implications. As a young MP in the 1950s he had been intrigued by hearing a trade union leader, Walter Padley, talk about the Levellers and Diggers with great passion. But during the Heath government of the early 70s, free of ministerial responsibilities and with some time on his hands, Benn finally began exploring the period properly. In 1973 he asked a fellow Labour MP, Jack Mendelson, a former university lecturer who knew the Civil War well, to give him an informal tutorial. 'We had about an hour in the [House of Commons] Tea Room on the Levellers and the Diggers,' Benn recorded afterwards. 'It was fascinating. He gave me a reading list including Christopher Hill on Cromwell.' Benn found the books revelatory: 'I had no idea that the Levellers had called for universal manhood suffrage, equality between the sexes . . . the sovereignty of the people . . . and even an attack on property.'

Over the next half dozen years, these political ancestors became increasingly important to Benn: as a source of material for his speeches and public writings, and as a validation. 'It is a real comfort for us [socialists],' he said in his 1976 speech in the church in Burford, 'to discover that we are the inheritors of such a strong and ancient tradition.' His speech was part of an annual commemoration called Levellers' Day, which had begun the previous year. It remembered the imprisonment in the church in 1649 of several hundred mutinous soldiers, radicalised by Leveller ideas, who had been defeated by forces still loyal to the more conservative Cromwell. Three of the rebellious soldiers' ringleaders were executed in the churchyard, and the Leveller movement began to fade away. 'The ideas of the Levellers were thought to be so dangerous,' said Benn, 'that the establishment wanted to silence them.'

During the late 1970s, the campaign against Benn which had suffocated him as industry minister did not go away. Reporters still watched his house. Cabinet colleagues and civil servants still briefed against him. Newspaper headline writers and cartoonists still presented him as a would-be dictator. In pro-Benn parts of the Labour party, as Jeremy Corbyn remembered, 'We always thought that the upper-class controllers of the media thought he was a class traitor.' Even theoretically friendly publications such as the *New Statesman* sometimes portrayed him as alien and strange. In June 1977 the magazine's political correspondent James Fenton, a poet with a strongly leftwing background, wrote a memorable portrait of Benn:

> What does it feel like to *be* Tony Benn? What's it like to wake up every morning inside Tony Benn, to shave Tony Benn's chin, to eat Tony Benn's breakfast, to kiss Tony Benn's wife, to go to work in Tony Benn's car, to sit in Tony Benn's office twiddling Tony Benn's thumbs, to consult the charts on Tony Benn's walls, to be blamed for Tony Benn's errors of judgement . . . to argue Tony Benn's case in cabinet and quite another case outside, to consult with Tony Benn's conscience about

whether to resign – and to do all this not once or twice, but *all the time*, without ever letting up?

Despite his modest, supposedly dead-end job in the Department of Energy, Benn still preoccupied people. Not just because of his unusual public persona or ideas, but for another reason: the Labour alternatives to his politics seemed to be failing.

The Callaghan government was often little more than an exercise in crisis management: negotiating wage agreements with the unions that did not worsen the already high rate of inflation; negotiating a loan from the International Monetary Fund (IMF) to stop sterling collapsing in the currency markets; arranging an alliance with the Liberals to make up for Labour's lost Commons majority – for nearly three years between the spring of 1976 and the winter of 1978–9, Callaghan and his ministers managed all these skilfully. But little the government did suggested that its improvised, sometimes weary centre-left politics had a long-term future in a country which was becoming increasingly polarised between right and left.

In the cabinet, Benn argued with eloquence against many of Callaghan's policies, such as cutting public spending to placate the IMF, but he was outmanoeuvred and outvoted. Yet his isolation in the cabinet meant that when the details of the fierce discussions inevitably leaked out, sometimes with his help, he was not fully associated with the government's compromises. He was still seen as a potential prime minister, despite his poor showing in the 1976 Labour leadership contest. After it, the bookmakers Ladbrokes had put the odds on him becoming premier in the next decade at 3-1.

That possibility may have been too much for some people. In October 1978, shortly after the Labour party conference in Blackpool, at which he had argued that MI5 and MI6 should be more closely supervised by MPs, that the army should be more deferential to ministers, and that the giant British oil company BP should be nationalised, Benn speculated darkly in his diary: 'It occurs to me that I have made quite a few enemies . . . I wonder whether they might just try to polish me off.'

Five months later, with the general election imminent, the fiercely rightwing Conservative MP Airey Neave, who was close to both

Margaret Thatcher and the security services, and well known for his plotting and web of connections, went to the Cumberland Hotel near Oxford Street in central London for a private meeting. It was with Lee Tracey, a former MI6 agent with similarly rightwing views who was now running an electronics business. Tracey later told the BBC's *Panorama* programme and the *New Statesman*'s respected investigative reporter Duncan Campbell, for whom Tracey had been a reliable source in the past, that Neave had phoned him and asked to meet.

At the hotel, which was large and busy and therefore discreet, Neave quickly explained to Tracey that he was worried Labour might win the election; that Callaghan, who was in his late sixties, might then retire; and that Benn would then be able to stand again for the Labour leadership, this time successfully. Neave asked Tracey if he would join a secret 'army of resistance', including a team of intelligence operatives, which was preparing a plan to 'make sure Benn was stopped' from becoming prime minister. 'According to Tracey,' Campbell subsequently reported, Neave told the former MI6 man that 'violent means' might be used against Benn if the plan was activated.

Neave and Tracey agreed to meet again. But a week later, before they could, Neave was killed outside parliament by a car bomb. The Irish National Liberation Army (INLA) claimed responsibility. Neave had hoped to become secretary of state for Northern Ireland if the Conservatives won the election, and to introduce a much more aggressive military strategy there against the INLA and other republican organisations. This was widely taken to be the motive behind his murder.

A distraught Thatcher presented him as a martyr: 'one of freedom's warriors' was her intriguing choice of words. Perhaps because of the strong emotions that now swirled around him, the story of his meeting with Tracey and the supposed plot against Benn took a long time to emerge. The *New Statesman* and *Panorama* revealed it in February 1981. At first, Benn was sceptical, saying in his diary that the story 'doesn't ring true'. He told the magazine: 'I sat in Parliament for many years with Airey, talked to him on many occasions and do not for one moment believe such a thought would have entered his mind.' Even as he became more and more interested in political forces outside parliament, both as allies and enemies, Benn retained a stubborn and possibly naive faith in some of the MPs he had got to know during his many years in the Commons.

But he did concede in his diary that the alleged conspiracy might have been 'the dirty tricks department' – of which organisation he did not say – 'trying to frighten me by implying that a serious assassination attempt was being planned'. And he was struck by the fact that every national newspaper except for the leftwing *Morning Star* ignored the *New Statesman*'s story, despite all its sensational details. 'That somewhat rouses my suspicions,' he said, 'that it may have been true.' Two days later, he watched the *Panorama* episode, which wove the plot against him into a wider study of the state of the intelligence services. 'I know a lot [of the programme] had been cut,' Benn said, 'but even so it was clear that the security services were completely out of control. Lee Tracey . . . was in the programme, and I was watching my potential assassin. It was a very strange feeling.'

No inquiry into the alleged plot followed.

Labour did not win the 1979 election as Neave had feared. After five difficult years in power, and particularly after being unable to cope with the strikes of the previous winter, the government was discredited in the eyes of too many voters. Yet Neave had been right, to an extent, about Benn's upward trajectory. Labour lost 50 seats to the Conservatives, but Benn's was not one of them, despite ongoing changes in his Bristol constituency that weakened Labour's position, such as an influx of wealthier voters from London and a local decline in manufacturing industry. His majority shrank by four-fifths to a vulnerable 1,890. But another general election was not now expected for four or five years, since the Conservatives now controlled the Commons comfortably. Benn had time to take advantage of the disarray among his Labour enemies.

After the election, Callaghan stayed on as party leader, a diminished figure. Benn chose not to stand for election to the shadow cabinet, so that he could promote his alternatives to Callaghan's exhausted centrism more freely. He did so with an intensity rare in British politics. For the next two years, according to one exhilarated observer,

Tony seemed to be everywhere: on radio and television, writing books and in crowded meeting halls all over Britain. Audiences of hundreds and often thousands listened as he analysed, examined, predicted and gave confidence that we could achieve socialism and, yes, it did involve the very people in that particular audience. Not only did each speech seem to produce a new idea or policy but each one was crafted with a care and a beauty the movement had not heard since the death of [the Labour leftwinger] Nye Bevan nearly two decades before. After the windy rhetoric of the Wilson/Callaghan years, Benn's speeches stood out like the paintings of a great artist amidst a display of painting by numbers.

The author of these gushing words was the usually deadpan Ken Livingstone. Despite his multilayered political career in Camden and Hampstead and on the Greater London Council during these years, and his own considerable self-involvement and ambitions, Livingstone saw Benn as the most important person on the British left: 'the first Labour politician to direct the attention of the left towards the nature of democracy and the need to open up British society . . . reducing the powers of patronage of the Prime Minister and bringing the civil service and its powers into the open . . . encouraging the involvement of women and black people [in the Labour party] alongside the traditional white male trade unionists.'

Diane Abbott was also excited by Benn in the late 1970s and early 80s. She often went to see him speak, at party rallies and conference fringe meetings. 'He was such a good speaker,' she told me, 'and he was the first senior Labour figure to talk about black politics and feminism. Like me, he was also a big civil libertarian. I thought, this is a politics I can relate to.' He quickly became one of her political heroes, and remained so. Almost a decade after his death in 2014, she read me a passage from one his speeches which she had stored on her phone.

Corbyn became a Bennite in the 1970s, too. As a trade union official and Labour activist, he met him at railway stations and drove him to meetings. 'I liked the way he listened to people,' Corbyn told me, 'his preparedness to learn about issues all the time.' The two men also shared the view that they should never make personal attacks on other politicians, however often they were attacked that way themselves. When Benn gave a speech, Corbyn sometimes stood just to the side of the stage, frowning with concentration, watching Benn and watching the audience, an alternately fierce and admiring look in his eyes, wanting all those listening to believe in Benn as much as he did.

In October 1980, almost 18 months after being defeated in the election, Callaghan finally resigned as Labour leader. Always a calculating politician, he had stayed on long enough to prevent the left from capturing the leadership in the immediate aftermath of the election, when a leadership contest could have turned into a referendum on the Labour right's recent failures in government. Yet by stepping down when he did, he also ensured that the election to replace him would be held under the same rules as the previous contest in 1976, when only MPs had had a vote and as a result Benn had done badly.

By the time of Callaghan's resignation it was clear that this restrictive electoral system, which ignored the views of the party membership and the trade unions, was not going to last much longer. The Labour movement, like Britain as a whole, was becoming less deferential. The party's quarter of a million members – some of them leftwing incomers, and others moving that way in the wake of 1968 and Wilson's and Callaghan's failures – were increasingly unwilling to let the party's two or three hundred MPs decide so much about the party's overall direction, from its leader to its policies.

The main vehicle for this growing dissatisfaction was the Campaign for Labour Party Democracy (CLPD). Founded in 1973, this was largely run by Vladimir Derer, a Czech exile from a leftwing but anti-Soviet background, and his wife Vera, from a house crammed with paperwork in Golders Green in north London. By the early 1980s the CLPD had expanded from a minor lobby group to one of the most powerful forces in the party. Rising leftists such as Corbyn and Livingstone joined it, along with some established leftwing figures such as Benn, all of them attracted by the CLPD's populist and egalitarian demands: that the Labour leader be chosen by a combination of party members, trade unionists and MPs; that the leader be unable to veto policies which the party had voted for, as Wilson had done with the manifesto commitments which Benn had tried to carry out at the Department of Industry; and finally, that every MP go through a competitive and democratic 'reselection' process in order to be a parliamentary candidate at each general election. The CLPD wanted Labour no longer to be controlled by cautious leaders and complacent, often centrist, almost impregnable MPs in safe seats. As Benn had been arguing since the late 1960s, the CLPD believed that as society was becoming less hierarchical, so political parties needed to become less top-down, more transparent in their workings – more genuinely democratic.

The Labour right resisted furiously. With the aid of much of the press, from rightwing tabloids to centre-left *Guardian* columnists, it portrayed the CLPD as a leftwing conspiracy and a bullying mob, made up of Trotskyists and members of the secretive, Labour-infiltrating sect the Militant Tendency, rather than the loose coalition of dogged and rather earnest party reformers that the CLPD actually was. Despite being so caricatured, the CLPD gradually made progress. After years of procrastination and deliberate delays, at the 1979 and 1980 Labour conferences the party agreed to introduce the reselection of MPs and to let Labour members and trade unionists have a say in choosing the party leader.

Callaghan resigned before the second change came into effect. Benn was advised by his allies that without it he would have no chance of winning the coming leadership ballot. He decided not to stand. Instead, he would try for the leadership in a year or two, once the new rules were in place, by which time he assumed that his standing with the Labour left and the party as a whole would also be stronger. 'I am in no hurry,' he recorded in his diary in October 1980, 'and I have lots of meetings [scheduled] in which I can talk about the issues.' The determinedly casual tone suggested a man still trying to convince himself.

The contest to replace Callaghan was narrowly won by Michael Foot, with Denis Healey second. Benn voted for Foot, but like much of the Labour left he did not see Foot as either a true leftist – Foot had been a less critical member of the Callaghan government – or as someone likely to be leader for long. He was barely younger than the retiring Callaghan, walked with a stick, and while he was a sweeping, compelling orator, he delivered his speeches in a quavering voice that suggested an early 20th-century statesman giving his final address.

The younger and much healthier-looking Healey was elected unopposed as deputy leader. The position came with few powers, but it was widely seen as the best stepping stone to the leadership. Yet Healey had vulnerabilities. Having been Callaghan's chancellor, he was implicated in that government's compromises and disasters. Some party members disliked him, as the public face of its squeeze on wages and state spending. Some MPs disliked him, too: he was ostentatiously clever and did not suffer fools. And having become deputy leader without a contest, he lacked a mandate. That would matter if his partnership with Foot ran into trouble.

It quickly did. In January 1981, the third month of Foot's leadership, a group of Labour MPs declared that they were leaving the party to set up a centrist rival – what would become the Social Democratic Party (SDP). In all, 28 Labour MPs eventually defected, including some of the Labour right's brightest and best-known figures, such as David Owen and Shirley Williams. About a quarter of Labour's support disappeared with them. The party that remained was weaker and more anxious, yet also more leftwing and, in theory at least, more receptive to change. The new, more inclusive system for electing the leader and deputy leader was now in place. On 2 April 1981, Benn announced that he was challenging Healey for the deputy leadership.

Benn began his campaign in a rush: hurrying into the House of Commons library after midnight, sealing up hundreds of letters to MPs there, putting them in the internal post, and sending a statement to the parliamentary press at 3am. But he had been thinking about standing against Healey for months. And for almost as long, allies and enemies had been trying to dissuade him.

Neither Benn nor many of these people expected him to win. He had too many enemies. In the 1976 leadership contest he had come a distant fourth. And Healey had only been deputy leader for a few months; an attempt to replace him could easily be portrayed as premature. The new threat to Labour from the SDP arguably made Benn's timing even worse.

But by 1981 he had long stopped thinking about politics in such tactical terms. Five years earlier, in his speech in Burford church, he had argued that politics was 'really about education', about conveying 'ideas and values' to voters. In his diary in December 1980, he justified his growing determination to challenge Healey in a narrower but still quite abstract way: 'to pinpoint the real issues for the Party'. After the first day of his deputy leadership campaign, much of it taken up by journalists asking him why on earth he was standing, he recorded defiantly and a little angrily in his diary that his campaign was intended 'to force people to make choices. That's what's called polarisation, divisiveness and all the rest . . .' He continued: 'I think this process is long overdue; the Labour Party are having a Turkish bath, and the sweat and the heat and the discomfort are very unpleasant. I am sure Denis will win . . . because the Party never sacks anybody . . . But I think there will be a sizeable body of opinion [which supports me] which can't be entirely ignored . . .'

Long after the deputy leadership race, appearing on the BBC's *Desert Island Discs* in 1989, he summed up his thinking about elections with greater calmness and clarity. 'Elections are a platform,' he said. 'People see elections much too much in terms of the outcome.' For Benn, the campaign was the point, not what happened on polling day. Many politicians and voters would disagree.

Yet in 1981 both the campaign and its outcome developed in unexpected ways. It became increasingly hard, even for Benn, to tell which was the most important. The length of the contest was partly responsible. It lasted for six months, four times as long as a typical general election campaign, with the result not announced until the Labour conference in late September. Through the spring, summer and autumn, Benn and Healey crisscrossed the country, which was already divided by the riots, strikes, and backfiring economic experiments of Margaret Thatcher's first term in office, and fought for what they thought was the future of the Labour party and of British leftwing politics.

Healey, a bull of a man with a broad head, huge, arching eyebrows and a cutting rhetorical style, had much of the establishment on his side. The Labour hierarchy, most trade union leaders, every national newspaper, most of the parliamentary Labour party, admirers in the business world won over by his austerity policies as chancellor, and even Conservatives who thought British politics needed a 'sensible' centre-left party – all admired Healey for his forcefulness and his supposed realism about what Labour politicians could achieve.

A more motley coalition backed Benn: shop stewards impatient with their union leaders, idealistic new Labour members, disillusioned old ones, young leftwingers such as Livingstone and Corbyn, and veteran political organisers from Trotskyist groups, who saw Benn as a 'transitional' figure on the road to more revolutionary change. The CLPD also joined his campaign, hoping that if he won he would be influential enough to democratise the party. Collectively these Benn supporters and activists became known in the media, and in the parts of the Labour party which were hostile to them, by a name that implied a cult-like devotion: Bennites.

One of the CLPD's most able activists became his campaign manager. Jon Lansman was still in his early twenties, less than half Benn's age. A Cambridge economics graduate from a comfortable north London background, whose father had been a Tory councillor, Lansman had joined Labour as a teenager. Disappointed by the top-down, increasingly centrist nature of the Wilson and Callaghan governments, Lansman became a CLPD member in 1977. He devoted more and more hours to the cause while living off unemployment benefit or working as a van driver – one young Briton out of millions who were living with the consequences of Labour centrism and Thatcherism's failures.

Lansman believed that Labour could be refreshed and radicalised by 'argument and persuasion'. Slight and intense, he was a good talker, on the phone or in person, unafraid of hostile journalists and tireless in spinning lines to them. He also had an encyclopaedic knowledge of the Labour party and union bureaucracies, where power lay in them, and how to exploit that or shift it in Benn's favour. Working from the big basement office in Benn's London house, or from a borrowed office at County Hall – in 1981 Labour had regained control of the Greater London Council – Lansman organised a campaign which largely ignored Labour MPs and trade union leaders. Instead, Benn tried to win over trade unionists and party members directly, through a continuous series of rallies, appearances at demonstrations, and speeches to fringe meetings at union conferences.

In some ways, it was a demonstration of the kind of populist, extra-parliamentary politics – as much a movement as a campaign – that Benn wanted to see spread through the Labour party and society as a whole. The campaign had little funding: Lansman worked unpaid. But it had extensive leftwing networks to tap into, such as the CLPD's list of sympathetic activists. And it had the compelling public persona of Benn himself. 'He wouldn't just make the big speeches,' Lansman told me,

> He'd go and do a factory gate meeting, or one in the canteen, before he did the main meeting in the town hall. He'd say, 'How long do you want me to speak for?' He'd put his watch on the table. And he'd end his speech and sit down at precisely the time he'd said he'd sit down. And the speech would all sound like it was precisely constructed and written. But it was all off the cuff ... I've never encountered anyone else on the left like that. He judged the crowd, and responded to their mood.

Benn made his campaign feel historic by speaking at events commemorating famous episodes in the story of the British left. May 1981 was the 600th anniversary of the Peasants' Revolt of 1381, when thousands of people from Kent and East Anglia marched on London in protest at high taxes and attempts to hold down their wages. For a few weeks, the revolt spread across the country, affecting both rural and urban areas, gaining recruits from both poor and relatively prosperous men and women, and forcing the king and his government into concessions, some of which remained after the rebellion was eventually put down. At Blackheath, then as now a big grassy open space just south of the City of London, the rebels were addressed by John Ball, a prominent radical preacher whose egalitarian ideas anticipated those of the Levellers. 'When Adam delved and Eve span, who was then a gentleman?' Ball asked the crowd. 'Matters shall not be well in England until all things are held in common.'

Benn spoke to a crowd in the same place exactly six centuries later. It was a cold, grey spring bank holiday, and he wore a parka. With his radicalisation had come a gradual change in his dress, from ministerial suits to more classless garments better suited to a political life increasingly lived outdoors, at protests and on marches – and also better suited to showing solidarity, consciously or unconsciously, with the working class. The Blackheath event also featured left-leaning bands and speakers from the anti-apartheid movement and Amnesty International. It was a broader, more vibrant coalition than was usually present at official Labour party events. When Benn spoke, the big, youthful crowd clustered tightly around the stage: parents with babies, men in leather jackets or charity shop coats with right-on lapel badges. He could make the left's causes echo down the centuries.

He also took part in political demonstrations with a more obvious immediate relevance. The first People's March for Jobs in May 1981 was a protest against the huge surge in unemployment caused by the Thatcher government. Five hundred jobless people walked to London – like the peasants in 1381, but this time starting in Liverpool and in Huddersfield in West Yorkshire. As a march to the capital beginning in parts of northern England particularly badly affected by redundancies, the action consciously imitated the famous Jarrow March against unemployment in 1936. The 1981 protest lasted a month, and received a lot of union support and media coverage, as even rightwing newspapers wondered whether Thatcher's economic policies were too harsh. Benn was among those who saw the marchers off in Liverpool. Halfway through their journey he joined them again, at Wolverhampton.

There, he was allowed to walk at the head of the narrow column as it moved quickly through the city centre under a heavy sky. A lot of the marchers were much younger than him, and quite fit after doing ten miles a day for the past fortnight. But he kept up, smiling and talking to whoever was striding beside him, seeming both invigorated and at ease. Photographers and TV cameras followed him hungrily.

The march stopped outside a church, for drinks gulped from plastic cups and a service taken by the sympathetic local bishop. One of the reporters approached Benn with a cameraman. 'Some people might find it rather odd,' said the reporter to Benn, 'that the Labour movement is praying to help the unemployment problem ...' In a quick, clear, almost patronising voice, Benn brushed off the question: 'Oh, socialism came out of the Bible, didn't it? I mean, it was the Christian message that all men and women were brothers and sisters.'

Also outside the church, a hulking young man with shaggy hair and a black anorak branded with the People's March logo came bouncing up to him. 'Mr Benn,' the young man said, grabbing his arm, and then throwing an arm around his shoulders, making him suddenly look quite small and old, even frail. 'When do you get to be our boss?' Benn patted him on the stomach and chuckled, a little theatrically but also with real delight. He was among his people, and there seemed to be ever more of them.

The sun came out, and he made a speech in the cobbled church square. 'Comrades,' Benn began, spacing out his words with almost Churchillian pauses, 'this ... is a march for human dignity. And against those forces which still try to persuade us that men and women should be crucified on a cross of gold, in the name of monetarism [the government's austere economic strategy] ... and profit and loss.' Benn shook his head like a 17th-century preacher denouncing Satan: 'We will not accept that.' For anyone appalled by Thatcherism – and in 1981, with her government sometimes behind both Labour and the SDP in the polls, that was a lot of people – Benn was offering the exhilaration and the reassurance of absolute opposition.

As the long deputy leadership campaign went on, so Benn's support and expectations rose. After the first week, he suggested in his diary that the result 'may not be a humiliating defeat'. After the first month, an ITV documentary was broadcast about his campaign, with the title *Benn's Bandwagon*. By August, he was predicting that Healey would beat him by only 53 per cent to 47 per cent. On 17 September, ten days before the vote, Benn wrote: 'I might squeak home.'

One observer of his campaign was Paul Foot, the celebrated investigative journalist who would later reveal how the intelligence services smeared Benn and other Labour figures. Foot was a dedicated member of the Socialist Workers Party (SWP), a relatively large and influential Trotskyist group which usually regarded all Labour politicians with both contempt and suspicion. Until 1981, Foot had thought of Benn as a careerist who had become an unconvincing radical, prone to 'wooden sermonising'. But when he went to Benn's campaign events, Foot found 'an explosion of political energy'. At 'mass meetings of the most extraordinary size and enthusiasm', he wrote afterwards, Benn 'was talking socialism in terms at once more easy to understand and more powerful than anything which had come out of the Labour Party in my adult life'.

Corbyn helped with the campaign, organising meetings and

demonstrations, handing out leaflets and badges, trying to amplify and create a legacy from the energy which Benn's speeches and walk-abouts generated. Meanwhile, less publicly, in private meetings, in quiet corners at trade union conferences, over the phone, Corbyn, Lansman and other activists steadily worked to win over the unions, branch by branch, region by region, calculating that if enough members could be persuaded to back Benn, then the heads of the unions – in whose hands the unions' political allegiances often ultimately rested – would have no choice but to do the same. The prestigious National Union of Mineworkers (NUM), the enormous Transport and General Workers Union (TGWU), the expanding National Union of Public Employees (NUPE), which was Corbyn's union – by September, Benn thought he might get the votes of them all. His son Joshua, like his father an enthusiast for new technology, used an early personal computer to calculate the different combinations of trade union, constituency party and parliamentary support which would lead to a Benn win. 'We felt we had a good chance,' Corbyn remembered.

Occasionally during the final weeks of the campaign, Benn allowed his thoughts to wander to what he might achieve, and the challenges he might face, beyond the deputy leadership. On 10 September, at a hotel in Clifton in Bristol, a much smarter area of the city than his constituency, he had a meeting with Salvador Allende's widow Hortensia. Since the coup in Chile eight years earlier she had become an exile and a leftwing political celebrity, travelling constantly, trying to keep up the spirits of the anti-Pinochet Chilean diaspora, and giving speeches to gatherings of her late husband's many foreign admirers. At their encounter in Bristol, Benn was respectful towards her, but also, in an unspoken way, focused on himself. 'May I ask you a question,' he said, 'because everybody asks me this. If we get a radical Labour government, how do we avoid suffering the same fate as Salvador Allende?' Hortensia briskly told him not to worry so much. In Chile, she said, the country's establishment, the US government and international corporations 'were determined to crush us and we were weak'. In more solidly democratic, more high-status Britain, she suggested, an elected leftwing government would be less vulnerable. 'You are much stronger.'

But Benn himself was not as strong as he seemed. A month into the campaign, in early May, he began to feel an unfamiliar tingling in his legs and hands. It persisted and spread as he carried on with his public events: the day he joined the People's March in Wolverhampton, seemingly full of energy, he actually felt like he was walking in 'wellington boots full of water', with numb sponges for feet. By 19 May, a general weakness was washing through him, and his throat felt tight. His hands were still tingling. By 27 May, he was finding walking difficult – like treading on glass. When he went to the House of Commons, he trod as slowly as possible, hoping that no one would notice what had happened to his gait. By 3 June, he could hardly walk: in a corridor in the Commons, 'I was pulling myself along by both arms.' That day, he still gave a speech at the annual conference of the train drivers' union ASLEF. The room was hot. There were television cameras. Onstage, Benn felt unsteady, but he hid it, and his speech got a standing ovation. The following day, he went into hospital.

As he left his London house, there were reporters outside the front door as usual, but again he walked slowly to disguise his symptoms. Before getting into the family car – his son Hilary was going to drive him to hospital – Benn talked to the television journalists, but only about what he thought should be Labour's policies: 'Get [Britain] out of the Common Market ... get rid of American nuclear missiles [from Britain] ... get back to full employment and ... abolish the House of Lords.' Then he was admitted to Charing Cross Hospital, and put out a public statement that he was being tested for a suspected virus.

He was given his own room on the tenth floor. Between medical examinations, which discovered that he had no reflexes in his arms or legs, but found no explanation for his sudden deterioration, he lay in bed watching a portable television he had brought with him. The programmes he chose were full of coverage of the deputy leadership contest in which he was no longer an active participant.

But he did not consider withdrawing from the contest. Instead he persuaded himself that his campaign now had enough momentum – 'the issues have got across' – that it no longer needed his constant presence. This was not necessarily a delusion or false modesty. Derer and others involved in the Benn campaign worried that it was becoming too presidential, too much about his compelling but divisive public persona and not enough about new ideas and mass participation. More democracy and a more equal society were not always best promoted by a charismatic, even messianic individual.

Benn also needed a rest. He had been trying to change himself, and the Labour party, and the country, almost non-stop since the late 1960s. While the doctors tried to work out what was wrong with him, he watched his television and received visitors, flowers, telegrams and thousands of letters. Two punks came to see him. They gave him a Mars bar, one of his favourite snacks, as a gift from the Tony Benn fan club.

Less friendly visitors were not permitted. Journalists waited outside the hospital and speculated about Benn's condition. Or most of them did. One reporter dressed up as a doctor and tried to get in. Another went to casualty, claiming to be in pain, and was found to have a camera concealed in his trousers. For the many newspapers increasingly worried by Benn's progress in the deputy leadership contest, any evidence that he was literally and permanently unfit for the position would be sweet relief.

After more than a week of tests, he was diagnosed with Guillain-Barré syndrome, a very rare nerve condition which causes the immune system to attack the body, and which can lead to lasting damage and even death. Benn was relatively lucky: after a fortnight in hospital, he was well enough to be discharged. But the numbness in his hands and feet, and his difficulty walking, receded only slowly. For much of the rest of the summer – much of the rest of the campaign – he felt tired, and had to shorten his working day. For the rest of his life, he walked with a slight shuffle and had to write with simple, jagged strokes, fingers sticking stiffly out.

Benn's illness and stuttering recovery did not take away the momentum of his campaign, which continued to close the gap between him and Healey through the summer and into the autumn. As Derer and Labour's other democratisers had hoped, the deputy leadership bid did take on some of the qualities of a social movement. Alliances formed between usually rivalrous factions. Experienced activists became unusually excited. Other people were drawn into politics for the first time. But Benn's illness also did not make his enemies any less determined to defeat him.

As ever, there were so many of them. The Labour leader Michael Foot had angrily tried to dissuade him from standing, arguing that a contest would be divisive. Union leaders had done the same. Clive Jenkins, general secretary of the large and fast-growing Association of Scientific, Technical and Managerial Staffs (ASTMS), invited Benn to lunch and gave him a gold-rimmed china cup. On the front of it was the inscription, 'Elections can be poisoned chalices, Tony', and on the back of it, 'Don't do it, Tony'. Benn thanked him for lunch, ignored his advice, and suggested that if his deputy leadership bid failed, he might stand again in a year's time.

Contrary to frequent claims in the press that they formed a sinister alliance, Benn had a cool relationship with many union leaders. He saw them as too cautious, as complicit in the failed compromises of recent Labour governments, and also as too controlling, running their unions from the top down – not in the spirit of '68 at all. Meanwhile they saw him as too much of a political risk-taker and individualist, and as a toff who was too romantic about the working class. This mutual lack of trust and respect made his deputy leadership bid much more difficult. However many union members he dazzled, there was no standard procedure across the movement for how their view of him should be taken into account. Sometimes union members were able to vote for their preferred Labour deputy leader; often, they were not, and the heads of their unions chose for them. The scope for shadowy moves against Benn was enormous.

The same applied in the parliamentary Labour party. The right of the party was never going to vote for him. Indeed, the fact that Foot – whom they considered a leftwinger – was leader made that faction even more determined to defeat Benn by any means. Meanwhile many MPs of the 'soft left', an emerging group of young and ambitious figures who thought of themselves as pragmatic socialists, as less confrontational and more careful in their choice of extraparliamentary allies than what they called the 'hard left' around Benn, decided to support neither him nor Healey but a third candidate for deputy leader, John Silkin.

A ponderous speaker who also worked as a lawyer, Silkin had no realistic chance of winning, given Benn's and Healey's higher profiles and greater charisma. He also entered the race almost two months after them, in late May. But he was a well-connected MP who had been a minister and chief whip, and was leftwing enough to be an alternative to Benn for MPs who considered Healey too rightwing. Silkin also astutely presented himself as the potential unifier of Labour's factions. In a party that had split once already in 1981, with the exodus to the SDP, his talk of unity had a psychological appeal and sounded respectable. Yet the fact that he had joined the contest so late suggested that his candidacy also had another, less high-minded, even sectarian motivation: to make the race messier, and to disrupt Benn's early momentum.

Meanwhile, for any Labour MPs who disliked all three candidates, or wanted to damage one of them without committing to another, there was always the option of abstaining. An election for a party position with little power had become a political labyrinth. None of the contestants would emerge undamaged.

During the last few weeks before the party conference at which the deputy leadership vote would take place, the campaign became quite vicious: 'the most intense power struggle I have ever witnessed', according to Chris Mullin, then one of Benn's lieutenants and subsequently a Labour MP for 23 years. When Healey appeared at a Labour rally in Birmingham on 19 September, he was booed and heckled so continuously that he was unable to give a speech. Benn was also at the rally, and was able to speak without serious interruption. Afterwards, he suggested in his diary that he disapproved of Healey's treatment: 'I will have to make it clear that there should be no shouting and that all the candidates should be listened to respectfully.'

Yet to many of Benn's critics, his condemnations of the crowd interventions which disrupted Healey's speeches – including chants of 'Out! Out! Out!'; heckling, booing and slow hand-claps – were performative and fake. Because Benn was backed by leftwing groups which were outside the party, they argued, he could distance himself from their behaviour while also benefitting from it. As during his time in the cabinet and shadow cabinet, this argument went on, Benn's gentlemanly good manners and pious air concealed an utterly ruthless and self-serving streak.

Sometimes, those who warned of what the *Sunday Mirror* called a 'Benn mob' took their claims further. The day after the Birmingham rally, Healey alleged on television that 'Mr Jon Lansman' had orchestrated the disruption, and had done the same at a campaign event in Cardiff two months earlier. The accusation set off an immediate media frenzy. Benn's campaign team phoned Lansman. He told them that he had had nothing to do with the trouble at either event: he had been away on holiday on both occasions.

Healey had to make a public apology. And it gradually became clear, for those who cared to look, that at least some of the trouble at his events was the work of anarchists, Trotskyists and supporters of Irish republicanism who were either only very loosely aligned with the Benn campaign or were not supporters of Benn at all. The deputy leadership contest was an opportunity to promote other causes, to express contempt for Labour, and to damage the party's public standing. There was disruption at some of Benn's events as well.

Yet the feeling that his campaign was bullying and in some sense undemocratic did not go away. To his enemies, and to most of the press, the fact that his campaign involved groups from outside parliamentary politics, and often took place away from the usual political venues, out on the streets, made it less than fully legitimate, even dangerous. That Healey himself was known to be one of the biggest bullies in Westminster and Whitehall, regularly crushing colleagues and subordinates; that British newspapers often behaved as a mob; and that Benn wanted more democracy, not less – all these inconvenient truths were ignored in the increasingly hysterical coverage of the Benn campaign. As ever, the left were held to different standards.

On 26 September, Benn arrived in Brighton for the party conference. Rain was blasting the seafront. The deputy leadership vote was scheduled for the next day. Benn and his small entourage set up an office in the Grand Hotel, a huge Victorian pile facing the churning sea, just along from the much plainer modern hall where the conference was being held, and Joshua got his computer out to calculate the likely voting permutations.

Benn knew that probably four-fifths of Labour MPs were not going to vote for him. He also knew that a similar proportion of Labour members, expressing their preference through their constituency parties, were going to support him. Such stark disagreements between Labour activists and the parliamentary party, and the urgent need, in the left's view, to make the latter take much more seriously the views of the former, was one of the main reasons why Benn was standing. But under the electoral system Labour had recently introduced for choosing its deputy leader, which gave 30 per cent of the vote to the MPs and the same to the members, their verdicts on Benn's candidacy were likely to cancel each other out. The distribution of the remaining 40 per cent of the vote, held by the unions, would be decisive. And with the more politically cautious unions favouring Healey, the Benn campaign believed that he needed the support of a less predictable one: the public sector union, Jeremy Corbyn's union, NUPE.

Unlike many unions, NUPE had decided to ballot its members about who should be deputy leader. Corbyn was one of the organisers of the effort to persuade them to choose Benn. Lansman was unimpressed by his work: Corbyn lacked the feel for power and the persuasive abilities of more seasoned union activists. Lansman also worried about the decision to ballot members, rather than hold a vote at NUPE's annual conference. Instead of being swayed by leftwing speeches there, perhaps including something stirring and seductive by Benn, NUPE members would be making up their minds more privately, at work or at home, probably with newspapers lying around full of attacks on Benn.

Yet Lansman and Benn still believed that NUPE might turn their way. The union's members were generally leftwing. And Benn's campaign was generally agreed, even by many journalists and his other enemies, to have been compelling political theatre, much more so than Healey's. In Brighton, up in his room in the Grand Hotel, the night before the deputy leadership vote was due to be announced, Benn recorded in his diary: 'The word is going round that we are going to win.' For its upcoming issue, the American news magazine *Time* prepared a cover referring to a Benn victory. His wish to loosen America's hold over Britain, in the middle of a tense phase of the Cold War, and his compelling political ideas and personality, meant that the deputy leadership contest had become a big international story.

The day of the announcement was a Sunday, so there was not much other news. The result was not revealed until early evening. For hours beforehand, reporters, photographers, television crews, pro-Benn and anti-Benn demonstrators, Labour delegates and politicians tried to occupy themselves by going to other conference events, walking back and forth along the promenade between the seafront hotels and conference venues, and milling around in lobbies, gossiping, speculating, waiting.

Benn went to a meeting of the Campaign for Labour Party Democracy. As he was walking in, someone told him that the NUPE members had chosen Healey. Democracy, Benn's great cause, had betrayed him. At 5pm, with Lansman, Caroline and a few other members of his campaign team, Benn entered the main conference building. It had a broad lobby and open staircases, so he was easy to spot. Journalists rushed towards him. Delegates shouted or cheered. News of the NUPE vote had not yet spread. Before going into the auditorium, as he was picking up a set of ballot papers so he could vote himself, he heard a rumour that the huge TGWU would not be supporting him either. Now expecting 'a massive defeat', he walked out on to the conference platform, and faced the delegates and the cameras.

His red tie was a little askew. The knot was small and tight, as if tied by tense hands. He took a deep, visible breath and sat down. He was 56 years old but his hair was already completely grey, the skin on his face pulled taut. As he waited for the result, he rubbed his jaw, shifted in his seat, leant back and looked from side to side. There were dozens of other politicians seated on the platform beside him, including Foot two places along, determinedly ignoring him. Yet the cameras were only interested in Benn and Healey. Given the talk about how the vote had gone, Healey seemed strangely nervous, his broad, fleshy face flushed as he looked around the hall.

The contest was in two rounds. Healey won the first easily, beating Benn by almost four to one in the unions, and by well over two to one among the MPs. Only the expected strong showing by Benn among the party members – he got 78 per cent of their votes – kept the race reasonably close. Silkin came third, and was eliminated.

But the second round was not so straightforward. While Benn was supported by only slightly more MPs than before following Silkin's exit, his support from the members went even higher, to 81 per cent, and his union vote more than doubled. The TGWU was backing him after all.

Benn did not learn all these details of how the vote had gone until later. Instead he sat up on the platform, waiting for the final result, drinking cups of tea and listening to a debate about apartheid South Africa which the party had scheduled to fill the time while the second round of votes was counted. Yet he did hear whispers that things had gone better for him than he expected. 'I got three separate messages that I had won.'

Offstage, Corbyn was approached by Arthur Scargill, the forceful trade unionist who would become NUM president the following year, and who was already a well-informed player in the Labour movement's upper echelons. Scargill was a Benn supporter. 'He said to me, "We've won it. Benn's got it,"' Corbyn remembered. 'I said, "How do you know?" And he said, "Don't you believe me?" I said, "I totally believe you, but where's the evidence?"'

Finally, the conference chairman announced that he would read out the result. It would be given as an overall percentage for the two remaining candidates. The chairman emphasised that the votes had been counted three times. The busy murmuring in the hall stopped. Benn sat expressionless, mouth slightly open, looking down at a piece of paper where he was going to record the outcome. He was an observer of politics as well as a participant.

'Tony Benn,' said the chairman, slowly and carefully, 'forty-nine point five seven four.' There were a few isolated shouts and cheers from the hall. Benn wrote the percentage down, still impassive. 'Denis Healey,' continued the chairman, 'fifty point four two six.' There was a roar from the hall. Benn wrote the numbers down, his face blank and still. Then something was released in him, and his tongue pushed forward inside the lower half of his mouth, making his chin bulge. Then he gave a small, cryptic smile. His eyes narrowed until they were almost closed. The smile lingered for a few seconds, and then his mouth went flat.

Was the result a disaster for Benn and the left, or a near-triumph? Was the tightness of the margin agonising, or a great exceeding of expectations? Was the contest the effective end of Benn's career as a major politician, or a sign of his surging momentum, a sign that his great breakthrough would soon come? Perhaps the result was several of these things simultaneously. In the immediate aftermath, little was clear. Benn left the conference centre still smiling, surrounded by reporters and clapping supporters, and walked back along the seafront to the Grand Hotel, where more supporters cheered him in the lobby and all the way up the stairs to his room. He and Caroline wolfed down some sandwiches. Then he decided to go straight back to the conference.

With proceedings in the main hall over for the day, he went to one of the many meetings on the conference fringe, where opinions tended to be more candid, especially at times of turbulence in the party. The meeting he chose was organised by a newish leftwing journal with a small circulation but a large and growing influence: *London Labour Briefing*.

The low-ceilinged room was packed, and everyone applauded when Benn came in. Camera bulbs flashed. A long table had been set up for a panel of speakers. At the table, either side of an empty seat which was immediately offered to Benn, were two youngish men in open-necked shirts, both involved with the magazine, Ken Livingstone and Jeremy Corbyn.

Livingstone had his arms folded, and sat almost languidly, leaning to one side as he watched Benn make a brief speech, as if he were looking out for rhetorical tips which he did not really need. With his moustache, slim build and utterly self-possessed air, Livingstone was a little like a cocky minor character from a 19th-century novel: charming but not necessarily to be trusted.

Corbyn seemed a more familiar sort of leftwinger. Unlike Livingstone, he wore a Benn campaign sticker. Corbyn's shaggy hair looked even more neglected than usual, great bushy tufts of it sticking out sideways above his ears. He hunched forward as Benn spoke, watching the audience intently, as if searching for anyone who dared dissent from what the defeated deputy leadership candidate was saying.

When it was Corbyn's turn to speak, he did so angrily, blaming Benn's loss on 'a number of [soft] left Labour MPs' who had abstained in the deputy leadership ballot. 'In reality,' said Corbyn, glaring round the room and wagging a finger, they had 'voted for Healey'. There was a burst of applause. 'And I think they must expect some discomfort from the rank and file in their own constituencies in the coming months.'

Benn's own speech was less recriminatory. 'I think everybody here knows,' he said, 'that what happened today was an enormous victory for us.' He nodded as he spoke, perhaps still in the process of convincing himself. 'We're nowhere near the end.'

A few days later, after the conference had finished, he recorded with a sense of vindication in his diary that one of the MPs who had voted against him for the deputy leadership, Dickson Mabon, had just defected to the SDP. 'One or two others may go,' Benn continued, 'so I should think that by next week Denis Healey's majority will have disappeared' – as each supportive MP had made up a quarter of his winning margin – 'and morally I will be the Deputy Leader of the Labour party.'

9

'Take the Power!'

Since the left is often outnumbered, inside the Labour party and other institutions, and in the electorates which decide party matters and the make-up of governments, it is rarely a good idea for the left to confront its opponents head-on. Guerrilla warfare, the gradual takeover of organisations, or the establishment of new ones, tends to be wiser.

London Labour Briefing, or *Briefing* as it quickly became known, first appeared in February 1980. It was not much to look at: a couple of dozen monochrome pages, laid out with no more verve than a competent student newspaper, containing comment articles, interviews and news about the London left, and coming out once a month. It was put together and mostly written by an editorial collective, with some contributions left anonymous. At a time when the British left produced a whole clamour of newspapers, magazines and journals, some of them covering the successes and failures of socialism across the world, at first sight *Briefing* seemed of local interest only, and about as stirring and controversial as its blandly matter-of-fact title. It did not even feature any red in its design.

But once you actually read it, the newsletter's true ambitions revealed themselves. It was intended to be a publication where leftwing politics was redefined and widened; where readers were radicalised; and, above all, where questions of power were addressed. In which parts of the British political system was power most available to the left? And what was the best way for the left to get a lot more of it?

'We lack the physical power to overthrow the Tories and their system,' wrote Chris Knight, one of *Briefing*'s founders, in its August 1980 issue. 'We are forced to make difficult choices. The task isn't to pass resolutions "demanding" the impossible. It is to fight for real power.'

Since the early 1970s Knight had been involved in a small leftwing group called the Chartists. Partly inspired by the 19th-century campaigners for extending democracy to the working class, the group oscillated between calling for a revolution and advocating a more gradualist politics. To give momentum to the latter, the Chartists wanted to draw on the radical energies being awakened in the Labour party by Benn and others.

'I realised the Labour party is colourless,' Knight told me. 'The colour of the Labour party depends on which faction has the most influence.' By the late 1970s, when the idea of *Briefing* began to crystallise, he and some of his Chartist comrades had concluded that local government was where Labour had the most potential. Unlike in national politics, where interest groups and orthodoxies from Westminster, Whitehall and big business put so many obstacles in the way of leftwingers – as Benn was discovering – municipal bodies such as city and borough councils were able to operate with relatively little scrutiny from the rightwing press or interference from the establishment, despite having considerable powers. Local election turnouts were also lower than national ones, which meant that leftwing candidates could win more easily, sometimes just by mobilising a few thousand dedicated supporters.

In this less hostile environment, the left could hone its electoral strategies, show what it could do in office, and make an immediate difference to people's lives – all as a preliminary step to one day gaining national power. Knight summarised the political approach advocated by *Briefing*: 'You don't preach. Practice is primary. The rest of the left always said, you've got to have a theory and a programme first. We said no, one thing leads to another. Success [in office] leads to more success.' Yet the newsletter retained a revolutionary edge. Its initial slogan was adapted from one of Lenin's: 'Labour – Take the Power!'

Since becoming councillors in the 1970s, Livingstone and Corbyn had reached essentially the same conclusion as the Chartists about the left and local government. Both men joined Knight and a few of his Chartist comrades in the *Briefing* collective: gathering and exchanging information about the Labour left in London, writing and commissioning articles, and above all discussing, together and in print, how the left's scattered activities in the capital could be better coordinated, and built into something of citywide and then national significance. 'We have set ourselves the ... vital task of keeping active militants inside the Labour Party and the unions in London in touch with each other and up to date on what is happening in the various battles across the capital,' read an editorial in the first issue. 'For far too long the largest local authority in Western Europe [the GLC] has been the "poor relation" as far as Labour Party organising and activity is concerned. We aim to rectify this ...'

For editorial meetings, the collective often used Livingstone's office in the GLC's main building, County Hall. This long, pale, labyrinthine block beside the Thames, which had taken over a decade to build, before, during and after the First World War, was so enormous that its security guards and party leaders often had no idea what gatherings were going on there, amid its miles of corridors. But the *Briefing* collective tried not to be too secretive or cliquey, at least at first. Another of their key ideas was that the left needed to build coalitions, rather than be sectarian, if it wanted to maximise its electoral strength and effectiveness in power. *Briefing*'s editorial meetings and pages were open to anyone in the London Labour party. Sometimes relatively junior figures such as Diane Abbott attended. Occasionally, enemies of the left were allowed to contribute articles, even ones attacking *Briefing* itself.

The content of the newsletter sent other important signals. The writing style was generally direct and accessible, avoiding theoretical jargon. The articles were often informative rather than polemical, telling readers about the state of selection contests between potential Labour candidates, about the political outlooks of the hopefuls and winners, and about the parts of London where the party was most likely to gain seats. As its name implied, *Briefing* was a kind of manual, explaining local politics and how readers might best take part.

Yet alongside this practical material were pieces about much wider topics: sexism, racism, feminism, gay rights, relationships, the politics of disability, the role of the family. Many of the collective had grown up in the 1960s and believed that the personal was political. That was not yet a common view on the left, where class remained the main lens through which the world was seen. *Briefing*'s interest in personal politics sometimes attracted a lot of attention, including from unlikely sources. At one GLC meeting in 1980, Livingstone wrote, 'The Tory Chair ... had to call Tory members of the Council to order because they were disrupting the meeting as they clustered round my desk asking to buy copies' of an issue of *Briefing* which dealt very frankly with the politics of sexuality. Such curiosity or prurience from the more socially traditional – and there were millions of them even in relatively liberal London – could easily turn to disgust, and a desire to shut down the debates which *Briefing* was encouraging; and indeed to suppress the whole brand of politics which the newsletter represented. But the ambitious young activists and politicians who put *Briefing* together in Livingstone's office were not put off by such possibilities. If they got more power, as they intended, they were going to exercise it in provocative new ways.

The very first issue of *Briefing* made it clear which part of the capital's local government would be the left's first target. 'Taking Over the GLC' was the headline of the main front page article, written by Livingstone. The next GLC elections would take place in just over a year, in May 1981, and it was likely that Labour would win them.

The Conservatives, and the British establishment in general, had for centuries had a fear of sometimes disorderly, always cosmopolitan London. Its huge number of poor inhabitants, and latterly its substantial population of middle-class liberals as well, meant there was always a potential appetite for political leaders who offered to make the capital more equal. The city's first elected government, the London County Council (LCC), had been continuously controlled by Labour for the last 31 years of its existence, from 1934 to 1965. The Labour LCC maintained its popularity partly by replacing hundreds of slums with council housing. Herbert Morrison, a particularly effective Labour LCC leader (and Peter Mandelson's grandfather), reputedly promised to 'build the Tories out of London'. Although Morrison was on the right of the party, Livingstone admired his administrative ability, and his ruthlessness.

In 1963, a Conservative government at Westminster passed legislation abolishing the LCC. The move was both administrative and political. London had far outgrown the LCC's boundaries, which only covered the inner city. But the Tories also hoped that incorporating the new outer suburbs and nearby home counties commuter towns and villages would add millions of wealthier and more rightwing voters to the city's electorate. This plan worked, up to a point. The new municipal entity of Greater London, governed by the GLC, became in effect a giant marginal constituency, with control of it alternating every few years between Labour and the Conservatives.

By 1980, the latest Tory administration had run the GLC for three years. GLC administrations rarely lasted much longer. London at that time seemed worn-out and gaunt, with potholed roads, a declining population, and public transport that was in a downward spiral of underuse and underinvestment. The Conservatives were unpopular in general, as the Thatcher government's risky economic experiments ran into trouble. So Livingstone and his *Briefing* comrades were hardly unusual in the Labour party for seeing that the Conservatives could be removed from power at the coming GLC elections, or in working towards that goal. But the *Briefing* collective also had a second, narrower objective. They wanted to ensure that when Labour took over County Hall again, the left would be in charge.

Well before the founding of *Briefing*, in the aftermath of Labour's defeat at the 1977 GLC elections, Livingstone had realised that the party would have a good chance of winning next time, and had begun looking around for other leftwingers whom he could persuade to try to become GLC candidates. Through the left's growing network in the capital, and sometimes over lunch at an Indian restaurant in Tooting, a south London suburb well away from Westminster journalists, Livingstone gathered around himself a group of young radicals and worked out with them how they could become GLC councillors. A typical recruit was Valerie Wise. The daughter of a leftwing former Labour MP and Benn ally, Audrey Wise, Valerie was still in her mid-20s and a political unknown. She seemed to say whatever was on her mind. But Livingstone spotted that she was ambitious, reliable and a good political organiser. Working with another clever young leftist and future GLC councillor, Michael Ward, Livingstone helped Wise get selected as the Labour candidate for a GLC constituency which was held – but not securely – by the Conservatives. Placing leftwingers in marginal Tory seats rather than safe Labour ones was a deliberate strategy. It was about maximising the left's influence over London rather than just its number of councillors. Livingstone told Wise: 'You only want to be there [in County Hall] if we win power.'

If that happened, the plan went, Livingstone would become GLC leader. There was only one problem. The position was always held by the head of one of the groups of GLC councillors, which were organised by political party. When the 1981 GLC elections took place, the leader of the Labour group was not Livingstone.

Andrew McIntosh, the incumbent, was a privately educated north Londoner who lived in wealthy Highgate. A part-time politician from the right of the party, he also ran his own market research company. In these and other ways, he was Livingstone's complete opposite. Yet both men were good at getting a surprisingly wide range of Labour politicians to support them. McIntosh was close to Michael Foot, despite Foot's more leftwing outlook. When the previous head of the Labour group, Reg Goodwin, had suddenly resigned in 1980, McIntosh quickly assembled a coalition of supportive GLC councillors while Livingstone was away, taking a rare holiday. On his return, Livingstone mobilised his own coalition as fast as he could. But McIntosh won by one vote.

Yet then he relaxed too much. Unlike Livingstone, he seemed not to appreciate that if their party won the GLC elections the following year, as was likely, then the accompanying increase in the number of Labour councillors would mean that McIntosh's victorious coalition from 1980 was no longer dominant enough within the Labour group to sustain his leadership. While Livingstone continued to recruit leftwingers to stand as Labour GLC candidates, McIntosh made little effort to widen his support among the party's existing councillors, or to ensure the selection of rightwingers as candidates. Even when Livingstone, with characteristic cheek, warned him that he would challenge him again for the leadership, after the elections – 'Look, Andrew, I am going to beat you … If there is a Labour administration, it will elect me leader' – McIntosh remained confident of his position. During the election campaign, the Conservatives repeatedly warned that if Labour regained control of the GLC a 'Marxist' administration led by Livingstone would follow. But the rightwing press, preoccupied by the seemingly much bigger threat of Benn's deputy leadership challenge, paid little attention.

On 7 May 1981 Labour won the GLC elections as predicted. Their victory margin was quite tight – 50 out of 92 constituencies chose Labour councillors – as the leftwing surge orchestrated by Livingstone did not fully materialise. Of Labour's successful candidates, he calculated that fewer than half – 22 – were on the left; 18 were on the right; and 10 were somewhere in the middle. It appeared that the Conservatives' warnings against a Livingstone takeover had had some effect. 'The Left Lose Out,' said the front page of the right-leaning *London Evening Standard* with satisfaction. 'Moderates "In Control".' Foot visited McIntosh in his County Hall office, congratulated him, and endorsed him as the leader of a new Labour administration. McIntosh and his team drank champagne. The *Evening Standard* took a photo of him by the Thames: smiling broadly and with his suit jacket slung over his shoulder, like a businessman having a riverside stroll after concluding a successful deal.

Livingstone agreed to appear with McIntosh in other post-election press photos. A dozen years younger and quite a bit leaner, the 35-year-old Livingstone stood with his hands hidden behind his back and a faint, fixed smile. It might have meant satisfaction, disappointment, or a mind that was somewhere else. Then he disappeared into the corridors of County Hall and got to work.

More than most on the left, Livingstone understood that political success often depended on winning over people with other allegiances as well as mobilising your loyalists. And he was not shy about passing on this insight. The previous year, he had been invited to a summer party at Benn's house in London. 'This was the left's equivalent of a royal garden party,' wrote Livingstone afterwards, 'and I felt I had finally arrived.' He told his host that 'he should also reach out to the centre' whenever he stood in internal Labour elections. Benn replied that much of their parliamentary party was so rightwing, such a move would be futile. The deputy leadership contest would prove him at least partially correct.

However, the Labour group in County Hall was more malleable than its parliamentary equivalent. Long before the 1981 GLC elections, Livingstone had realised that he could win over a wide range of councillors, even ones supposedly close to McIntosh. One of the key converts was Illtyd Harrington, who had written the approving 'Young Turks' article about the new London left back in 1971. A leftwinger himself but also a pragmatist, Harrington was now McIntosh's deputy, and increasingly unimpressed by his performance as Labour group leader.

Another pivotal, similarly disillusioned figure was the group's long-serving chief whip, Harvey Hinds, who was adept at listening to the complaints of councillors and then steering their decisions. Both Hinds and Harrington sometimes found Livingstone too self-serving and theatrical in his politics. Yet his energy and new ideas about what the GLC could do impressed them. Livingstone was careful to cultivate both men, meeting with them privately during the early months of McIntosh's group leadership, sharing dissatisfactions about him, and discussing how he could be replaced.

The morning after Labour recaptured County Hall in 1981, Livingstone, Hinds and Harrington met again. While McIntosh was giving a triumphalist press conference in his leader's office, with Hinds and Harrington in attendance, Livingstone slipped into the room and waited at the back for the event to end. When it did, McIntosh rushed off out of the room to do more interviews, and all the journalists left with him. Livingstone, Hinds and Harrington lingered in the office, alone. One of the older Labour operators closed the door. Then Harrington said to Livingstone, 'You've got it all sewn up. For God's sake, don't do anything to blow it today.'

Overnight, Livingstone, not always as calm as he looked, had been fretting that Labour's narrow victory margin over the Conservatives would make seizing the GLC for the left, let alone using it to enact leftwing policies, very difficult. But Labour's failure to win the GLC easily in favourable political circumstances also fed the disillusionment with McIntosh among the party's GLC councillors. And Livingstone had carefully organised a way for them to turn their discontent into action.

In the final days before the GLC elections, he had spoken to every Labour candidate likely to win, and likely to support a leadership challenge by him against McIntosh, and had invited them to a gathering of the GLC left which would take place the afternoon after the election results were announced. Livingstone also persuaded allies on the executive committee of the London Labour party, which oversaw some of the party's operations at County Hall, to slow down the process by which Labour would choose a new GLC leader, if the party returned to power. Instead of a 9am meeting and ballot of all Labour's councillors on the day after the election, which McIntosh wanted, as it would leave Livingstone and any other leadership challengers little time to get organised, this crucial gathering would happen at 5pm.

The day after the election came. Once Livingstone, Hinds and Harrington had finished their discreet conversation in McIntosh's office, they prepared for that afternoon's meeting of leftwing councillors and other potential Livingstone backers. Its existence was not mentioned to McIntosh and his subordinates and supporters. But the attendees Livingstone wanted were told that it would start at 2pm – three hours before the meeting which McIntosh expected to be his coronation.

At 2pm, as planned, a couple of dozen councillors who were excited or curious about Livingstone's scheme to take over the GLC congregated quietly in room 166 of County Hall, one of hundreds tucked away in its mazy interior. At the head of a boardroom table, Livingstone made a brief pitch for the job of GLC leader, then invited others who wanted roles in his administration to do likewise. More councillors drifted in during these speeches, until two-thirds of the Labour group were present – more than enough to attempt a coup against McIntosh. With the mood in the room rising, Livingstone was nominated as leader unopposed, as were most of the other candidates for senior positions, including Hinds and Harrington. But there were contests for dozens of more junior roles – a sign of frictions to come – so the meeting went on for almost three hours, until 4.45pm. By then, the absence of so many councillors for so long from the rest of County Hall had been noticed by McIntosh and his team. When the whole Labour group gathered for the leadership ballot at 5pm, Livingstone's plot was no longer a secret.

Yet it was too late for McIntosh and his supporters to do much to stop it. They managed, just, to prevent Livingstone winning by a show of hands, which required a two-thirds majority. But the result of the secret ballot that followed was clear enough: Livingstone 30, McIntosh 20. Most of the promises of support made to Livingstone in room 166 had been kept. So stunned were McIntosh and his allies, and so unprepared for what had just happened, that they did not contest any of the ballots that immediately followed for the 25 most important GLC roles. 'Not a single person who had voted for Andrew held a position in the new administration,' wrote Livingstone afterwards. Despite the secret ballot, he was confident that he knew exactly who his opponents were. The whole meeting had taken three-quarters of an hour. The whole coup had been carried out in an afternoon.

*

The ingenuity and apparent ease with which Livingstone had ousted the Labour GLC leader whom Londoners had just voted for, and the fact that the Labour left, for the first time ever, now controlled the government of the country's run-down but still dominant capital – these twin shocks horrified and fascinated the national press. 'Red Ken Crowned King of London,' declared the *Sun*. The *Daily Mail* warned: 'The Left's victory in London could be repeated up and down the country where Labour has won control of county halls.' The *Mail* connected Livingstone's coup to a speech that Margaret Thatcher had just given in Scotland, in which she claimed that extremists were manipulating the Labour party in order 'to impose upon this nation a tyranny which the peoples of Eastern Europe yearn to cast aside'.

In fact, Livingstone was a frequent critic of the Soviet bloc. Like the other British leftists who had been politicised by the anti-authoritarian explosion of 1968, he regarded the lack of freedom and democracy and the excess of state control in the Eastern bloc as far too high a price to pay for its patchy egalitarian achievements. A few weeks after he became GLC leader, a *Mail* interviewer was puzzled to discover that the man the paper called 'the Commissar of County Hall' was actually 'contemptuous of the Soviet Union'. At one point, Livingstone described the GLC's bureaucracy as 'the worst outside the Soviet Union'. The interviewer also found him 'eager to espouse ... the Polish Solidarity movement', the campaign for trade union rights and democracy which the Soviet-aligned military government in Poland was trying to crush.

But despite such anti-Soviet statements, the idea that Livingstone and the wider Labour left were literally or metaphorically agents of the Eastern bloc was a belief, or a useful weapon, which the British right were not prepared to give up. In 1984 the bestselling thriller writer Frederick Forsyth, who was close to both the Conservatives and the security services, published *The Fourth Protocol*, a crude but readable novel which became both a computer game and a film, about a Soviet plot to bring a leftwing Labour government to power in Britain, which would then get rid of its nuclear weapons and American bases and take the country out of NATO.

In the book, a fictionalised version of the British defector to Russia Kim Philby helps initiate the plot by sending a memo to the general secretary of the Soviet Communist Party. The memo describes how a 'little fellow with a nasal voice', who is 'a consummate politician', has been 'using his base in County Hall . . . to build up a personal Far Left political machine that now spans the whole country', and 'has effectively superseded Anthony Wedgwood Benn [as] a leading mover in the Hard Left capture of the British Labour Party'. In case any readers have not worked out the identity of Forsyth's villainous politician, the memo continues: 'The Livingstone coup d'etat [at the GLC] is the model upon which is to be based the final takeover of the Labour Party.'

Shortly before a general election, the Soviet plan goes, a nuclear weapon is to be smuggled into Britain, detonated, and presented as an accident that fatally undermines the case for Britain's nuclear deterrent and ensures the election of a unilateralist Labour government. That government will then be quickly overthrown, as MacIntosh was, by a Livingstone-like figure – Forsyth did not risk saying that this would necessarily be Livingstone – who would become 'Britain's first Marxist-Leninist Premier'.

In reality, Livingstone was not a dogmatic politician. 'Marxism? I'm not even sure what it means,' he told the *Mail* interviewer early in his GLC leadership. 'I've never even read Marx; I prefer science fiction.' As much as he had an ideology, it was a belief that his cohort of 1960s leftists were the representatives of a rising generation that was more liberal, democratic and egalitarian, and that they had the right to change Britain accordingly. 'The thing about the GLC in '81,' he told me years later, 'was that it was the first time that my generation had got its hands on anything [political].'

Not everyone on the left immediately recognised the significance of this. Not even Benn. Most of his diary entry for the day of the GLC coup was taken up with thoughts about his worsening health, about whether he had taken on too much by standing for the deputy leadership, and about the failure of his son Stephen to win a difficult GLC seat. Right at the end of the entry, Benn added: 'Also Ken Livingstone was chosen as Leader of the GLC over Andrew McIntosh.' In that understatement was the germ of a rivalry.

By contrast, the first edition of *Briefing* after the coup was ecstatic. 'LONDON'S OURS!' bellowed the front page of a 'Special Victory Issue', in thick, black, almost tabloid-style capitals. The accompanying article by Livingstone continued: 'No one will be left in any doubt that the GLC is now a campaigning organ.' That campaigning would be 'against the government', but also in favour of radical causes:

> County Hall is a vital resource – so let's begin to make use of it! The meeting rooms in this empty building will provide an ideal central meeting point for left-wing groups, women's organisations, movements of ethnic minorities etc. Let us know when you want to meet here.

Both this open-ended social inclusivity and aggressive political partisanship were new to British local government. Both would quickly become central features of Livingstone's administration – and consequently would so provoke the rightwing press, the millions of rightwing London voters, and the Conservative government, including Margaret Thatcher herself, that the GLC's right to exist at all would be challenged. Under Livingstone, Britain's oversized capital would become the site of a pioneering and sustained experiment in leftwing government. One way or another, the left's enemies were determined that it would fail.

After Livingstone, probably the most important conductor of this experiment was John McDonnell. To a surprising degree, his participation was an accident. In the Labour party in Hayes, where he was still living and working as the 1980s began, 'We all used to treat the GLC almost like the House of Lords: it wasn't relevant to us,' he told me. 'Our work was more about the local council, the local party, the local MP.' County Hall seemed a long way away, literally and politically. 'I'd only been there a couple of times.'

Rather than try to become a GLC councillor, or an elected representative of any sort, McDonnell planned to remain a behind-the-scenes leftwing organiser, at least for the time being. He was still in his twenties. Then a friend, Chris Rogers, decided to seek the Labour GLC candidacy for Hayes. McDonnell agreed to be his election agent. Before their campaign had got very far, Rogers changed his mind, and took an elected position in a trade union instead. McDonnell became the GLC candidate in 1981 in his place. He was successful, and became part of the influx of new leftwingers to County Hall.

At first, Hayes remained his focus, and he saw the GLC mainly as a way of getting the relatively neglected area more resources. For example, 'Hayes needed a bypass, because all the [Heathrow] airport traffic was going through the town centre. So we set up the Hayes Bypass Campaign, which included direct action – sitting down in roads.' McDonnell's participation in the stunt as a GLC councillor got it plenty of attention.

When he did go to County Hall, he was initially unimpressed by many of his fellow Labour councillors. 'I turned up at my first Labour Group meeting. It was supposed to be this radical thing ... And I looked around and thought, "This is quite rightwing, actually."'

Before being selected as a candidate, he had never met Livingstone, and in some ways they were very different. The new GLC leader had been an increasingly well-known figure in London politics for a decade. McDonnell was six years younger and had never held elected office. Livingstone was a pragmatist, prepared to retreat or cut deals when he felt that would advance or protect his political projects. McDonnell could be tactically flexible, too – 'I've always been a coalition-builder,' he told me, 'to get to an objective or divide your opponents' – but he was more set in his objectives: advancing the interests of the working class, and remaining alert to any sign that any leftist was betraying them. He was also much less interested than Livingstone in having an adaptable political identity, or being liked. 'I work on the basis that eventually people will understand what you're doing, and if they don't understand, tough.'

While Livingstone wore relatively relaxed and unconventional clothes for a politician – safari jackets and creased corduroy – McDonnell wore smart raincoats and suits. He wanted to look serious. While Livingstone was a publicity-seeker who gave candid interviews and sought to create and exploit controversies, McDonnell was more guarded. In public, he often used dry political language. He would talk about there being 'a number of issues', about policies being 'delivered'. He would sometimes highlight his capacity for desk work, honed by his years as a researcher for trade unions, by describing himself as 'a bureaucrat'.

Yet in more private political contexts, such as one-to-one conversations with comrades, he could be more openly ideological and more emotional: sometimes furious, sometimes cuttingly funny, sometimes menacing. At one typically acrimonious GLC meeting early in Livingstone's administration, he passed the GLC leader a piece of paper and said in his soft Liverpudlian voice: 'It will be in your own best interests to sign this.'

The meeting was in January 1982, one of many during the early months of Livingstone's administration about a surprisingly explosive issue: its transport policy. The Labour manifesto for the 1981 GLC elections, which in the absence of much new thinking from McIntosh was full of ideas from Livingstone, McDonnell and other leftists, had promised that 'the needs of public transport will have priority over private cars'. The document included a commitment to cut bus, train and tube fares by up to a third, with the reduction funded by a new property tax, mostly levied on businesses. To Livingstone, a non-driver and an avid user of London's ailing public transport, making this form of travel much cheaper was a way of reversing the long decline in passenger numbers, increasing mobility for the city's often isolated poor, and helping the environment – a growing preoccupation among the urban left. The policy was given a clever and memorable name, 'Fare's Fair', and the price reductions were implemented in October 1981.

Four months later, the policy was declared illegal by the courts. Despite the fact that passenger numbers had surged, and traffic congestion and accidents had fallen, legal action against the fare cuts by the Conservative-controlled borough of Bromley – a relatively wealthy and car-dominated outer suburb which resented subsidising public transport which its residents rarely used – was heard by the High Court, the Court of Appeal and the House of Lords, and ultimately upheld. McDonnell and a few other leftwing GLC councillors urged Livingstone to defy the ruling. The piece of paper McDonnell handed him to sign in January 1982 was a plan to set up a mass civil disobedience campaign, in which GLC politicians and other passengers would refuse to pay any public transport fares when they were increased back to their original levels, as the courts had told the GLC to do.

Livingstone responded to the plan with a characteristic mixture of enthusiasm and calculation. 'As an ex-anarchist, I found the idea of millions of Londoners defying an unjust law instantly appealing,' he wrote afterwards. But he doubted that would actually happen 'in a country without any anarchist traditions'. He also worried that the many Labour-voting London Transport employees – and also any leftwing GLC councillors who refused to pay fares – would be put in a very difficult position. Without his support, the campaign fizzled out.

McDonnell was disappointed by what he saw as Livingstone's unprincipled and erratic performance in this and other controversies during their first year on the GLC together. 'I thought I was joining a left group,' he told Livingstone's early biographer John Carvel, 'and then all of a sudden we were . . . capitulating on a number of issues.' At Labour group meetings in County Hall, McDonnell was the loudest of Livingstone's leftwing critics. If the GLC leader did not do better, these interventions implied, there was an alternative to his left: McDonnell himself.

During McDonnell's first year as a councillor, he became interested in the GLC's revenue and expenditure. 'I wanted to know where the power was, where the resources were,' he later told me. In 1982, he decided to try to become chair of the GLC's finance committee, the most powerful of a network of elected committees, each chaired by a councillor, which took many of the GLC's key decisions. County Hall had always been a self-important place, and its workings were modelled to a large extent on those of the House of Commons and Downing Street. McDonnell saw the finance chair as 'London's chancellor'. In national politics, chancellors were often known for wanting to be prime minister.

When McDonnell told Livingstone he was planning to stand for the finance job, Livingstone reacted unexpectedly. He told McDonnell he would vote for him. 'He looked really shocked,' Livingstone wrote:

> I could see from his face that he thought I was lying. But I had several reasons for supporting John. First and most important was his competence and capacity for hard work, which was equalled by only two other members of the [50-strong Labour] Group. Secondly, as I told him at the time, 'I'd rather have you using your talents to get control of the finance department than constantly . . . looking for issues to strike holier-than-thou positions on.' Keeping John on the backbenches would have meant endless divisive rows splitting the Labour Group as he struggled to build his reputation on the left.

To Livingstone, politics was a world of constantly evolving alliances. 'There's no permanent friendship,' he told me in 2013. 'People who you were totally close to, and working with . . . ending up hating you.' Throughout his career, he believed that a politician's ambitions, ideals, and the interest groups he or she represented had a chance of being satisfied only if he or she was always attentive, and responsive, to shifts in power and in voting patterns – whether within their party or outside in society. Thus Livingstone saw the rise of McDonnell as both a threat and an opportunity. If McDonnell was elected as chair of finance, Livingstone would find out more about his potential rival: 'I knew that the demanding post . . . would soon reveal whether John was a democratic socialist or, as some of his critics suspected, a slightly Stalinist centralizer incapable of devolving and sharing power.'

And looking several steps further ahead, as Livingstone always tried to, if McDonnell made a success of the job, and turned himself into a strong candidate to be the next GLC leader, then ultimately he might liberate rather than usurp him. 'Red Ken', as he was becoming nationally known, had not given up on the idea of getting into parliament. He anticipated, correctly, that the next general election would be in 1983. 'If that happened,' he wrote,

> I would need to stand down as [GLC] leader in time for someone else to establish themselves before the 1985 [GLC] elections . . . I therefore wanted [a] candidate to support. If John . . . indicated the desire to hold together the broad left-centre coalition . . . I would prefer him to be my successor . . . It seemed to me that a successor from the far left might be the only way to extend the initial radical phase of the administration.

In May 1982 McDonnell was elected finance chair. Soon afterwards, Livingstone made him his deputy. The two men became a political double act. Livingstone used his charm and tactical nous to build rickety coalitions within the Labour group, keeping the party's small GLC majority intact. 'He's a really good negotiator,' McDonnell told me, 'a really good team-builder.' Meanwhile the blunter, more intimidating McDonnell pushed through policies, and deployed his bureaucratic patience and attention to detail to sift through the mass of legislation covering the financing of local government, looking for unexploited sources of revenue to fund their administration's radical programme – of which transforming London's public transport was just the start.

Their working relationship was often intense. They had similar personal ambitions and a shared sense of mission, that they were somehow going to rescue London. Like Livingstone, McDonnell treated having a political career as a multi-level process, where you kept your options open, and in 1983 he stood for parliament. He tried to capture the Conservative seat of Hampstead, which apart from some boundary changes was the same constituency that Livingstone had attempted to take four years earlier. By almost exactly the same narrow margin as Livingstone – just over 3,000 votes – McDonnell failed. He refocused on his part in their County Hall double act. The partnership had a self-mocking but also self-mythologising quality. In the 1984 GLC staff pantomime, Livingstone played Dick Whittington, the fictionalised, poorer version of a real medieval merchant who rose to become lord mayor of London four times. McDonnell played Whittington's cat: valued both for his companionship and for his outstanding facility at killing rats.

Under Livingstone, the GLC became an attractive, or at least intriguing, place to work for people from across the left. With the failure of Benn to achieve a breakthrough by winning the deputy leadership; with the shortcomings of Foot's leadership becoming increasingly obvious, such as his antique public speaking style and his lack of ideological clarity; and with the SDP squeezing Labour in the polls and making a quick return to national office less likely – in this generally deflating time for the left, joining the socialist experiment in County Hall was one of the few appealing prospects.

There were also more positive reasons to take part. In the 1968 uprisings and the wider counterculture afterwards, an idea had spread that urban areas could become strongholds and showpieces for radical politics, sometimes called 'red bases'. In Italy, a country with a long tradition of independent-minded city governments, and where the ideas of 1968 particularly lingered, the northern city of Bologna was run by an innovative communist administration during the 1970s, which consulted residents at regular neighbourhood meetings and distanced itself from the Soviet Union. The administration received quite a lot of attention from the British left, including a 1977 book, *Red Bologna*, which Livingstone and his circle read carefully.

Another influential book which indirectly encouraged leftists to get involved in the GLC was 1979's *In and Against the State*. Written by a collective of British public sector professionals, it combined a critique of the modern state as a paternalistic ally of capitalism with an interesting solution: 'Those of us who work for the state . . . must find ways to oppose it from within our daily [professional] activity, which means . . . creating alternative forms of organisation.' As its title neatly encapsulated, the book suggested that socialists who were suspicious of the state could work for it, nevertheless, in order to transform it from within. McDonnell, who was heavily influenced by the book, believed that he and other such socialists could turn the GLC into one of the 'alternative forms of organisation' that the book called for, by, as he put it later, 'opening the doors [of County Hall] and saying to people, "You come in, you tell us what's needed, you tell us how it should be delivered, and you participate in the delivery."' If you were an ambitious leftist, and conscious that Britain was becoming a less deferential place, then Livingstone's GLC was one of the few leftwing institutions that seemed to understand the change – and one of even fewer where you might be able to make a difference.

Livingstone's administration also had flair. In 1981 the Thatcher government was causing an almost unprecedented surge in unemployment. In response, the GLC used County Hall's vast frontage and highly visible position, right on the river and opposite parliament, to put up a huge white banner, leaning against the building's steep roof and lit up at night. 'London's Unemployed', the banner read in giant black letters, and then gave the precise, awful figure, which GLC staff clambered out on to the roof and updated monthly. The banner embarrassed and enraged the Thatcher government, drew attention to the relatively neglected issue of joblessness in London – the crisis was more associated with the North and Midlands – and made the whole country aware of the GLC's defiant and rebellious existence.

Leftists of all kinds came to work at County Hall: ideologues, pragmatists, technocrats, nostalgics, revolutionaries, gradualists, veterans, prodigies. Other people were drawn in who were not primarily leftists at all, but feminists, gay and lesbian activists, environmentalists,

anti-racists, black and Asian rights campaigners, Irish republicans or
often a combination of these identities. Labour's 1981 GLC manifesto had promised, 'We will introduce positive discrimination', which
was a broad-brush way of saying that the council would prioritise the
disadvantaged, in its hiring as well as its policies. More clearly, articles
in *Briefing* had shown that Livingstone and his circle saw socialism as
being about minority rights as well as the class struggle. And his
record as a councillor, on the GLC and in Camden and Lambeth, suggested that he was more likely to follow this rhetoric with action than
most other white male politicians.

One person was particularly interested to see whether the new
London left's plans would work in practice, across the whole of the
capital rather than just in individual boroughs. On the evening that
Livingstone was elected GLC leader, Diane Abbott waited outside the
room where the Labour group had gathered. 'Everyone [in the group]
trooped in,' she told her biographers, 'and when they came out Ken
was leader. He looked completely different, it was the effect of power,
suddenly he was transfigured!'

Abbott was now working in County Hall, as a journalist. The previous year, she had left the National Council for Civil Liberties,
alienated after only 13 months there by what she saw as the limits of
its thinking on class and race. She felt that the organisation found it
hard to see black Britons as anything other than victims – rather than,
as she intended to be, also agents of their own upward mobility.

Journalism appealed to her bookish side, to her appetite for
research, and to her curiosity about how power worked in Britain. It
also had more potential than a behind-the-scenes pressure group for
acquiring a lasting public profile. In early 1980, she started as a
researcher for Thames Television, a respected maker and broadcaster
of news and current affairs programmes which held the ITV franchise
for London. She was attached to an early evening news programme.
In the turbulent early 80s the job often involved researching stories
about politics. The early working hours also gave her time afterwards
to write for leftwing publications such as *Briefing* and the *Leveller*, a
fortnightly paper with a name that referenced Tony Benn's favourite
17th-century English radicals. The *Leveller* never achieved *Briefing*'s
influence, and was produced not in County Hall but in a basement on

the Caledonian Road, then a scruffy shopping street in north London. Yet Abbott saw writing for the paper not just as worthwhile in itself but also as a step towards bigger things. On her first visit to the basement, she told other members of the unpaid editorial collective that she was going to become Britain's first black female MP.

She had been a Labour party member for just two years, and had never held elected political office. Only in her mid-twenties, in public if not in private she already seemed impregnably sure of herself, partly because she had succeeded or at least survived in so many white-dominated contexts. She also believed that for all black Britons, as for any disadvantaged group, confidence was an important political weapon. In May 1980, she wrote in the *Leveller* about a riot the previous month in St Pauls in Bristol, the most serious in Britain for years. Years of repressive, often racist policing of a predominantly black area had provoked young, mainly black men into damaging a dozen police cars and effectively taking over the streets for several hours. Abbott described the disorder as an 'urban insurrection' and 'one battle won'. She continued:

My mother is a black working-class lady nearing 60. Eminently respectable and conservative-minded, she was pleased and excited by the ITN film of policemen running away from black youth and and said firmly: 'It shows they can't push us around any more.'

The tone of this passage – formal, precise, educated in its phrasing, but with a provocative conclusion – would become Abbott's tone in public settings. It was a good way of getting attention, and also of making enemies. As the quote from her mother suggested, she had inherited some of her tough-mindedness from her parents. But unlike them, she never talked about permanently going 'home' to the Caribbean at some future date. Like many black Britons of her more politicised generation, Abbott planned to stay in the country for good, and therefore believed that she needed to help change it.

Yet first she needed to observe and make contacts among more experienced political operators who broadly shared her goals. During 1980, she tried to persuade Thames Television that the rise of Livingstone and his allies, even before they had taken over the GLC, was such an important story that she should cover it full-time, based at County Hall. The sheer size of the building and the GLC's self-importance meant that it had its own broadcast studios. Abbott's bosses were not instantly won over by her proposal, but once Labour won the 1981 GLC elections and Livingstone mounted his coup, both events that Abbott had told her bosses were likely to happen, Thames appointed her as their County Hall reporter.

She saw the life of the building change. While under previous administrations it had been an elaborately hierarchical place, with staff required to put on a suit and tie if they needed to visit the 'principal floor' where the councillors had their offices, now County Hall was semi-officially renamed 'the People's Palace'. The committee rooms and corridors became busier, the visitors to the complex younger, less overwhelmingly white and male. Instead of hosting endless drinks receptions for councillors and businessmen, sometimes so extravagant that as a backdrop animals were borrowed from London Zoo, in the evenings the building was now the venue for gatherings of activists in denim jackets. Itinerant London leftwingers who were not GLC councillors but were close to Livingstone, such as Jeremy Corbyn, were allowed to treat the building, with its photocopiers and spare desks, as an operational base.

Abbott became a participant as well as an observer, spending time in the GLC press office every day, and discussing with Livingstone and McDonnell what the council might achieve. In her biography, she refers to the GLC using the first-person plural: 'We were across the Thames [from parliament], with the unemployment figures on the roof. It was exciting, it was about transforming reality, it was about changing the institution [of the GLC] . . . and about offering a real alternative to Thatcherism.'

The new London left, or at least some of it, had made it out of the basements and borrowed living rooms of the capital's less prestigious postcodes and into a new realm of chandeliers and wood panelling, like revolutionaries who had seized an actual palace. The question was: what to do next?

PART THREE

The Red Base

10

A Beginning and an Ending

The takeover of County Hall had consequences in unexpected places. One of these was the constituency of Islington North. It ought to have been a political backwater. Held by Labour for almost half a century, usually comfortably, in 1981 its seemingly haphazard, zigzagging boundaries enclosed a typical slice of north London. With its tight knot of council estates and immigrant cafés, fraying Victorian houses and thundering main roads, the constituency was not much like the more fashionable Georgian Islington which was beginning to gentrify rapidly a couple of miles to the south.

Until 1981, one of the few notable political facts about Islington North was that it was the smallest and probably the most crowded constituency in the country. Many of its large working-class population came from Ireland, the poorer parts of the Mediterranean, and the Caribbean. Wages in the constituency were well below the national average, and unemployment was much higher: approaching one in five adults. In the 1970s and 80s, 'inner city' was a constantly used euphemism for social tension, crime and poverty. Since the election of the Thatcher government in 1979, a Whitehall subsidy paid to the constituency and the many other struggling urban areas like it had been steadily and severely cut. Islington North did attract some middle-class incomers, drawn by its roomy old properties and relatively central location, but it was better known for its pollution: before the existence of the M25 orbital motorway, lorries crossing the capital used the constituency as a shortcut.

Its MP in 1981 was suitably hopeless. The Venesses' old enemy Michael O'Halloran still held the seat, as he had done since 1969. According to his fellow Labour MP Tam Dalyell, O'Halloran was 'the least coherent man ever to come to the House of Commons'. He told Dalyell that he had not planned to become an MP, but had been selected by an 'Irish mafia' of churchmen and party officials, which ensured that areas of London with large Irish populations were represented by Labour members with Irish roots and traditionalist social views.

During the 1970s and early 80s, O'Halloran's conservatism, lack of political initiative, and allegations that his position as an MP owed much to fraud and vote-rigging in the local party – allegations repeatedly investigated by Labour's national executive committee – all sustained the campaign against him, which was led by the Venesses. It was similar to the one being led by McDonnell against the Labour rightwinger Neville Sandelson in Hayes and Harlington. Right across the city, the Labour left was increasingly coordinating its activities, trying to create a much bigger space for itself – and for that to happen, often the Labour right would have to be pushed out.

Yet in Islington as in Hayes, for a long time the left failed. O'Halloran hung on: the allegations against him were never sufficiently proven for him to be removed, while at general elections, even though the turnout was tellingly low, he retained his seat four times, with unspectacular but consistent majorities. Then in 1981 the politics of the constituency finally shifted. A powerful local priest, Father McNamara, who drank with O'Halloran and helped get the Catholic vote out for him at elections and for internal Labour battles, was found dead from booze in his car. Meanwhile the broader political picture also changed. Livingstone's coup at County Hall and Benn's stronger than expected campaign for the deputy leadership convinced many people on the Labour right that their party was moving unacceptably leftwards. The founding of the SDP gave them somewhere else to go.

In Islington North, rightwing Labour members started defecting. In September, O'Halloran did the same. He specifically blamed Benn and Livingstone: 'bigoted and unrepresentative of millions of Labour supporters'. Like the other Labour MPs who switched to the SDP, O'Halloran did not resign his seat so that his decision could be tested at a by-election. But when the next general election came, Islington North would need a new Labour candidate.

The years of acrimony in the constituency meant that finding some-one from the local party who would be acceptable to enough activists and voters – common practice in candidate selection – was pretty unlikely. The leftwing Labour members in Islington, who were now the dominant faction, also feared that if any of them stood they would be badly damaged by accusations that the campaign to remove O'Halloran had been motivated by personal ambition. Yet Labour did need a candidate who knew the constituency well. At the last gen-eral election the party's majority had fallen quite sharply, to a less than impregnable 4,456. In the 1970s and 80s, the capital was not as strongly Labour as it has since become. If the party chose a bad can-didate, it was not inconceivable that Islington North could go Tory.

Corbyn lived a hundred yards from the constituency. His area, Hornsey, was socially quite similar to Islington but more Conserva-tive, with a Tory MP whom he and other activists had been trying to dislodge for years. Corbyn had stayed in touch with the Venesses, and often collaborated with them and other Islington leftists. 'Jeremy was just someone you saw everywhere,' Keith Veness told Corbyn's biog-rapher Rosa Prince. 'It was always the same people turning up to things. Everyone thought that Jeremy was a good bloke, very active . . . He supported us in the battle against O'Halloran.' Corbyn also had the beginnings of a profile beyond this kind of small-scale politics, thanks to his writing for *Briefing*, his work on Benn's deputy leader-ship campaign, and his fiery televised intervention at the 1978 Labour party conference. Even the limitations of his public persona could be a political advantage: they could mark him out as a new kind of Labour MP, one who would remain primarily an activist. At a time when the left particularly valued grassroots activism, and wanted absolutely no compromise with Thatcherism, Corbyn's seemingly tireless, almost ego-free brand of socialism potentially had strong appeal.

There could also be a strategic value to his presence in parliament. With the GLC captured, the *Briefing* collective and other London leftists saw getting a foothold in the Commons as one of their next targets. This switch of focus was partly driven by anxiety. The aggres-sion and ambition of the Thatcher administration's national policies, and the funding reductions that it was imposing on local government, were reminding the London left that municipal radicalism was not enough. More positively, there was a growing appreciation at *Briefing* that being an MP, even if you were a lone voice and outside the parliamentary mainstream, would bring status, publicity, facilities, and access to political intelligence. Radical causes can acquire momentum and credibility when they are raised on House of Commons headed paper. And if an MP has a relatively safe seat, such as Islington North, these tools can be used for decades. 'It was extremely important for us to have an MP,' *Briefing*'s co-founder Chris Knight told me. Corbyn was meant to be 'the first'.

But did he actually want to do it? Unlike his hero Benn, who became an MP at 25, Corbyn had spent his entire twenties in non-parliamentary politics. He believed that much of what was most politically important – strikes, marches, foreign causes, innovations by local councils, the involvement of ordinary people – happened outside the Commons. Also unlike Benn, he did not have the education, or the articulacy, or the appetite for confrontation to find parliament easy. Most of Corbyn's political life so far had been among people who basically agreed with him. He had attacked enemies, but generally as political categories, and rarely to their faces. He liked people, and he liked people to like him – to think, as Keith Veness put it, 'that Jeremy was a good bloke'.

There was also a diffidence about him. When it came to high-profile political roles, as opposed to less personally exposing everyday activism, 'Jeremy's never up for anything', said Veness. 'You ... have to talk him through it.' One of Benn's most loudly voiced principles, thoroughly absorbed by Corbyn, was that politics should not be about personalities. Benn's charisma and ego meant that he could never quite extend this principle to himself. But the less compelling and self-involved Corbyn managed to, at least for a while. He was known for his causes much more than his personality.

And yet, trying to become an MP would be a new political experience. Corbyn knew Islington and the strength of its left well enough to know that he would have a good chance. The role might be very fulfilling, and make his campaigning more effective. Like Benn, Corbyn had an idealistic view of democracy, and he could see how Islington was being damaged by Thatcher's policies, and that as an

MP he might be able to lessen that. He also knew that his comrades at *Briefing* wanted members of the collective to start becoming MPs. He had a sense of duty.

By 1981 there was nothing else in his life to stop him taking on even more political responsibilities. His relationship with Abbott had not lasted very long. They went on holiday to France on his motorbike. Later, wishful thinking in the media and Westminster would turn this into a much more intriguing trip to communist East Germany. She moved into his flat. But after less than a year, the relationship fizzled out. She had tired of how single-mindedly he focused on politics, of how rarely he came home. But they stayed close.

During late 1981 and early 1982, with persuasion from the Venesses and other activists in the constituency, Corbyn finally came round to the idea of standing for selection in Islington North. The local left got to work. In late 1982, he was chosen as the Labour candidate.

After that, things went less smoothly. In early 1983, with a general election expected imminently, adjustments to constituency boundaries partly driven by inner London's shrinking population reduced Islington's Commons representation from three seats to two. Islington North survived; but convention dictated that Corbyn should stand aside in favour of an existing Labour MP, John Grant, whose Islington Central constituency was to be abolished. Yet before Corbyn could be forced to step down, in another of the changes of fortune – or rather, changes of political circumstances – that would accelerate Corbyn's career, Grant defected to the SDP. Corbyn remained the Labour candidate.

The chaos of Islington politics continued regardless. The SDP chose Grant as their candidate for Islington North, and not O'Halloran – despite the fact that he was its current MP. O'Halloran left the SDP and tried to rejoin Labour. The party rejected his application, but decided to do its entire candidate selection process again. Again, Corbyn won. Still O'Halloran did not give up: he decided to run against Corbyn in the general election, as the representative of 'Independent Labour'. To get into parliament, Corbyn would have to beat two sitting MPs – an almost unprecedented level of competition.

Yet despite all these obstacles, Corbyn occasionally allowed himself to see the potential of the path he was embarking on. At the 1982

Labour party conference, he met Bob Clay, another Labour leftwinger who had recently been selected as a parliamentary candidate. 'We were introduced to each other in a pub,' Clay told me, 'as two people who were going to get elected as the main troublemakers of the '83 intake. Getting a bit carried away, one of us cracked a joke: "One of us will probably end up as leader of the party!"'

While Corbyn thought things might be opening up for him, Benn was beginning to think the opposite. The defiant optimism he had felt in the immediate, adrenalised aftermath of his narrow deputy leadership defeat did not last long. Just over a fortnight after the result, on 14 October 1981, he went to a meeting of the committee which had overseen his campaign. One of its most important and perceptive figures, Vladimir Derer, told the gathering that the movement to democratise the Labour party, which had given Benn's campaign much of its momentum, had now 'waned'. 'Our support is weaker,' Derer said. Benn noted the remark in his diary.

The next day, Benn learned from a hospital consultant that his illness over the spring and summer had done 'serious damage'. How far he could recover might not be known for two years. 'I am beginning to realise that I may be handicapped for life,' he wrote. 'I would like to be able to run and jump about before I die but I've got to face the possibility that I never will.' He was only 56 years old.

A couple of weeks later, he heard that three Labour MPs wanted to meet him in the House of Commons. He agreed, even though he knew they had not supported him in the deputy leadership contest. When they met, instead of moving on from that battle, the MPs told Benn he was 'a hated figure', who 'would bring the party to disaster'. Again, he recorded the bleak encounter in his diary.

Labour had recently come third in a by-election in Croydon in south London, behind both the Conservatives and the SDP. Five months later, in March 1982, the same thing happened at the other end of the country, in the Glasgow constituency of Hillhead. Both seats had been key Labour targets, and during this period it became commonplace to hear journalists and prominent party figures from Foot downwards say that Labour's declining popularity was largely because of Benn and his divisive behaviour.

Even Benn himself eventually seemed to accept that the time for leftwing rebellions had passed, at least for the time being. In December 1981, after acknowledging that it had been 'a traumatic year' he wrote: 'I think now – and my friends agree – that we [Labour] should fight the General Election on a status quo agreement, whereby ... policy is agreed ... [party] constitutional changes are accepted, the left holds off on further constitutional change ... and the leadership is not challenged.'

In early January 1982, at a suitably neutral venue, a country club belonging to a trade union in the pretty home counties market town of Bishop's Stortford, a truce was agreed between the Labour right and left, on roughly the terms Benn had laid out, which was intended to last until the general election. The following weekend, this New Year's resolution was assessed by a gathering of Benn's circle and other leftists at his house in London. Livingstone and several of his GLC comrades were there – a sign of their growing importance. Yet the most revealing contribution came from Benn's clever young fixer and organiser, Jon Lansman.

Only a few months earlier, responding to the deputy leadership result, he had animatedly told the television cameras outside the Labour conference in Brighton that 'nothing' was 'going to be stopping' the left's campaign for more radical policies and more Labour democracy. But now, in London, Lansman admitted that 'the left was at a low ebb', as Benn recorded. Lansman argued that 'therefore a truce ... was the best way to protect our gains'. Benn addressed the gathering in even more downbeat terms: 'We have to face the fact that we want a Labour victory – we have to trundle those awful old duds in the Shadow Cabinet back into Whitehall offices ...' His own days as a minister in the Department of Industry, believing that he could help create a radically different Britain, seemed a long way away.

The left's loss of confidence and leverage from late 1981 onwards – at the level of national, as opposed to local, politics – was not just a product of Benn's setbacks and frailties. It was also caused by less public forces. Probably the most lethal of these was John Golding.

Golding was the son of a pottery worker. Six years younger than

Benn, with a bruising wit and a quick brain, Golding had been shaped by centre-left institutions during the 1950s and 60s. Through a union-funded university scholarship and junior clerical positions for the government, he had escaped the world of factory work for a white-collar career, which led him into trade union jobs and then politics. In 1969 he became the Labour MP for the industrial town of Newcastle-under-Lyme in the west Midlands. He had two main political preoccupations. The first was protecting the working class from low wages and patronising professionals: tasks he pursued as employment minister in the late 1970s. And the second was protecting the Labour party from impractical leftists.

Golding regarded Benn as the worst of them. In a relentlessly score-settling but revealing memoir, *Hammer of the Left*, Golding portrays Benn as an 'aristocratic' and sanctimonious politician, 'exceedingly bright' and 'attractive', but with a messiah complex and no judgement: 'Like Toad of Toad Hall ... [he] always appeared to be chasing the latest fad.' In Golding's view, Benn led a narrow, overly metropolitan alliance of 'mad' Trotskyists, 'social workers', and 'the bedsit brigade' – rather than the 'ordinary working people' that Labour ought to be representing. 'He was God's greatest gift to Thatcher,' wrote Golding, 'and had to be stopped if Labour was to survive.'

As a member of Labour's national executive committee (NEC) in the early 1980s, and in many other, more hidden roles, Golding orchestrated a fightback by the Labour right against the left. It continued despite the truce agreed between the two sides at Bishop's Stortford. Golding's memoir describes how the right started 'organising the union vote' at Labour conferences, persuading 'union moderates to join the party and sign up as [conference] delegates'; and above all, 'fixing the constituencies' – getting 'moderate' union branches to affiliate to them 'to help in the reselection of sensible MPs'.

Sometimes, the campaign sought to subvert the left itself: 'to persuade individual left-wingers to look after themselves by doing deals with us and ratting on deals with the left'. At other times, the counter-revolutionaries carefully agreed 'slates' of appropriate candidates for union or Labour positions. To coordinate all this activity, Golding and a small group of centre-left union leaders and MPs held clandestine meetings at London hotels:

'Fixing' was far better done in secret ... Documents considered would be gathered up at the end. All correspondence would go to home addresses. As a result, except for two minor breaches [of confidentiality], while documents from the left were constantly provided [to us], the left did not receive those of the moderates.

In many ways, Golding's manipulation of Labour and the unions' structures and rules deliberately copied work done by the left. He regarded Lansman as a 'very skilful' organiser and a 'superb fixer'. As the left's impetus faded from the 1981 Labour party conference onwards, the counter-revolutionaries gradually recaptured the party machine, starting with the powerful NEC. The day after his deputy leadership defeat, while trying to recover in his hotel room in Brighton, Benn recorded in his diary that the results that morning from the annual NEC elections had been 'a disaster', with four of the left's candidates defeated. At the next party conference, in 1982, he wrote: 'The NEC swings to the right and I am more and more isolated . . .'

But Golding was not content just to marginalise Benn. He wanted to squeeze him out of parliament altogether. 'He and his barmies had done for so many decent folk in the Labour Party,' wrote Golding. 'It was time, in true Sicilian style, to pay him a visit, return the compliment and do for him and his leadership ambitions.'

Golding had spotted that Benn's position in the Commons was more vulnerable than it seemed. Although Benn had been an MP since 1950, and was revered in the Commons as a parliamentary presence even by many of his worst enemies, his relationship with his constituency of Bristol South East was less solid. At the 1979 general election his majority there had shrunk dramatically, from a formidable 9,373 to a flimsy 1,890. This deterioration showed what a divisive figure he had become during the 70s. It also suggested that some of his constituents saw him as an increasingly disengaged figure.

Benn did not live in the constituency – a plain inner suburb of small terraced houses and council tower blocks, petrol stations and lines of basic shops. When he was in Bristol overnight, which was not often, he stayed at the Grand Hotel, a handsome and quite plush Victorian building in the city centre, a couple of miles from his seat. Usually, he did not stay in Bristol at all, but took an evening train or drove down the motorway, usually late at night and very fast, back to his home in London. Rather than a dislike of Bristol, the habit reflected how close he was to his family, and how many political commitments he had in the capital and around the country. But his lack of rootedness in Bristol gradually became a problem.

On 1 April 1982 he recorded in his diary:

> To Bristol, and talked to Meg, now chair of the [constituency] Party, who expressed the widely shared anxiety that I'm not active enough in Bristol: a serious criticism. They are afraid that all the hostile press coverage is having an effect in the constituency. I feel a sort of fatalism about it ... I no longer believe that in Bristol views are any different from those of people in London, though I used to think they were. Every time they turn on their TV sets and see me engaged in some controversy or other they ask why they don't see me in Bristol ... The price may very well be my defeat.

Defending his now thin majority would have been a difficult enough prospect. But actually his situation was worse: his constituency was being abolished as part of the redrawing of the country's electoral boundaries. To remain a Bristol MP, which he was determined to do, he would have to be selected as the candidate for either the new seat of Bristol South, which Labour was likely to win, or the new seat of Bristol East, which it was not. Given his divisive reputation, getting selected for the second seat would be much easier than for the first, which was likely to attract more contenders.

While Benn was trying to decide on his best course, Golding got to work. In November 1981, he took a train to Bristol. He claimed afterwards that by coincidence Benn was on the same service, and that they ran into each other 'in the buffet car'. Golding's account continues cuttingly: 'As he travelled first class, there was no danger we would meet in our seats.' Benn's usually candid and comprehensive diary makes no mention of the encounter.

Either way, both men record that later that day Golding addressed a meeting of Bristol trade unionists, and told them that if they wanted to 'defeat the influence of the far left' in the city, they needed to affiliate to local constituency Labour parties, especially Bristol South.

Golding later told *The Times* that the gathering was not part of 'a conspiracy', but part of 'a determined effort to make certain that Mr Benn does not depose Mr [Michael] Cocks' – an opponent of the left – 'who could be in competition with Mr Benn' for the Bristol South candidacy.

After the meeting, Golding and other organisers from the Labour right spent a year and a half encouraging local trade unionists and residents of the constituency to join the Bristol South party, and to choose Cocks as their Labour candidate when the time came. Having served as a Bristol MP for so long, and also fuelled by a volatile mix of fatalism, over-confidence and defiance, Benn decided to stand for selection in Bristol South regardless. When the selection vote finally came, in May 1983, Benn made his pitch to the constituency party first:

> I . . . went into a huge room where they were all sitting. I could see a few friends, but there was a sea of trade unionists, who had been brought in under the Golding aegis, and women in their early sixties from the Co-op Women's Guild. I swear many of them had never been to a political meeting before in their lives. I knew I was going to lose . . .

He did. Golding gloated afterwards: 'We had sewn up Bristol South.' The following day Benn was selected as the candidate for Bristol East instead. He would try his best to win it, but he knew his chances were slim. Almost a month before the general election, with the great majority of the campaign still to come, he drove to parliament, parked his car, and loaded it up with much of the contents of his Commons office.

Labour's election chances were even worse than Benn's. In the week that Thatcher called the election, the respected polling firm MORI put the Conservatives 15 per cent ahead. In fact Labour had been well behind the Tories, and sometimes narrowly behind the SDP as well, for over a year, since April 1982. The weakness of Labour's position was one of the reasons that Golding had been so determined to squeeze Benn out of parliament. After the general election, it was widely expected that a defeated Labour party would be looking for a new leader. Benn would be a contender – but only if he was still an MP, as party leaders have to be.

The unstable and fragile state of Labour in 1982 and 1983, like the opposite state of the Conservatives, had many causes: Foot's inadequacies and Labour's public divisions; the still-novel presence of the SDP, which meant the anti-Tory vote was even more split than usual; and an improvement in the economy, which was beginning to recover from the Thatcher government's brutal surgery. But there was another more random and probably more decisive factor: the war in the Falklands.

An Argentinian invasion of the islands, a possibility for decades, did not happen until Thatcher's government disastrously mismanaged both its military and diplomatic approaches to the remote archipelago. Yet through her boldness, bloody-mindedness, superior fighting resources, and a great deal of luck – such as Argentina impatiently invading too early in the year, before the Falklands' frigid winter made recapture impossible – Thatcher was able to turn a potentially fatal crisis into a political as well as a military triumph. During the ten febrile weeks of the war, from early April 1982 to mid-June, British politics suddenly emerged from the long period of flux it had been in since the early 1970s, which had presented Benn and the left with lots of opportunities, and entered a new period of relative stability and rightwing dominance. For the left, it would be a much more hostile environment.

In private, Benn admired some things about Thatcher. 'I give her full marks,' he wrote after watching her in the Commons in 1981, 'she certainly fights her corner and gets across her propaganda.' In 1982 he described her as 'a leader and a teacher of a . . . formidable kind' – an echo of his speech in the church in Burford six years earlier, where he had argued that politics was 'really about teaching'. He also saw in her a shared desire to replace the postwar status quo – 'that old decaying corporatist, liberal, capitalist structure', he called it in 1982 – with something more dynamic. Like him, she was an iconoclast, sometimes an ideologue, and often a workaholic whom colleagues found hard to get on with. They both had an intensity which their enemies in politics and the media presented as a kind of madness.

Yet while he wanted a society which somehow combined freedom with equality, she wanted one where freedom was paramount, but narrowly defined as economic self-advancement. And unlike him, she had powerful forces on her side, or at least available for her to deploy.

While the armed forces retook the Falklands, urged on by almost all the press, Benn watched disapprovingly – 'it's a colony we grabbed years ago,' he wrote, 'and we have no right to it' – feeling unable to do much to stop the conflict. Foot and most Labour MPs supported Thatcher's Falklands policy, appalled by the aggression and authoritarianism of the Argentinian government, and also too timid to break with the stifling Westminster tradition that parliamentary unity is crucial in wartime.

Away from the Commons, the Labour party was more independent-minded. Livingstone spoke against the war, and in favour of the islands' sovereignty being decided by the International Court of Justice. Corbyn called the war a 'Tory plot', and proposed a motion against it at Haringey council. In the righteous, over-stuffed rhetorical style which would become his trademark as he went up in the political world, he condemned all the aggressors equally, and tried to place the war in a wider context:

> We resent this waste of unemployed men who are being sent to the Falklands to die for Thatcher and Galtieri [the Argentinian military dictator] ... It is a nauseating waste of money and lives ... at a time when we can't find money for houses, hospitals or wages, not for world hunger, not for aid to north-east Africa ...

Benn did speak and vote against Thatcher's Falklands policy in parliament, and also at public anti-war meetings. But appearing at the latter was considered sufficiently dangerous for him, given his profile and the general atmosphere of jingoism, that three stewards had to walk him to a bus stop so that he could travel home safely after an anti-war rally in Hyde Park. His feelings of impotence and vulnerability were not helped by a bout of pneumonia, which was reported excitedly by some newspapers as a grave illness. He quickly recovered, but his political mood did not. 'I feel somehow that we are at a real turning-point in politics,' he recorded in July 1982, the month after the Argentinian surrender. 'Victory in the Falklands War, Thatcher's strength, the counter-attack of the right of the Labour Party on the left, the fact that unemployment has weakened the unions ... I feel we have just come to the end of an era.'

*

The following year's general election campaign was unusually short. It lasted exactly a month, from 9 May to 9 June. Yet it decided so much.

Given the weakness of Labour's position, and the apparently waning influence of Benn and the left, the party's manifesto was astonishingly, even bafflingly, radical and ambitious. It promised 'to bring about a complete change of direction for Britain': not just the reversal of the militaristic, socially polarising policies that the Thatcher government was pursuing, but the beginning of a national transformation beyond that achieved by previous Labour governments. This transformation would include shortening the working week and introducing a minimum wage; increasing opportunities for women and ethnic minorities; widening home ownership; giving workers a say in the running of their companies; standing up for gay rights; and making the activities of government more transparent. At the same time, Labour promised to curb long-established centres of power, such as the banks and the security services, and abolish others, such as the House of Lords and 'concentrations of press ownership'. Labour would also ban fox hunting, stop 'arms sales to repressive countries', and get rid of Britain's nuclear weapons. It would take the country out of the EEC – an 'obstacle' to 'radical, socialist policies' – and 'increase aid to developing countries towards the UN target of 0.7 per cent'. It would restrict imports that threatened British industries.

Over the next four decades, a striking number of these proposals would become government policy, under Tory as well as Labour premiers. Yet for many people in 1983, and since, the lengthy, sometimes clumsily worded manifesto – 'Here you can read Labour's plan to do the things crying out to be done in our country today,' ran its opening sentence – was spectacularly ill-judged, 'the longest suicide note in history' in the famous words of the acerbic Labour rightwinger Gerald Kaufman. Even for a party with a long history of election blunders and setbacks, the 1983 manifesto quickly became a notorious document.

In many ways, 'The New Hope For Britain', as the 1983 document was awkwardly titled, was also Benn's last stand as a major politician. Most of its ideas were ones he had come up with or adopted during the 1970s and early 80s, and had helped push through Labour's policy-making machinery. That these radical proposals had made it into the manifesto at a time when Benn and the left were past the peak of their power was partly down to the slowness with which the party sometimes changed.

Yet in 1983 there was also another force at work in Labour politics, in the run-up to the campaign and during the election itself. For some canny people on the right of the party, the fact that Labour were almost certain to lose created an opportunity. 'I was determined that the left would get the blame,' wrote John Golding afterwards. 'I was going to hang [Benn] by going along with some of the barmiest policies he had got through ...' That the resulting manifesto would lead to many Labour MPs losing their seats, Golding and his comrades believed, would not be unfortunate collateral damage, but precisely the point of the exercise. For the sectarians of the Labour right, saving the party required them first to destroy much of it.

In 1982, as part of this counter-attack against the left, Golding had stood against and replaced Benn as chairman of the party's influential home policy committee. Through his membership of this and other party bodies, Golding helped ensure that the 1983 manifesto was both recklessly bold and indigestibly long – 'a wish list' as he later described it. At the final manifesto meeting, he successfully opposed a suggestion that the document should be made more concise. 'John Golding made a very strong point,' Benn noted in his diary. He recorded Golding as saying: 'You can't condense a document like this, and it has had a very good reception [in the party].' For Benn, worrying about why this Labour rightwinger and sworn enemy of his was supporting a leftwing, essentially Bennite manifesto, and whether that was a warning sign, appeared to be less important than the fact that such a manifesto had been adopted. For Benn, 'the issues' had become much more important and interesting than manoeuvres or tactics. This was not always a good strategy.

With this mixture of motives, the Labour campaign began. There were a few hopeful moments. At the end of the first week, one opinion poll showed a halving of the Tory lead over Labour, to a less than impregnable 7 per cent. In other polls, the SDP, now in an alliance with the Liberals, seemed to be taking away support from the Conservatives as well as from Labour. Meanwhile, Michael Foot displayed his old-fashioned oratorical gifts to thrilled audiences. 'There were a thousand people at my meeting last night,' he told Golding, 'who gave enormous cheers to my statement on nuclear disarmament.'

In Islington North, Corbyn proved a decent campaigner. He presented himself to voters as an insurgent: still shaggy-haired, lanky and intense, making angry speeches and always canvassing, up and down the narrow, polluted pavements. He attacked the government for 'cuts, closures and poverty', and promised a better future under Labour in populist terms: 'Only the Labour Party has a plan that puts people first.' Unlike in much of the country, many Islington voters were increasingly receptive to rebellious leftwing politics. The previous year, Labour had recaptured the borough council from the SDP. The new administration hoisted a red flag over the town hall, where it flew for the next five years, and elected as council leader Margaret Hodge.

A few years older than Corbyn, Hodge was ambitious and confrontational, advocating policies such as refusing to set a budget for the council if the government tried to rein it in by imposing spending cuts. From a very wealthy family which owned an international steel-trading business, she appeared to be one of the London left's rising stars. Islington was promising territory for such politicians, with its obvious social problems and increasingly politicised middle class, including many employed in socially conscious professions such as teaching and local government. Hodge quickly became a well-known figure, in Islington and beyond.

Corbyn did not have her flair for publicity. But he showed during the 1983 election campaign that he did have a rare gift for getting on with voters: for listening to them properly, about local concerns as well as national and international ones; for forging bonds on street corners and in people's homes. He found apparently ordinary lives, lived in the constituency's leafy but run-down council estates, its subdivided and draughty old houses, its constantly changing parades of small shops and import businesses, endlessly fascinating. His determination to canvass as many addresses as possible led him to mistakenly door-knock the campaign headquarters of his Tory rival.

In Bristol East, Benn campaigned with less gusto. In the newly formed constituency Labour party, 'The organisation is fairly minimal,' he wrote, almost ten days into the campaign. 'My anxiety at the moment is that things ... haven't started, or, if they have, there's no sign of it.' A reporter from the *Financial Times* – whose editors and readers were unlikely to wish him well – attached himself to Benn's campaign. Other newspapers watched from London and waited for the campaign to end in disaster. Yet Benn stuck to his old routine – better suited to his previous, safer seat – of often staying the night in London rather than Bristol. He wanted to conduct a 'low-key' campaign, he wrote: 'no frantic handshaking, no loudspeakers, no razzmatazz'. He had a growing interest in the less personality-driven politics of movements such as the Campaign for Nuclear Disarmament. After all his recent bad health, he also had less energy, not least for all the walking that canvassing involved. Bristol East was a spread-out constituency with many hills. Some of his campaign visits had a weary quality:

> To the boot and shoe factory in Kingswood, where men and women were sitting in front of sewing machines which must have been sixty years old ... It was sheer wage slavery. HTV and [the] BBC were there to take a picture of me ...

His expectations about his Bristol contest changed frequently. Sometimes he saw defeat as inevitable. At other times, he thought he might just win. From talking to voters and collating their responses, Benn and his campaign volunteers estimated that the likely Labour vote was not quite big enough to beat the likely Tory one, unless the Liberal candidate attracted a large number of Conservatives.

A similar complexity tightened the Islington North contest, with Corbyn competing against both the former MP Michael O'Halloran, standing as Independent Labour, and another former Islington Labour MP, John Grant, now standing for the SDP. On polling day, Corbyn's campaign sent activists to polling stations, to walk up and down outside wearing sandwich boards which said, 'Corbyn is the real Labour candidate.' At one polling station, his activists also brought a banner reading, 'Vote for your Labour candidate.' O'Halloran supporters were at the same polling station, holding an identical banner. There was a fight between the two groups, which had to be stopped by security guards. Corbyn's radical, pro-peace campaign seemed to have ended up as an old-fashioned turf war.

Episodes of farce also punctuated Labour's national campaign. A plan was drawn up for the shadow chancellor Denis Healey, one of the few Labour figures whose abilities the press respected, to explain the party's economic policies at a morning press conference, using a blackboard. But no one remembered to bring any chalk. On another disastrous day for Labour, Foot's sometimes recklessly frank wife Jill Craigie, a pioneering feminist film-maker, told a local newspaper – in what Craigie later said was an off-the-record conversation – that 'even if the party wins', her 69-year-old husband would be unlikely to stay on long as leader. He would 'make way for a younger man'.

Yet in truth such gaffes, like the manifesto, were not Labour's biggest problem. Their biggest problem was the widespread feeling that whatever Labour offered or said or did, the Conservatives deserved to be re-elected because of the victory they had won in the Falklands, and because of the lift in the public mood, not universal but substantial, which had followed. Thatcher made sure that the war remained in voters' minds by visiting the islands for the first time four months before calling the election. The near-impossibility of challenging her status as a heroic war leader was made clear in the last week of the campaign, when Healey said in a speech that she had 'wrapped herself in the Union Jack, exploiting the sacrifices of our troops'. She was a prime minister, he continued, 'who glories in slaughter', while her government, with the war over, was 'lending the military dictatorship in Buenos Aires millions of pounds'. Healey's claims were all essentially correct, and Benn, despite their nasty fight for the deputy leadership, defended them in public. But most of the press and a chorus of other politicians, including the leaders of the SDP and the Liberals, claimed to be appalled by what Healey had said.

Four days before polling day, the *Observer* published a survey of voters' attitudes to the record of the Thatcher government. The only areas where more people were positive than negative were her leadership and the Falklands conflict. But that approval, and the divisions and inadequacies of the opposition parties, were enough to win the Conservatives a Commons majority of 144, the largest for almost 40 years.

Benn, following events on his portable television, saw dozens of Labour MPs lose their seats, as he waited in a back room at a school where the Bristol East votes were being counted. He did not want to watch, or be watched, as the ballot papers piled up for him and the other candidates. The school was ringed by camera crews, he recorded in his diary, 'as if they had come to witness ... executions'. His wife Caroline went back and forth into the counting hall to bring him news. At first she said that he looked narrowly ahead of the Conservative candidate, Jonathan Sayeed, and Benn began to believe that he might scrape home. But at about 1.30 in the morning, with almost all the votes tallied, she told him he had lost.

Onstage for the announcement of the result, Benn stood behind the returning officer, as if trying not to be the centre of attention. Sayeed stood in full view: a very upright former Royal Navy sailor in a double-breasted suit, his dark hair floppy in the 1980s Tory style, a quarter of a century younger. Benn had never lost a parliamentary election. He felt as if he were in a dream.

When his total vote was read out, he looked at Caroline, who was standing beside him, then looked down. His face was almost expressionless, but tight, his mouth clamped shut. There were defiant cheers and surprisingly strong applause from the Labour supporters in the room. Benn lifted his head and managed a brief smile. Even Sayeed applauded. Then the Tory candidate's vote was read out. The cheers and boos were so loud that some of the figures were inaudible, yet it was clear that he had won. Benn kept his head up, but he stared into the distance, seemingly close to tears.

Sayeed had beaten him by 1,789 votes: not a tiny margin, but dwarfed by the 10,404 votes that had gone to the Liberal candidate. Despite Benn's long record as a defender of civil liberties and other liberal causes, the Liberal voters of Bristol East, perhaps persuaded by the press caricature of him as a potential leftwing tyrant, had decided not to support him.

Golding heard the news on the radio while he was at his own election count in Newcastle-under-Lyme, a hundred miles to the north. After listening to endless BBC reports about MPs from the Labour right losing their seats, Benn's defeat lifted his mood: 'We counted it as a Labour gain.' By the logic of the Labour right, as tribal as the most dogmatic leftwingers they despised, a Tory MP was preferable to a man who had represented the party in parliament for four decades. Golding survived the night with a reduced majority.

In Bristol, Benn rallied sufficiently to make three concession speeches: first from the stage, then for the reporters outside the school, then for tearful Labour activists at a local trade union headquarters. 'I shall carry on,' he said, 'outside parliament.' The street politics that had inspired and begun to change him, starting in 1968, suddenly seemed a lifeline.

The same morning, shortly after breakfast time, he and Caroline drove back to London. Three cars of photographers followed them, through Bristol's twisting streets and down the motorway. He tried and failed to lose them. As the Benns neared the capital, the pursuing cars overtook them, to set up camera positions outside their house in time for their arrival. When the Benns got home, the intrusiveness of the photographers – and perhaps also a delayed reaction to his rejection in Bristol – left him furious. 'If there was any violence in me,' he raged in his diary afterwards, 'I would have knocked them all down.' But instead, the Benns walked up to their front door, entered, and shut it behind them. The photographers knocked and rang the doorbell. Benn stayed in the house and slowly began to unpack.

11

Man of the People

In politics, even the worst defeats often contain victories. For Labour in 1983, one came in the ex-industrial constituency of Sedgefield in County Durham, where the 30-year-old Tony Blair was elected as an MP for the first time. Another came in Islington North. Corbyn, at 34 also young for a successful Labour candidate, won fairly comfortably in the end: increasing the party's majority by a quarter to 5,607. His enemies from the Labour right, Grant and O'Halloran, came a distant third and fourth, respectively. In Islington at least, the left seemed to have a parliamentary future.

But in much of Britain Labour was massacred. Its share of the vote was 27.6 per cent, only just ahead of the SDP–Liberal Alliance, and its worst since 1918, when Labour was still a relatively new party and had never been in government. Across the country, people who hated and sometimes feared the party rejoiced that, after four decades during which it was either in power or had a good chance of recapturing it, Labour's prospects seemed to have drastically receded. At my cold boarding school in the Tory seat of East Berkshire, where the Conservatives thrashed Labour by 43 per cent, my friendly and very rightwing maths teacher rushed up to me on the playing fields and said gleefully, 'This means they will never be in power again!' I was 13, interested in politics, but not sure which side I was on yet. But I knew enough to be unsettled by what he meant.

Benn tried to persuade the public, and probably himself, that the result was better than it looked. He told an interviewer: 'For the first time since 1945 a political party with an openly socialist policy has received the support of over eight and a half million people.' Yet in his diary he recorded: 'The full scale of the losses is enormous.'

Three days after the election, he and two dozen leading leftists gathered in the large south London back garden of Chris Mullin, the Bennite editor of the Labour newspaper *Tribune*, to talk about what had gone wrong and what the left should do next. It was quite a warm Sunday. On an assortment of non-garden chairs, amid mugs of tea and unopened beer cans, sat Livingstone, Lansman, Benn's economic advisor Stuart Holland, and a small circle of Labour MPs, including Corbyn. Most of the men were in shirtsleeves. The older Benn had put on a jumper. But the new member for Islington North wore a creased, undersized T-shirt with a deep V-neck – like something he might have worn in bed. He showed no sign of being intimidated by the more senior and experienced people present, as they sat watchfully with their arms folded, their body language a bit despondent and slack.

After being congratulated on his win, Corbyn made one of the blunter contributions to the election post-mortem. There had been 'great incompetence in the party machine', he said. 'The leaflets put out were absolutely bland crap.' Just because he was now an MP and a public figure, rather than a largely behind-the-scenes activist, he was not going to speak in euphemisms. Many would see this refusal to play the Westminster game as naive and counterproductive. But it was also a signal that parliament had a distinctive new member. In his first year, he would be the sixth most rebellious MP, in terms of voting against their own party, out of 650.

The meeting in Mullin's garden concluded with a downbeat discussion about who on the left should stand for the party leadership once the defeated Foot inevitably stood down. With Benn now ineligible, the favoured choices were Michael Meacher and Eric Heffer, respected but not compelling leftwing figures. Corbyn had joined the parliamentary left just as it was entering a crisis of confidence and talent.

Yet he quickly showed himself to be quite politically self-sufficient. Three weeks after the garden meeting, he made his first Commons speech. The tradition is that these are not contentious, but he ignored that convention. He began by saying that parliament 'seems a million miles away from the constituency that I represent and the problems that people there face'. His constituency had been treated by the government with 'contempt'. Local health and education services had been badly cut, wages were 'well below the national average', and long-term unemployment was common. In Finsbury Park, one of the most deprived areas, he continued, 'There are black people . . . who have never worked . . . They have little regard for [the] system . . . The people in my constituency are bitter and angry.' He warned: 'I shall convey that spirit to the House as often as I can.'

His speech was part of a debate about the problems of inner London. Even after their huge election victory, the area contained few Conservative seats. Regardless, Corbyn seemed outraged at the near-empty government benches during his speech: 'It is incredible that only 13 Conservative members can be bothered to attend today's debate.' He believed that he was dealing with bigger political questions than mere parliamentary arithmetic. 'We shall return to these issues,' he concluded, 'because justice has to be done.'

In the Commons, he quickly established himself as a moralist, who treated fine rhetoric and formal parliamentary dress as fripperies. Many MPs found his unvarnished style provocative. One of his first enemies was the Tory Terry Dicks, who had also been elected in 1983. Dicks was an abrasive rightwinger who wore showily smart suits with waistcoats. He had captured the outer London suburb Hayes and Harlington from Labour after Neville Sandelson defected to the SDP. In 1984, seeking controversy as usual, Dicks suggested that 'Labour scruffs' such as Corbyn should be barred from the Commons until they dressed more appropriately.

Corbyn rarely spoke to parliamentary reporters, regarding them as part of the Westminster machine and of little use to his constituents. But on this occasion he agreed to be interviewed and filmed by the BBC2 programme *Newsnight*, dressed in one of his typical Commons outfits. Standing outside parliament on a winter day, he wore old brown shoes, shapeless grey trousers, a creased corduroy jacket and a rustic-looking oatmeal jumper, with no tie and shirt collars poking unevenly out. With his beard and a lock of wavy hair dangling across his forehand, he looked like a young farmer. But in his small voice he responded to Dicks' criticism with impressive vehemence. 'It's not a fashion parade,' Corbyn said. 'It's not a gentleman's club, it's not a bankers' institute. It's a place where the people are represented . . .'

Trying to steer the interview on to less serious ground, the reporter asked him if he was wearing a jumper that his mother had knitted.

'Yes it is,' Corbyn said. He opened his jacket to show off her handi-work, also revealing pockets busily stuffed with notebooks and pens. 'It's very comfortable,' he continued, 'and it's perfect for this kind of weather, because I'm hopping in and out of buildings all day long, going to meetings . . .'

Then he narrowed his eyes and went back on the attack. 'Late at night here it's quite disgusting,' he said, shaking his head. 'After the dinners are over and the division bell rings for ten o'clock, there are fleets of limousines drawn up, and out get large Tory MPs with even larger stomachs, wearing dinner jackets, and they stride in to vote . . .' The reporter asked if he was jealous. 'Not at all,' said Corbyn. 'I turn down dinner invitations all the time. I don't think that's the job of an MP. The job of an MP is to represent their people.'

Even during his first few weeks as an MP, when the most iconoclas-tic leftwing incomers can find themselves intrigued – or paralysed – by the Palace of Westminster's maze of buildings and rituals, Corbyn took a determinedly utilitarian approach to being in parliament. The month after he was elected, he wrote an article for *London Labour Briefing*, headlined 'Turning the Party Outwards'. The Commons, he wrote, 'abounds with bars and restaurants but seems strangely incap-able of providing all members with an office. It shows an odd sense of priorities to allow this nonsense.' For his first nine years as an MP, he had to share an office with the Labour leftwinger Bob Clay, also elected in 1983. For Corbyn, the problem with such cramped arrange-ments was not the lack of prestige but the impracticality. He regarded himself as one of a new generation of leftwing MPs 'who have a wealth of experience outside Parliament,' he wrote, and who 'see their main job as not retreating into Parliamentary procedure but building links with the movement outside and using the platform [of the Com-mons] to advance these connections'. He and his comrades intended to act as the parliamentary representatives of causes and campaigns, rather than parliament's representatives in those campaigns – as MPs with activist pasts often became. Being in parliament, in other words, was a means, not an end.

However, for most of its history his party has believed the opposite: that the Commons ought to come first, with Labour trying to capture as much of it as possible, and then using its considerable powers to change the country. Everything else in politics ought to come second. In that approach, Labour has followed the older, usually more powerful Conservative party, which has generally been much more interested in dominating Westminster than in mounting protests or constructing social movements. Widely seen as one of the most successful parties in the world since modern democracy began – in terms of winning elections if not running effective governments – and also regarded as the political default by most of the British press, the Tory party sets an example that Labour, much less secure about its place in public life, often finds itself imitating.

And yet, Labour and the Tories are in many ways profoundly different: not just in their ideas and policies, but in the nature of their support. The Conservatives, as the party of hierarchy and inequality, will probably always have a greater ability to attract the approval of elites. This means that Labour needs to draw strength from other interests, such as egalitarian campaigns and pressure groups, as well as from left-leaning voters. If it neglects these extraparliamentary forces, and instead concentrates all its energies on Westminster – itself a profoundly conservative place – then both in government and opposition Labour will often be outgunned, and achieve less than it could.

In 1961, the revered British Marxist theoretician Ralph Miliband made similar arguments in a withering and often convincing book, *Parliamentary Socialism*. He described Labour's readiness to strike deals with the establishment, rather than reduce its powers or give serious consideration to less privileged interest groups, as 'the sickness of Labourism'. The book and the phrase became briefly famous. But by the time Corbyn entered the Commons, almost a quarter of a century later, the book's influence had faded and was largely confined to academia. Corbyn and the handful of other Labour MPs who shared his vision of politics were on their own.

Corbyn's openness to extraparliamentary causes also meant that his job as an MP soon expanded far beyond the already ambitious one of improving the difficult lives of his constituents in Islington North. Residents there with immigrant backgrounds were often preoccupied by political situations in their countries of origin. 'Jeremy knocks on a door, and some guy from Paraguay starts telling him about all the issues,' said Keith Veness, who later became his constituency agent. 'And then you can't get Jeremy out of there.'

In the early 1980s the cold war was in a turbulent phase again, causing conflicts and injustice from the tropical island of Grenada, which the United States invaded in October 1983, to the cold deserts of Afghanistan, which the Soviet Union had been trying to occupy by force since 1979. There were also Corbyn's own global political interests, formed by his wide reading and travel as a young man. And there was his tendency to see the whole world in the same, quite simple terms: as an almost infinite series of malign relationships between oppressors and the oppressed – relationships in which it was his duty to intervene.

During 1983, in the few months of parliamentary time remaining after the election, he made Commons contributions about Grenada, Cyprus, Turkey, Bangladesh, El Salvador and Nicaragua; about the World Bank and the Commonwealth; about experiments on animals and interrogations by the Royal Ulster Constabulary. 'Whenever you saw him,' a leftwing Labour MP told me, 'he always had a large pile of documents. Arriving late for a meeting, departing early for the next one.' As in his years as an activist, Corbyn became known in Westminster for his total dedication to politics and terrible timekeeping.

But as an MP he now had the authority and funds to travel abroad and see the foreign situations that preoccupied him at first hand. Within weeks of being elected, he flew to Nicaragua in Central America. There, a revolutionary government established by the Sandinista National Liberation Front – a leftwing movement with similar aims, and a similar appeal for Western leftists, to Salvador Allende's Chilean government a decade earlier – was trying to transform the country while simultaneously fighting off counter-revolutionary groups, including the American-backed Contras. Corbyn was thrilled by what he found:

> Every public building is festooned with posters proclaiming the fourth anniversary of the Sandinista victory [over the dictator Anastasio Somoza] and 'Todas las armas al pueblo' (all arms to the people) as the way to defend the gains made. This spirit is proclaimed on every

street and every workplace where press cuttings and information about the military situation are posted. In the street, in taxis, and in shops and markets people are delighted to talk about the gains and the problems . . .

This account was one of several he published on his return to Britain. It appeared in *Socialist Organiser*, a newspaper put out by a coalition of small British leftwing groups who sometimes worked with Corbyn and Livingstone but considered themselves far more radical. At times in these pieces, Corbyn sounded almost as if he had joined the Sandinistas. 'The demands of defence of the revolution obviously have to take priority,' he wrote,

in the allocation of resources by the government. But the achievements are impressive in every field – in health, education and in popular involvement in running the country . . . The Council of State has 51 members drawn from popular organisations, trade unions, women's organisations, churches, private industry . . . Each Barrio (neighbourhood) has series of local committees who deal with the collective needs of defence, public health, education and housing. In one very poor Barrio we were able to visit, 472 families had divided themselves into 25 committees and are working together to transform ten acres of former Somoza land into a decent place to live. Their current problems are to get running water put in each house, and to ensure that the school has sufficient chairs . . .

But Corbyn had not completely forgotten the barrios of Islington. He continued:

The contrasts of attitude in Nicaragua with Britain are enormous . . . A very poor country, under threat from all sides, is actually creating employment, undertaking major rail and heat and power projects, building houses and schools, and improving health care: planning national spending for need not private profit. In Britain, incalculably wealthy by Central American standards, our government claims not to be able to afford to build houses and health centres or even to be able to maintain the existing number of hospitals . . .

In another report on Nicaragua, for *London Labour Briefing*, he argued that the country was having to cope with far greater external pressures than Britain ever had to. Nicaragua was 'facing the classic strangulation of its liberation that all third world countries face when they try to unshackle themselves from western domination'. The United States, he claimed, wanted 'to enslave everybody south of the Rio Grande', the river which ran along the Mexican–Texan border. For Corbyn, the US was as ubiquitous a villain in world affairs as the Soviet Union was for many Tories.

Other MPs, including some in his own party, soon became sceptical about his attachment to foreign causes, seeing them as gesture politics. One former leftwing MP, who was in the Commons with him for over 20 years, and worked closely with him on some issues, told me: 'Many of his causes were things you couldn't do anything about.'

Corbyn's office mate Bob Clay disagreed. He said that the moral authority and the network of contacts in troubled countries that Corbyn built up, year by year, sometimes had practical uses. 'During the civil war in Colombia in the 90s,' Clay said, 'when the thugs picked up a trade union leader, they'd usually be dead in 48 hours. Jeremy would get a fax saying, so-and-so's been lifted. There would be no interest from the [Labour] front bench. He and I would get as many MPs as possible to sign a letter of protest to the Colombian embassy. Very often, it did the trick.'

Corbyn was also prepared to put himself at some risk. In July 1984, he took part in an anti-apartheid protest outside the South African embassy in Trafalgar Square in London, which had been banned by the police on the dubious grounds that it was disrupting the embassy's 'peace and dignity'. Dozens of protesters had already been arrested when Corbyn joined in. He was arrested, too, along with two other Labour MPs. A photograph of him being led away by police officers became iconic in anti-apartheid and leftwing circles: Corbyn, his face defiantly expressionless, being frogmarched along the dirty pavement outside South Africa House, squeezed between the two officers, with a placard hanging by a string around his neck, reading in large, hand-written letters, 'Defend the Right to Demonstrate Against Apartheid. Join this Picket'. For anyone looking for a Labour messiah, he even looked a bit like Jesus.

His arrest did not have serious consequences. A magistrate dismissed the police case against the protesters and awarded each of them £250 compensation, which they all donated to the anti-apartheid movement. But other Corbyn causes became more perilous for him. Like Livingstone, he became a high-profile – to many people, infamous – advocate for a totally different British approach to the conflict in Northern Ireland. With many Irish immigrants in his constituency, and a loathing for British imperialism and militarism, Corbyn was a supporter of the Troops Out movement, which campaigned for the withdrawal of British forces from Ulster. He also believed it was necessary for British politicians to 'reach out' to Irish republicans in order to negotiate an end to the violence. That position would later become the Westminster orthodoxy, but in the 1980s and for much of the 1990s it was seen as unacceptable and immoral by most of the media and most MPs, including in the Labour party.

In July 1983 Corbyn and Livingstone invited Gerry Adams, who had just been elected as the Sinn Féin MP for Belfast West, to visit them in London. Adams met Labour councillors at County Hall and gave a press conference alongside Livingstone. Adams said that the aim of his visit was to start a dialogue with British voters and politicians. Yet in his meetings with the GLC councillors he was sometimes much less mild, saying that unless the British troops withdrew, 'We shall have to go on fighting.' With British soldiers still regularly being killed in the conflict – 39 of them in 1983 – for Labour politicians to talk to a party connected to this violence was widely seen as at best naive and at worst traitorous. Corbyn, who had been an MP for barely a month at that point, was particularly easy to portray as a 'useful idiot' for the Provisional IRA.

Characteristically, he paid no notice to his critics. In 1984, two weeks after the IRA had almost assassinated Margaret Thatcher by bombing the Brighton hotel where she was staying for the Conservative party conference, he invited two IRA members who had served prison sentences for terrorist offences to the House of Commons. He spoke to them in a private room about prison conditions in Northern Ireland, which were often brutal and had become one of his causes, and also 'about the possibility of . . . a political solution' to the conflict. For several weeks the media and the Labour hierarchy were unaware that the visit had taken place. The Commons was constantly full of visitors coming and going, especially people seeing busy MPs such as Corbyn. Yet news of the visit eventually got out. The new Labour leader Neil Kinnock was appalled. He had replaced Foot the previous year and was attempting to make the party more appealing to centrist and even rightwing voters. Corbyn was summoned to a meeting with Labour's chief whip, Michael Cocks, who had helped push Benn out of Bristol and out of parliament, and who was renowned for his general hatred of the left and his ferocious manner.

But Corbyn emerged from the encounter seemingly unflustered. 'Mr Cocks and I don't agree,' he told reporters. 'He thinks it was unwise to have such a meeting in the House of Commons. I think otherwise. I made it very clear that I felt it important that any individual MP who wishes to meet anyone from anywhere should have the right to do so.' Corbyn was learning, as Benn had done decades earlier, that dissent could be more effective when expressed in reasonable-sounding language. It was a way of making the status quo seem unreasonable – and of neutralising negative assumptions about you held by voters and opponents. In Britain's often intolerant political climate, maintained as such by the rightwing press, few people expected leftwing radicals to be polite or nice.

During the 1980s and 90s, Corbyn kept pushing the boundaries that existed in British politics regarding acceptable behaviour on Northern Ireland: inviting senior Sinn Féin figures to the Commons and the fringe of the Labour Party conference; speaking at Troops Out rallies in Britain and Ireland, sometimes alongside Sinn Féin politicians; and employing as a researcher Ronan Bennett, who had been convicted in 1974 of murdering a police officer during a bank robbery by the Official IRA. Bennett's conviction had quickly been quashed because the evidence against him was false, but his past was considered too controversial regardless by the parliamentary authorities, who took away his Commons pass. As was the case with Livingstone, Benn, McDonnell, Abbott and anyone else on the Labour left who challenged the Westminster consensus on Northern Ireland, almost anything Corbyn did or said about the subject was considered suspect.

At the root of this suspicion was always the idea that he was too comfortable with people who used violence for political ends. There is clear evidence that in the 1980s he felt that the latter was sometimes justified – in his support for the Sandinistas' war to protect their revolution, for example. He was not a pacifist. But the war in Northern Ireland was very different. It was not about defending a leftwing revolution, even if the Provisional IRA and Sinn Féin did sometimes use leftwing rhetoric. And by the 1980s the conflict had been going on for over a decade, and fewer and fewer people, on all sides, still believed it could be won militarily. Corbyn was not one of those diehards. 'I wanted the fighting to stop,' he said in 2015, when asked by Andrew Marr to justify his 1980s activities around Northern Ireland, 'and I said that to many, many people on many, many occasions. I don't want violence. I don't want killing. I don't want all the horrors that go with it.'

Some will always see something inauthentic in such repetitive, overemphatic denials. But the arc of Corbyn's political life supports the sentiment. Someone who joined CND two years before he joined the Labour party, and has never left it, and has campaigned against wars for half a century, seems unlikely to be a secret admirer of violence. And if that is accepted, then the charge against him becomes smaller: that he shared platforms with and collaborated with Irish republicans earlier than he should have done, before Sinn Féin and the Provisional IRA renounced the armed struggle. Moreover, even that charge also loses much of its force when placed alongside the still-emerging story of contacts between British governments and the IRA. A Conservative secretary of state for Northern Ireland, William Whitelaw, had met the IRA leadership for covert talks in London as early as 1972. At the time, Corbyn was still trying to be a local newspaper reporter in Shropshire.

His association with Irish republicanism, however misunderstood or misrepresented, has had consequences. Sometimes these threatened to be more serious than reputational damage. During the 1990s, Keith Veness told me, 'One bloke turned up for one of Jeremy's constituency surgeries, saying he wanted to talk about Northern Ireland. He said he was a republican, but he talked about "the Provisional IRA" – in my experience, only loyalists do that.' Veness prevented the man from seeing Corbyn. Shortly afterwards, 'I tried to persuade Jeremy to wear an anti-stab vest. But he wouldn't do it. Jeremy's got a very poor sense of personal security. I said to him, "Sometimes, you're actually courting martyrdom." '

If Corbyn's political life was beginning to develop a religious quality, its main place of worship in Islington was a modest, boxy red-brick building on the busy Seven Sisters Road. Built by the cooperative movement, the detached Victorian property had a meeting hall and two offices downstairs, and a tiny caretaker's flat above. Behind was a large council estate, and in front was the incessant traffic. In 1983, the building was about to be sold to a Bengali clothing company when the Islington North constituency Labour party came across it. Property was still cheap in this poor and polluted area of inner London, especially after the early 1980s recession, and the party was looking for a local base. Shortly before the general election, it bought the premises.

The party had in mind not a standard constituency office but something more ambitious – almost a miniature version of Livingstone's County Hall. It had part of the ground floor converted into a bar. Another section was to be rented out to a suitable political organisation. The hall was to host political and cultural events. And the upstairs flat was to become the local MP's office. The idea was that selling drinks and tickets to events in the hall would subsidise the use of the building for workshops, electioneering, speeches by visiting Labour and trade union figures, and constituency surgeries. In a sometimes fragmented but strongly politicised constituency, the local left would have a new focus, a place which reproduced on a small scale the vibrant mix of politics, culture and socialising found in leftwing strongholds in continental Europe and South America. The building was named the Red Rose Centre.

The space for rent was let to the Chile Solidarity Campaign, a British organisation set up in response to the coup against Allende. It campaigned against the Pinochet dictatorship, and also against the Thatcher government's close diplomatic and defence relationship with Chile. Ten years on from the coup, Chile was fading as an issue in Britain, but Corbyn was still energetically involved in it, using his new status as an MP to put down anti-Pinochet motions and ask the government awkward parliamentary questions. At the Red Rose, he spoke to people from Chile Solidarity almost every day.

Meanwhile on Friday evenings, in the tiny upstairs flat, he held his constituency surgery. Once he became known locally as an MP with an almost infinite capacity for listening, people flocked to the building. People with immigration problems. People struggling to get state benefits. People desperate for council housing, the supply of which the Thatcher government was steadily cutting off. Sometimes, there would be a hundred people waiting to talk to him, sitting on the stairs up to the flat, queueing through the building and out into the street. Often, he did not have the power to solve their problems. But he would patiently hear them out. Veness thought Corbyn was like Marjorie Proops, then the *Daily Mirror*'s famous agony aunt. The new MP offered constituents tea, and toys and a TV to keep their children occupied. He arranged for the many local residents from Turkey to speak to him through interpreters. His surgeries could last six or seven hours.

At the same time, the rest of the life of the building carried on: activists coming and going; lefties from all over north London cramming into the hall to hear Tony Benn and other Labour luminaries, or to see alternative comedians, with their Thatcher-bashing routines. Noisiest of all were the drinkers in the bar. The local party found that the building's overheads were much higher than they had anticipated, so, as Veness put it, 'You had to appeal to Labour members to come in and get drunk.' The bar became known locally for its low prices, and for serving people who were banned from pubs in the area. Islington North had a lot of itinerant hard drinkers. At the Red Rose, with its prominent position on a main road, they mixed not always harmoniously with feminists, black activists, trade unionists and pacifists. Sometimes, volunteer bouncers had to be used in the bar, and to prevent Corbyn's queueing constituents from being jostled or alarmed.

But little of this bothered Corbyn – in fact, the opposite. 'Jeremy had no problem pushing through a group of drunks to get up to the office,' said Veness. Although Corbyn barely drank himself, 'He thought it was all marvellous. Because he was a man of the people.'

The raucous bustle of the Red Rose raised his profile, and suggested that he stood for a more expansive politics than the puritanism with which the left were often, if not always fairly, associated. The Centre also increasingly became his refuge. As the Thatcher government went on and on, and Kinnock made Labour ever less hospitable for leftists, and Corbyn's never rosy view of the House of Commons darkened still further, to something close to contempt, he spent more and more of his days at the Red Rose, doing his constituency and broader campaigning work there, and only heading to parliament in the evening, when most of the votes were.

In some ways, it was and is easier for London MPs to be rebels, to be politically self-contained. Members with distant constituencies, such as the many Labour MPs from the north of England, could find it hard to get away from the claustrophobic Palace of Westminster, with its many bars and its pressures to conform, since they often could only afford small flats or rented rooms in central London. By contrast, Corbyn and the leftwing London MPs who would join him in parliament had proper homes and their personal political territories quite nearby. He had an old car, but he insisted that he could drive from the Red Rose to the Commons in eight minutes. Even in the less congested London of the 1980s and 1990s, the journey took over twenty minutes. But Corbyn was always an optimist.

12

Socialism in One City

By the mid-1980s, despite Benn's recent defeats and their party's general election disaster, the new Labour left had a foothold in British political life. Corbyn was using this energetically but modestly, as a single MP, generally a marginal figure in parliament, trying to gradually make a difference to deep-seated local and global problems, through alliances with outside activists and a few kindred spirits in the Commons. His attitude to time was much more patient and elastic than that of most politicians. That would become both a great strength and a great weakness.

Livingstone used his opportunity differently. His ego was bigger than Corbyn's, and so, it seemed, were his prospects. As the politician who was in charge, to a degree, of Britain and Europe's largest city, and as the only Labour figure who held real power in an era of otherwise near-total Tory supremacy, he could do significant things now, and possibly even bigger things in the future.

'After Benn hadn't won the deputy leadership at party conference in Brighton,' Livingstone told me later, 'I remember walking back to the station and thinking that, for all my political career up to that point, I'd been taking up issues that others had raised. But now I was leader of the GLC, and had been for four or five months. I felt . . . a real responsibility. I was part of setting the agenda now. And a lot of people on the right did think that eventually somebody like me would take over the Labour party. They'd managed to block Benn . . . But here I was, this little oik from south London who had managed to overturn the Labour leadership of the GLC. I might be able to do it nationally . . .'

This was not just not his ego talking. For much of the 1980s, Foot's struggles as Labour leader, the slow progress made by Kinnock as his successor, and the often more compelling politics of Livingstone's GLC tenure meant that a small but growing number of serious observers saw the 'oik from south London' as a leadership solution for Labour. As early as June 1982, when he had been running the GLC for barely a year, Livingstone was talent-spotted by the influential *Sunday Times* columnist and political editor Hugo Young. The often astute Young was not a supporter of the Labour left – his own politics were centrist – but he was always interested in able radicals. After spending a long train journey with Livingstone, whom he had not met before, Young wrote in his private notes that the GLC leader was good company, 'humorous' and 'open', yet also formidable: unusually, both 'very committed' to leftwing politics and 'extraordinarily detached' from the stresses it generated. Unknown to Young, Livingstone had low blood pressure. Young noted that he was 'a good political analyst', and 'very adept and knowledgeable with electoral figures'. About Livingstone's future, Young wrote: 'One remembers that he can afford to wait, unlike Benn. I think he will be leader of the Labour party before the end of the century.'

Characteristically, Livingstone pursued his ambitions by multiple routes simultaneously: not just leading the GLC but also trying again to get into parliament. Ahead of the 1983 election, this involved attempting to be selected as the Labour candidate for the London seat of Brent East. It was a tatty but vibrant inner-city constituency, similar in some ways to the seat Corbyn sought in Islington, with a large and racially diverse working class which was loyal enough to Labour to usually give the party a solid majority. But unlike Islington North, Brent East already had quite a leftwing MP, Reg Freeson, a renowned anti-racist and peace campaigner who had represented the area for almost 20 years.

In middle age the sometimes prickly Freeson had begun moving rightwards, falling out with some of the more dogmatic leftwing activists in his constituency party and voting for Healey rather than Benn as Labour deputy leader. During 1982 and 1983, these activists tried to remove him as the Labour candidate for the next general

election, and to replace him with Livingstone. This already acrimonious situation was given an additional edge by the fact that the Jewish
Freeson was a Zionist, while Livingstone and some of his backers
were strong critics of Israel.

By the early 1980s, 'A cause dear to my heart was the struggle of the
Palestinians,' Livingstone wrote later. Like an increasing number of
Labour leftwingers, he had acquired what he thought was a clear view
of the Israel–Palestine issue: the Palestinians were the victims, and the
Israelis were the aggressors.

This perspective had taken a long time to become a common
Labour position, and was still far from universal in the party. Labour
support for what had become Israel was almost as old as the party
itself. It predated the British government's 1917 Balfour Declaration
recommending 'the establishment in Palestine of a national home for
the Jewish people', and had been sustained by senior figures such as
Harold Wilson and Michael Foot. During the postwar period, many
in the party continued to see Israel as a unique, essentially left-of-
centre country, created for victims of fascism and centuries of
persecution, and characterised by collectively farmed kibbutzim and
generally left-leaning governments. The Labour party had a strong
bond with the Israeli Labor party, which was always a member of
Israel's postwar coalition governments. What criticism there was of
Israel in Britain often came from the Young Liberals, the radical youth
wing of the Liberal party. After campaigning against apartheid South
Africa during the 1960s and 1970s, they began to argue that Israel
was a similar society in its treatment of its Arab citizens, its occupation of Palestinian territory and its aggression towards its other
neighbours.

In 1982, one of the first Israeli governments not to include Labor
invaded Lebanon, and then facilitated the massacre of thousands of
Palestinian and Lebanese civilians by Israel's local allies. The Young
Liberals' controversial critique of Israel was adopted and taken further by the Labour left. *Labour Herald*, a small campaigning
newspaper which Livingstone had co-founded, published a cartoon of
the Israeli prime minister Menachem Begin in a Nazi uniform, giving
a Nazi salute, while standing on a pile of corpses.

It was at best hugely provocative and at worst utterly offensive.

Livingstone and the newspaper were condemned by the Board of Deputies of British Jews, but they did not soften their stance on Israel. As with the campaign led by John McDonnell a few years earlier to deselect the centrist Labour MP for Hayes and Harlington, Neville Sandelson, who like Freeson was Jewish, the Labour left was unafraid of making Jewish enemies, just as it was unafraid of making enemies elsewhere. It was hard to argue that McDonnell and Livingstone were driven by antisemitism. They were lifelong anti-racists, and their campaigns against Sandelson and Freeson were motivated by ideology, personal ambition and a general contempt for centrism. Yet at the Board of Deputies these battles would not be forgotten.

In Brent, the Livingstone–Freeson contest became an attritional struggle over party procedure, which drew in lawyers, Labour headquarters and Tony Benn's nemesis John Golding, who was beginning to see Livingstone as just as big a threat to sensible Labour politics as Benn had been. In April 1983, Labour's NEC, which Golding and the right now dominated, ruled that Freeson could not be deselected. The relevant committee of the Brent East constituency party responded by voting to replace Freeson with Livingstone anyway, by 71 votes to four. Before the situation could be sorted out by the courts, Thatcher called the 1983 election. The ever-opportunistic Golding successfully put a motion to the NEC that it was now too late for Labour to change any of its parliamentary candidates. Freeson remained in place. 'This will freeze Ken Livingstone out,' wrote Golding in his local paper, with some satisfaction.

But he was only partly right. While Livingstone had no time to find another winnable seat – and thus potentially become eligible to stand for the Labour leadership, once he had some parliamentary experience and once the party's difficulties made his unorthodoxy appealing – he still had his other political role: leading the GLC, which already gave him a higher profile than most MPs. Livingstone wanted the council to be a model for a future Labour government. He also wanted it to be a demonstration of what 'the post-1968 generation', as he called it, could achieve as politicians and social reformers. And perhaps even more than either, he wanted to change London. 'We didn't want to see London continue to decline,' he told me.

The unusual ambitiousness of his administration was very public. It promoted and organised its activities around big themes: 1983 was named Peace Year, 1984 was Anti-Racism Year, 1985 Jobs Year. The implication was that the GLC was playing a significant part in solving the main problems of the era, with the capital setting an example to Britain and the wider world. 'We came in with incredible confidence and optimism about what we could do,' remembered Michael Ward, one of Livingstone's key lieutenants. That confidence was everywhere in the council's communications: from its combative press releases to its suddenly ubiquitous 'Working for London' slogan; from its unusually slick municipal branding and logos to the billboards it put up across the city, which were collages of provocative messages and imagery. 'Keep London Out of the Killing Ground', urged one Peace Year poster, showing Tower Bridge and St Paul's cathedral menaced by giant Soviet and American missiles. In their visual style, the posters were halfway between clever modern advertising and Weimar-era agitprop. 'We were certainly never knowingly undersold,' said Ward.

But the GLC was still only a local council, a couple of decades old, in an ancient and centralised country, which was becoming more so under the rule of a Conservative government profoundly hostile to Livingstone's small Labour faction. His party had won power in London narrowly, under a different leader. And the GLC's official functions were limited: either complicated emergency roles such as flood prevention and running the fire service, or tricky strategic ones such as city planning, or seemingly minor ones such as managing parks and cultural venues, which it had to share with the capital's three dozen often highly territorial borough councils.

The Thatcher government reduced the GLC's powers further. In 1984, in the aftermath of Livingstone's failed attempt to slash tube and bus fares – his outlawed Fare's Fair policy – the Tories took away the GLC's responsibility for public transport. This was only part of a more fundamental attack. The successful Conservative manifesto at the 1983 election described the GLC, which the Tories themselves had created, as 'a wasteful and unnecessary tier of government'. The manifesto promised that the government would solve this problem, by taking up an idea that had been floating around in Conservative circles ever since the early 1970s, when the previous Labour GLC administration had briefly threatened to create a more equal London. The GLC would be abolished.

Though Livingstone's GLC fought determinedly and ingeniously against it, spinning out the struggle for years, the prospect of abolition sat under his administration like a ticking bomb. Meanwhile, an actual unexploded bomb, probably from a Second World War air raid, lay undetected in the silt of the Thames a couple of hundred yards from County Hall. The bomb was only discovered, well into Livingstone's tenure, when the GLC had the river dredged for a new pier so that visitors could arrive by boat at the Festival Hall. The bomb was so powerful that much of central London was evacuated for its removal.

Livingstone's administration responded to the hostile circumstances in which it was forced to operate with a mixture of ingenuity, urgency and magical thinking. The urgency was evident in the rapid succession of policies the council enacted, right up until the last days before it was abolished. Staff still working at County Hall then were unofficially told, 'Get whatever resources you can out of the building.' Photocopiers and other office equipment were removed and distributed to community organisations that the council had been funding.

The GLC's magical thinking was evident in its belief that a city council with little power by European or North American standards could, for example, opt out of the Cold War, by declaring London a nuclear-free zone. As the home of the Ministry of Defence, and of a prime minister absolutely committed to nuclear weapons, the city remained one of the Cold War's main capitals, whatever the GLC did or said. But for Livingstone's administration, symbolic gestures were sometimes as important as practical measures.

In many ways, ingenuity was his GLC's most striking quality. And this ingenuity was most usefully applied to finding money. How exactly the council was funded was such a complicated question, so tangled and knotted by years of wrangling between the council, central government, the courts and the boroughs, that even Livingstone himself found aspects of it 'incomprehensible' when he first became leader, despite his huge appetite for the minutiae of local government and the decade he had already spent in County Hall. But he was a fast learner, and so was his chair of finance, John McDonnell. They mastered the basics of GLC finance: that the council was funded by a patchwork of grants from Whitehall and by a property tax, the rates, which the GLC set and levied on London's homeowners and business properties. Then McDonnell and his staff combed through the legislation covering all this, to see if it contained any revenue-raising powers which previous administrations had not sufficiently exploited.

It did. In 1972, the Conservative government of Edward Heath had passed a Local Government Act. A typically elaborate Heath reform, almost 450 pages long, it reorganised the structures, administrative boundaries and some of the financing of local government across much of England and Wales. Buried deep in the legislation, under the bland heading 'Miscellaneous', was clause 137. 'Power of local authorities to incur expenditure for certain purposes not otherwise authorised,' it began, intriguingly. 'A local authority may ... incur expenditure which in their opinion is in the interests of their area or any part of it or all or some of its inhabitants.' The only limit on this essentially undefined spending was that it had to be funded by an increase in the rates not greater than '2p in the pound ... for that year.'

Two pence in the pound did not sound much. But London had so many ratepayers, and by the 1980s so many of them had valuable properties, thanks to several property booms during the 1970s, that the Livingstone administration was able to use this discretionary power to raise about £40 million a year. This was over 40 times as much as the previous, Conservative-run GLC had obtained through clause 137, and represented an increase in the council's revenue of almost 5 per cent.

Moreover, by permitting local authorities to spend their clause 137 money on anything, as long as 'in their opinion' it was 'in the interests' of their residents, the legislation created a huge opportunity for any council which wanted to test out radical ideas. Such a scenario had probably not been envisaged when the Act was drafted in the early 1970s, when London's new urban left was still in its infancy, and most local authorities were still conservative institutions. The legislation was also a product of a more politically permissive age: the Heath government was less concerned with hoarding power and controlling spending than Thatcher's would be. Yet it was her government that would have to deal with the consequences of the Act's loose drafting.

Other extra funds flowed unexpectedly to Livingstone's GLC. The Fare's Fair policy had put the council £125 million in debt, because the GLC had subsidised the reduced ticket prices. When the policy was outlawed, the council increased the rates to pay off the debt in a single year, 1982, and then did not lower them again, so in each subsequent year the GLC had an extra £125 million to spend. Added to the clause 137 revenue, this money meant that while Thatcher was imposing austerity across much of the country, in London Livingstone could outspend his GLC predecessors by roughly a fifth in real terms.

'It was the nirvana!' McDonnell told me with uncharacteristic excitement, 41 years later. 'You could raise the rates ... We could borrow cheaply from the City ... There were bits of creative accounting that went on ... I started with a £1 billion budget and ended up with £3 billion.'

Another section of the Local Government Act was exploited by the Livingstone administration. Clause 142 allowed any local authority to 'make ... arrangements whereby the public may ... readily obtain ... information concerning the services ... provided by the authority'. The legislation helpfully provided examples. A council could 'arrange for the publication within their area of information on matters relating to [its] local government'; or 'arrange for the delivery of lectures and addresses and the holding of discussions on such matters'; or 'arrange for the display of pictures, cinematograph films or models or the holding of exhibitions relating to such matters'. Thus the Heath government inadvertently encouraged Livingstone's GLC to produce a constant stream of newspapers, newsletters, reports, pamphlets, posters and stickers promoting its activities and stances. McDonnell believed that not nearly enough Londoners knew what the council actually did. One of its responsibilities was road management. 'So I had someone go round putting GLC stickers on every push-button pedestrian crossing.'

Much of this promotional material was more visually striking, and therefore more memorable, than the left's usually dour and inky publicity because the council had the money and the initiative to hire visual professionals: both commercial advertising agencies – the

GLC's use of them would influence New Labour – and leftwing artists such as Peter Kennard, a maker of angry photomontages who was already working for the Campaign for Nuclear Disarmament. At the GLC, as throughout his career, Livingstone would take his collaborators where he could find them.

He worked from a desk thickly covered in neat piles of papers, in a palatial County Hall office which was nevertheless smaller and less grand than the traditional GLC leader's quarters, which were still occupied by the leader of the Tory opposition group. Livingstone was aware of the value of populist gestures. He was the first GLC leader to be addressed by his first name by the 7,000 County Hall staff. He was more visible there than his predecessors: loping along the endless corridors, rarely wearing a suit, chatting to staff and councillors in his nasal drone, dropping in on the council's key committees, listening, making interventions, cajoling people, gathering intelligence, forming new alliances.

His administration had a majority of eight, unusually small for the GLC, and it soon shrank to four when two Labour councillors defected to the SDP. The remaining Labour councillors divided into three groups: 22 leftwingers, 16 rightwingers and 10 from the centre of the party. So he could rely completely on less than a quarter of the council – with further defections to the SDP expected at any moment. For his administration to survive, let alone get anything significant done, he had to manoeuvre carefully. Rightwing Labour councillors were offered positions on committees to keep them busy. Centrists were listened to by Livingstone with apparent respect, and reassured that he was not a leftwing fanatic but a pragmatist. Like the House of Commons on which it was partly modelled, County Hall served a lot of alcohol. Labour councillors who drank too much were tracked down in the toilets when their votes were needed. At least once, Livingstone got the support of a paralytic Labour councillor by holding their hand up for them in the debating chamber.

He also protected his regime in subtler ways. A lover of meetings and how they could be manipulated, he scheduled the extra council sessions which the Conservatives often requested, in the hope of defeating his fragile administration, for Friday afternoons. He knew that by then some of the wealthier Tory councillors would have left London for their weekend houses. Still a broad reader despite all his GLC duties, he got the idea for this ruse from the Roman historian Suetonius, who had recorded that Julius Caesar took the same approach with landowning senators.

One of Livingstone's strengths as a tactician was his eye for others' weaknesses. Yet about his own political flaws, he could be less clear-sighted. In public, he was a great talker: cheeky, direct and colloquial, never flustered, always quotable. But sometimes he talked too much. During his first two years as GLC leader, the buzz he got from being frank, from breaking taboos, combined with his desire to get the council and himself more attention, became a kind of addiction to controversy – an addiction he never completely conquered. Three decades later, he self-admiringly titled his autobiography *You Can't Say That*.

In the early 1980s, as subsequently, the press were an almost insatiable audience for his views: on everything from the conflict in Northern Ireland ('the last colonial war') to relationships ('everyone is bisexual') to the wedding of Prince Charles and Diana Spencer ('I would like to see the abolition of the monarchy'). The problem was not always the views themselves. Though controversial, they were the views of a large and growing minority of leftwing and socially liberal Britons. The problem was how little these views sometimes seemed to have to do with his presumed job of running the troubled capital. He was often stretched too thin, and too caught up in the drama of being a controversialist: saying risky things, justifying them, sometimes having to qualify them, often having controversies follow him around. The more publicly cautious McDonnell sometimes found Livingstone's outspokenness maddening. 'He'd drive you up the wall at times,' he told me. 'He'd say something, and you'd think, "Who thought that one up?"' But Livingstone could not resist talking to journalists. With County Hall directly across the river from the Commons, where so many of them were based, 'Red Ken' became the next bogeyman for the rightwing papers as Benn's public profile gradually diminished from 1983 onwards.

Much of the Labour party, including its leaders, Foot and then Kinnock, distanced themselves from Livingstone during the early 1980s, just as they had distanced themselves from Benn since the mid-1970s. County Hall received few supportive or inquisitive visits from mainstream Labour politicians, despite all the interesting experiments in modernising Labour politics that the GLC was conducting inside. More often, the national party briefed journalists against the council. Only Corbyn and a few other leftwing MPs, plus a handful of leaders and councillors from the left's strongholds in the inner London boroughs actively supported Livingstone in his first, often difficult years as GLC leader.

Some of the reactions to his tenure were extreme. In October 1981, after a Provisional IRA nail bomb outside a barracks in Chelsea had killed two Londoners and injured dozens of soldiers and civilians, the *Sun* misrepresented Livingstone as an 'apologist' for such violence, and described him as 'the most odious man in Britain'. The next day, he was due to give a widely publicised speech to the City of London's Junior Chamber of Commerce. He liked to seek converts in unlikely places. As he walked up to the venue in the normally peaceful City of London, as usual without a security escort, he was approached by two smartly dressed men. One of them said, 'Good evening', shook his hand, and then sprayed his face and eyes with red paint. Livingstone grappled with the man, grabbed the can, and ran into the building. He cleaned himself up and gave the speech anyway. A group calling itself the 'Friends of Ulster' claimed responsibility for the assault. It was reported in the press but not condemned. There was a widespread feeling that he was getting what he deserved.

As well as his outspokenness and Machiavellian brand of leftwing politics, there was also something about Red Ken's masculinity that provoked people. In Britain, one common conception about socialist politicians or leftwing union leaders was that they were tough working-class figures: usually middle-aged men, from industrial backgrounds, who to an extent had earned the right to be bolshy, even in the eyes of the right in parliament and the media. Later on in his career, John McDonnell would benefit from being seen in this way. But Livingstone was different. While from a working-class background, he was not a former coalminer or factory worker, but a former lab technician who famously kept newts: in other words, a bit of a nerd. Still in his thirties, he was skinny, wore sometimes dapper clothes that did not hide it, and spoke in a small, needling voice that suggested bureaucratic meetings rather than rousing oratory at mass rallies. Like the even less macho Jeremy Corbyn, who would also enrage people more deeply than his policies alone could explain, Livingstone was not a muscular socialist of the sort that the British establishment had learned to semi-tolerate. He was a smart alec, scientifically trained, media-savvy and a little sexually ambiguous: a socialist suited to a more fluid age.

But in the Britain of the early 1980s that age had yet to properly begin. For much of 1981 and 1982, he and his GLC administration were extraordinarily unpopular. In August 1981 his personal approval rating dropped to 11 per cent. For many Londoners, he was too radical. To some leftwing voters and activists, including some of his *Briefing* comrades, he was not radical enough: making seemingly bold moves on issues such as public transport fares, but then retreating when the establishment pushed back. He felt vulnerable to an internal coup, to his own methods being turned against him, and believed that the only thing preventing one was an absence of possible alternative leaders. But that vacuum was not going to last. The GLC's new intake of councillors was more able than usual, thanks partly to the talent-spotting he had done. Its most promising and ambitious members, such as McDonnell and Valerie Wise, were gaining experience all the time.

Livingstone worked harder and harder: over 70 hours a week. He did not have much else in his life. His first marriage, to Christine Chapman, a teacher he had met at the start of his political career, had ended in 1980. He moved out of their basement flat and into a bedsit in a house full of medical students. He was happy living in unflashy places, having lived with his parents until well into his twenties, but his bedsit was modest even by those standards. Much of the middle of the room was taken up by a quarter-sized snooker table which he had bought himself for his first Christmas apart from Chapman. He would come back from long days of difficult GLC meetings and practise his shots on his own. Snooker was an appropriate game for him, with its need for precise manoeuvres, planning ahead, and blocking off opportunities for your opponent. But interviewers who visited the bedsit once he became GLC leader focused instead on how minimal, eccentric, even pathetic his home life seemed to them, for a man in his mid-thirties with such major public responsibilities. They portrayed him as a kind of hair-shirted fanatic. Another way of looking at these encounters, and the access he was allowing journalists who were essentially hostile, was that he was exposing himself too much. If he did not change his approach to leading the GLC, he would be eaten up.

He did change. From late 1982 onwards, he led with more focus on what the council could actually achieve, with the powers it still had, rather than on how disruptive of political norms he and the GLC could be. He stopped picking fights so continuously. In 1984, he was contacted by Buckingham Palace and told that the Queen would like to unveil the Thames Barrier in east London, a spectacular and high-profile defence system against flooding which had finally been completed after a decade of stop-start construction. Livingstone was still a republican, and some leftwing GLC councillors wanted the ceremony to be conducted by the longest-serving worker at the construction site or by an East End celebrity. But Livingstone saw a political opportunity in doing things differently. With the Thatcher government in the process of trying to abolish the GLC, and the prime minister widely believed to have a cool relationship with the Queen, he agreed to let the Queen officially open the barrier with him.

Before the ceremony, 'We encouraged media speculation that this revealed the Queen's opposition to abolition,' he wrote afterwards. The increased coverage the ceremony received because of her involvement was also a chance to publicise the GLC's value, flood defence being one its responsibilities. And most deftly, in some ways most shamelessly of all, Livingstone used his elderly, more traditionally minded mother as a way for him to avoid having to spend a politically awkward amount of time in the royal presence. His mother sailed downstream with the Queen and Prince Philip on the royal barge, while Livingstone waited for them at the barrier. His mother chatted to the monarch and her husband about horse racing. When they disembarked, Philip told Livingstone, 'Your mother's a lively old stick.' The GLC leader, smartly dressed for once, bowed to the Queen, so deeply and correctly that it was possible to see the gesture as ironic. Then she pressed a button to raise the seven gates of the silvery, improbably beautiful flood barrier. Two of the gates got stuck in the mud of the riverbed for a few moments, but Livingstone was one of the few people who noticed.

It was an era when spectacle and symbolism were becoming more important, in politics as in culture and consumerism. Thatcher understood this: she had used the Falklands War as an advertisement for her brand of patriotic Conservatism. And so did Livingstone, unlike most 1980s Labour politicians. His GLC hired more press officers. It reintroduced herbaceous borders to local parks, which had been pared back to bland expanses of grass and trees by government spending cuts. At the Crystal Palace athletics stadium in south London, the council hung a 'GLC Working for London' banner beside the running track, right where the 1500 metres began, because recent British Olympic success at that distance meant that the races got TV coverage. The council's canny self-promotion became part of the London landscape. Beside a busy slip road leading on to the huge roundabout at Brent Cross in north London, a sign read for years: 'GLC Waste Disposal Unit Working for London'.

Meanwhile, Livingstone also began to turn his notoriety into a more palatable, sometimes almost apolitical, form of celebrity. His quick, dry wit – 'Quite frankly, *I* wouldn't agree with what I was quoted as saying,' he said after one attempted monstering by the *Sun* – meant that he became a frequent guest on *Question Time* and other TV and radio discussion programmes. Britons who did not live in London, along with many who did, discovered that he was more fun than the dogmatic, dangerous leftist portrayed by the papers. In BBC radio's Man of the Year poll in 1982, he came second behind the Pope, the widely admired political liberal John Paul II.

The government's wish to abolish the GLC raised Livingstone's profile and popularity further. He became an underdog. Many people who did not share his politics nevertheless believed that the way to remove his administration was through the ballot box, rather than by legislation which would leave London without a municipal government. That the Conservatives' motives were so blatantly partisan further helped his cause. In 1984 the trade and industry secretary Norman Tebbit, one of Thatcher's most aggressive ministers, told a gathering of London Tories that the GLC was 'typical of [a] new, modern, divisive form of socialism. It must be defeated. So, we shall abolish the GLC.' Even Kinnock began appearing at County Hall to lend the anti-abolition campaign his support.

Livingstone also got better at using the council's bureaucracy. Like the civil service on which it was modelled, it was large, able, sometimes conservative and self-regarding, and very capable of obstructing its supposed political masters. Thirty-seven thousand people worked for the GLC in an almost incomprehensible scattering of buildings across London. While the council's ruling politicians changed frequently, thanks to the capital's volatile politics, the more senior GLC officials did not. In key places such as the legal department – 'the largest in Britain', according to Livingstone – white men from elite universities were accustomed to conducting the council's business largely as they saw fit. 'The day after we were elected,' remembered Ward, 'we, the new members, all got a memo [from a senior official], saying that in a week's time there would be a seminar for us on how the council was run.' The strong implication was that it was not run by politicians.

The seminar never happened. Livingstone and his lieutenants made it clear that this time they wanted the GLC to be under political control. The officials should not have been surprised. A suspicion of bureaucracies, and sometimes outright hostility towards them, had been a central feature of the 1968 uprisings which had politicised Livingstone in the first place. He also had a history of clashing with officials whom he considered unhelpful, first as a borough councillor in Lambeth and Camden, then during his first eight years as a GLC councillor. As GLC leader, his initial plan was to 'take over the machine', by forcing two-thirds of the council's senior officers into early retirement, replacing them with less powerful and less independent figures, and then being able to intimidate these more junior officials into being more cooperative. But his small majority made that impossible. The Labour rightwingers among the councillors, whom he now needed to keep onside, would not have supported such a ruthless and partisan scheme.

So instead he sought to make converts among the senior County Hall officers. A crucial one was the council's 'Comptroller of Financial Services', Maurice Stonefrost, a deceptively charming man who had overseen the deep spending cuts by the previous Labour administration, which Livingstone had vehemently and unsuccessfully opposed. Despite this history, the two men warmed to each other once Livingstone became leader. Unlike many of his colleagues, Stonefrost considered it his primary task to serve whoever was GLC leader. An enthusiast for fast cars in his time off, he was also intrigued by Livingstone's appetite for risk. Both men were intensely interested in the detail of government as well. Stonefrost patiently explained to Livingstone and McDonnell the complexities of how the GLC was funded, and relished trying to keep the council afloat financially once the Thatcher government began to cut those funding sources off. The guerrilla war quality of Livingstone's GLC made working for it more compelling than the usual routines of local government.

To McDonnell, who had a more favourable view of the County Hall civil service than Livingstone, 'It was almost as if they were waiting for us, those people in the bureaucracy who wanted to *do* things.' As finance chair, he had 'a team around me' of council officials that was 'unchallengeable'. 'When I went into negotiations with ministers, I was always better briefed than the minister.'

Whenever the administration wanted to test the boundaries of what it was legally allowed to do, which was quite often, it sought advice from outside barristers known to have Labour sympathies – rather than from those with Conservative leanings, as had been the case during previous, more cautious Labour administrations. And whenever the chair of one of the council's committees had had enough of that committee's chief official, the official would be removed. Through this gradual purge, Livingstone was able to clear out 'most of the officers I was determined to get rid of', he wrote afterwards, 'within two years'. Grounds for dismissal, in his view, were 'incompetence', 'racism', 'Tory sympathies' or a 'simple inability to understand what we were about'. Traditional civil service neutrality was acceptable, in his view, only if it meant accepting and facilitating whatever his administration wanted to do.

This internal revolution did not succeed entirely. 'I'd got no more control over the legal department at the end of my time than I had at the beginning,' Livingstone told me. 'They were implacably conservative. When we brought in our first gender and ethnic monitoring' – a policy which the GLC pioneered – 'some of the highest refusal rates when it came to filling in the forms were among the lawyers.'

When the monitoring forms were completed, they revealed that the GLC's progress towards racial and gender equality was significant but hardly complete. Between 1981 and 1985, the proportion of female council employees grew by almost a third, and of black employees by over half. But the proportions were still low, at 21 per cent and 11 per cent respectively. Some powerful parts of the council were diverse, such as the innovative women's committee, set up under Livingstone to make the GLC and the capital better for women. Yet elsewhere at County Hall, 'White men did most of the senior professional jobs ... Women and black people worked as cooks, cleaners, messengers and junior clerical and administrative staff,' wrote Paul Soto in *A Taste of Power*, a broadly positive but sometimes critical collection co-written by close observers of and participants in Livingstone's GLC. 'In any of the GLC's canteens you were almost certain to be served by a black woman.' By 1983, the third year of the Livingstone administration, out of 550 senior council officials, only 15 were black and 35 were women.

In a country where parliament and many other powerful institutions were still all white and overwhelmingly male, however, the GLC's efforts to diversify did stand out. Not so much for their achievements as their seriousness: the council established an equal opportunities unit, one of the first in Britain, to reform its recruitment, promotion and disciplinary processes. The chance to job-share was introduced for all positions. Two workplace nurseries were set up, and a childcare allowance was paid to staff on low wages. In many ways, the GLC behaved like an enlightened corporate employer, decades before such businesses became common.

The council also pioneered the use of procurement contracts and conditional public funding to pressure companies and other organisations into reflecting the actual population mix of London. One of the enterprises it subsidised was *City Limits*, a listings weekly with a leftwing edge which was run as a cooperative by former staff from the once countercultural, now increasingly commercial magazine *Time Out*. The radical politics of *City Limits* did not save it from scrutiny by the council's diversity monitors. 'At one of our meetings of leftwing councillors,' Ward told me, 'Paul Boateng [a black Labour GLC councillor] turned up and said, "All the staff at *City Limits* are white! They can't have another penny until they integrate their staff."'

Ward was chair of the GLC's industry and employment committee, which gave grants to new small businesses, to try to revive London's economy and simultaneously reshape it in favour of the disadvantaged. With *City Limits*, 'I got in one of the people who was running it, and said: "Look mate, no more money until you integrate. Your next appointment is going to be a black person." And it was.'

Unlike Benn at the Department of Industry a few years earlier, Livingstone and his comrades could not easily be overruled by a higher Labour authority. There was no Harold Wilson or array of other senior party figures with whom discontented GLC officials could form alliances in order to kill off Livingstone's ideas or water them down. Since Labour was not in power nationally, and since the shadow cabinet had no formal say over what Labour GLC leaders did, Livingstone had relatively free rein. At least for now.

Where the council made the most difference to London, both during the 1980s and for decades beyond, was in changing the city's sense of itself. Rather than being an essentially traditional, officially monocultural, in some ways tired and declining former imperial capital, London began to turn into a place where multiculturalism and other new ways of living were supported and celebrated by politicians. This idea of London as a modern and innovative city is now a commonplace, even a cliché, among politicians on the right as well as the left. But during Livingstone's GLC, rethinking and reshaping the capital in this way was intensely controversial.

To a degree, it was also an accident. 'What we'd really wanted to do was build housing and modernise the transport system,' Livingstone told me. 'But those we were blocked on.' So instead of transforming the city physically, in the manner of past municipal socialist reformers such as Livingstone's hero Herbert Morrison of the London County Council, the GLC sought to change its collective psychology.

One part of this huge project was to get Londoners to accept their city's new social realities. After postwar immigration, after the shrinking and fragmentation of the capital's old working class by deindustrialisation, and after the social reforms of the 1960s such as the legalisation of homosexuality, 'London was now a collection of minorities', Livingstone acknowledged in 1987 – long before most British politicians. 'The only way it could work as a city was if each group tolerated the others.'

But Livingstone wanted more than just social peace. 'I came into politics because I wish to change society,' he told his early biographer John Carvel in 1984. 'And that means changing the hearts and minds of people ... I've no doubt that by the end of this century, if we continue to fight for ... women's rights, gay rights and a proper equal opportunities policy for blacks, we'll ... change attitudes nationally.'

Yet that could not be done just by sitting in County Hall and telling Londoners that diversity was a good thing. The GLC needed to listen carefully to people's experiences of their ever more multicultural city, with its multiplying inequalities, opportunities and frictions. And they needed to address the social problems that this great flux produced in a new way. Rather than centrally design and then disseminate solutions, as the paternalistic postwar state had done, London's government, in Livingstone's view, should provide the disadvantaged with advice and funds, and then let them improve their own lives. 'People have to do it for themselves,' Livingstone told the *Guardian* journalist Terry Coleman in December 1981. Coleman was the paper's star interviewer and a specialist in lightly mocking scepticism. He summarised Livingstone's worldview as wanting 'each factory run by its own workers, and each school by the parents and teachers'. Without fully appreciating its significance, Coleman had found the libertarian, even anarchic strand in Livingstone's thinking that connected him back to Benn and Allende and 1968. Coleman suggested to Livingstone that, in fact, 'Few people could run anything.' Livingstone completely disagreed: 'The potential's there in everybody.' To unlock it, the GLC gave out grants: to women's groups, peace groups and gay groups; black groups, Asian groups and disabled groups; nurseries and playgroups; law centres and tenants' groups; leftwing groups and green groups; youth centres and pensioners' groups; Christian groups and Jewish groups.

McDonnell was in charge of the grants programme. In some ways, it was an extension of his work with community groups and anti-racist bodies in Hayes. Thanks partly to that experience, he understood how more socially conservative Londoners could be persuaded to support, or at least tolerate, radical initiatives to help minorities. He explained the GLC's approach to me: 'If we can get the bread-and-butter issues right, people will give us a bit of leeway on other issues which they may not support at first, such as the equalities issues. They will think, "God, what have they come up with now? But actually they have just reduced my bus fares."'

A decade before New Labour, the Livingstone administration used private polling and focus groups to test its policies. 'You'd watch the focus groups through two-way mirrors,' McDonnell remembered. 'We'd say to the participants, "This is what we are going to do [as a policy]. What do you think? And what language do we need to use to persuade you?"'

While the GLC tried to mould public opinion, outside interests naturally tried to influence the grants programme. The Board of Deputies of British Jews, which had been founded in 1760 and saw itself as the pre-eminent Jewish body in the country, worked with Livingstone's GLC from 1981 to 1983. But this relationship, already tense due to differences over Israel and the Palestinians, unravelled when the board told the council that it wanted to vet all grant applications by Jewish organisations. Some of these applications came from entities such as the Jewish Socialists' Group, which was much more left-leaning and critical of Israel than the board. When the GLC refused to hand over this vetting role, the board stopped working with the council. The council carried on giving grants to Jewish groups of which the board disapproved. The basis had been laid for a long feud.

By 1986, the GLC was funding over 2,000 organisations and annually distributing grants worth over £50 million. Its approach was often proactive. Some GLC staff working for the grants teams were given cars, fuelled from County Hall's own petrol pump, their boots filled with application forms for funding, and sent off across London, looking to make contact with organisations with whom they had only had a brief introductory phone call – or just to knock on doors. Potential recipients of grants were sometimes advised by the GLC about how best to apply for GLC funds.

As a way to spend public money and try to change society, it was new and risky. The radicalism of some of the groups funded, the lack of close supervision of how they spent the money, and the potential electoral benefits for the Livingstone administration all had the potential to enrage the GLC's many enemies. McDonnell told Carvel that the 'political returns' from the grant system were 'absolutely enormous'.

There were also more subtle frictions and tensions in the grant system. Volunteers in community groups, who were often unpaid, worked alongside paid GLC employees. And for all its talk of giving power and resources away, the council controlled the distribution process. Sometimes, its decisions were ideological. It refused a grant application from a group campaigning for a new airport to be built in London's then empty and derelict docklands – the scheme would later become City Airport – on the grounds that the project was against GLC policy.

Ultimately, a city government with a charismatic and powerful leader and a distinct vision was only going to give local groups so much say. And yet, as the groups receiving GLC funding grew in confidence and experience, so they were likely to want more say: over their corner of the city, or the city as a whole, or the practices of the council itself – or quite possibly all of these. The longer the Livingstone administration went on, the harder it might be for it to reconcile the centralising and decentralising forces which it had unleashed.

Yet this future conundrum was not what bothered the rightwing press. 'Militant lesbians, babies for peace, Irish and black extremists, prostitutes' collectives, left-wing theatre groups and revolutionary "creatives" of all kinds have soaked up millions of ratepayers' money,' claimed the *Daily Mail* in May 1983. 'Terroristic rates [on businesses] have produced a rash of bankruptcies and a flight of firms' away from London. The fact that the GLC also funded hundreds of utterly conventional social organisations such as sporting bodies and community associations, a reflection of Livingstone's own conventional side, with his love of London buses and gardening, was ignored by the press in its rush to condemn the GLC as 'loony'.

The choice of adjective was inadvertently revealing. Not just that it had previously been applied to Benn, but also that it suggested that there was an instability, even a feeling of insecurity, within the rightwing critique of the GLC. 'Loonies', at least in the tabloid sense, were scary as well as silly. The papers could not decide whether Livingstone's GLC was eccentric, deluded or deeply threatening. As with the government's plan to abolish the GLC, there was a haste and crudity to the press attacks which suggested a degree of panic. Red Ken had to be stopped, before his council began not just to alter London for good, but to 'change attitudes nationally', as he put it.

A few people were so enraged by the 'loonies' at County Hall that they turned to violence. 'I had my windows smashed,' McDonnell told me. 'Bottles broken into my children's sandpit in the back garden. It was horrendous. On one occasion, I was driving my car, and there was a knocking sound going on. So I took it to a local garage. They checked all over, and then they checked the wheels. All my wheel nuts had been unscrewed.' The consequences could have been fatal.

For many younger Londoners – the people who would establish the capital's social norms in future – the GLC's subsidising and advocacy of diversity was at the least intriguing, sometimes politically formative, and sometimes life-changing. In a city where previously most people had paid little attention to their municipal government, supporting the GLC became a strong political marker: on T-shirts, badges, window stickers, car stickers and posters; in pop songs and interviews with famous musicians; in fashion magazines and at leftwing gatherings of all kinds.

Non-Londoners were sometimes intrigued by the GLC as well. In 1984 I was 14 and living on a suburban army housing estate in a Tory town in Surrey. One evening, I went to London with my parents and older sister to see a play at the Festival Hall. The GLC's now infamous headquarters at County Hall, which I had been reading about in my father's copies of *The Times*, was only a couple of hundred yards away, further along the south bank. In the Festival Hall, the GLC had overhauled the programming and catering to make them more accessible to London as a whole. I can't remember what play we saw, but I do remember eating my first ever rice salad, from the Festival Hall buffet – in its food choices Livingstone's GLC sometimes showed its hippy side – and feeling that I was getting a tiny taste of another England, excitingly different from the one I knew.

*

For the curious and committed alike, there was one particularly vivid expression of what the GLC was about. Again it was made possible by the 1972 Local Government Act. Heath's high-minded legislation had suggested that councils could organise 'lectures', 'discussions' and 'exhibitions' about what they did. Characteristically, Livingstone's GLC interpreted this in the broadest possible way. It would put on festivals.

Before his administration, the GLC had already been involved in outdoor public celebrations, for example around the Queen's Jubilee in 1977, and in putting on live music, for example in park bandstands. But the models that Livingstone and his comrades had in mind were more radical. In Italy and France, the Communist Party had for years been organising big outdoor gatherings where political messages and loyalties were consolidated and converts were made, in theory at least, while rock bands played and people of all ages ate and drank in the sun. In Britain during the late 1970s and early 1980s, the Rock Against Racism movement had staged boisterous free carnivals in London and a few other cities, facilitated by sympathetic leftwing councils and featuring multiracial line-ups of punk and reggae bands. The divisiveness of Thatcherism and the era's general political turmoil meant that more pop musicians than usual were prepared to take political stands. Attendances at these events were huge: up to 100,000.

Livingstone's GLC was much more comfortable with popular culture than its Labour predecessors in County Hall, which had instead prioritised widening access to high culture, by expensively subsidising some tickets for the opera and ballet. Livingstone had been a rock fan since the 1960s, and his generation of leftwing London politicians were often into contemporary African and South American music as well, which played an important part at anti-apartheid events and fundraisers for liberation movements in Latin America. The Livingstone administration concluded that a lot of the GLC's previous cultural policies had been too conservative, too narrow in their impact, and an inefficient use of public money.

Instead, the GLC would hold pop music festivals to promote itself and its annual campaigning themes. To help put together these ambitious events, it hired Mark Hollingsworth, a precocious management graduate in his mid-twenties who had recently helped both to professionalise and to radicalise the Glastonbury festival, by weaving into it speakers and messages from the Campaign for Nuclear Disarmament. To secure the best bands, the GLC also set up its own booking agency, Campaign Events. With an annual budget of over £1 million, it quickly became one of the most powerful booking agents in the world.

The GLC's attempt to combine politics and entertainment on a challengingly large scale started in 1983 with three free festivals to amplify its Peace Year campaign, held in local London parks. The experiment had mixed results. Huge numbers of people came, up to 80,000 at the biggest festival, from right across the spectrum of London subcultures: hippies, punks, black and white rude boys, middle-aged blues fans. The music ranged from mainstream pop groups such as Madness to the pantomime punk band The Damned, to the smooth leftwing soul of the Style Council. Anti-nuclear activists, such as women from the famous peace camp at Greenham Common, also appeared onstage. But the political content sometimes got lost amid the usual festival distractions of mud, drinking and drugs, and tribal rivalries between different groups of fans, which in the early 1980s were very strong. After The Damned, like all the other acts, were only allowed to play an abbreviated set of songs, some of their fans threw mud, cans and bottles at the performers that followed, including the women from Greenham. A model of peace and happy diversity it was not.

But the GLC's festival organisers were quick learners. The following year, the most high-profile event they staged was in a more controllable and more obviously political place: the south bank in central London, including County Hall. The Jobs for a Change festivals were partly conceived by Michael Ward, one of the council's most important and innovative economic strategists. He and his colleagues on the industry and employment committee felt that the GLC's approach to unemployment, which included Benn-style policies such as supporting cooperatives and subsidising workers to run struggling factories, was not 'getting through' to Londoners. For these and subsequent festivals, instead of trying to convey political messages mainly through a few speeches, as before, the council followed Hollingsworth's advice and did something more modern and, for politics, still quite novel.

The GLC sought to integrate its ideas into almost every element of the festivals, and into their overall feel – to influence festival goers' thinking without them always noticing. Familiar with the methods of contemporary marketing and branding, and aware that the connotations of leftwing politics were becoming increasingly negative as Thatcherism became more dominant, Hollingsworth wanted the GLC to stage political events that were both 'positive' and in some of their propaganda 'subliminal'. In the divided Britain of 1984, with the miners' strike recently begun, this was quite a task.

Moreover, Hollingsworth and the GLC had another ambition for the festivals. They wanted them to give people an experience which combined an unusual degree of both freedom and equality. On the one hand, Hollingsworth explained in 1987, 'The festival as a whole should be fluid, non-fixed. You have to set up a structure that people can play in. It has to be left to them to use the occasion how they want. You have to design it to give choices.' But at the same time, as the coordinator of the GLC's Jobs Year Dick Muskett put it, the festivals had to avoid feeling 'oppressive' to anyone. 'You have to make sure,' he went on, 'that women don't feel offended by what is going on ... You make sure that there are facilities for ... people with disabilities ... that there is plenty of space – and safe space – for children ... that there's a diversity of music that will appeal to the different cultures that exist in London, that are part of London ...'

In other words, the festivals were designed both to cater to individualism, which by the 1980s was such an obviously powerful force, and to make allowances for social disadvantage, so that the collective experience could be as equal as possible for all. Essentially, the festivals were supposed to be giant, day-long demonstrations of what Livingstone's GLC was about.

The first of two Jobs for a Change festivals took place in June 1984. For most of a midsummer day, from mid-morning until well into the evening, the south bank was effectively turned into a giant, immersive political installation. As well as two music stages, featuring overtly leftwing musicians such as Billy Bragg and the Redskins and more subtly subversive ones such as the Smiths, there were exhibition stalls for community groups and cooperatives, piles of GLC pamphlets, public debates, film showings, workshops, talks and exhibitions. Cast members were interviewed from the hugely popular recent TV drama about life on the dole, *Boys from the Blackstuff*.

County Hall itself was opened to the public. In its elaborate wood-panelled council chamber, there was a rolling debate about unemployment, in which everyone was invited to participate, and which lasted for five hours. Elsewhere in the building there was an exhibition about the work of the industry and employment committee, and a maze for festival goers to explore, in which doors printed with the government's policies led to dead ends, while those marked with the GLC's offered ways forward. But often people just chose to roam the building, or sit on the grand staircases, relishing the sense of a world turned upside down. In the polished corridors along which the council's senior officers usually strode, there were now skinheads, Rastafarians and Londoners of all sorts. Livingstone took in the scene, and his usually cool manner turned to giddy enthusiasm:

> People were sort of wandering in and just getting really happy and excited and talking. And there was an incredibly mutually supportive atmosphere in the whole building. I've just never felt anything like it before . . . in a political gathering . . . The buzz people got . . . from each other was incredible. You just saw the enthusiasm, that could be unleashed by a genuine socialist movement . . .

The freewheeling nature of the festival also left it open to disruption. While the Redskins were playing, dressed in their customary skinhead outfits, about eighty very different skinheads, members of the racist National Front who had been prevented by police from marching to nearby Trafalgar Square, forced their way through the crowd. They invaded the stage, and assaulted one of the musicians, who had to be taken to hospital. The National Front mob was then chased off the festival site by striking miners whom Hollingsworth had hired as security guards, partly as a way of giving GLC money to their strike fund. There was an idealistic side to the GLC festivals, an echo of politicised countercultural gatherings back in the 1960s – which was unsurprising given Livingstone's personal history – but there was also an enterprise and a tough-mindedness that was very 1980s.

As the day went on, Livingstone made a series of increasingly impassioned speeches from the music stages. The final one was just before the Smiths, then approaching their peak as Britain's most obsessively followed cult band, were due to take to the stage. Twenty thousand people had squeezed into the County Hall car park, and dozens more had scrambled up to risky vantage points, high among the columns and balconies of the building's starchy Neoclassical facade. Thinking that he was essentially the warm-up act, the GLC leader, incongruously wearing a tie, spoke only for a few minutes: a standard rant against the Thatcher government. But the applause he got was louder than that for the band.

In 1987, after the festivals were over, Livingstone talked about what he thought they had really been about. As well as promoting the GLC, and a new, more diverse idea of London, they had been against 'puritanism', he argued. He defined puritanism as

> an inability to come to terms with yourself physically and emotionally, to relate easily to others ... It's obviously a very important part of the engine of capital, in the sense that it drives people ... to control, to dominate ... And therefore an alternative world, a cooperative one, is going to mean ... [that] people will relate easier to each other, they will be able to come to terms with themselves, their own bodies, their own sexuality ... if you start to loosen those [attitudes], you actually call into question a whole lot of property relations as well – the whole balance of power between capital and labour. That is an absolutely frightening thing for the British establishment ...

In some ways, Livingstone's argument was simplistic. In Britain, the next few decades, with their frequent Conservative governments but gradual loosening of social mores, would demonstrate that social liberalism could spread without socialism. Meanwhile, big business would commodify much of the lives of many of those who did 'come to terms with themselves, their own bodies, their own sexuality', as he put it, through the fitness and sex industries and social media.

However, just because the social revolution that Livingstone's GLC helped start was partly co-opted does not reduce its significance. If anything, it suggests the opposite. And as for the other argument he made in 1987, about his GLC's festivals and other inclusive, culturally open activities being a 'frightening thing for the British establishment' – by 1987 he had already been proven right. At midnight on 31 March 1986, after a final festival outside County Hall, the GLC was abolished.

13

'A Lot of Hope Rides on
Our Victory Tonight'

The termination of the GLC was a brutal political act, even by the Thatcher administration's standards. It showed how far she and her ministers would go to shut down any opposition which they saw as a serious threat. In that sense, the abolition was a kind of coup, peaceful but profoundly anti-democratic. It also left London without a government, seemingly ignoring the fact that the city was only just emerging from its postwar slump. The problems that Livingstone's GLC had been beginning to address, such as the city's old and fragile public transport, could easily worsen again.

And yet, abolition also created new possibilities. Just as Livingstone's takeover of County Hall in 1981 had drawn in all kinds of leftists to work with him, so abolition dispersed them again, determined to apply the council's ideas to the wider world – or at least to find another way of making a political living.

One of this diaspora was Diane Abbott. Starting in 1984, she had become directly involved in the council, doing freelance shifts as a press officer. By that stage, despite the GLC's determined and inventive campaign against abolition, which recruited allies ranging from sympathetic advertising agencies to pro-democracy Tories in the House of Lords, it was fairly clear that the council would soon be erased, thanks to Thatcher's crushing Commons majority. Partly for that reason, and partly out of curiosity and ambition, Abbott had kept a career going in politics and television.

In 1982, she had left Thames Television for a younger and more risk-taking media company, TV-am, a London start-up which intended to transform the country's viewing habits and broadcast journalism itself by experimenting with a format then new to Britain, breakfast television. She was hired as a researcher and reporter, and also became the company's National Union of Journalists (NUJ) representative. Both jobs quickly turned into quite an education. Within a few weeks, TV-am's initial approach, of providing not bite-sized, easily digestible early morning news for busy viewers but a whole hour of current affairs, produced according to what the company's ostentatiously clever chief executive Peter Jay called a 'mission to explain', became a ratings disaster and a national laughing stock. The company's investors were horrified. Jay was persuaded to step down, and was replaced by an aristocratic Conservative MP and journalist, Jonathan Aitken, who had more charm and fewer fixed ideas about what constituted good television. Aitken allowed a complete and shameless overhaul of TV-am's programme, including the introduction as a presenter of Roland Rat, a relentlessly perky and nasal children's puppet; and also a drastic reduction of the company's generously sized workforce. As the NUJ's representative, Abbott's job was to negotiate with Aitken about the redundancies.

They got on surprisingly well. After Cambridge, she was used to posh people with different politics, and sometimes intrigued by them. She also agreed with Aitken that the TV-am workforce needed to be shrunk if the company was to survive. Despite her radical politics, she could also be pragmatic – you could say, selective in the application of her ethics – in the tradition of her tough ancestors in rural Jamaica. The redundancies were made, the programme was moved downmarket, and the ratings and advertising revenues eventually recovered. Meanwhile in her non-NUJ work at TV-am, Abbott acquired a reputation for being able but sometimes overcommitted and not always thorough. She stayed with the company for three years, quite a long time by the impatient standards of her twenties and early thirties. Afterwards, she and Aitken kept in touch, becoming close friends. He eventually became godfather to her only child.

One of the attractions of breakfast television for her was that her work was usually done by lunchtime. That left much of the rest of the day free for her main interest, politics. As well as her involvement with the GLC, from 1982 she also had a more formal and public role, as a local councillor in the central London borough of Westminster.

On the face of it, it was a strange place for an ambitious young leftist to begin their political career: a generally prosperous, normally Tory-controlled borough, with a council led for much of the 1980s by Shirley Porter, whose efforts to make her party's dominance permanent, through gerrymandering, were later found to be illegal. Yet in the poorer northern part of the borough some wards usually voted Labour. One of them, Harrow Road, included the area where Abbott had lived as a young child, and which still meant a lot to her. In 1981 she bought a small top-floor flat in the ward, using a mortgage scheme operated by the council. Becoming a property-owner with Tory help was another sign of her pragmatism. Then she won selection as one of Labour's ward candidates. In the following year's local elections, she promoted herself as 'Harrow Road's first black Labour candidate', committed to 'Giving Black People a Fair Share' of council services. It was a risky approach. Despite being racially diverse, the borough had never had a black councillor. But she won. Her victory made the national press, with a mention in the *Guardian*. As at Cambridge and Harrow County School for Girls, she now had the double-edged prestige of being a pioneer.

With her party in opposition in the borough, she devoted much of her time as a councillor to asking Porter and her administration awkward, attention-getting questions, for example about Westminster's preparedness for a nuclear war, which was much more limited than the council wanted to admit. Abbott's cross-examinations irritated the Tory councillors, who in the era of Margaret Thatcher would have been less bothered by such behaviour from a white woman, and quickly convinced her Labour colleagues that she would go on to greater things. Becoming an MP was the obvious next step. Yet as a black woman, and also a member of the Labour left, it was not that simple.

Britain had never had a black female MP. In the early 1980s, it hardly had any women MPs of any sort: after the 1983 election, only 4 per cent of the Commons was female. And Britain had not had a black or Asian MP for over half a century, since the defeat in 1929 of Shapurji Saklatvala, an Indian immigrant from a wealthy mercantile family who had briefly been the Communist MP for the then working-class inner London constituency of Battersea North. Before Saklatvala there had been a dozen other non-white MPs going back to the 1760s.

But that narrow lineage had then been interrupted for half a century, despite postwar mass immigration, the many thousands of black and Asian Britons joining trade unions and political parties, and the increasingly multiracial nature of British society.

At the 1983 election, Conservatives with Turkish Cypriot and Anglo-Indian ancestry had won seats: respectively, Richard Hickmet, and Benn's nemesis in Bristol, Jonathan Sayeed. But they were not seen as and did not identify as ethnic minority MPs. In the Commons, non-white Britain still effectively did not exist, except as the subject of occasional, often anguished, patronising or frankly racist debates about the dangers of too much immigration or the deep problems of the inner cities. To Abbott and other black and Asian activists, MPs of all parties had a 'colonialist' attitude to their non-white constituents: whether they neglected them or worked hard for them, they considered that representation by white MPs was sufficient.

In 1983, a campaign was launched to change this, in which Abbott would play a big role, and which would both crystallise and help realise her desire to become an MP. She and other activists chose Labour as the focus for the campaign, because it was the party which most non-white Britons voted for, and because the party was increasingly reliant on this support, as Thatcherism drew parts of the white working class away. In the 1983 election, 1 million of Labour's paltry 8.5 million voters were black or Asian. Without them, the party would have come third in its share of the vote, behind the SDP–Liberal Alliance, and would have faced the prospect of losing its status as the main opposition to the Conservatives.

At the centre of the campaign was a demand that Labour allow its non-white members to create what were called Black Sections: organised groups that would represent those communities and lobby for them within the party, and also push the party to belatedly get non-white MPs back into parliament. At first, Abbott and her fellow activists believed that this demand would be fairly uncontroversial, since Labour already had women's sections and youth sections. But they were wrong. For a range of reasons, some high-minded and some grubbily calculating, many Labour politicians saw Black Sections as a terrible idea.

They believed that acknowledging the importance of race in this

way would segregate the party. It would distract from Labour's traditional emphasis on class. It would be a public admission that the
party had let down its non-white members. And it would alienate
Labour supporters who were racist – as well as racist voters it needed
to take from the other parties. Even worse from the perspective of
some white Labour MPs, the creation of Black Sections would
threaten their monopoly on representing multiracial constituencies.

Worse still, the campaign was seen by the new party leader Neil
Kinnock as a threat to his efforts to make Labour more respectable.
Led by outspoken young leftwingers such as Abbott, the Black Sections movement riled the rightwing newspapers he was trying to
impress, which distrusted black activists in general and socialist ones
in particular. Finally, the Labour leader, like much of his parliamentary party, regarded the new species of Labour politician which had
been evolving in the capital since the early 1970s as too exotic and
metropolitan in their liberalism, radical gestures and concern with
diversity – alien to the party's steadier, more puritan, monocultural
industrial-town traditions. Kinnock had been born in Wales, and represented a Welsh seat. Abbott summarised his outlook to me with
typical bluntness: 'He hated the London left.'

For almost a decade, from 1983 to 1990, the Black Sections issue
caused uproar at Labour conference and within the party. In the end,
Abbott and her comrades had to settle for a compromise: not the official recognition of Black Sections but the creation of a Black Socialist
Society affiliated to Labour. Yet the campaign succeeded in other
ways, by forcing the party to take its black and Asian councillors,
activists, members and voters more seriously; and to accept that they
should be represented in parliament as a matter of urgency. In 1985,
well before the next general election was due, black Labour activists
drew up and publicised a list of constituencies with significant non-
white populations, and began to lobby the party for these seats to be
contested by black or Asian Labour candidates.

As one of the most prominent Black Sections campaigners, Abbott
was able to advertise her Commons potential. At the 1984 Labour
party conference, she made a memorably fierce speech which attacked
'some opponents of Black Sections' as 'straightforward racists'. There
were jeers from some delegates in the mostly white audience. She was

not intimidated. Instead, she ingeniously wrapped up her critique of Labour racism inside a reference to one of Kinnock and the party's foreign causes. In the Black Sections movement, she said,

> We've been accused of apartheid. I'll tell you what's apartheid: all-white parties in multiracial constituencies, that's apartheid. An all-white House of Commons, that's apartheid. We are providing a remedy for that apartheid, and there are no practical alternatives coming forward.

Wearing a white T-shirt with 'Black Section' printed on it in large letters, she stood out amid the conference's sea of sensible jumpers and blouses. Some who worked closely with her in the Black Sections movement felt she was more interested in her own advancement than the cause itself. She was sometimes late to arrive at meetings and early to leave. She could improvise too much when preparation was required, making broad-brush speeches without notes. Yet on other occasions she was as focused as a good barrister, demolishing the arguments of her opponents. She also had strong defences, built up over years as the only black person in the room. As much as anyone could be ready to become the first black woman in parliament, with all the prejudices that would stir up, she believed she was.

In early 1985, Abbott was contacted by Labour activists from one of the most multiracial constituencies in the country, and asked if she was interested in trying to become the party's candidate. The seat had been Labour-held since its creation, its existing MP would not be standing at the next election, and almost a third of its voters were black or Asian.

There was only one problem. The constituency was Brent East in London, and other activists there had already promised the candidacy to Ken Livingstone. With the abolition of the GLC looking more and more probable (the necessary legislation would finally be passed by a narrow margin a few months later), Livingstone was even keener than usual to keep his political options open. That he had already tried hard to become Brent East's candidate during 1982 and 1983, and had only been stopped by his enemies at Labour headquarters, only increased his determination to get the seat this time. He planned to use it as his escape route from municipal politics, into what he expected would be the wide open spaces of Labour politics in the House of Commons.

When he heard that Abbott was also trying for the seat, Livingstone's usual calm amid even the trickiest political manoeuvres momentarily deserted him. He asked Corbyn, who was still close to both of them, 'What's her game?' For Livingstone, who prided himself on being several steps ahead of most politicians, who was especially canny at getting himself elected, and who had probably done more for women and black and Asian Britons through his work at the GLC than any other current Labour figure, the idea that he could be beaten to the Brent East candidacy by a black woman who was a more junior leftwinger, and who had worked for him only a few years earlier, on his abortive campaign to become MP for Hampstead – the possibility was excruciating.

He soon recovered his composure. He reminded Brent East's Labour members that they had backed his previous attempt to become their parliamentary candidate, and that their choice had been unfairly overridden by the national Labour hierarchy. Nine of the constituency's eleven wards nominated him again. The general committee of the local party, which had the final say over who should be the candidate, was much less enthusiastic. Some on the committee no longer regarded Livingstone as a reliable leftwinger, after all the U-turns and tactical retreats of his GLC leadership, such as over cutting public transport fares. Others now believed that Brent's substantial black population ought to be represented by a black MP.

The selection contest lasted several months. Before the final vote, with the contest between Abbott and Livingstone seemingly close, an intriguing Labour document surfaced and was passed to the *Guardian*. Apparently written by Abbott, it said that she and her part of the Labour left were 'not interested in reforming the prevailing institutions of the police, armed services, judiciary and monarchy', but were 'about dismantling them and replacing them with our own machinery of class rule'. Compared to Livingstone, a radical flexible enough to have bowed to the Queen at the recent opening of the Thames Barrier, the document made Abbott seem utterly dogmatic, and likely to be a disruptive MP.

But most of the document was fake. A few months earlier, she had written a less sensational early draft of a discussion paper about the Labour left's future strategy, for a conference in London. Someone had got hold of a copy, added the provocative passages, and presented the document to the press as Abbott's work alone. She had her suspicions about who might have organised the smear. One lunchtime at County Hall, where she was still working as a press officer, she challenged Livingstone in person about whether his campaign for the Brent East candidacy had produced the forgery. According to the *Guardian*, he admitted that 'maybe his supporters had been getting a little over-enthusiastic'. But he neither confirmed nor denied to her or the press that he had had anything to do with the document. Over a quarter of a century later, in his lengthy and often candid memoirs, he did not mention the incident.

The vote to select Brent East's Labour candidate was held in two stages. In the first round, Livingstone beat Abbott narrowly, by 31 to 26, with 18 votes going to other contenders. She seemed to still have a chance. But in the second round, her support dropped back while his surged, as more rightwing members of the local party, who had initially supported neither of them, decided to back him. He won comfortably, by 50 to 25. Whenever the next general election was, unless it included a big shock in Brent, Livingstone had the next stage of his political career seemingly mapped out.

For Abbott, the selection battle was a nasty but enlightening experience. On the Labour left, she now realised, personal ambition could trump comradeship, and people could be used – politics here was not so different from how it was everywhere else. By encouraging her to try for the Brent East candidacy, activists there had really sent her on 'a kamikaze mission', as she put it later: they were more interested in her damaging Livingstone than in her actually winning. And the fact that she had lost so heavily, despite Livingstone's many enemies, demonstrated how minor her political status was, for all the press interest she was starting to attract. She was just a councillor, with three years' experience, and a black woman in a political world still dominated by white men. She had been put in her place.

The day after her defeat, she ran into Corbyn on Westminster Bridge, which connected County Hall with the House of Commons.

They were both on foot: she was heading home despondently from a freelance shift in the GLC press office; he was going in the opposite direction, to a meeting with Livingstone or one of his lieutenants. As they greeted each other on the bridge, she started crying. He tried to cheer her up. 'These things happen,' he said, with the sanguine air of someone who had already made it into parliament. 'Get your head up, do it again, and you'll get elected.'

Not for the last time, he was too optimistic. Within weeks of losing in Brent, she tried for another candidacy, this time for Westminster North, a Conservative seat in London with a small majority. Her council ward was in the constituency, which was starkly divided between wealthy and poor residents. Her well-spoken radicalism meant that, in theory at least, she could appeal to both groups. She started as the favourite. But then Jennifer Edwards, a council officer from the nearby borough of Camden who had credentials both as a municipal administrator and as an anti-nuclear activist, entered the contest. Abbott lost again: by almost exactly the same margin against Edwards, who was white, as she had against Livingstone. Abbott was now 31 years old. Her early promise seemed in danger of being unfulfilled.

'I was fed up with running for selections,' Abbott told me. She stopped looking at the notices for upcoming contests that were published in *Tribune*, the long-established Labour newspaper. She believed that by challenging Livingstone, the most influential person in London Labour politics, in the contest for Brent East, she had destroyed her chances of becoming a parliamentary candidate in the capital, which because of its diversity and strong left was by far the best place for ambitious black politicians. Then one day, while she was at work in her latest trade union job, for the Association of Cinematograph, Television and Allied Technicians (ACTT), her secretary, who was interested in Labour politics and wanted Abbott to make a mark in it, spotted a particularly promising selection notice in the paper. 'She said, "Look, look, Hackney North,"' Abbott remembered. 'And I said, "Pat, I'm sick of selections." And she said, "I just have a feeling about Hackney North." So she wrote the application letter, and put it in front of me to sign.'

Hackney North and Stoke Newington was right next to Corbyn's seat, but even more removed from the London mainstream. A maze of tucked-away streets and overgrown green spaces, unlike Islington Hackney North was not connected to the tube network. The area had been a haven for dissenters for centuries: religious nonconformists, early feminists, anti-slavery campaigners, communists, anarchists, refugees, Rastafarians, Jewish socialists, Irish republicans, squatters, punks, terrorists and activists for causes from environmentalism to nuclear disarmament to Black Sections. By 1985, the area had also experienced centuries of immigration, from Ireland, continental Europe, Africa, Asia and the Caribbean. Almost 40 per cent of local voters were non-white.

The seat had been Labour since its creation in 1950. In 1961 it had elected David Pitt, the first non-white councillor to serve on the London County Council, the GLC's predecessor. But by the 1980s the constituency was not a particularly happy place politically. Despite its activist traditions, general election turnouts were low. Despite its diversity, support for the National Front was high. The racist group came fourth at the 1974 and 1979 elections, behind only the main parties. Local political life could have an element of violence: bricks through windows, bigoted graffiti, aggressive demos, even arson and bomb plots.

Some of this confrontational atmosphere was created by social conditions. The area was both depopulating, as many of its old factories closed down and white working-class residents left for outer London or beyond, and overcrowded, since many of its hastily built Victorian terraces had been subdivided, with thin party walls and neighbours often living incompatible lives. Local doctors' surgeries were swamped, local schools were generally poor, the local police were corrupt and violent, and crime was very high. In 1981 alone, the number of robberies in the borough of Hackney (of which the constituency took up half) was the equivalent of one burglary for every sixteen dwellings, and one break-in for every four cars.

In 1983, these and other frightening facts about the area were included in *Inside the Inner City: Life Under the Cutting Edge*, a sometimes lurid but thoroughly researched and well-reviewed book about the problems of urban Britain by the journalist Paul Harrison. He used Hackney as his cautionary example. Yet social trends in complex urban areas do not always all go in the same direction. The book acknowledged that parts of the borough, such as the prettier, originally medieval streets of the centre of Stoke Newington, were being discovered and changed by young middle-class gentrifiers, teachers and social workers who liked the area's radical associations and relatively cheap property. Some of these largely white incomers became influential in the constituency Labour party, along with some black residents who were part of the upsurge in black politics in the early 1980s. Increasingly, the area's existing Labour MP did not meet their expectations.

By 1985 Ernie Roberts was 73 years old. He did not live in the constituency, and had first been elected partly on the understanding that he would not represent the area for long. A former communist and an outspoken supporter of Irish republicanism, he had repeatedly been prevented from standing as a parliamentary candidate by the Labour hierarchy, until in 1979 he finally won Hackney North, becoming the oldest new MP for decades. He had his strengths: he was dapper and charming, known in the Commons for his colour-coordinated outfits, and was supported locally and across London by some on the Labour left because he had campaigned for decades against nuclear weapons and racism. But he was also an old white man, with plenty of non-parliamentary interests to fall back on if he stepped down, and he was representing a seat increasingly populated by young non-white voters, and which had already pioneered the election of black politicians. If a black Labour parliamentary candidate could not be successfully inserted here, Black Sections activists asked, then where?

For months, their campaign worked on the constituency, ward by ward, getting Black Sections activists and sympathetic local party members to put down and pass motions saying that the seat needed a black candidate. Then Abbott put herself forward: young, clever, charismatic, already a bit of a media personality, already known to some activists in the constituency, and potentially part of a leftwing double act in north London with her close friend Corbyn.

But Hackney North's secure Labour majority – even in London there were not many such constituencies, with Thatcher then at her peak – meant that competition for the candidacy was fierce. There was another non-white contender, Sunhail Aziz, an Asian trade unionist; and another female one, Hilda Kean, leader of the borough's radical new leftwing council. And then there was Roberts: enjoying finally being an MP and determined to serve a third term. The generally leftwing local party and the local unions – all of them white-dominated – regarded him as more reliably socialist than Abbott. As well as his years of activism, he had a long history as a trade unionist, and his first job had been in an engineering factory at the age of 13. Her Cambridge education and work for commercial television companies were seen as a bit suspect by comparison.

She believed there was a further reason why she was not the favourite to win the selection. In the eyes of many white leftists, she told me, 'black women are never left enough'. She went on, 'The big leftwing figures in Britain in the 80s were all white men: Benn, Livingstone, Scargill.' For all the pioneering diversity work that the GLC and others on the London left had done, it was still hard for a lot of Labour activists in Hackney and elsewhere to imagine a black woman joining this elite socialist club, and that became a self-fulfilling prophecy. Abbott campaigned hard for the Hackney North candidacy, but 'I did not expect to win.'

Over a hundred people, an unusually large number, came to the decisive selection meeting, which was held in the handsome Art Deco council chamber of Hackney Town Hall. The would-be candidates were to be interviewed and then make speeches. The local party officials present were Roberts supporters. So were most of the ward representatives, who had been mandated to back him by their party members. Altogether, there were enough people in the room for him to win, Abbott realised, unless her interview and speech persuaded them otherwise.

There were also some of her supporters: 'a mix of leftwingers and other members who wanted a black MP, and also feminists, some of them quite rightwing [by Labour standards], who wanted a woman MP'. But the excitement of her backers was mixed with resignation. 'Two of my women supporters came up to me and said, "If you can come a good second, that would be great."'

Waiting for her turn, she paced the corridor next to the council chamber. 'There were photos of Hackney mayors from between the wars,' she remembered. 'They were all Jewish men. And I felt like they were talking to me – whisper, whisper – saying, "We came to this country, like your parents, and we did it. You can do it."'

In her speech, she shrewdly made both a practical and philosophical case for her candidacy. She promised to live in Hackney North if she became its MP, and to open a constituency office. Roberts, though popular locally, had provided neither form of access. She also argued that choosing her would be a vote for the area's increasingly multicultural and multi-class reality, rather than its past as a partly industrial inner suburb arranged primarily around the lives of working-class white men. 'You can select an MP that looks back,' she said, quite brutally but accurately characterising Roberts, 'or you can select one that looks forward, to the new Hackney.' Her clear voice filled the large room. It was not hard to imagine it doing the same in parliament.

'I could see people listening, agonising,' she remembered, 'because they had been mandated to vote for Roberts, but they now knew they had to vote for me.' She ended with some lines from 'Still I Rise', a 1978 poem by the black American writer and activist Maya Angelou. 'I am the dream and the hope of the slave,' the last line went. The gesture was both self-important and very powerful.

Roberts got 35 votes: a solid total. But Abbott got 42. She was now the Labour candidate. 'The Labour officials there looked gutted,' she told me. Yet she was elated, and so were people far beyond Hackney Town Hall. The headline in the Caribbean diaspora newspaper *West Indian World* was 'Di Does It'.

A few days later, the *Observer*, the British white liberal's Sunday newspaper of choice, gave her a 1,000-word profile, almost unheard-of for a newly selected parliamentary candidate. The paper praised her for winning by generating 'genuine enthusiasm', rather than relying on 'an organised cabal', as the Labour left usually did, the article implied. The profile also described her, however, as 'pushy' and 'out-spoken'. She was 'the kind of person about whom no one feels neutral'.

When her victory was announced at the town hall, Roberts walked out of the building without congratulating her. For months afterwards, he claimed to journalists that her win was illegitimate, on the grounds that some party members who had been mandated to vote for him had acted otherwise. The claim was baseless: Labour rules allowed its members to decide for themselves in selection contests. But for rightwing newspapers, the chance to allege a leftwing plot, while also weaponising her blackness, was irresistible. 'Black Diane "won after vote swap"' was one headline in the *Sun*. The *Daily Express* described her as a 'black extremist', and the Black Sections movement as 'illegal'. Abbott found the abrupt changes in how she was seen by the media, and by some in her own party, simultaneously ridiculous, dizzying, frustrating and intimidating. 'Until I became a parliamentary candidate, I wasn't leftwing enough,' she told me. 'Once I won the selection, I was an extremist.' Her monstering had begun, before she had even had a chance to stand for parliament.

When she did so, at the 1987 general election, the process was as bruising and exhilarating as the selection battle, but on a bigger scale. This time, the noteworthy newspaper profile of her was in the *New York Times*. Alongside Corbyn, Livingstone and three others, she also featured on an anti-Labour poster put out by the Conservatives' national campaign. 'So This Is the New Moderate Militant-Free Labour Party', the poster said, alluding to Kinnock's efforts to push the party towards the centre, which had included expelling members of the leftwing Militant Tendency. Neither Abbott nor Livingstone nor Corbyn had ever been in Militant, which disagreed with their focus on inequalities of all kinds and not just class. But factual accuracy was never a priority for attacks on the left. The point was to make them look and sound sinister, and to a degree the poster succeeded. It was designed like a wanted poster, with two rows of mugshots. Corbyn stared out from his with a faraway look and a rigid, humourless mouth, like a member of a cult. Livingstone was pictured seemingly giving a speech, head tilted back, pale, stubbled and wearing a black polo neck, like a 1960s revolutionary. The photo of Abbott was more neutral. Perhaps she had not been a public figure long enough to provide a properly alarming image. She was smiling, and wearing pearls and what looked like a smart dark jacket. But underneath there was a recent quote from her: 'All white people are racist.'

The campaign in Hackney North was fractious. The Conservative candidate was Oliver Letwin, a young Thatcherite who had been educated at Eton. He presented himself to the many journalists who visited the constituency as a charming underdog, while accusing

Abbott of being, as *The Times* reported it, 'a revolutionary with no genuine allegiance to British parliamentary democracy'. He quoted from the partly faked document which had been used to smear her in the Brent selection contest.

The Conservative campaign office was firebombed. Their party chairman Norman Tebbit rushed to Hackney and insinuated that the arson might have been the doing of Labour 'extremists', which was also how the rightwing press regularly described Abbott. Her own campaign office had its glass front smashed. No one was arrested for either incident. She responded aggressively to the Conservatives' personal attacks, telling *The Times* that Letwin would 'play the race card ruthlessly'. 'In a place like this,' she went on, 'what other cards does an Old Etonian merchant banker hold?' The rhetorical question had a proper Commons sting.

But in other ways she was less deft. When the Labour-supporting *Guardian* sent a reporter to the constituency, she refused to talk to him, and gave no explanation. While the paper was broadly pro-Kinnock and often critical of the Labour left, the gesture seemed a bit paranoid and thin-skinned – and likely to be counterproductive. In Hackney newsagents, the *Guardian* often outsold every other paper.

She faced other obstacles. The National Front protested in the constituency against her candidacy. Senior Labour figures stayed away from her campaign. Some white Labour activists in the seat did not turn up to canvass for her. Corbyn heard about this unofficial boycott, and lent her volunteers from his local party, despite the fact that he had his own election to win. Abbott took similar risks with her campaign literature, getting posters and leaflets designed that were dominated by photos of her rather than by the Labour logo. She emphasised rather than played down who she was.

A few days before the election, she agreed to be interviewed by the *New York Times*, even though none of its readers were likely to be relevant to the Hackney contest. She met the reporter not in the constituency but in the River Room of the Savoy Hotel, one of the swankiest dining spaces in London, which she had never been to before. She dressed in bright, socialist red, and ordered the biggest breakfast on the menu. She talked about her admiration for black American iconoclasts from the 1960s such as Angela Davis and

Malcolm X, and said she believed that, after 'a time lag', black British politics was about to undergo a similar upsurge. Continuing in a very confident future tense, she said: 'I'll be representing a strong anti-racist, anti-fascist district, an old immigrant stronghold.'

On the day of the election, she was more nervous. There was talk of a high turnout – unusual in the constituency – in the more Conservative parts of the seat, such as the Orthodox Jewish enclave of Stamford Hill. The rumours were correct, to an extent: the total Tory vote in the constituency went up by almost a tenth. Support for the SDP–Liberal Alliance also increased, by almost a third. In all, nearly 20,000 people chose candidates other than Abbott: likely evidence that her race and possibly her gender had put some voters off. Yet there were also other shifts on polling day. 'Around teatime', she remembered over 30 years later, 'the streets of Stoke Newington came alive with people going out to vote in a really determined way ... black people ... And I suddenly realised, the community is on the move ... I still meet people who say, "I voted for the first time in '87, and I voted [for] you."'

She received 18,912 votes: only 77 fewer than Roberts at the previous election. She beat Letwin, who came second, by 7,678.

The result was declared at 3am. By then it was becoming clear that Margaret Thatcher was going to win her third consecutive election, and by a landslide. But in the crowded room where Abbott made her victory speech, that was all momentarily forgotten. She wore bright red again, with more pearls, and her hair in long Afro-Caribbean braids. She was not going to fit in with any previous notions about how an MP should dress. After a big intake of breath, she spoke in a very loud voice. 'I have come a long way to stand here before you tonight,' she said at the climax. 'And I am aware that a lot of hope, not just in Hackney, but across the country, rides on our victory tonight. I hope and believe that I can fulfil those hopes.'

PART FOUR

Into the Wilderness

14

Exile at the Westdale Hotel

Abbott's greatest political hero – or at least her greatest white one – also enjoyed success at the 1987 election. Like hers, Tony Benn's victory was in a constituency long held by Labour, and his majority was similar: a comfortable 8,577. Despite the alarm and hostility they both aroused in traditionally minded voters of all parties, the two well-spoken leftwingers could reasonably expect to provoke the Commons for many years to come.

Yet there the similarities between their trajectories ended. While Abbott was 33, typically young and confident for a new MP, Benn was 62, and scarred by decades of defeats, controversies and hard-won victories. His health seemed fragile: his handwriting, balance and walking were still affected by his bad case of Guillain-Barré syndrome in 1981. Always quite thin, he now looked bony, his eyes blazing or twinkling from a face with no spare flesh. He habitually wore cardigans under his jackets as an extra layer of warmth. As the climate for British socialists chilled dramatically during the mid-1980s, almost everywhere except in London, Benn needed a place to shelter, to recover from his political wounds, and to start again.

Chesterfield is an old Derbyshire market town on a hilltop, over 150 miles from Benn's previous public arenas in Bristol and London, and not much like either. Its handsome but slightly underpopulated town centre has cobbles and medieval and Tudor buildings; yet in the 1980s much of the life of Chesterfield and the surrounding area was Victorian in origin and industrial. In the town and for dozens of miles across the flatter land to the east, one industry often dominated, culturally and psychologically if not always economically: coalmining.

By the time Benn became Chesterfield's MP, at a by-election in

1984, a year after losing his Bristol seat, many of the pits in the Derby-shire coalfield had already closed: part of the long postwar contraction of the British coal industry under both Labour and the Conservatives. In Chesterfield, a different economic future had been set, for good or ill, by the opening of an angular new shopping complex by the newly married Diana, Princess of Wales in 1981. But in the mid-1980s the region's mining tradition was still a powerful presence. Just outside the town centre, a florid and stout Victorian building, fronted by two statues of trade unionists who had been important in the 19th-century Derbyshire coalfields, housed the local offices of the National Union of Mineworkers (NUM). Almost directly across the road from its dozen high-ceilinged, ornately decorated rooms was the Chesterfield Labour Club, a plainer building where much of the town's most important political business was conducted, and where Benn had his constituency office.

He had become the local MP partly by chance. For five months after losing his Bristol seat in 1983, he had led a less stressful but also less anchored life than he had for decades. He reflected. He considered writing a book. Without any constituents or Labour parliamentary positions to represent, he was able to be pickier about which television programmes he appeared on. He also made foreign trips he had been planning for years. In Japan, he visited the Hiroshima Peace Memorial Museum, where the brutally frank exhibits reinforced his opposition to nuclear weapons. In Cuba, he swam in the warm sea, met government officials and arranged to meet Fidel Castro. The latter prospect, Benn recorded, made him and Caroline 'as excited as a couple of kids would be at the prospect of Santa coming down the chimney'. The encounter between the great pioneer of authoritarian but effective socialism and the great advocate of a much more democratic but barely enacted British variant never happened. Castro's attention was suddenly taken by an American invasion fleet setting sail for Cuba's tiny Caribbean ally Grenada.

Back in England, Benn sometimes found it hard not being an MP. To answer the hundreds of letters he still got every week, he now had to pay for his own stationery and postage. 'I have been using House of Commons letter-heading for thirty-three years,' he complained. 'The cost of stamps is astronomical.' He also had to keep going back to

Bristol for valedictory events and other party gatherings, which he found melancholy and unsettling. Had his parliamentary career ended, or had it just been interrupted? Given how many enemies he now had in the party, and given how much harder it was becoming for Labour in the mid-1980s to get anyone into parliament, it was difficult to know.

Yet during one of these Bristol trips, in November 1983, he learned that the Labour MP for Chesterfield was about to resign and take a job in the coal industry. For Benn, the sudden appearance of this opportunity had some justice to it. Eric Varley, the departing MP, was a Labour rightwinger worn down by the party's leftward shift over the past dozen years, a shift which Benn had led, ultimately at huge personal cost. But now there could be a belated pay-off for the exiled leader of the left.

Benn quickly became desperate to secure it. On his first visit to Chesterfield to meet Labour members and try to persuade them to choose him as their candidate, his train went through the station without stopping, and instead halted half a mile further on. Unaware that the driver was planning to back the train into the station, and worried about being late, Benn opened one of the doors of his carriage, which was much easier for passengers to do in those days, and walked back along the track towards the town.

He made it unscathed to the station, and through the selection process, and on 1 March the by-election was held. Much of the media hoped that Benn would lose. During the selection process the *Daily Mail* campaigned against him becoming the Labour candidate, and claimed that the party's new leader Neil Kinnock was against that happening, too. Yet in fact circumstances within the party had – to an extent – changed in Benn's favour. With Kinnock now leader for the foreseeable future, Benn was considered less of a threat by the Labour right. Kinnock also needed a by-election win to demonstrate that his leadership was making progress. So in the run-up to polling day the voters of Chesterfield and the packs of Benn-hunting journalists who had arrived in the town were treated to the unlikely sight of senior Labour figures who until recently had been some of Benn's most vicious enemies, such as Denis Healey and Kinnock himself, campaigning energetically for him. Healey and the teetotal Benn even went to the pub together in a small town outside Chesterfield. With television cameras feet away, Healey played the piano while he and Benn sang: 'Here we are again, happy as can be, all good pals and jolly good company!'

In public, Benn was happy to take any help he could get. Yet in private, too, he was pleased, even a bit moved, by the by-election support he received from the shadow cabinet. 'I must say Denis played it like an old trouper,' Benn recorded in his diary after their pub singsong. Benn's enemies were always saying that he would destroy the Labour party, either deliberately or inadvertently. In fact, he loved it too much.

He won the by-election by 6,264 votes – smaller than Labour's usual margin in Chesterfield, but decisive enough. At the count, young Labour activists chanted, 'Tony Benn! Tony Benn!' He made his victory speech, then had to make another to a crowd outside the Labour club, then another inside the club, standing on a table, to party members. He finally went to bed at five in the morning. In a Labour town, among the industrial working class he revered, and far from his enemies in Fleet Street and across the Tory south, Benn believed he was making a fresh start.

Less than two weeks later, before he had even had time to read all his by-election post, the 1984 miners' strike officially began. As a former energy minister, and a close ally of the miners' leader Arthur Scargill – and as an advocate of workers' power, and opponent of the measures the state took against it – Benn correctly and quickly understood that the strike would be a pivotal economic and political event. Yet his involvement in the dispute also marked a shift in his politics. He was changing from someone who had been preoccupied by the future, by the latest radical social movements and how a new socialist society could be constructed, to someone who was preoccupied by the present and the past, and trying to save as many as possible of the socialist traditions which ran through them.

In parliament, he quickly became one of the best critics of the aggressive way the strike was policed; of the weaknesses in the case for closing dozens of pits, the plan by the National Coal Board which had prompted the strike; and also of the Thatcher government's intention to destroy the NUM, arguably the last powerful union, as a significant political force. Whatever you thought of his politics, Benn's knowledge of the economy, built up while running economic ministries in the 1960s and 70s, supplied him with plenty of strong arguments in favour of the miners. In a Commons debate on 7 June 1984, he responded to the government's and the coal board's claim that pits had to be closed because they required too much subsidy and were therefore 'uneconomic', by pointing out that 'Agriculture is subsidised up to the hilt ... by a government which has poured money into uneconomic land.'

Such interventions had a value; but it was limited, given that the Conservatives had a Commons majority of 144. It was in Chesterfield that Benn's commitment to the strikers became more practical and more intense. From the first month of their walk-out, he often got up before dawn, sometimes as early as 4am, in order to go on 'the soup run' to miners' pickets at nearby collieries. It was often very cold, and he would put on two pairs of socks and two jumpers. Then he would meet a few party and NUM activists outside the Labour club, and they would drive off with their cargo of soup and their anxieties about the picket line police, down the hill into the country darkness.

Usually, the arrival on a picket line of Benn, still one of the most famous politicians in the country, would make the police moderate their behaviour or change it altogether. On the morning of 23 March 1984, he visited six collieries. At one of them, 'There were 200 police in buses,' he recorded. 'As soon as I appeared, the buses went off in convoy. The word has got round that if Tony Benn turns up at a colliery the police go away, so the demand for me gets greater. It was a useful piece of work.'

But sometimes he got a more real taste of how the strike was being policed. On 22 June 1984, he and some activists visited a camp which a few dozen striking miners had set up in a wood near a colliery in the neighbouring Nottinghamshire coalfield. The miners were being kept away from the picket lines by the NUM, because they were all on bail, having been arrested for picket line offences, which the police often defined with intimidating vagueness. To keep themselves busy and useful, the miners were picking up deadwood from land belonging to a supportive local farmer, which could then be distributed as fuel to the strikers' increasingly impoverished households, with strike pay sometimes only £1 a day.

The miners' camp was near a dirt track. While Benn was there, talking to its inhabitants and admiring them for being 'just like Robin Hood and his gang', a police car came down the track. It stopped beside the miners, he recorded, 'and a sergeant asked them what they were doing before turning [the car] round and leaving'. Shortly afterwards, when Benn and his companions drove back up the track themselves,

> We were stopped at a road-block set up by the police. They asked, 'What are you doing here?' I sat in the back (with my tape recorder running) and we said, 'We're just going home. We've been distributing soup.' Then we saw another police vehicle with dogs ... so we decided to turn back. When we reached the camp ... the dog patrol ... had parked about 200 yards ahead. Then a police bus with riot wire over the windows arrived carrying about fifteen or twenty constables. For the first time in my life, I felt really threatened ... I trembled physically. I thought I might need to be there if a fight began ...

This time, unlike on other occasions during the strike, there was no such confrontation. Perhaps Benn's presence put the police off. His mind quickly turned to how the police's strike tactics could be beaten. The following month, he came up with a plan to distribute a form of identity card to constituents of his who were involved in the strike, which would state that they were helping him with his duties as their MP, and thus enable them to get through police checks and roadblocks.

Yet cumulatively, as the strike continued through the summer, the autumn, and into the winter, and as he saw at first hand how the state dealt with the strikers, and how that treatment was wearing them down, his view of the dispute darkened: 'I never understood until now ... the true nature of class legislation, class law, class judges, class magistrates, class use of the police, class use of the media. It has completely shaken me. I knew it in theory, but I know in practice now what is happening.'

In March 1985, almost exactly a year after walking out, the strikers went back to work. Benn watched it happen at a huge colliery near Chesterfield which would be closed under the Conservatives eight years later, despite having just achieved record production. As elsewhere, the returning miners carried banners, to try to show that their collective spirit and traditions had not been crushed. 'Every emotion swept through me,' Benn recorded in his diary. 'Wanting to weep ... then tremendous pride ... then feelings of intense hate as a scab came forward dressed in his pit clothes and photographed them ...' The strikers shouted 'scabby bastard!' But Benn did not. With his companions, he 'stood there and applauded as they all marched into the colliery'.

Throughout the strike and for half a dozen years afterwards, when Benn was in Chesterfield he lived in a hotel, rather than buying or renting a local property. He had done the same as an MP in Bristol. Yet whereas there he had habitually stayed at the large and prestigious Grand Hotel, in Chesterfield he chose somewhere very different. The Westdale Hotel was a tiny, plain establishment with half a dozen bedrooms which occupied a narrow, net-curtained Victorian house with a small front garden. It was across the street from both the NUM offices and the Labour club. Benn made himself even more available to the town's tight community of leftwing activists by taking the ground floor room which faced the garden and the street. When they wanted him to come with them to early morning strike meetings or picketed pits, his comrades would sometimes wake him up by banging on the room's bay window.

The extreme accessibility and modesty of Benn's new constituency life was an expression of his politics, of his ongoing flight from family privilege and running ministries towards raw outdoor activism and hourly mugs of what he called 'workman's tea'. For someone who had been arguing for over a decade and a half that politics should become much less hierarchical and easier to participate in, removing most of the barriers between himself and local activists and voters was appropriate, and a potentially powerful symbol. But it did not come without risks. Benn remained a politician who received death threats, who was of interest to the security services, and whom the rightwing press regularly depicted as a dangerous and essentially traitorous figure. His metamorphosis into an indulged national treasure was still many years away.

His room at the Westdale was really two rooms: a medium-sized bedroom at the front, and a slightly bigger room behind, which contained a galley kitchen. Benn would cook there for most of his meals, because he was worried that food from elsewhere might be poisoned. At least one of the leftists who regularly visited him from London, often to support the striking miners, worried that Benn's living quarters were also vulnerable to another form of attack. There was a small hole in the glass of his bedroom's street-facing bay window. The owner of the hotel, an Irish Catholic with whom Benn got on very well, said the hole was just a flaw in the glass. But Jeremy Corbyn was convinced that it was a bullet hole, and that someone had tried to shoot his mentor.

Other visitors were more relaxed. Ken Livingstone offered to sleep on a spare mattress in Benn's bedroom. Caroline combined seeing her husband with giving lectures about education in nearby Sheffield. Their grandchildren jumped on and off the low walls around the Westdale's garden. Yet at other times, the most famous leftwing politician in Britain was on his own in the dim hotel. He would sit in a heavy red armchair in his room, which he saw as his best place for thinking; or he would sit in the same chair with his door open on to the narrow entrance hall, listening for hours to Irish music that the hotel's owner put on for him. Sometimes the two men would talk, about politics, or about their different Christian faiths – 'By God, he could quote the Bible from one end to the other!' the hotelier told me. The two men came to trust each other. Benn knew that the hotelier would tell journalists who phoned nothing, except for Benn's phone number. Partly in return, Benn occasionally became the hotel's night porter, letting in guests or even booking them in. According to the hotelier, none of these guests ever realised who was serving them. Benn had become an ordinary worker. Although when the hotelier bought him a suitable work coat for the job, he never wore it.

After the miners' strike, Benn worked hard to keep his life as an MP with no ministerial prospects in a neglected region useful and interesting. He absorbed himself in the problems people brought to him at his regular constituency surgeries: a woman whose home was infested with rats; an old couple in tears because they could not find anywhere decent to live; young homeless people who had been unable to get housing benefit. He was a good listener, intensely curious about other lives, and he could tell people many helpful things about how the state they were trying to deal with actually operated. Yet there was no disguising his change of role. Far from shaping a government, as he had in the 1960s, or trying to radicalise one, as he did in the 1970s, he was now trying to deal in small ways with Thatcherism's consequences.

Occasionally, he was able to use Chesterfield as a base for something larger. In 1986 he helped organise an unofficial summit in the town between the United States and the Soviet Union, featuring representatives from the London embassies of both countries. After a lunchtime and afternoon of polite civic events, including the presentation to both diplomats of pictures of a Chesterfield church with a famously twisting spire – appropriately for a summit intended to ease Cold War tensions, from a distance the spire looked a little like a malfunctioning missile – the diplomats gave speeches and then answered questions from the public. The American got a more hostile reception than the Russian. Benn was delighted at this small undermining of Western Cold War orthodoxies, and at the local and wider attention the summit received. 'Instead of organising on the far left as a fringe,' he recorded afterwards, 'this was quite different – organising within a town.'

The following year, he helped stage a weekend-long Chesterfield Socialist Conference, held shortly after the official party conferences. Its timing proved even better than intended. Earlier the same week, on Black Monday, a huge stock market crash had begun, and many leftists suddenly hoped or believed that the 1980s supremacy of free-market capitalism and rightwing politics was coming to an end. Two thousand people of all ages came to the conference, including Corbyn, Livingstone and Scargill, but also less predictable participants such as green activists, members of the African National Congress and observers from Nicaragua.

Long queues for events formed in chilly late autumn sunshine. Benn ran into and hugged old comrades. There were debates and workshops about democratising the economy, shortening the working week and other forward-looking themes, as well as old-fashioned battles between leftwing sects to control the conference agenda. On the

Saturday night, hundreds of people slept on the floor of a hall in the town, on mattresses provided by the fire brigade, and kept warm by portable heaters the council usually provided for people whose homes had been damaged by floods. On the Sunday, dressed smartly for the occasion in a red tie and crisp white shirt, Benn was interviewed by a news reporter from ITN, Eleanor Goodman. 'I think you're here, actually, at a turning point in postwar British politics,' he said, smiling. 'Of that I'm quite sure.' Her report on the conference was a respectful six minutes long, and took the event seriously. Less encouragingly, she described those present as 'the outside left'.

Away from Chesterfield, Benn's re-entry into parliamentary politics revealed a reduction in his status. It took over three months for him to be given a desk in the Commons. The late and grudging allocation of office space was one of the ways that the Labour hierarchy publicly marginalised and humiliated new MPs from the left.

Since 1982, the Labour left in the Commons had tried to counter this bullying and isolation, and their party's general shift to the right, by operating as a parliamentary collective, the Socialist Campaign Group. Founded by Benn and two dozen other leftwing MPs in the aftermath of his failed bid for the deputy leadership, it met weekly, assessed Labour and Conservative policy, and organised Commons revolts. Important leftwing figures from outside parliament, such as Livingstone, also attended. At its best, the Campaign Group, as it was known for short, was a stimulating and influential political environment, where different generations of leftists had frank arguments, educated and supported each other, and planned effective Commons interventions. Yet with at most a few dozen members, the group had a limited ability to challenge the Labour leadership. Even at its smallest under Kinnock, the party had 209 MPs, so the group could easily be outvoted. Many of the group, such as Benn, were middle-aged. As the 1980s, 1990s and 2000s went by, and successive Labour leaders kept the party moving rightwards, a dispiritingly steady trickle of Campaign Group members left parliament, died, or moved to the right themselves, leaving the group behind.

Benn remained a committed and energetic member. But the group was not enough in itself to satisfy his appetite for London-based politics, which remained large despite his excitement at 'organising within a town' in Chesterfield. In 1985, he became involved in another project to revive British socialism. The Independent Left Corresponding Society took its rather archaic name and its inspiration from the 18th-century London Corresponding Society, a network of debating and reading groups which had agitated for more democracy in Britain during the febrile years following the French Revolution. The 1985 update was intended to be an informal but intellectually serious leftwing think tank, where radical Labour politicians such as Benn would meet and exchange ideas with socialist thinkers and activists who were independent of the party, such as Tariq Ali, Hilary Wainwright and Ralph Miliband.

But the corresponding society also had a more emotional, more personal purpose. The defeat of the miners, coming not long after Benn's defeat in the 1983 election, and his deputy leadership near-miss, had left Benn even more vulnerable than usual to periods of deep gloom. 'The corresponding society was very much meant to be a refuge for Tony,' Ali told me. 'Ralph said to me, "Tony's in a depressed state. We should do something to cheer him up."'

The society met monthly on Sunday evenings at Benn's London house. A rough circle of chairs would be drawn up in the living room or the small, tightly walled back garden. Those present would try to avoid sitting in one particular chair, which was plain in design and very uncomfortable. It had once belonged to Keir Hardie, the first leader of the parliamentary Labour party, also an intense, iconoclastic leftwinger with powerful enemies, about whom Caroline was writing a biography. Often, the chair would end up being occupied by Corbyn, while pushier or more senior attendees grabbed the better spots.

The talk would then range widely, from almost academic discussions of the state of the modern economy, trade unionism and democracy, often led by historians and theorists from the journal *New Left Review*, to gossip about who might be the next leader of the Labour party. Corbyn did not say much, but listened reverentially. 'In many ways this was my university education,' he wrote later.

Benn also did a lot of listening. Despite his Oxford degree and reputation as a thinking politician, he knew he was actually not that well-read. He tended to read bits of books, or to absorb other people's best verbal arguments, and then use them as jumping-off points for his political imagination. The Sunday evening gatherings also helped him feel at the centre of things still. In a sense, the people who came to his house then were competing for his approval: showing off their debating skills, unveiling their formulae for improving the left's fortunes, and auditioning to replace him as the Labour left's leading figure.

But Benn was not fully reconciled to giving up that position. In the late 1980s and into the 1990s, whenever there was a big disruptive event in the party, his ambition to play a major Labour role would stir again. In June 1987, the party was heavily defeated once more at a general election, after mounting a highly professional centre-left campaign which impressed journalists much more than voters. Over the next nine months Benn gradually convinced himself that he should challenge for the party leadership. In December 1987, he recorded in his diary: 'The old war horse in me sniffs the gunpowder, and prepares for battle.'

Few on the left, including almost certainly Benn himself, thought he had much chance of succeeding. But a challenge would be a chance to 'get across issues', Benn argued, to Labour members and the wider electorate. The vagueness of this aim was easy to criticise, and a third of the Campaign Group opposed him standing. Many of his political confidants outside parliament, such as Caroline and Miliband, also advised him against. But for the Labour left to do nothing in response to the clear failure of the Labour right at a general election – that was also a questionable strategy. If the left did not present an alternative now, would it ever do so again?

From March to October 1988, Benn went through his usual election routine – warm and packed campaign meetings, frosty media interviews – and soon realised that the result was going to be 'an absolute disaster', as he put it on 29 May. In the parliamentary party, the constituency parties, and above all in the trade unions, many people believed that Kinnock was improving Labour's position, however thin the electoral evidence. Meanwhile, many Kinnock sceptics did not believe that a Benn leadership would do any better.

When the vote came in October, Kinnock crushed Benn by 88.6 per cent to 11.4 per cent. The result was announced at Labour's annual conference. Immediately afterwards, a reporter from the

BBC's *Newsnight* programme asked Corbyn, who had been heavily involved in Benn's campaign, whether the contest had ended up as 'a euthanasia of the left'. 'Not at all,' said Corbyn. 'We had a rally here last night of over 500 people . . . It's the rebirth of a serious, thinking left that's looking forward, beyond the 80s.' His tone was surprisingly calm – almost like that of a professional spin doctor. But the speed with which his head bobbed nervously as he spoke said otherwise.

Whatever Corbyn claimed, the scale of Benn's defeat revealed an imploding Labour left. To win barely a tenth of the vote, in a party which itself had the support of less than a third of voters – to judge by the previous year's general election – suggested that the left was no longer a mass movement but a marginal faction, exactly as the right of the party wanted. And that faction was itself divided. In London, one of the left's few remaining strongholds, Ken Livingstone and John McDonnell had fallen out.

It happened during the final, feverish pre-abolition phase of the Greater London Council. The contentious issue was a fundamental one: how far leftwingers in local government should go in order to protect their municipal revolution against an ever more hostile right-wing central government. Should the GLC accept at least some of the cuts imposed on it by the Thatcher government, and spend its last months using this reduced budget as radically as it could? Or should the council see attack as the best form of defence – and even try to help bring the Thatcher government down?

In July 1984, her administration told the GLC and a dozen other leftwing councils, including Liverpool and Sheffield, that from the next financial year the level of the local taxes they set to raise much of their revenue, known as the rates, would be limited or 'capped'. In essence, the Thatcher government intended to stop these councils being able to afford to practise municipal socialism, which often cost more than conventional local government.

Yet far from being intimidated into moderating their policies, the councils decided to try to turn the threat into an opportunity. Aware that the government was straining to cope with the miners' strike, which Livingstone and other leftwing councillors supported, sometimes in person, the councils formed a plan to defy the coming cuts and undermine the government at the same time.

At a meeting of the London Labour party in January 1985, the plan was outlined by Livingstone and McDonnell. When the time came in early March for the councils to set their next rates and annual budgets, as they were legally required to do, the councils would simultaneously pass resolutions refusing to do so. The councils would then continue to pay their workers and provide services for their residents for as long as possible, using money which usually went to the banks in interest payments for council debts. Faced with this mass default – a kind of financial strike in town halls across the country – the banks and the markets in the City of London would panic. Meanwhile, the government would face the prospect of essential local services such as rubbish collection collapsing altogether once the councils ran out of money. The government would be forced to abandon its cuts to council funding. Such a humiliating setback, if it came at the same time as a defeat by the striking miners, would badly wound the government – and could even cause its collapse.

For this plan to work, Livingstone told the meeting, London would need to become 'a city in revolt', with 'members of councils and trade unions physically taking control of their town halls', in order to carry on 'delivering services to the people they represent'. He went on dramatically: 'We will effectively operate within the state in defiance of the state. That will prove the most dramatic challenge, apart from the challenge of the miners, that this government has faced since 1979.' In his speech, McDonnell employed a metaphor that might have come from a military textbook, or from his guru Gramsci, to sum up the councils' strategy: the municipal revolt would open 'a second front' against the government. On the question of whether some of the GLC's Labour councillors, not all of whom were leftwingers, might baulk at taking part in mass law-breaking, McDonnell went into his icy, dogmatic mode: 'There is a need to enforce socialist discipline on GLC councillors to ensure that they carry through this policy.'

In some ways, the plan was Livingstone and McDonnell's municipal leftism taken to its logical conclusion. It was defiant, disruptive, highly ambitious, and hugely risky – ignoring the conventional political logic that said it was not a good idea for a council to take on a national government with a huge majority. At first, in early 1985, the two GLC men seemed as committed to the scheme as they were to the rest of their council's approach. 'In the preceding three years,' wrote Livingstone later, 'we had worked so closely together that it had almost become a joint leadership.' His partnership with McDonnell had grown into 'the closest political relationship of my life' – rare praise from the usually self-contained Red Ken.

Yet in fact the tension between Livingstone the pragmatic radical and McDonnell the consistent socialist with a revolutionary edge had never completely gone away. They complemented each other more than they mirrored each other. And like a lot of what Livingstone said, his talk about turning London into 'a city in revolt' through refusing to set a rate was not a promise to be taken literally, but one tactical option of several that he was considering.

During the weeks leading up to the early March deadline for councils to set their rates, he delegated the GLC's work in this area to McDonnell and his staff. Livingstone respected his deputy's head for figures, and also needed to be available to front the GLC's anti-abolition campaign. The two men persuaded their fellow Labour councillors that any new financial documents that McDonnell and his team produced, about the size of the existing GLC budget and how it would be affected by government cuts, should not be published or discussed by the Labour group until just before the deadline for setting a rate. That way, the government would not gain useful intelligence. Even more importantly, the inevitable split in the Labour group between those who did and did not support the rates revolt would be delayed as long as possible, and would therefore remain manageable.

Or at least, that was the theory. In reality, the GLC's supposedly cunning rates strategy became a slow-motion car crash. First, the government announced that the maximum rate that it would allow the council to set, which was always expressed as a fraction of a pound, was 36.5p. When Livingstone asked McDonnell what this figure would mean for the GLC's next budget, McDonnell told him that cuts would be necessary of £140 million, or over 15 per cent. During January and February 1985, the GLC noisily publicised what it said would be the consequences:

Big cutbacks on free travel for London's million old people . . . the end of the popular dial-a-ride service for people with disabilities . . . more people . . . on the dole, including many GLC workers . . . council tenants' rents up . . . reductions in the fire service . . . the end of road improvements and maintenance . . . less money for flood prevention, controlling pollution and other hazards . . .

As well as this depletion of essential services, the GLC claimed that the cuts would lead to 'the virtual end' of its huge and innovative grants programme for community organisations and disadvantaged groups. Thus both the radical and the almost apolitical but highly valued sides of the council's work would be severely damaged or made impossible.

Not everyone, however, believed the GLC's dire forecasts. Local councils were known for producing pessimistic budget projections, in order to get proposed cuts scaled down, as the *Guardian*'s expert on London government John Carvel pointed out. Another of the doubters about the frightening figure that McDonnell had produced was someone with over a decade of experience of the financial and political games that could be played with municipal budgets: Livingstone himself.

According to the political autobiography he published in 1987, *If Voting Changed Anything, They'd Abolish It*, at first he had not been particularly alarmed when the government produced its 36.5p rate limit. The GLC, he wrote, 'had just lost control of London Transport, which had consumed 19 per cent of our budget, [so] I was sure that we would be able to get by . . . without having to make any real cuts'. Yet McDonnell's insistence that the figure would mean £140 million in spending reductions had persuaded Livingstone – up to a point: 'I was in no position to question his judgement, although I suspected that he was exaggerating . . . somewhat.' While the GLC publicly talked up the dangers of the cuts, in private its director-general Maurice Stonefrost, one of the officials Livingstone trusted most, worked out the ways in which the council's budget would have to be adjusted if the 36.5p rate became a reality.

In late February, barely a week before the deadline for the council to agree its rate and budget, Stonefrost revealed to Livingstone that the 36.5p figure would actually require a spending reduction of only £30 million – and could even allow a spending increase of £24 million, if the council did some creative accounting with its debts. In one sense, all this was great news: the government's rate-capping tactic did not seem likely to cripple the GLC after all. But in another sense, the news was a disaster, because it discredited the whole argument that the GLC and the other leftwing councils planned to make, that the government cap on their rates would require cuts so awful that it was better not to set a rate at all.

Livingstone wrote that he was 'shocked' by Stonefrost's revelations. He then asked another senior GLC official who worked with Stonefrost, a former leftwing Labour MP called Reg Race, why the council was 'still pumping out propaganda saying £140m cuts'. According to Livingstone, Race replied that McDonnell was responsible. 'We gave John a report,' Race said, 'which showed [the GLC] could have between two and four per cent [spending] growth' if it accepted the Conservative cap. 'He told us to shred all copies.'

Livingstone confronted his deputy in one of County Hall's corridors. McDonnell insisted that Stonefrost's calculations were wrong, and that the £140 million forecast was still correct. 'We went round and round the figures for over half an hour,' Livingstone wrote. He told McDonnell that he still did not believe that such cuts would be needed, and that he had instructed Race to draw up a document showing how a spending increase would be possible instead, which would be presented at the council's imminent budget meeting. According to Livingstone, McDonnell then said: 'If you don't stop Race you'll have destroyed the whole fucking [anti-government] campaign.'

Livingstone replied: 'And if these figures are right, we're going to look like the biggest fucking liars since Goebbels.'

The two men stormed back to their offices. Over the next few days, their positions diverged further. Livingstone's conviction that the GLC needed to find a way out of what he saw as the collapsing no-rate strategy grew stronger when he learned that some leftwing London borough councils were beginning to back away from the plan by drawing up motions for their own budget meetings which said only that they could not set a rate 'at that stage'. Livingstone also believed that his deputy had distorted the GLC's true financial position, and had then tried to get him and the rest of the Labour group to go along with that fiction, regardless of the consequences. In uncharacteristically stern language, Livingstone wrote: 'John had made a grave error of judgement.'

McDonnell, meanwhile, believed that his boss was 'bottling out', abandoning a principled and highly potent policy which had been collectively agreed by the GLC and other leftwing councils, in order to protect his political career, which could be badly affected if Livingstone was found to have broken the law over the rates issue. McDonnell was also furious that his fiscal rectitude as a politician, which was central to his creed that the left should wield power as effectively and sustainably as possible, had been fundamentally questioned. 'They accused me of cooking the books,' he told me, still quietly outraged almost 40 years later. 'I said to them, "Don't be ridiculous." Every budget at the GLC had to be signed off, both by the finance officers and the legal officers.'

Finally, he believed that accepting the Conservative spending cap was effectively 'accepting abolition' of the GLC, because the council's services would become so underfunded and run-down. To prevent the cap being accepted at the coming budget meeting, he even obtained a legal opinion to reassure the GLC's Tory councillors that they could vote against accepting their own government's 36.5p rate, without punishment, by voting for a lower rate instead. Thus he hoped that neither rate would be accepted, and the no-rate plan would be enacted. Unlike Livingstone, McDonnell was an ideologue; precisely because of that sense of certainty, and his belief that great political prizes were at stake, he gave himself permission to manoeuvre in unexpected ways.

In the days running up to the budget meeting, the bitter disagreement became public. McDonnell spoke to the London radio station LBC. 'Well, Ken is a friend,' he began, with ominous politeness. 'But there is no doubt that he has betrayed the whole campaign in order to save his political career.' McDonnell then told the influential north London newspaper the *Ham and High*: 'I will never trust him again . . . When it came to the crunch he chickened out.' McDonnell summoned up one of the worst possible insults that could be used against a Labour leftwinger: 'He is a Kinnock.'

Livingstone called a press conference and gave an equally furious summary of McDonnell's behaviour, accusing him of deliberately misleading his colleagues. Livingstone then made what he described afterwards as 'a long and bitter personal attack' on the man who had been his closest comrade only a week earlier. For years, the rightwing press and the right of the Labour party had been caricaturing the London left as sectarians obsessed by questions of ideological purity and internal battles. Now Livingstone and McDonnell seemed finally, after years of flexibility and collaboration, to be proving the right's case.

Three days later the budget meeting finally began. It lasted 23 hours: through large parts of a Friday, Saturday and Sunday, ending just before 8pm. The already sour mood in County Hall's circular, sometimes claustrophobic debating chamber, from which the world beyond County Hall was not visible, was not helped by the fact that the miners' strike had ended a few days earlier. The anti-rates strategy, if it survived the budget meeting, would no longer be a 'second front' against the government. The GLC and the handful of other councils would be taking on Thatcher's centralising machine on their own.

Leftwing activists mobilised by McDonnell filled the public gallery. They barracked Livingstone when he spoke. By the second day, the usually composed GLC leader was rubbing his eyes with tiredness and frustration. First, he tried to persuade the Labour group that they should vote for the 36.5p rate purely as a back-up, in case the no-rate plan was not passed and the Conservatives seized the opportunity to impose a stricter rate cap. Yet each time, this partial climbdown was rejected by McDonnell and over half a dozen other leftwing Labour councillors – enough to prevent the motion from passing, given that the party only had a GLC majority of four. Meanwhile, time slipped by towards the Sunday evening deadline for the council to set a rate, or not do so and break the law.

As councillors on the Labour right began to panic at the latter prospect, the Tory councillors saw their chance. They proposed a series of motions for a lower rate, starting at 27p and gradually moving upwards to 33p – all figures which would require deep cuts. These motions were all voted down; but Livingstone was now anxious that sooner or later the Labour right would support one of the

Tory proposals. He urged the Labour group to support the 36.5p rate. Again, McDonnell and his allies refused. Finally, seconds before the deadline, a motion was proposed by the Labour right for a rate of 33.8p. The Conservatives and some of the Labour right supported it. The Labour left, including McDonnell and Livingstone – momentarily on the same side again – opposed it. The motion passed. After months of radical rhetoric and careful planning, the GLC, the Labour left's municipal showpiece, would now have to make do with a budget considerably lower than the one the Thatcher government had originally tried to impose on it. In Livingstone's 1987 book, the chapter dealing with the saga is appropriately titled 'The Rate-capping Fiasco'.

The aftershocks went on for years. Livingstone and McDonnell, and their respective factions, publicly blamed each other for the rates disaster. Both men had a point. McDonnell's behaviour had combined panic with stubbornness, clinging on to the no-rates strategy, regardless of what new information emerged about the GLC's finances. Meanwhile Livingstone's endless searching for compromises had emboldened the Labour left's enemies. To make the GLC's chaotic climbdown look even worse, other leftwing councils such as Lambeth and Liverpool stuck to the no-rates policy for several months longer. They made the supposedly streetwise GLC seem more vulnerable to political pressure.

In April 1985, the GLC Labour group voted to sack McDonnell as the council's deputy leader and chair of finance. Livingstone survived as GLC leader, but was now considered a traitor by much of the London left: 'I was on the receiving end of ... personal hatred from many activists, including close friends,' he wrote. They 'completely cut me out of their lives'.

He was self-sufficient enough to cope. He also believed that political feuds within the left, like alliances there, were always temporary. In July, he wrote to McDonnell and invited him to lunch, to see if they could discuss 'doing something to heal the rifts on the left'. He got a letter back from McDonnell's local Labour party in Hayes. 'The left is defined within certain parameters,' it began, in a formal, tightly wound style which sounded very much like McDonnell's. 'The acceptance of class struggle, and a determination to fight in comrade-ship and solidarity . . .' The letter went on:

> You have placed yourself permanently outside of the left . . . The Hayes and Harlington [Labour party] meeting at which your correspondence was discussed was unanimous in the view that we should have no deal-ings with someone who has scabbed on the movement and his former comrades for personal political gain.

15

A Desk in the Corridor

The time that the five Labour heretics spent in the wilderness varied in its length and degree of isolation. Some of them remained nationally known. By the late 1990s, for the first time, all of them were members of parliament. Some of them even began to be seen as national treasures, with their prickliness and potentially disruptive beliefs increasingly indulged as harmless, old-fashioned expressions of integrity and principle. Yet others received tougher treatment: mockery, smears, threats and ostracism, often from their own party. These less revered leftists kept their political careers alive, and began to extend them into new areas, but often so slowly and erratically, and so far away from parliament, that for decades Westminster journalists barely noticed.

Meanwhile in the Commons, none of the five were treated as figures of current significance. They were MPs who represented a politics whose time had supposedly gone. And even when that judgement was exposed as premature, and some of the five finally became powerful, the taint of the wilderness years – the supposedly extreme things they had thought and done then; the supposedly extreme people they had associated with – would damagingly linger on.

McDonnell was first into exile. After being sacked from his main GLC jobs in 1985, he remained a backbench councillor until the council's abolition the following year. Then he spent a dozen years in less obviously political roles. He worked as head of policy for the Labour leader of Camden council, then as chief executive of the Association of London Authorities, an organisation of Labour-run boroughs, then as chief executive of the Association of London Government, a cross-party body. He took satisfaction from the detailed work, from helping to distribute as many of the GLC's functions as possible to sympathetic local authorities and specially established new bodies. But over the next few years, with the national political climate still hostile thanks to the Conservatives winning the 1987 and 1992 elections, this kind of GLC-in-exile 'just got eroded', McDonnell told me. 'Resources dried up.'

Meanwhile, his personal loss of power and status, and of taking part in the GLC's intense ideological debates and dramas, took years to adjust to – as much as he ever did. 'Personally, it was distressing,' he told a BBC2 documentary in 1998, in a rare moment of public vulnerability. 'I was [GLC] deputy leader and chair of finance, and then all of a sudden I was gone.'

He tried to become a Labour parliamentary candidate. His refusal to back down in the battle over the GLC's rate level had cemented his reputation as a person of principle among some on the London left. But there were not enough of them: during 1985 and 1986 he failed three times to be selected for a constituency in the capital. The 1987 election, at which Corbyn, Abbott, Benn and Livingstone all won or held their seats, took place without him.

By remaining highly active in the Hayes Labour party, and as a community activist in the area, he finally managed to become a parliamentary candidate there for the 1992 election. But by then Hayes was no longer a Labour seat. Instead its MP was Terry Dicks, the rude, waistcoat-wearing Tory who had wanted to bar Corbyn and other Labour 'scruffs' from parliament. Dicks had ridden the Thatcherite tide which swept up support from first-time homeowners, skilled factory workers and small businessmen in Hayes, as it did right across the outer London suburbs. Some of the seat's Labour voters also switched to the SDP. They were following the example set by Neville Sandelson, the seat's previous Labour MP, who had moved to the SDP in 1981, thus inadvertently justifying the years of attempts of McDonnell and other local leftwing activists to deselect him.

With the anti-Tory vote split, the Conservatives took Hayes at the 1983 election by over 4,000 votes. At the 1987 election, Dicks increased his majority to almost 6,000. Like some of the people who voted for him, he was a middle-aged, working-class white man with sour, often offensive views about race and immigration. He described the black Labour MP Bernie Grant, who was elected at the same time as Diane Abbott and sometimes wore traditional African robes in parliament, as looking 'like a Nigerian washerwoman'. In 1983, Dicks said that immigrants who did not like the British way of life 'could always leave and go elsewhere'. Pro-death penalty, anti-abortion and an advocate of birching football hooligans, Dicks was a reactionary and a self-publicist even by the ostentatiously illiberal standards of the late 80s and early 90s Tory party.

McDonnell despised him. 'This malignant creature,' he called him in public in 1997. In 1992, he campaigned fiercely to unseat him. Dicks had visited Iraq as a guest of Saddam Hussein's government, and McDonnell accused him of being an apologist for its atrocities.

McDonnell also knocked on thousands of doors along Hayes' meandering roads of semis and council flats. Yet despite his decade and a half as an activist in the area, the doorstep conversations he had this time came as a shock. Labour's election manifesto included a commitment to raise taxes on the top fifth of earners, while cutting them for considerably more Britons. But a lot of the voters McDonnell spoke to, even those on low wages or unemployment benefit, told him, 'I can't vote for you, because you'll increase my taxes.' A national Conservative poster campaign warning of 'Labour's Tax Bombshell', amplified by the rightwing press, had scared many people – despite great efforts by Labour to reassure them, including the unusual step of publishing a shadow budget during the campaign. McDonnell came to an unorthodox conclusion for a leftist: that it would be very hard for Labour to gain seats in a general election without first winning the fights about tax that the Tories would always start.

Steadily, his campaigning ate into Dicks' majority. But not quite enough. On an election night when Labour lost narrowly all over the country, leaving the Tories in office with a majority of 21, McDonnell's result was one of the most agonising for Labour. After four recounts, he lost by 53 votes. Dicks then sued him for libel over his Iraq allegations. Dicks won £15,000 in damages and £55,000 in costs. McDonnell reluctantly paid up, and then recommitted himself to local Labour and community activism, hoping to win the seat next time. Over the next four years, while the party finally worked out a formula for winning power, under John Smith and then Tony Blair, McDonnell did not appear in a national newspaper.

Livingstone did not have that problem. After the abolition of the GLC, he remained one of the best-known politicians in the country. His profile was sustained as much by his instantly recognisable voice and seemingly insatiable appetite for publicity as by his provocative political opinions. He gave endless quotes to journalists about the state of the Labour party. He frequently appeared on both political and non-political TV shows. He published his first autobiography, *If Voting Changed Anything, They'd Abolish It*. He even appeared in a TV advertisement for cheese: eating at an ordinary, cluttered kitchen table, tie knot pulled down like a naughty schoolboy and suit jacket rumpled. 'My favourite cheese has always been Red Leicester,' he said. Hammily, he raised an eyebrow and then frowned. 'Can't think why.' He was happy to play a cartoon of himself – in other words, to be a real celebrity, one of the first in late 20th-century British politics. After the constant stress and administrative headaches of his GLC leadership, and the decade of hard learning and manoeuvring in local government that had led up to it, he seemed to be relaxing and having a good time for a while.

He went trekking with friends in Nepal for four weeks, cutting himself off from almost all British political news for the first time since his 1960s African travels. The following month, in November 1986, he went to Israel. Along with general curiosity about a country he had never visited, this trip did have a political element. He had been invited by Mapam, a small leftwing party with a history of supporting coexistence between Jews and Arabs, and of opposing the building of Jewish settlements on Arab land. He spent two weeks in Israel, meeting Mapam activists and Jewish and Arab politicians, staying on a kibbutz, visiting the main holy and contested sites, and being interviewed by the Israeli media. 'The interviews went well,' he claimed afterwards, 'as journalists discovered I wasn't the anti-Semitic monster I'd been painted.' At the kibbutz, he was impressed by how the communal childcare liberated women. 'Everywhere I went I found myself at home,' he said later, 'primarily because I was dealing with the left of the Israeli political spectrum who already shared my views . . . I enjoyed Israel immensely.' For those who saw him as a hater of the country, his enthusiastic visit was awkward contrary evidence. In the decades of controversy to come about his views on Israel, its immensely complex history and its treatment of the Palestinians, his critics never mentioned the 1986 trip. But nor did Livingstone show any sign that the visit had made him think again. On Israel, this most flexible of leftwing politicians was rigid.

In June 1987, his year of freedom after the GLC came to an end. He became an MP. His victory in Brent East at the general election was unconvincing: Labour's usually solid majority in the seat fell by two-thirds, to a skimpy 1,653, which was no guarantee of a lasting parliamentary career. Yet with his extensive self-confidence and knowledge of psephology, Livingstone attributed the fall to the fact that he had replaced a sitting Labour MP, a process which typically caused 'about 10 per cent' of Labour supporters, in his estimation, to abstain or defect to other parties. Those voters, he believed, would come back to the party in due course.

Other Labour figures were not so sure. They noted that while the party had taken voters from the Tories at the general election in Wales, Scotland and much of England – not enough to prevent another large Thatcher majority, but a recovery of sorts – in London the flow of votes had gone the other way. The Conservatives beat Labour's vote share in the capital by 15 per cent. During the election campaign, the future Blairite minister Patricia Hewitt, then a cautious Labour strategist, had written an internal memo about the state of the contest in London. 'It is obvious from our own polling, as well as from the doorstep,' she said, 'that . . . the "loony Labour left" is now taking its toll; the gays and lesbians issue is costing us dear amongst the pensioners and fear of [Labour] extremism is particularly prominent.' The memo was leaked to the press.

For the rest of the 1980s and well into the 90s, the party continued to underperform in the capital, reducing its chances of regaining national office. Among Labour rightwingers, political analysts and journalists, this supposed tainting of the whole party by the metropolitan left became known as 'the London effect'. The fact that parts of the capital had benefited more from Thatcherism than the rest of the country was left out of this analysis. Meanwhile, the possibility that Livingstone and his comrades might in the long term be the future of the party in the capital, rather than liabilities from Labour's past, was considered far-fetched.

This suspicion of and anger at the London left followed Livingstone into the Commons. He arrived there as a new MP feeling excited, eleven years after first being selected as a parliamentary candidate. He knew that the Commons could be an inhospitable place for socialists, but so had been County Hall, and he had mastered that labyrinth. Yet while County Hall had been a huge, loosely controlled institution, full of empty spaces, literally and politically, which ambitious leftists could occupy, the Commons was a much tighter place. The Conservatives and the narrow mindset of their press allies dominated most debates. Meanwhile Kinnock was shifting Labour steadily to the right, and making the parliamentary party more centrally controlled and disciplined. Mavericks such as Corbyn, Abbott and Livingstone – who on the night he was elected an MP told the BBC on live television that Labour's national defeat was largely Kinnock's fault – were deliberately marginalised.

Livingstone discovered this as soon as he tried to set up a parliamentary office. Rooms for MPs were, as ever, in short supply. The rightwing Labour whip who allocated his party's share, Ray Powell, followed the traditional practice of rewarding the leadership's favourites while leaving likely rebels with minimal facilities. He kept a list of new MPs, ordered by how quickly he intended to give them office space. He put Abbott second-last, and Livingstone last. The former head of the GLC, who the previous year had had a palatial room in County Hall, was now forced to work in various Commons corridors, wherever there was a communal phone he could use, with all his paperwork – a vital element of his evidence-based radical politics – balanced on his lap, or on his briefcase, or spread out on the floor. He had little privacy. Parliamentary guides pointed him out to tourists. The public humiliation carried an unsubtle message for Livingstone, and for anyone who saw him: being a famous leftwinger outside parliament counts for nothing in here.

After several weeks, Livingstone, Abbott and other Labour MPs who were working in the corridors were given desks there. After eight months, Abbott was finally given an office, uncomfortably shared with three other female MPs, despite the fact that female MPs were a small minority. By the end of April 1988, 11 months on from the general election, all the corridor exiles had been given office space, except for Livingstone. Telling the *Guardian* he had had enough of 'drifting round the Commons like some medieval ghost', he gathered up his papers in a Selfridges carrier bag, picked up his briefcase in his other hand, walked out of the Palace of Westminster, stopping to pose for a photographer, smiling, and then took the bus home. He would be doing his parliamentary work there from now on, the *Guardian* reported, and would only return to the Commons to vote 'on issues dear to his heart', or if 'he thinks there is a chance of bringing down the government'.

Shortly afterwards, a Commons office space for Livingstone miraculously materialised. But he still found it hard to settle in the Commons. Its old-fashioned rules and practices frustrated him. MPs were not allowed to do paperwork in the chamber while waiting to speak, which disrupted his habit of working as continuously as possible that he had followed since his earliest days as a politician. He was also disappointed by the quality of many of the debates, especially the ones that extended impractically far into the evening and beyond. At his first 'all-nighter', he sat in the back row, as far as possible from the Commons speaker, so that he could work on his papers undetected, and half-listened to a drunk Conservative MP and a drunk Labour MP make rambling speeches. Livingstone decided that the debate was 'a complete waste of time' and went home to bed. He came back to the Commons at 7.30 the following morning and found the debate still dribbling on. He never stayed in the chamber for a whole all-nighter. In 1988, after less than a year as an MP, he summed up his impressions of the Commons for the press: 'Parliament is worse than I thought it would be. It's like working in the Natural History Museum, except not all the exhibits are stuffed.'

For his first few years in the Commons, he did his best to wake it up. He used his maiden speech to make sensational allegations about the behaviour of MI5 and the SAS in Northern Ireland during the 1970s, which he connected to Thatcher's mysterious ally Airey Neave. Livingstone repeated and expanded on recent media stories, which had been based on the testimony of two former army intelligence officers, Fred Holroyd and Colin Wallace.

They claimed that an SAS officer based in Ulster, Captain Robert Nairac, a hero in military and rightwing circles, who had been awarded a posthumous George Cross after being killed by the IRA in 1977 while operating undercover, had actually been involved in assassinations and collusion with the violent Protestant paramilitary organisation the Ulster Volunteer Force. Three of this alleged conspiracy's victims, Livingstone told parliament, had been musicians from a hugely popular Irish group, the Miami Showband. They were shot late one night in 1975 in the Ulster countryside, near the Irish border, after their minibus had been stopped at a supposed British military checkpoint. This infamous atrocity had allegedly been committed, Livingstone continued, in order to wreck a ceasefire between the IRA and Harold Wilson's Labour government, and as part of a wider plot by rightwing MI5 officers to destabilise Wilson's premiership.

Despite Livingstone's keen interest in Irish issues, he did not know enough about the murky war in Ulster to be completely sure that the allegations were true, and he made that clear in his speech. He called for the Thatcher government to 'either deal with the allegations or demonstrate they [are] untrue'. Yet by raising the issue of lethal and illegal violence by the state, or by rogue elements within it, and also by questioning the reputation of a military hero, Livingstone was stepping well outside the conventions of Commons discourse. Thatcher and many of her MPs were outraged – or pretended to be – and most Labour MPs were not supportive. Kinnock said with typical feebleness that Livingstone's speech had been 'probably unfair'. But Livingstone was undeterred. When Thatcher used prime minister's questions to denounce his speech and deny its allegations, he noted that instead of her usual, proudly upright, eyes-blazing body language when challenged, she shiftily 'crouched and did not make eye contact'.

Over the next two years, Livingstone asked 360 parliamentary questions about what he called 'the dirty war' in Northern Ireland. Many MPs and journalists felt he had turned into a crank. Without London to run, and without many prospects in the parliamentary Labour party, at least in the short term, all his energies, it could be argued, had too little to focus on. Yet alleged illegal killings and political manipulation by the state and its proxies, a conspiracy involving Westminster, Whitehall and the most unstable and violent part of the UK, were only minor issues if you subscribed to the view that Northern Ireland did not matter – a view which was increasingly hard to sustain as the undeclared civil war there continued into its third decade.

Livingstone's activities as an MP attracted the attention of the security state, watching him as he watched them. In 2015, a whistleblower who had worked for the Metropolitan Police's special branch, Peter Francis, would reveal that it had secretly kept files on the political activities of ten Labour MPs, including Livingstone, Corbyn, Abbott and Tony Benn. However marginalised and dissatisfied the left became in parliament during the 1980s and 90s, their perceived threat to the status quo remained.

For a time in the late 80s, Livingstone also remained a big figure in the wider Labour party. In 1987 he was elected to Labour's powerful national executive committee (NEC), despite not having stood for it before. In 1988 he was elected to it again. The crushing failure of Benn's leadership challenge that year meant that Livingstone – still only 43 – now seemed the one remaining leftwinger with a chance of eventually becoming leader.

Acknowledging that possibility, in 1987 the KGB sent an agent, disguised as a charming and deferential journalist from *Pravda*, to interview Livingstone and befriend him. They got on well. Livingstone started writing articles for *Pravda*, and visited Russia in 1988. But his longstanding scepticism about the Soviet Union's methods and achievements did not diminish. During his visit, he was particularly struck by being turned away from a restaurant, even though it had no other customers. The staff, he learned, were allowed to keep any unused food. 'Without a profit motive,' he wrote afterwards, 'the staff had no interest in anyone dining there at all.' Red Ken was never quite as red as his rightwing enemies, or leftwing purists, expected.

But he remained divisive enough to repel support, instead of attracting it, when the political context did not suit his tactics and message. In 1989 the Eastern bloc collapsed, and a related panic and retreat began across the Western left. Socialists such as Livingstone could be caricatured as out of date. Meanwhile, controversies lingered in the media and the Labour party about his attitude to the IRA. 'As with other colonial situations,' he had dared to suggest in 1987, the IRA's armed revolt would ultimately force Britain to negotiate and remove its troops. He also made enemies by continuing to criticise Kinnock's leadership, sometimes using arguments about contradictions within Kinnock's policies which could then be borrowed by the Tories. At the 1989 Labour party conference, all these anti-Livingstone feelings came together. To his surprise, he was not re-elected to the NEC.

His first reaction was shock. After 'twenty years as a workaholic activist', he wrote, 'my life had been turned upside down'. He partially retreated into his private life. He had recently bought his first home, a terraced house with an overgrown garden in Cricklewood, an inner suburb in north-west London, similar in its diversity and tattiness, and its psychological distance from Westminster, to Corbyn's seat in Islington. Livingstone began digging and stocking a pond and doing wildlife-friendly landscaping and planting. He called the result the Kinnock Memorial Garden.

In 1990 he became a father, having the first of two daughters with Philippa Need, a journalist from the *Ham and High*, a north London newspaper in which he had often featured. He and the girls' mother were friends rather than partners: she was single and had asked him to help her have children. He agreed that he would help bring the girls up, from a distance. The arrangement was kept private, partly because of its delicacy, and also to protect all concerned from the consequences of his reputation. Two decades later, I was interviewing Livingstone in his kitchen in Cricklewood when there was a knock on the door. It was Need. She and Livingstone chatted warmly and unselfconsciously in front of me for a while, then he gave her some money and she left. One of the reasons that he was such an effective – and to some people on the right, dangerous – advocate of looser, more accommodating social values, was that he lived by them.

However, having a fuller home life and a career as a backbench rebel was not enough to satisfy him. When Kinnock resigned after the 1992 election defeat, Livingstone stood for leader. He knew he had no chance of winning. Labour was still moving rightwards. The overwhelming favourite for the leadership was John Smith, a precisely spoken Scottish lawyer from the social democratic wing of the party who exuded caution and rectitude – seemingly as different a Labour politician from Livingstone as it was possible to imagine.

Livingstone knew that even being nominated to run against Smith, thus earning himself and the left's ideas more of a serious hearing for a few months, was pretty unlikely. After Benn had challenged Kinnock in 1988, the irritated Labour hierarchy had changed the rules for leadership contests, doubling to 20 per cent the proportion of MPs required to nominate a candidate. In 1992, that meant Livingstone needed the support of 55 MPs: more than there were in the Campaign Group and Labour's other leftwing factions put together.

For ten days, he made a show of seeking nominations, and enjoyed the increase in press attention. But he had been too much of a loner during his five years in the Commons, and too unpredictable in his stances, to get the support of the whole parliamentary left. Unlike them, he criticised Smith for proposing tax rises on too many Britons as Kinnock's shadow chancellor. Like many commentators and politicians outside the left, Livingstone argued that the policy had badly hurt Labour at the 1992 election. Meanwhile, winning over MPs from the Labour right proved even harder for him. In the end, he got an embarrassing 13 nominations from across the party. At that point, he wrote later, 'I knew . . . I would never lead the Labour party.'

He retained hopes of becoming a minister in a future Labour government. Smith was a more inclusive leader than Kinnock: he saw the left as a legitimate and useful part of the Labour coalition. Despite Livingstone's criticisms of his tax policies, the two of them sometimes had lunch when Smith was leader, 'to make sure we understood each other's positions', as Livingstone put it. For someone who had long been presumed by many of his enemies to be a nasty leftwing sectarian, Livingstone could be surprisingly positive, even sentimental, about Labour centrists who tolerated his rebellions. Smith's broad-church approach also had some similarities with Livingstone's as GLC leader, when he had recognised that he needed some alliances with the Labour right. Under Smith, Labour also quickly established a strong poll lead over the Conservatives. John Major's accident-prone, incompetent and increasingly tired government struggled in the Commons against his exacting, sometimes witty cross-examinations.

Yet in 1994, before Smith could assemble a Labour government of diverse talents – perhaps keeping Livingstone busy and out of trouble by putting him in charge of a tricky Whitehall department – he died suddenly of a heart attack. Livingstone felt 'devastated'. Again, he went through the motions of standing for the leadership, and again he failed to get enough nominations to become a candidate. Tony Blair became leader instead.

At first, Livingstone underestimated him. 'I thought he was a nice young man,' he told the *Guardian* journalist John Carvel, 'who hadn't been prepared for leadership and hadn't thought where he stood on the great global issues.' In fact, Blair was not that much younger than Livingstone: the age gap was eight years. And Blair had been an MP for four years longer. Moreover, he and his handful of equally clever and ambitious close allies, such as Gordon Brown and Peter Mandelson, had a plan for taking over and transforming Labour which was as radical, practical and democratically questionable as Livingstone's takeover of the GLC had been back in 1981.

Once Livingstone realised during the late 1990s that New Labour was going to define an era rather than be a brief centrist gimmick, he stopped regarding Blair so patronisingly and began thinking about how he could survive and even thrive under him. He had managed to be a highly successful politician for five years in the more hostile political environment of Margaret Thatcher's government, after all. The more dominant the prime minister, the greater the vacancy for someone who would defy them, to provide voters of all parties with an underdog, and general discontent with an escape valve. Livingstone knew how to play the rebel role.

Yet by the time New Labour took power in 1997, 'Red Ken', as fewer and fewer people called him, at least in a respectful way, had been making outrageous statements and asking awkward questions in the Commons for a decade. The returns were diminishing. Blair's majority was also so large that effective rebellions by the left were going to be hard to mount. Livingstone was now in his early fifties, and if his political career was going to have a second act, it was increasingly clear that it would not be in parliament. 'At the end of the day,' he told Carvel, 'I'm interested in governing.'

But in the highly centralised political system that Thatcher had created, and which Blair had largely left intact, in England at least, power resided more than ever in Downing Street, in a few influential ministries such as the Treasury, and in the massed ranks of loyal government MPs in parliament. If Livingstone could not or would not play a significant role in any of those power centres, then where else?

Diane Abbott spent over a quarter of a century as an MP struggling with similar questions. Like Livingstone, she was interested in power. And like him, she found parliament a difficult place to convert her public profile into political gains. But the inhospitality she faced there was deeper.

Not being given a parliamentary office for months after arriving in the Commons was just the start of it. Many staff in the Palace of Westminster simply refused to believe that Abbott and the three other black or Asian MPs elected in 1987 – Bernie Grant, Paul Boateng and Keith Vaz – were MPs at all. They had hardly arrived in the Commons as unknown figures: their election campaigns and victories had got plenty of media attention. During her first months as an MP, Abbott was endlessly interviewed by newspapers and magazines and news programmes, and also appeared on big current affairs shows such as *Question Time*. Still in her early thirties, she was suddenly one of the most famous young women in the country. Yet in parliament, she and the other three non-white MPs were often stopped by security staff and other attendants, and asked what they were doing in the building, and told to identify themselves. Sometimes, they were manhandled. Black and Asian constituents whom the MPs invited to visit them in the Commons often got the same treatment.

'In those days, all the Commons staff were white,' Abbott told me. 'Even the catering staff were white. Black MPs provoked fear and hostility.' Her gender singled her out even further: 'I was the only black woman in parliament for ten years.' Even MPs from her own party often treated her as an alien. 'I was in the queue in the Commons tea room behind another Labour MP. Trying to chat to him, I said, "Where are you going for Christmas?" He said somewhere in the north of England. When he asked where I was going, I said, "Jamaica". And he said, "Do they celebrate Christmas in Jamaica?"'

She was used to operating in white environments, but in the

Commons the scrutiny was more intense. Sometimes, people just stared at her, as if the idea that a black woman could become an MP had only just occurred to them, or because they thought such a thing should not happen at all. While noting all the ambient and overt racism, she also tried to tune it out. 'Life had taught me, you just had to get on with things. If you allow yourself to be derailed by racism, you won't do anything.' At times, she turned the long history of prejudice in the Commons back against the racists. At the official opening of parliament after the 1987 election, she deliberately sat in the spot on the opposition benches that had once been habitually occupied by Enoch Powell.

A few white MPs tried to make her feel she belonged. 'Jeremy [Corbyn] was very supportive.' While others kept their distance, he sat with her and the other three new non-white MPs in the Commons. Tony Banks, a more flamboyant leftwing MP who had been a key figure in Livingstone's GLC, took her to the Smoking Room, a Commons bar long associated with Conservative MPs and boozy machismo, on her very first day. Pointedly, he bought her a bottle of champagne.

Support also came from outside parliament, from black people and others not just in her constituency but all over the country. As she had acknowledged in her election night speech, 'a lot of hope' had been invested in her. With this hope came demands. There were thousands of letters, telephone calls, requests for meetings, requests for her to intervene in people's troubles, to take a stand on race-related issues. She and the three other black and Asian MPs were expected to act as role models, to make non-white Britain proud and clear the way for others to follow.

At times, the burden of all these roles was too much. Often during the first few months after being elected, Abbott said later, 'I was in a kind of daze.' 'She used to ring me up all the time,' an old ally of hers from the Labour Black Sections movement told me. 'She was quite needy.'

The abolition of the GLC the year before she became an MP meant that she and the other three new non-white MPs had lost a powerful ally outside parliament, which had been there when the Black Sections movement started. Now the four MPs were on their own.

The media regarded her with a mixture of fascination and hostility. For women's magazines, softer television interview programmes, and newspapers read by the Jamaican diaspora such as the *Gleaner*, she was a pioneer to be praised and defended. Meanwhile, for some Conservative newspaper journalists she was an exotic novelty, rather than just a typical modern Londoner. In November 1987 Colin Welch complained leeringly and mock-seriously in the *Telegraph*: 'It's illegal to call her dusky or alluring.' More often, the rightwing press was hostile. The day after she won Hackney North, a leading article in *The Times* warned that 'the far left' had 'chalked up considerable gains' in the election, citing wins by 'Mr Bernie Grant ... Mr Ken Livingstone ... [and] Ms Diane Abbott ... all extremists [who] stand between the Labour Party and any prospect of a Labour government'. The next day, another *Times* leader – it was rare for the self-important paper of the establishment to opine on the same subject two days running – described the Labour MPs as 'ambitious demagogues claiming to represent blacks, homosexuals, women and so on'. 'Mr Kinnock,' the newspaper declared, 'must ... expel them.'

A week after being elected, Abbott appeared on *Question Time*. One of the other panellists was Cyril Smith, a Liberal MP then generally seen as a jolly, harmless figure, though after his death he was revealed to be a prolific child abuser. Smith argued that one of the reasons for Labour's unpopularity was 'Diane Abbott and people like her'. When the applause from the studio audience had died down, Abbott responded. 'If Mr Smith believes that having black people in parliament for the first time is in some sense a backward step,' she said, 'thousands of people that voted for me in Hackney North would disagree.' As she was speaking, an angry murmur rose from the audience, almost loud enough to drown her out. Whether the anger was at her accusation of racism, or was an expression of racism, or was a combination of the two, it was impossible to tell. But the whiteness of the audience and the nasty atmosphere which had suddenly filled the studio were undeniable. For some people, from the very start of her parliamentary career, Abbott was intolerable.

In her constituency there were other perils. As well as racists, she was threatened by black separatists who believed she should not work with white MPs. More mildly, the establishment image of the

Commons meant that 'A lot of people in the black community said to me, "You've sold out."' Meanwhile, others expected her to help solve poisonous local problems such as the culture of Stoke Newington police station, which had become notorious for deaths in custody, usually of young black men. The constituency's mazy streets and hidden yards also housed black, white and Turkish gangs; IRA cells planning London attacks; and many active leftwing factions, some of which continued to see her as insufficiently socialist – the usurper of, and inadequate replacement for, the still-revered Ernie Roberts. Some of these disgruntled activists wanted to deselect her. As a new MP with a decent but not huge majority, she quickly became aware of these dangerous currents and of her position's general precariousness. 'If you live in Hackney,' she said in 1997, 'the question is, are you paranoid or are they out to get you?'

When she moved house to the constituency, she chose one of its few gated streets. Palatine Avenue was and is a short road with less than a dozen properties, its electric entrance gate half-hidden up an unpaved side street with disintegrating tarmac. It was a suitable address in many ways. Some of its buildings had been constructed in the 18th century to house refugees from the Palatinate region of what became Germany, who were fleeing French invasions. During the early 19th century, one of the properties had belonged for a time to John Caspar Mais, a Jamaican immigrant, entrepreneur and lawyer, who made a pioneering but unsuccessful claim for compensation to be paid to '76 enslaved people' in Jamaica. In Hackney, Abbott joined a long line of persecuted minorities and nonconformist campaigners.

Reducing local violent crime became one of her preoccupations. 'Sometimes, it took a lot of courage,' said Keith Veness, who worked with her in the constituency for decades as a Labour activist and general fixer. 'We had one meeting with predominantly older black women. Diane said to them, "If your son comes home with a gun, report it." None of the women said anything. They all just looked round the room.'

During the 1990s, her constituency gradually became less affected by crime and more gentrified. When I first went there in 1993, staying with a friend in one of Stoke Newington's more middle-class streets, a drug dealer's jeep sat idling at the end of the road all day long. When

I moved into the same street the following year, the jeep was gone. Another dealer lived next door to me, but he was less intimidating, apologising for waking me up by selling from his front doorstep in the early hours of the morning. By the time I moved out in 1997, he had also moved on.

Abbott's local status steadily improved as well. At the 1992 election she increased her majority by over a third, to over 10,000, and at the 1997 election she increased it again, to over 15,000. She was not loved in Hackney North, as Corbyn increasingly was in next-door Islington North. Casual conversations I had about the two MPs with fellow residents in both places during this period made the contrast obvious. Unlike Corbyn, Abbott could lack tact and patience with constituents. But she was admired, for her path-breaking, for her resilience against racists and other enemies, and for speaking her mind.

Sometimes the latter habit brought trouble. In 1996, she used a fortnightly column she wrote for the *Hackney Gazette* to criticise a local hospital for hiring 'blonde, blue-eyed girls from Finland, instead of nurses from the Caribbean who know the language and understand British culture and institutions'. Rarely able to resist pushing a provocative argument as far as possible, she went on: 'Are Finnish girls, who may never have met a black person before, let alone touched one, best suited to nurse in multi-cultural Hackney?'

An international row followed. Abbott was accused of racial stereotyping and even racism. There were complaints to the British police and the Commission for Racial Equality. The Finnish embassy in London pointed out that 'not even 20% of Finns are blonde and blue-eyed'. For a day, Abbott tried to justify her stance as being motivated by concern for her constituency rather than by national prejudice. 'The issue is not one of colour,' she told the *Guardian*, 'the issue is that people should not be recruited from overseas in an area of mass unemployment.' The Royal College of Nursing supported her, to a degree, by saying that recruiting from overseas was a short-term solution to staff shortages in British hospitals, which were chronic after 17 years of Tory rule. But Abbott's clumsy language and use of national stereotypes made an apology unavoidable. She made it with limited grace, while also belittling the newspaper that had given her a column: 'I very much regret that one sentence of my article for a local paper has led to a widespread misunderstanding of my position ... My priority is the best possible health service for my constituents, employing the very best people irrespective of race.'

Saying sorry, in any public context, was difficult for Abbott. The reluctance was partly down to her stubborn, in some ways introverted personality. But it was also a sign of her vulnerability: she was too isolated and unusual a public figure to be forgiven for her mistakes like more mainstream politicians. But her critics were rarely interested in her disadvantages. They saw her surface certainty as arrogance. And black politicians, unlike white counterparts such as Margaret Thatcher, were not allowed that.

On occasion, however, Abbott's unapologetic and outspoken manner won her admiration in parliament, or at least a sort of startled respect. She showed little deference towards Kinnock or Blair as Labour leaders. In 1996, when Blair was at the peak of his power and prestige as prime-minister-in-waiting, Labour backbenchers were summoned in groups to see him. Abbott was supposed to be in one with her fellow leftwinger Chris Mullin, still a member of the Campaign Group but beginning to find common ground with New Labour on issues such as crime. Mullin recorded in his diaries that Abbott 'waltzed in' to the meeting with Blair '20 minutes late'. She then told her leader that New Labour made people feel 'talked at rather than listened to'. As a result, she went on, the party was 'losing sight of those who traditionally voted for us', leftwing people and the working class.

When Labour won power the following year with a crushing majority of 179, Abbott's warning, like similar warnings during the mid-1990s from Livingstone, Benn and Corbyn about the electoral risks being taken by New Labour, seemed hopelessly off the mark. The party's win was so dramatic and such a relief, after 18 years out of office, that even Blair sceptics in the party celebrated. Abbott was one of them:

When I finished my count [in Hackney], my friends and I went down to [the] Southbank [where Labour's victory gathering was], and it was just the most amazing feeling. We parked, and we walked up. People were stopping and saying well done, well done ... It felt like I had waited my whole life for this.

But in fact her warnings about New Labour were not wrong, just premature. Over the next three general elections, under Blair and then Brown, the party would shed almost 5 million voters, over a third of its 1997 total, and end up almost back where it had been when Kinnock had begun moving it to the right a quarter of a century earlier. At the 2010 election, as in 1983, Labour would spend much of the campaign trying to avoid coming third.

During New Labour's long decline, Abbott's own majority, despite her distance from Blair and Brown, also fell. Hackney voters were meant to admire dissenters; but they did not give her enough credit, it appeared, for being one of parliament's most frequent rebels. What credit she did receive did not outweigh the apathy and alienation among many voters which New Labour gradually created. The same forces eroded Corbyn's majority too, despite his greater local popularity. Under a Labour government as under a Conservative one, the wilderness in which the left was trapped seemed to go on and on.

16

'A Wasted Resource'

Corbyn was better suited than Abbott, Livingstone or McDonnell to life on the margins. His ambitions were more modest: to serve his complex constituency, and to stand up for neglected foreign causes. He was more interested in acquiring knowledge than power; and in becoming an effective campaigner rather than a minister or leading Labour figure. So although his stances were often radical, at odds with the status quo at home and abroad, and the stubbornness with which he maintained them was a challenge to less principled MPs, Corbyn was generally not seen as much of a threat by the Westminster establishment. 'You really don't have to worry about Jeremy Corbyn suddenly taking over,' Blair told Joe Murphy, a veteran political journalist for rightwing papers, during a conversation about Labour's future in 1996.

Corbyn's parliamentary manner reinforced this unthreatening reputation. His speeches remained strident: the sound of a lifelong activist trying to make himself heard above the murmuring cross-party consensuses and rhetorical conventions. But outside the chamber Corbyn avoided confrontations. Even the fiercest Labour whips, whose pressure to vote with the party leadership Corbyn routinely ignored, found that he would not get into an argument with them. Instead, he would state his dissenting position in the fewest words possible, and look at the floor. He rarely explained his rebellions to the whips, or to other MPs; nor, increasingly, was he expected to. Everyone knew where 'Jeremy' stood, and that it was not with most MPs.

Yet at the same time, on an individual level, he wanted to get on with everyone in parliament, whatever their party. He was polite. He rarely raised his voice. He did not spread malicious gossip or slag people off. Gradually, these benign qualities were noticed, and appreciated, by other MPs of all parties, as was the consistency and determination of his stances. He became a fixture in the Palace of Westminster: sometimes in a huddle with Abbott, Benn, Livingstone and other Campaign Group comrades; or sitting alone at the very back of the Labour benches in the chamber, generally listening rather than speaking; or rushing along the corridors from one meeting to another, clutching a mass of documents, usually running late. He was seen as a purist; and even, with his beard and plain clothes, a kind of political holy man. He was admired, and he was seen as an irrelevance.

He voted repeatedly against the Labour leadership: 64 times during Blair's first government, more than any other Labour MP. He regularly railed against the Conservatives, with a moral force less principled MPs lacked. Otherwise, his main contribution to the life of the Commons was to sponsor, co-sponsor or sign lots of early day motions, a parliamentary device commonly used to draw attention to an issue. One issue of many that he kept returning to during his decades as an MP was antisemitism.

On 7 November 1990, he signed an early day motion condemning an increase in antisemitic publications in Britain. On 2 November 1992, he was the main sponsor of a motion condemning a planned march by the National Front, as 'an insult to the memory of all victims of the Nazi holocaust'. On 30 April 2002, he was the main sponsor of a motion condemning the vandalism of a synagogue in his constituency. On 8 March 2006, he signed a motion condemning an Iranian newspaper for soliciting cartoons about the Holocaust. On 14 November 2007, he co-sponsored a motion calling for more effort to reduce poverty and social exclusion in the east London Jewish community. On 27 January 2009, he signed a motion welcoming action against antisemitism on university campuses. On 22 February 2010, he co-sponsored a motion urging the government to allow more Jews from Yemen into Britain. On 13 June 2012, he co-sponsored a motion calling on the BBC not to drop a Jewish programme, *Jewish Citizen Manchester*, from its broadcasting schedule. On 1 March 2013, he signed a motion condemning antisemitism in sport.

In all, Corbyn was involved in 46 early day motions either

opposing antisemitism or supporting the Jewish community, or both, between his election as an MP in 1987 and 2015. He also helped the Jewish Labour MP Margaret Hodge, whom he knew from her time as leader of Islington council in the 1980s, but whose politics had since moved well to the right of his, when her constituency of Barking in east London was targeted by the antisemitic British National Party (BNP). Between 2005 and 2010, the BNP won council seats there, and almost overtook the Conservatives as the second-placed party behind Labour at general elections. Hodge later told Corbyn's biographer Rosa Prince:

> Jeremy must have come down two or three times, brought a car full of people from Islington to help me . . . That's Jeremy – I think he appeared more often than any other London MP. I was fighting fascism and that would be completely up his street.

Yet most of his work received little attention from Westminster journalists, and was often unnoticed even by his own constituents. I became one of them in 1997. I voted for him at the 2001 general election, regarding him as a worthy, idealistic, but slightly hazy figure: a critic and unofficial conscience of the less consistent but more important politicians of New Labour. Despite the fact that I had been covering British politics as a journalist for half a dozen years, I did not know much else about him.

A few years earlier, I had been given a copy of *The Islington Cookbook*, a 1993 collection of recipes for charity contributed by an exhaustive selection of the borough's well-known and locally known residents. Tony Blair, then living in Barnsbury, one of Islington's more elegant southern neighbourhoods, and sharing in the era's middle-class enthusiasm for Italy, contributed 'pasta with sun-dried tomatoes'. Chris Smith, the 'soft left' – or in other words, periodically leftwing – Labour MP for Islington South, provided a recipe for gingerbread. And Abbott offered her take on 'West Indian rice and peas', despite not being an Islington resident. Yet there was no contribution from Corbyn. Perhaps he had been too busy, or was still too uninterested in cooking. Whatever the reason, his absence felt appropriate. Among the book's striving, self-publicising minor and major celebrities – typical worldly middle-class Islingtonians from politics, the media and the arts – he might have seemed out of place.

In private, and among close comrades, he could be less earnest. With a sudden cheeky grin, one front tooth poking out slightly more than the others, he would mock the intransigence of the left's enemies – 'Some things never change … like the Daily Telegraph!' – exactly as they sometimes mocked his. Treating the power structures as absurd was a way of making the struggle against them less all-consuming, at least for a moment, so that the struggle could then be continued afresh. It was an old leftist trick.

Occasionally, Corbyn even made risky jokes about politics in public. For a period in the early 2020s, a café at the British Library in London employed a barista who could make particularly intricate patterns with cappuccino foam. One day, Corbyn came into the café. He got talking to its staff, as was his habit with almost all members of the public, and learned about the barista's aptitude. The barista then offered Corbyn a decoration of his choice. Corbyn asked the barista to make him a coffee topped with a hammer and sickle.

Corbyn met his second wife at a leftwing event. In 1986, he was in the audience for one of Livingstone's speeches when he got chatting to a young Chilean woman whose background immediately fascinated him. Claudia Bracchitta came from a family of Chilean and Spanish leftists. One of her grandfathers had fought against General Franco in the 1930s, and one of her uncles had been Salvador Allende's personal physician in the 70s. The uncle had been in the presidential palace with Allende when the Chilean military attacked it in 1973. After the coup, Bracchitta, then 11 years old, and her mother escaped to London, and built a new life among the capital's extensive network of Chilean exiles and supportive local leftists.

The Bracchittas moved to Haringey, Corbyn's first political territory in the capital, and mother and daughter both became involved in the activism and socialising of the north London left. When Claudia and Jeremy finally, perhaps inevitably, met, they quickly started a serious relationship, marrying in 1987 and having a son, Benjamin, the same year. Corbyn wanted to keep his family life private, perhaps mindful of all the malicious prying Livingstone and Benn had experienced from the Tory press, and for the first few years he succeeded. He was the only MP to refuse to confirm his marital status to Andrew Roth, a much-read observer of Westminster who published a regularly updated potted biography of every MP. People who met Corbyn and Bracchitta at parties were sometimes startled when the ungroomed MP introduced the glamorous Chilean as his wife.

In 1994, after eight years with Corbyn, she finally agreed to being interviewed, for a *Guardian* article about women married to MPs. She did not hold back. Her husband's work took up too much of his time, she said. He had even left her bedside when she was in labour with Benjamin to make a speech to the hospital's trade unionists. 'The problem with Jeremy,' she said, 'is that he does not know how to say no. So he's always attending some meeting or other when not in parliament. I am therefore the one who has to be there all the time for the kids.' They had had a second son, Sebastian, in 1991. 'I would love to see him [Corbyn] more,' she continued, 'because [our children] need us both. He tries to find the time and is getting better, but politics is very consuming.' His absences and the lack of childcare in parliament – 'not one nursery or crèche,' she said – were frustrating her plans to become a mature student or a graphic artist.

In private, further tensions built up between them over Ben's education. Corbyn believed that their sons should go to local state schools, partly because that was what less privileged children had to do, and partly because he wanted their sons to have a more egalitarian education than his own. But there was a problem with this principled stance: Islington schools were officially among the worst in the country. Inner London's struggling education system, often avoided by the middle class, was a lingering symptom of the city's postwar decline.

For several years, Corbyn and Bracchitta sent Ben to a troubled local primary school, where he was unhappy and unsettled. Bracchitta became determined that he should not have the same experience at secondary school. In 1997, she and Corbyn applied for him to attend the one good comprehensive that was relatively close to their home, but it was too popular for him to get in. Instead, Islington Education Authority offered him a place at Holloway Boys School, then classified as 'failing'. To Bracchitta, the offer was unacceptable, yet for a time Corbyn, away from home a lot as usual, simply avoided the issue. Avoidance was often his approach when confronted with difficult situations, as it was with difficult people.

Then a potentially explosive solution to the problem presented itself. As a long shot, Bracchitta had also applied for a place for Ben at a grammar school in outer London. It required an entrance exam that she thought he was unlikely to pass, since he had had no special coaching for it. But he did pass. For months, Corbyn told Bracchitta that he was implacably against their son going to a selective school in a distant borough, and she told him that she felt the same way about Ben going to Holloway Boys. In the end, in 1998, Bracchitta got her way: as the more present parent, she ultimately had more say over the family's school choices. Shortly afterwards, she and Corbyn separated.

For a year, they kept their break-up secret. But in 1999 the press found out. Journalists feasted on the rich mixture of parental and political issues, and revelations about a previously private couple, that had suddenly been provided. Generally, the articles took Bracchitta's side. 'Jeremy thinks as a politician first, and as a parent only second,' was one headline in the *Mail on Sunday*, as if Corbyn's personal moral code, which had partly cost him his marriage, was mainly about self-promotion and popularity.

He hated the attention. Not only did it make him famous, or infamous, for a few weeks, in a way that he had never sought or previously experienced; the episode also trivialised his politics, so that his belief in equality and in practising what you preached was presented as priggishness, as an inflexibility that made him impossible to live with. For the powerful interests they threatened, it was important that people of the left such as Corbyn were presented as difficult and limited people: as fanatics.

In fact, he and Bracchitta had remained close since their separation. When the school story broke, they were in the middle of having a house they had recently bought together converted into two flats, so that they could bring up their children as jointly as possible. Between 1998 and 2000, they also worked together closely as political campaigners. It was on an issue central to both their political lives and preoccupations.

In October 1998 Augusto Pinochet, who had unwillingly stepped down as dictator of Chile eight years earlier after losing a referendum on the issue, was arrested in London. An international warrant had been issued by a Spanish judge who was investigating some of his regime's atrocities against Spanish citizens, and who was seeking his extradition. Allegations of murder, kidnapping and torture against Pinochet were not new, and the evidence for them was undeniable, but never before had any country, including Chile, acted decisively to bring the ex-dictator to justice. During the early and mid-1990s, when the Conservatives were still in power in Britain, Pinochet had regularly visited the country, helping arrange arms sales to Chile, and seeing political allies such as Margaret Thatcher, whose government had shared some of his regime's enthusiasm for freeing business from regulation while repressing dissident citizens. Pinochet also enjoyed the old-fashioned shops and restaurants of smart parts of London such as Piccadilly. Meanwhile Corbyn and other British and Chilean leftists fumed, protested, and called in vain for his detention.

Now, in 1998, a Labour government had finally done it. By chance, the home secretary Jack Straw, whose view of the situation was pivotal, had visited Chile in the 1960s, like Corbyn, and like him had been excited by the promise of the Chilean left. For a year and a half after his arrest, Pinochet was held under house arrest near London, while the acceptability of his extradition to Spain was repeatedly considered by the House of Lords. Chilean and British protesters, for and against Pinochet, mounted loud and tireless demonstrations, distributed leaflets, and awakened an argument about the dictatorship which had been largely dormant in Britain for decades.

Corbyn was a key figure in the pro-extradition campaign: making speeches in parliament and in the streets, signing Commons motions, submitting petitions, giving interviews to British, Chilean and other foreign journalists, and constantly encouraging and advising the anti-Pinochet exiles. After his quarter of a century campaigning on Chile, which had become an increasingly lonely occupation, the arrest and detention of Pinochet and the renewed awareness of his crimes was exhilarating for Corbyn, and also a relief and a vindication. His prominence in the pro-extradition campaign also brought threats. In February 1999 hundreds of posters appeared on walls in his constituency. They read: '3000 missing. Jeremy Corbyn MP, you're next.' The Pinochet regime was infamous for abducting, torturing and killing exactly that number of dissidents. But Corbyn claimed not to be intimidated. 'These fascist thugs don't scare me at all,' he told the *London Evening Standard*. 'I shall carry on my campaign.'

In March 2000, Pinochet was released by Straw on the questionable grounds that he was too frail to be extradited, and flew back to Chile. Like anti-Pinochet activists worldwide, Corbyn was intensely disappointed. The ex-dictator would live for another six and a half years. His release from Britain could be seen as a typical New Labour compromise: challenging the forces of the right, but only up to a point. However, in Chile and elsewhere Pinochet's already damaged reputation was weakened by the humiliations and revelations of his arrest, incarceration and flight from Britain. In Chile, a belated reckoning began about what his regime had done. Corbyn's anti-Pinochet work had finally helped make a decisive difference.

But questions of success or failure, at least as conventionally understood in politics, rarely preoccupied him. Instead, like Benn and other patient, idealistic leftists, he saw political participation as an end in itself, and victories as being won over decades or even centuries, often in unnoticed increments. From the early 1970s to the early 2010s, Corbyn was a ubiquitous presence at leftwing events: on marches, at rallies, on picket lines, at occupations and on vigils, however tiny or seemingly futile – events at which few or no other Labour MPs were present. He rarely made the most memorable speech, or attracted much attention. Still skinny as he moved through middle age, he wore his usual baggy, low-key clothes to public protests and spoke in his usual limited but fierce rhetorical mode through borrowed megaphones. More charismatic leftists such as Benn or Livingstone were sometimes needed to give the protests a spark. But Corbyn always turned up. In a country that often values these qualities, he was reliable, dogged, humble, and seemingly not in any way hypocritical. Gradually, more and more activists and other leftwing people across the country met him, worked with him, liked him, and owed him political debts. One day in the future, unimaginable during these slow decades of demonstrating in the cold and the rain, those connections and debts would be decisively cashed in.

*

Very gradually, and not consciously, he began to supersede his hero Benn. From the late 1980s onward, Benn's activities slowly became less of a threat to the status quo, in the minds of his enemies and in his own. One sign of this withdrawal from frontline politics was the increasing importance to him of keeping a diary. He had done so since childhood, partly to satisfy the puritan impulse he had inherited from his father, to make use of all his time and to keep an account of how he had done it. As a new MP in the early 1950s, he had begun focusing the diary on his political experiences. During periods of personal crisis, such as his ejection from the Commons on inheriting his father's peerage in the early 60s, he had stopped writing the diary for long stretches, but with time these gaps became shorter and less frequent. Keeping a record of his political career, including his day-to-day feelings about his performance, the state of the Labour party and the country, and his dealings with colleagues and vice versa, became almost as important to him as the career itself. Unsettlingly for many of his comrades, and unusually for a politician with strong, supposedly all-consuming convictions, he was an observer as well as a participant. It was one of the reasons he was not trusted.

When he became minister of technology and a member of the cabinet in 1966, he began dictating his diary into a tape recorder, to get round the Whitehall rule that accounts of cabinet meetings could not be directly dictated to secretaries, who were not covered by the Official Secrets Act. Benn built up a huge archive of tapes, without knowing whether he would ever have time to transcribe them, or would ever have them transcribed by someone else. If the tapes were to be turned into a book, or books, he assumed that publication would not happen in his lifetime.

During the mid-1980s, as his prospects narrowed and he neared his 60th birthday, he began to change his mind. He transcribed several months of tapes to see how they read on the page. He was still busy trying to keep the socialist flame alive in Chesterfield and beyond. So he hired someone to begin transcribing the others.

Ruth Winstone was a polite, efficient, and self-contained young woman, with politics similar to Benn's but an independent mind, who had previously helped his Labour ally Chris Mullin with a book project. She did not actually know much about Benn when she started working for him, other than that he had stood up for a lot of lost causes, and was now at a low point. While she transcribed the tapes in the basement kitchen of his London house – the only space on that floor which was not piled with his accumulating papers, mementoes and other office paraphernalia – she quickly became aware that Benn was frustrated and looking for a new outlet. His courteous manner and endless comforting mugs of tea did not disguise it.

Within a few months of her starting, the transcription had acquired a concrete goal: what Benn called 'the diary project'. He asked her if she would edit the transcripts into a series of books, while supervising other people who would take over the transcribing. She agreed. The first volume was published in 1987, and the books soon became a success. They sold well, perhaps unsurprisingly for diaries by a controversial politician. More strikingly, they were sympathetically reviewed – more so than anything he had done in public life for decades.

The diaries gave him renewed energy and purpose. His home office became busy with volunteer typists and researchers, called 'teabags', because of their tea-making duties, and also as an acronym for 'The Eminent Association of Benn Archive Graduates'. Some of them were teenagers from families that Benn knew through the incestuous London left, such as Ed Miliband, one of Ralph Miliband's sons, who chose to spend most of the summer holidays after his O-levels in Benn's basement. If Benn could not change Labour through his actions in the party, perhaps he could do so through his diaries, as both a corrective to the traditional account of events and a kind of miniature political academy.

On the page, he was almost as compelling as in the flesh: indiscreet about his colleagues and party without being nasty; open about his wild mood swings between optimism and gloom; frank about his health problems and his dependence on his family; and alert to the big but not always obvious shifts and turning points in British politics. Yet on the page he was also tamed in some ways. The titles of the volumes that covered 1968 to 1990 were downbeat – *Office Without Power*; *Against the Tide*; *Conflicts of Interest*; *The End of an Era* – as if his career was doomed from the moment he turned leftwards. And by definition 'the diary project' looked backward, not forward: it was about defeats and lost opportunities much more than future possibilities.

The diaries were not always melancholy and introspective. People whom Benn saw as promising new Labour talents, such as Corbyn and Ed Miliband, were regularly identified. For a supposed political narcissist, Benn was very interested in other people and generous towards them. But by publishing his diaries, and on such an epic scale, he tacitly accepted that he would be seen increasingly as a writer rather than a doer from now on. Rather than roaming through ministries and party conferences, constantly threatening vested interests, on the pages of his diaries he was contained. It was the beginning of his comfortable confinement as a national treasure.

Taking refuge in the diaries seemed ever more necessary during the late 1980s and early 90s. Labour's relentless creep to the right under Kinnock; the post-Soviet sweep of free-market policies across eastern Europe; the growing enthusiasm for the EEC among trade unionists and other British leftists; even a more cautious, more pro-Kinnock mood in his constituency party – all these developments alarmed and depressed Benn. 'I feel a bit left behind somehow,' he said in November 1988. The following year, he organised another socialist conference in Chesterfield. About 1,200 people came: 'not quite as many as last year,' he recorded. 'People on the left are extremely demoralised . . .'

In 1990, his shrinking prospects appeared to narrow drastically. He was diagnosed with leukaemia, and told he might have only another three or four years to live. The condition was chronic rather than necessarily terminal, so he decided not to make it public, fearing that it would immediately create a competition to succeed him in Chesterfield, which would make continuing as the MP very difficult. As long as his health allowed, he would represent the seat, checking with doctors before each election about whether standing again was a wise decision. In the event, his condition did not worsen. Right through the 1990s and into the early 2000s, it remained secret to everyone except his family. After a long run of bad luck and defeats, stretching right back to his illness during his deputy leadership bid in 1981, the remission of his leukaemia was a huge reprieve. But could Benn do more with his remaining years than be a famous chronicler of the left's retreat?

*

One evening in May 1990, he met up with Corbyn at the Commons. At Benn's instigation, they had smuggled into parliament a toolbox containing screws and a Black & Decker drill, a framed photo and an inscribed brass plaque. The photo and plaque honoured Emily Wilding Davison: a suffragette who on census night in 1911 had hidden in a broom cupboard in the crypt of the parliamentary chapel, so that her address would have to be recorded as the House of Commons, and so that in that sense at least, her political status would be the same as a man's.

Seventy-nine years later, after a quick dinner in the Commons cafeteria, Benn and Corbyn set off for the chapel, as inconspicuously as it was possible for two troublemaking MPs carrying a toolbox to manage. The evening corridors and hallways were quiet, but a policeman spotted them and asked what they were doing. Corbyn, who despite his heart-on-sleeve reputation could be cunning, put on his most saintly air and told the policemen that he and Benn were going to the chapel, saying nothing about the toolbox. The officer insisted on accompanying them, explaining that the chapel was locked and he had the key. He even carried the toolbox for them, never asking why they had it. He unlocked the chapel and walked away.

Benn and Corbyn went to the cupboard Wilding had hidden in, and attached the plaque and the photo to the inside of the door. The inscription on the plaque emphasised that the suffragette had acted 'illegally' by her incursion, and that two years later she died 'from injuries sustained when she threw herself under the King's horse at the Derby'. 'By such means,' the inscription concluded, 'was democracy won for the people of Britain.' The illicit memorial was not meant to be a cosy heritage plaque. But after initial resistance, the parliamentary authorities allowed it to remain.

With help from his protégé, Benn had won a small, satisfyingly concrete victory about the past. In 1990 he also began work on a much larger-scale and less achievable project, which he hoped would shape the future. The Government of Britain Bill, later renamed the Commonwealth of Britain Bill, was an attempt to create 'a completely new constitution from scratch', as he put it. The resulting document, published as a paperback in 1993, included:

devolution of power from London to Scotland, Wales and the English regions ... votes at [the age of] sixteen ... equal representation of the sexes in Parliament ... replacing the monarch with an elected President ... [and] the House of Lords with a House of the People ... reform of our legal system under which magistrates would be elected ... a Freedom of Information Act and the parliamentary supervision of the security services.

The bill did not cover Northern Ireland, except to say that 'the jurisdiction of Britain [there] shall cease'. It also proposed that 'every citizen' of Britain should have 'social rights', such as 'warm housing' and 'free and equal access to child care'; and 'economic rights', such as 'a fair wage ... sufficient to maintain a decent standard of living', and the right 'to participate in all decisions ... affecting the workplace'.

For anyone dissatisfied with the status quo – and by the early 1990s Britain in its second decade of Tory rule was a stuck and fraying place – Benn's clearly written, wide-ranging document was an intriguing and potentially intoxicating read. I came across it as a recently formed, still quite ignorant leftist at Oxford University. I was studying modern history, which on the British part of the syllabus mostly meant 20th-century Toryism. I was also encountering precocious undergraduates who would go on to be New Labour ministers. Compared to the depressing insistence of these assured young politicos that the big battles between left and right were now over, or too difficult for the left to continue fighting, and compared to the cynical calculations of the Tory governments I was studying, Benn's call for a whole new political order in Britain felt thrilling. It included so many of the left's demands and wishes, some of them going back centuries. It also integrated them with seemingly all the causes Benn had been pursuing, such as workers' control, since his radicalisation had begun in the late 1960s. In some ways, the document was his ultimate statement.

But most of it was also a dead end, at least in the short term. While versions of some of what Benn wanted would eventually happen – devolution, freedom of information, more women in parliament, the living wage – his constitution's more radical, more disruptive reforms, such as the abolition of the Lords and the monarchy, were politically impossible in the early 1990s without a much bolder Labour party, and they remain so today. Benn introduced the Commonwealth of Britain Bill to parliament in 1991 as a private member's bill, seconded by Corbyn, but unsurprisingly with no official support from Labour. The bill did not make it to a second reading. Over the next decade, Benn introduced it several more times, but the result was always the same.

This probably did not come as a surprise to him. Having seen the conservatism of parliament and of most of his party up close for half a century, he almost certainly knew that his bill's impact, if it had much at all, would be symbolic rather than practical. But in the unlikely eventuality of there ever being a truly radical Labour government, Benn's constitution, if anyone thought to consult it, could give ministers plenty of good ideas.

By the early 1990s, Benn and Corbyn had formed quite an effective double act. But it was hardly a partnership of equals, given their differing levels of fame and political experience. Then, in 1997, New Labour's first electoral triumph inadvertently provided Corbyn with another parliamentary comrade to make trouble with: this time someone of similar age and seniority. John McDonnell finally got elected to the Commons.

Hayes and Harlington was one of dozens of seats across southern England that New Labour gained from the Tories. That McDonnell was the beneficiary, rather than a less leftwing, more biddable candidate – of the sort that New Labour imposed on most other constituencies – was down to his unusual reputation. While its radical aspects meant that 'some elements' on the right of the party, as he put it, 'tried to block me', he also had acquired a respectability through his hard work for the London local government associations, which included collaborating with the Labour right and sometimes even Tory politicians, and advising Labour shadow ministers about the capital's problems. Like Livingstone, with whom he gradually, if not completely, mended fences during the 1990s, McDonnell had much more administrative experience than the average leftwing parliamentary hopeful or MP.

He also had a pre-existing public profile in Hayes. Since being narrowly defeated for the seat by Terry Dicks five years earlier, he had kept up his activism there. He had a seemingly inexhaustible appetite for meetings, whether public, private, or secret. He knew every corner of the constituency, where he had lived for almost a quarter of a century. And he knew the local issues, from the provision of public toilets in the town centre to the particularly deep poverty of the ward where he lived. 'John's meetings were always packed tight: white working class, lots of Sikhs,' Valerie Veness, the veteran London Labour activist, told me. 'They all loved John. People in the local party who didn't share his politics still loved him. The work John did in Hayes was like what Jeremy had done in Islington: involving party members, constantly campaigning.'

Boosted by the national enthusiasm for Blair, he won with a majority of 14,291 – far greater than Corbyn or Abbott achieved when they first won their seats. Unlike Hackney or Islington, Hayes was not obvious territory for the radical left. Instead of politicised incomers, lots of public spaces for gatherings, and busy networks of squats and cooperatives, it had quiet suburban streets of small businesses and semis, with new cars squeezed into tight driveways. Cannily, McDonnell presented himself to his constituents not as the iconoclastic former deputy leader of the GLC but as an unideological figure, working non-stop for local causes. He summed up for me how he wanted locals to see him: 'They say he's "loony left" in the papers, but I know the bloke, and actually he helped my family. And I saw him at the community centre, and at so-and-so's funeral . . .' His constituency office was almost comically no-frills: a large pebble-dashed hut, the door paint ripped by years of taped-up notices. His new comrades in the parliamentary Labour left quickly discovered that it could be hard to get him to leave the constituency.

When he did, it was often to campaign with Corbyn. They became bonded by their differences as much as their similarities. Corbyn admired McDonnell's organisational ability, his grasp of detail, his fierceness and, less openly, his working-class credentials. McDonnell admired Corbyn's ability to get on with almost anyone, his personal integrity, his global political interests and much greater Commons experience.

At leftwing mobilisations away from parliament, from tiny picket lines to major demonstrations, they became a familiar pairing: McDonnell neat and intense, Corbyn baggier in his dress and his sentences, both speaking with utter conviction, listening patiently to each other's unvarying speeches, patting each other lightly on the shoulder afterwards. In parliament, meanwhile, their voting behaviour was almost identical. During Blair's first government, McDonnell defied the Labour whip 59 times, only five times fewer than Corbyn, and almost always on the same issues. They were the two least obedient Labour MPs, and remained so throughout the party's 13 years in office, and afterwards, right up to 2015. As the layers of shared experience built up, Corbyn began describing McDonnell publicly as his 'best friend in politics', suggesting that a loneliness had been alleviated – a loneliness that his relationship with Benn had not been able to fill. McDonnell, more guarded than Corbyn in his public tone, would simply say again and again how much he agreed with 'Jeremy'.

After taking part in central London demonstrations, they would habitually go together to Gaby's, a long-established Middle Eastern café just up from Trafalgar Square. Behind the mounds of salad half-blocking the front window, the narrow but deep interior of Gaby's had formica tables, ceiling fans and discreet nooks and crannies. As the centre of London became slicker and pricier from the late 1990s onwards, partly because of the Blair government's desire to create a more 'dynamic' capital, Gaby's, founded in 1965, seemed more and more of an anachronism. The renewal of its lease became a fraught process. But its cosmopolitan food was cheap. McDonnell particularly liked the grainy, homemade hummus. And the café was often convivial, with middle-aged regulars talking politics at the closely packed tables, sometimes with placards from demonstrations resting beside them. As an example of the sort of milieu the two MPs liked, it was as appealing as it was precarious. Would Gaby's survive for much longer? As with the Labour left in the Blair era, it was hard to say.

New Labour's approach to dissident socialist MPs was not to crush them but to isolate them. Blair's big majorities meant that rebellions by the left were expected to be, at most, irritations and embarrassments, rather than decisive parliamentary threats. Appearing to tolerate the left could be a demonstration of strength. Mixed in with this confidence was also an anxiety: that confronting the left directly would remind voters of Labour's splits during the 1980s. Blair himself was also particularly aware of how difficult it might be to get rid of some leftwing MPs. Having lived in both Hackney and Islington before becoming prime minister, close to both Corbyn's and Abbott's constituencies, he knew how entrenched they had become. At the 1997 election, Abbott and Corbyn beat their nearest challengers by 48 per cent and 56 per cent of the vote respectively. 'Blair kind of accepted you'd have some left MPs in the party, because some local parties wanted them,' Abbott told me. Blair also had a residual reverence for the socialist who had captivated him and Cherie back in the 1980s. 'He respected Tony Benn,' said Abbott, 'partly because of the continuing strength of Benn's support.' To a small but significant extent, this respect legitimised Benn's protégés in Blair's eyes. As Abbott saw it, 'Benn gave us cover.'

So Blair and the New Labour hierarchy resisted intermittent pressure from people on the right of the party to have the rebels expelled or deselected. Instead, they sought to starve them politically. New MPs were discouraged from joining them in the Socialist Campaign Group – or even from talking to them. Alan Simpson, a leftwing MP during the 1990s and 2000s, told me: 'The whips would say, "You want to be careful having conversations with Jeremy Corbyn. Careers can be ruined that way."' The rebels were generally kept off Commons select committees by the party hierarchy. Much of their life at Westminster became a kind of limbo. They were not controlled: Corbyn was not given a pager, New Labour's electronic prod for herding MPs. But the remaining leftwingers were rarely influential in parliament. They would grow old together, the party hierarchy hoped, and no one would take their place. Blair's strategist Peter Mandelson had a phrase for what he wanted the parliamentary left to become: 'a sealed tomb'.

McDonnell was even more isolated from the party mainstream than other MPs on the left. His character was seen as the reason. When in Westminster mode, he had none of Corbyn's affability; instead, he was curt, at best, towards people that he disagreed with or did not respect. At other times, he was openly furious with them, or full of undisguised contempt. 'I've had to have a few run-ins with people,' he admitted to me. 'I've had to be a bit hard with people. Saying to them, "Why did you vote that way?" Those situations were embarrassing for them. So I got a bit of a reputation for being hard and ruthless.'

After waiting decades to become an MP, there was something pent-up about him. His vicious falling-out with Ken Livingstone was also widely remembered, and how long it took them to make up. McDonnell bore grudges. He drew red lines. He was happy to have enemies – indeed, he believed that that was what politics was largely about.

The Commons likes aggression, as long as there is something theatrical and slightly insincere about it. Genuine anger is less admired, even feared. In 2009, without a parliamentary vote, Gordon Brown's government approved the building of a third runway for Heathrow, something that McDonnell had long opposed. McDonnell made a speech in the Commons that switched in a few seconds from studied calm to finger-jabbing rage. Then he stormed down the steps from his place on the backbenches, grabbed the heavy ceremonial mace with both hands, and strode off with it across the chamber. It was a gesture of disgust and breach of parliamentary rules that few MPs ever dared. As the speaker of the Commons rose from his seat to tell McDonnell to put the mace down and that he would be punished, the MP shouted over him: the government's Heathrow decision was a 'disgrace to democracy in this country'.

He was suspended from the Commons. MPs and Westminster journalists saw the episode as a sign of dangerous immaturity. Around parliament, it was common to hear people mutter that McDonnell was 'a nasty piece of work'. Some people outside parliament said much the same thing. Well into the 2000s, advisors to Livingstone talked about 'Mad McDonnell'.

But others saw his intensity differently. 'Young green activists, suspicious of traditional politics, made an exception for John,' said John Stewart, a veteran environmentalist and opponent of Heathrow expansion. Like Corbyn, McDonnell often seemed to be working on behalf of protest movements, inside the Labour party, rather than the other way round. Unlike most MPs, he sometimes advocated 'direct action', a vague but potent political concept which the rightwing press regularly tried to turn into a bogeyman. In reality, direct action usually meant non-violent but often illegal activities such as occupations, tres-passing, and strikes and mass street demonstrations held without the right permissions. Such tactics had long been commonplace among anti-roadbuilding and anti-arms-trade campaigners, for example. But for an MP, supposedly an upholder of Britain's system of pacifying representative democracy, to call for direct action: this had a transgres-sive, even revolutionary edge.

And as the relatively calm, small-stakes politics of the 1990s and early 2000s gave way to turbulence and more fundamental battles, over the Blair government's support for the Iraq War and then the coalition government's imposition of austerity, so direct action seemed increasingly appropriate to the times. When the streets of Whitehall were full of tear gas, smashed placards and protesters boiling with anger as they were held for hours in police 'kettles', as happened during demonstrations against austerity, McDonnell's calls for direct action could not be dismissed just as a pose or wishful thinking. A broad dissatisfaction with the status quo was beginning to build during the later Blair years and the first years of the coalition, and the Labour party, at least as it currently existed, was not bold enough to contain it.

Yet while McDonnell was becoming nationally known as a fire-brand, he was also strengthening his more conciliatory reputation. 'John has always been comfortable dealing with people who aren't in the Labour party,' said Stewart, who had known him since his GLC days. 'Because he is so sure about his own ideological position, it gives him a bit more freedom, in his own mind, to work with others.' McDonnell explained further: 'When I'm collaborating with someone [from outside the left] on an issue, I make it clear, it's just about that issue, full-stop.' Sometimes people ignore the warning. 'They'll come up to me, and say, "Can you help us with this, because we worked together on that?" And I say, "Sorry, I can't." Sometimes people don't like that.'

On Heathrow, McDonnell collaborated with a wide range of people, from young climate activists to wealthy green Conservatives such as Zac Goldsmith. He chaired an unofficial cross-party Com-mons group against the airport's enlargement 'in a very consensual way', Stewart recalled. 'He would give equal time to everyone around the table. He never brought party politics or his particular political perspective to the meetings.'

Opposing the airport's remorseless growth was not straightforward for McDonnell. Many of his constituents worked there. Plenty of the people in the villages threatened by the expansion were home counties Tories. Yet at anti-Heathrow gatherings away from parliament, Stewart felt that McDonnell was 'able to outline [our] campaign strategy in terms ordinary people understood. And he was clear what his role in that strategy was, even if that role meant going to four meetings on a Saturday afternoon.' As the struggle over the airport dragged on for years, Stewart noticed something surprising about McDonnell: 'More mainstream people I met through the Heathrow campaign – centrist Labour people, Westminster lobbyists – would say to me, "John McDonnell is a wasted resource. If only he would modify his politics."'

17

The Limits of Leftism

For much of the 1990s, Ken Livingstone also seemed to be achieving less than he should. Increasingly frustrated and marginal in the Commons and the Labour party, he seemed to be looking for things to do. He appeared on TV programmes that were only loosely connected to politics, such as the comedy panel show *Have I Got News For You*. With his quick wit and sense of mischief, the sense that at any moment he might say something outrageous, he was a compelling screen presence, and he began to become a mainstream rather than merely political celebrity.

His instantly recognisable voice also got him work. In 1995 the Britpop band Blur, then at the height of their fame, hired him to narrate 'Ernold Same', a not very subtle, spoken-word song about a commuter whose life never changes. Newspapers began to ask him to write regularly for them. The usually Conservative-supporting *London Evening Standard*, becoming friendlier towards Labour politicians as a Blair premiership loomed, made Livingstone the restaurant critic for its magazine.

It was a less improbable appointment than it first seemed. As a hedonistic rather than hairshirt socialist, he had always liked a drink and eating out, often in cosy, boozy Soho institutions such as the Red Fort and Vasco & Piero's. Less easy to understand was his decision to start writing a column for the *Sun*, which had called him 'the most odious man in Britain' in his GLC days. With his prospects of high office apparently gone, Livingstone seemed to be drifting into the more comfortable role of semi-retired politician and media personality, producing one-liners rather than proper speeches, reducing his former radicalism to a cheeky but unthreatening one-man show, performed for whoever would pay.

It was a similar process to the one undergone by Tony Benn, as he gradually became better known as a diarist than as a challenging politician. During the tumultuous 1970s and 80s, the left had been kept in check through Whitehall and the Labour right's dirty tricks. During the more placid, less politicised 1990s and 2000s, at least some of the left appeared to be being indulged, offered a degree of celebrity and respect in return for political irrelevance.

Yet as was often the case, Livingstone's cheekiness and attention-seeking concealed more serious political activities. He used the *Evening Standard*'s generous restaurant reviewing expenses to pay for lunches with leftwing activists from inside and outside the Labour party, who were more used to conspiring over crisps and pints in sticky pubs. At these long lunches he exchanged gossip and political intelligence, nurtured relationships, and encouraged the left's factions to put aside their disagreements and prepare for the day when Blairism lost its dominance. Meanwhile he used his *Sun* column to criticise Blair for moving Labour away from its 'long tradition of solidarity with workers', and to promote anti-establishment causes such as republicanism in blunt, populist language. 'Abolish the royals,' wrote Livingstone, 'and save [Prince] Wills from a screwed-up life.' In an era increasingly characterised by centrist, gradualist, euphemistic politicians, Livingstone was still trying to make the creation of a socialist Britain and other big, disruptive reforms sound like common sense.

Even more quixotically, it seemed, he had acquired a strong interest in the weaknesses of Western economies, despite capitalism's apparent triumph over communism. His new preoccupation was partly prompted by an unsuccessful argument over lunch with an editor of the free-market magazine the *Economist*. Livingstone had claimed that British manufacturing was being stunted by a lack of investment. His assertion was basically correct: decades of politicians from both the left and the right, from Tony Benn to Rishi Sunak, have come to the same conclusion. But he did not have the facts to back it up. He had spent most of his career in local government, which had limited economic powers, and had never bothered to read Marx. At lunch with the *Economist* editor, he felt suddenly out of his depth. For a politician who prided himself on his grasp of detail, it was not a comfortable state.

To educate himself, he began going to the meetings of a group of economists who had worked for the GLC, including Robin Murray and Doreen Massey. They were on the left, but they were intensely interested in technological and social trends, and how socialists might adapt to the ones they could not change. As a pragmatic leftist who was always interested in modern things, Livingstone was receptive to their exploratory thinking.

Yet the person who became his biggest economic, and arguably intellectual, influence was a less self-questioning figure than he was. John Ross had a first from Oxford, decades of experience in dogmatic leftwing sects, and a liking for grand, often counterintuitive theories, which he would sometimes expound to his comrades without warning for many minutes at a time. In 1983, the year of Margaret Thatcher's biggest landslide victory, he had published *Thatcher and Friends*, a book which argued with a lot of determination and voting data that the Conservative party was actually in long-term decline. The same year, Ross helped launch the Socialist League, soon known as Socialist Action after the name of its newspaper. It was a small revolutionary group which instructed its members to follow a strategy of 'deep entryism': joining the Labour party, shedding their previous Socialist Action identities, and becoming trusted advisors to leading figures on the Labour left, in order to influence them.

With his interest in psephology, Livingstone read *Thatcher and Friends* and was intrigued by it. A few years later, Ross came to see him, officially to do an interview for *Socialist Action*, but really to see if they could strike up a relationship. When the conversation got on to economics, Livingstone was impressed by his visitor's cleverness and range of knowledge. He hired Ross as his Commons researcher – in reality his tutor.

'We talked three or four times a week,' Livingstone told his biographer John Carvel, 'and he explained what was happening in the national and international economy. He said you could never trust the Treasury's statistics and needed your own database. So I spent £35,000 for a five-year lease on what was then the biggest computer in private hands in Britain. We set up an enormous database about all the main world economies since 1860 and others since 1960, updating it each month with the latest statistics and reports from the OECD, the World Bank and the Treasury.'

With some satisfaction at the ironies of the arrangement, Livingstone funded the research through his frothy media work and his TV ads for Red Leicester. Then he and Ross drew conclusions from their data, and published them in a monthly newsletter, the *Socialist Economic Bulletin*. Available to subscribers for £5 an issue or £20 a year, it was slim and highly assertive in its content. A typical issue, from June 1994, argued that a future Labour government 'must correct the fundamental distortions of the British economy – its obsession with investment overseas instead of investment at home, its excessive military spending, and its subordination of the interests of manufacturing to those of the City'. These broad critiques, which sometimes echoed points that Tony Benn had been making for two decades, were often backed up by unBennlike graphs, with scales in tiny print, which plotted highly technical economic indicators such as 'gross domestic fixed capital formation as % of GDP' across long periods of time, and did plenty of bragging about the quality of the publication's data and analysis. The March 1998 issue, for example, claimed that the bulletin had 'consistently presented a more sober, and realistic, assessment of the development of the UK and world economies than the Treasury'.

The idea that two middle-aged lefties with a big computer could understand the economy better than Whitehall's supposedly brainiest ministry had a certain appeal, especially as it became steadily clearer during the 1990s that many of the Treasury's policies under the Tories were not yielding their promised results. Livingstone claimed that the bulletin was read by thinking people on the left in Britain and abroad, and inside the Treasury itself. But the publication also had a cranky quality. Its air of total certainty, when economics was such a treacherous subject, and the fact that Livingstone had never shown much interest in the field before, made some journalists and fellow MPs wonder what on earth he was up to. After meeting him for the *Independent on Sunday*, the renowned interviewer Lynn Barber complained in her article: 'He is obsessed with economics ... He talks so much about it that I eventually wailed, "This is terribly boring – can't you talk about gay rights or Ireland or something?"'

He kept putting out the bulletin for ten years, from 1990 to 2000.

From 1992, he had to do much of it on his own, as Ross had been lured to Russia, where he had been hired by the general secretary of a trade union to analyse the increasingly anarchic workings of post-Soviet capitalism. In Moscow, Ross advised a succession of left-leaning figures, collaborated remotely with Livingstone, and produced a Russian version of the bulletin. It urged Boris Yeltsin's government to abandon its free-market policies 'and copy the success of China's economic reforms', as Livingstone put it, 'where strong state regulation of the banks guaranteed higher levels of investment'.

To anyone who during the 1990s had grown used to seeing Livingstone as a kind of leftie light entertainer, his and Ross's economic concerns might have seemed 'terribly boring', if they were noticed at all. But with China on the rise, and Britain opening up to visitors and investment from there and elsewhere in the post-communist world, Livingstone and Ross were actually ahead of the curve, at least compared to most British leftists. For Livingstone, getting socialists and capitalists to work together, in big cities, so that the benefits of economic growth could be distributed to millions of residents as quickly as possible – which was basically what China was doing, albeit at great social and environmental cost – became a fascination. He just needed somewhere in Britain to try this magic formula out.

The opportunity to do so came from an unlikely source. 'I rather admired Ken's style,' writes Tony Blair in his memoirs, 'his quirkiness . . . and his ability to communicate.' Someone close to Blair told Livingstone's biographer John Carvel: 'Tony always hoped that Ken would come on board when we came into power.'

Despite Livingstone's public criticism of Blair, the desire to work together was mutual. Motivated as ever by a mixture of personal ambition and the wish to maximise the left's influence by any means possible, Livingstone 'wanted to be part of the struggle inside Blair's government', he wrote later, rather than 'campaign from the back benches'. Even though in opposition New Labour had steered the party relentlessly rightwards, Livingstone hoped that once in office Blair would be nudged back to the left by pressure from MPs and by the need to address the disastrous social inequalities he had inherited from the Tories.

There was also a deeper kinship between the two men, a shared sensibility so politically awkward to discuss that neither of them would ever acknowledge it. Both of them despised what the Blairites called 'Old Labour'. For Livingstone, it meant the party he had first encountered and fought as a young councillor, a party controlled by socially conservative, predominantly working-class white men, who could not, or would not, see that Labour's future depended on greatly broadening its membership and electoral support into the kind of cross-class, multiracial, less masculine, more sexually diverse coalition which participated in and voted for his GLC. To Blair, 'Old Labour' meant something a bit different: almost anyone in the party who was tied to its traditions, or simply to the left of him. Yet there was overlap in their analyses of Labour's past problems. Neither man had much time for its compromising centre-left 1970s governments, for example. Just as importantly, both men believed that a new Labour politics was now required. That made them potential collaborators. It also made them potential rivals.

A few weeks before the 1997 election, Livingstone went to see Blair. He had been encouraged to do so by Margaret Hodge, the former Islington council leader, who lived near Blair and had transformed herself from a rebellious leftwinger into a keen foot soldier for New Labour. Livingstone and Blair spoke alone in the leader's office. According to Livingstone, the only one of them to offer an account, he told him that he was keen to serve in a Blair government. He also 'explained what needed to be done with the economy', and advised his party leader to avoid 'being ground down by bureaucracy and the media', and 'to push big reforms at the start'. Blair politely disagreed with the latter piece of unsolicited advice. New Labour intended to govern with great caution at first, in order to reassure rightwing voters and journalists. But Blair ended the meeting by saying that, while he could not make any specific promises, he hoped to have Livingstone in his government.

Nothing happened in the immediate aftermath of Labour's 1997 election victory. But six months later Blair invited him to another one-to-one meeting. Livingstone's political stock was rising: a few days before, he had been elected to Labour's national executive committee after nearly a decade of failed attempts, defeating Peter Mandelson,

Blair's key lieutenant. It was an early sign that parts of the party were shifting back to the left.

The prime minister asked Livingstone how he thought the government was doing. Labour were at 60 per cent in the polls, 35 per cent ahead of the Conservatives – probably as popular and dominant as any British government has ever been. 'Much worse than I expected,' Livingstone began. Then he launched into a long list of criticisms, covering everything from the government's failure to raise taxes on the rich, to its restriction of public spending to limits set by the previous Tory administration, to its granting of independence to the Bank of England. According to Livingstone's memoirs, 'Blair's pleasant demeanour evaporated, his face hardened and although I can't remember the exact words he used, it was along the lines that if I obstructed his reforms he would destroy me.'

According to Livingstone's later biographer Andrew Hosken, Blair was not as aggressive as that. Although the prime minister did not accept Livingstone's criticisms at the meeting, Livingstone went back to his office fully expecting the phone to ring and Blair to offer him a job. But it never did. Livingstone's candour had been either horribly misjudged, heroically principled, a sudden episode of self-sabotage or, most likely, a mixture of all three. The two men did not meet again one-to-one for seven years.

Yet long before that happened, Blair inadvertently offered Livingstone another chance to become an important politician again. Throughout the late 1990s, he backed the idea that London should have its first elected mayor.

The years after the abolition of the GLC saw a steady deterioration in the capital. Traffic congestion thickened. Tube trains got stuck in tunnels. Rough sleepers appeared in more doorways. Public spaces became worn and tatty. There was still a lot of private affluence: Thatcher's pro-City of London policies had created big new enclaves of bankers. But that only made the public decay seem starker and more unjustifiable. 'London's fabric is rotting,' wrote the journalist Peter Kellner in the *Independent* in 1989. 'Londoners are more likely to be assaulted, burgled and run over than anyone else in mainland Britain, and the capital's villains are less likely to be caught . . .' When

I moved to London five years later, it still seemed thrilling and full of cultural energy, but also neglected and a bit anarchic: the only large city in Europe without a city government.

During the 1990s a feeling spread and solidified among leftwing, liberal and even some Tory Londoners that this absence of administration and democratic accountability was at the heart of the city's problems. Its three dozen underfunded borough councils and the business-focused, only semi-democratic City of London Corporation were incapable of addressing citywide issues such as pollution and fraying transport. In 1994, Labour began advocating an elected Greater London Authority (GLA), essentially a more modest successor to the GLC. Two years later, the party suggested in a consultation document that the city might benefit from having an elected mayor as well. 'Such an approach would be quite new in Britain . . . leaving one person in a much more powerful position than has been customary,' the document cautioned. But Blair, who enjoyed having a great deal of individual power himself, quickly turned the tentative suggestion into a strong recommendation. Inspired by what he saw as the dynamism of American big-city mayors, he pushed successfully for his party to offer Londoners a referendum on whether they wanted both a GLA and a mayor. In 1998, the vote was held and almost three-quarters of those who took part backed the mayor and GLA proposal. The first mayoral election was scheduled for May 2000.

Initially, Livingstone was against the idea of a mayor. 'I thought the idea was barmy,' he wrote afterwards, 'just another example of New Labour's obsession with all things American.' He thought London should be run solely by the GLA, with greater powers than Labour were proposing for it. Whether he wanted to play a part in this arrangement he did not publicly say. But then, during 1997, as the momentum for a mayor grew in the run-up to the referendum, and media speculation started about who might be the mayoral candidates, Livingstone's name inevitably came up. His previous experience running London, his celebrity, and his independence from New Labour – all these made him an obviously appealing choice. He was invited to participate in lots of pre-referendum public discussions about the shape London's government should take. Perhaps inevitably, being part of these events also got him thinking even more than usual about the city's problems, and then about what he would do to address them, were he to stand for mayor – as more and more people clearly wanted. As someone who loved power and the challenges of government even more than most politicians, he eventually found running for the mayoralty impossible to resist.

The lure of it was strengthened by the absence of other plausible candidates. The seemingly good long-term prospects of the Blair government, and the possibilities for ministerial jobs in it, as well as uncertainty about how much power the mayor would actually have, discouraged other senior Labour figures from standing for the job. Meanwhile the Conservatives' unpopularity in London, which grew sharply and became less cyclical during the 1990s, put off senior Tories. In early 1998, when the deputy prime minister John Prescott formally presented Labour's mayoral plan to the Commons, Livingstone quickly stood up in the chamber to respond. 'Let me be the first to thank the deputy prime minister,' he said, 'for placing before Londoners this exciting and radical new job opportunity.' The fact that previously he had been against a mayor, and had said so repeatedly in public, was now of no importance, his brazen intervention suggested. Like a snake, he found old identities easy to shed.

But deciding to stand was the easy part. Over the next two years, he faced a succession of obstacles erected by the Labour hierarchy to block his path to the mayoralty. Since their falling out in 1997, Blair had decided that Livingstone was infuriating rather than intriguing. Other senior Labour people disliked and distrusted him even more. 'The feeling about Ken among the top brass was unbelievably strong,' Blair wrote in his memoirs. For Prescott and the chancellor Gordon Brown, Blair continued, their hostility towards Livingstone was 'visceral'. As figures to the left of Blair, who had largely suppressed their more radical sides for the good of New Labour, as they saw it, Livingstone uncomfortably reminded them, consciously or not, of how much they had compromised.

During 1998, 1999 and early 2000, in waves of speeches, articles, interviews, anonymous briefings and open letters to party members, Labour grandees from Blair downwards, as well as New Labour-aligned trade union leaders, argued that Livingstone was totally unsuited to becoming mayor. He was 'a self-obsessed, vain and manipulative opportunist who is temperamentally unable to deliver for London', concluded an exhaustive 4,651-word *Guardian* article on 19 January 2000 by the usually even-handed political reporter Will Woodward, which laid out 'the case against Ken Livingstone'. Much of this case, which was made right across the national press, was based on portraying his leadership of the GLC as an extremist experiment that had been disastrous for London and for Labour. The fact that some of the Livingstone GLC's social liberalism, for example on gay rights, and also some of its slick, poster-based presentational techniques, had been adopted by New Labour was never mentioned. Instead, success for Livingstone in the mayoral election was widely presented as a major threat to Blair. 'Opponents ranging from members of the cabinet to former colleagues on the Greater London Council warn that Mr Livingstone as mayor would become the de facto opposition to Tony Blair's government,' Woodward wrote. As is often the case when a prominent leftwing politician is being targeted by the establishment, Livingstone was presented as both a foolish radical – 'in a state of near-permanent adolescent rebellion', said the *Mail* in March 2000 – and a profound threat to the status quo.

'We [New Labour] had a formidable machine in those days and it did its job formidably,' Blair wrote in his memoirs. But to New Labour's surprise and frustration, against Livingstone the machine struggled. The press attacks did not damage him much. Many people with doubts about him knew his history already, and other Londoners remembered the GLC more positively than many journalists and New Labour wanted them to. The attacks also made Livingstone look like an underdog and a plucky rebel – often effective identities in British public life, and especially so by the end of the 1990s, with the Blair government no longer brand new and beginning to be seen as too powerful and intolerant. Shrewdly, at first Livingstone campaigned for the mayoralty under the slogan 'Ken's Right to Stand'. It reminded people that he and London had had their democratic rights attacked before, when the GLC was abolished, and it also appealed to voters beyond the left: to libertarians, centrists, even Tories, and anyone else who believed that the mayoral contest should be as open as possible.

His campaign quickly became both an uprising and a bandwagon. Graffiti in pub toilets said, 'Go on Ken!' Celebrities supported him:

both predictable leftwing ones such as Billy Bragg and Jo Brand, and more fashionable figures such as Fatboy Slim, the Chemical Brothers and Damien Hirst. The London left mobilised, lending organisers and MPs with connections to hard-to-reach voters – Diane Abbott among them. Livingstone's campaign was directed from a small house with dirty windows, three phone lines and a small staff, including two members of Socialist Action: Simon Fletcher, a deceptively mild young organiser who had worked for Tony Benn; and Redmond O'Neill, an older, fiercer Irish republican. Behind the scenes, they coaxed together the capital's quarrelsome leftwing factions, many of whom distrusted Livingstone almost as much as New Labour did, into a temporary but potent coalition.

John McDonnell co-chaired the 'Right to Stand' campaign, and wrote a caustic piece in the *Guardian* mocking New Labour and the press for their scaremongering about 'the recurrence of the biblical pestilence of Livingstone', and also reminding readers of the GLC's considerable achievements. At the end of the piece, McDonnell even claimed Livingstone had 'a sincerity and personal kindness rare among politicians'. Exactly how sincere McDonnell himself was being was hard to tell. Yet their show of reconciliation sent a useful message. Livingstone might be maddening sometimes, but he was such a valuable politician that even his worst enemies wanted to bury the hatchet.

Throughout the campaign he roamed the city: always by bus or tube, constantly being recognised, ready to chat to passers-by, and surrounded by reporters and cameras, turning each day of the campaign into one continuous photo opportunity. I interviewed him on a freezing street corner off Tottenham Court Road one morning in early 2000. I was writing a piece about him for the *New York Times* magazine – his campaign had caught the attention of newspapers far beyond London. With his cheeks pink from the cold and from talking non-stop, he began to describe what he would do as mayor. 'I'm demanding that we get back the police we've lost,' he said, not raising his flat voice despite the traffic roaring past. 'The mayor's got to get back from the national government the money that we pump into it. London contributes £19bn more than it receives . . . And the mayor's going to have to advocate tolerance. One of the reasons that we've got openly gay government ministers now is that the GLC stood up for tolerance 16 years ago . . .' I interrupted him to ask if, given the centralising tendencies of New Labour and almost all British governments, his plans for the mayoralty were not too ambitious. 'If I can't make a difference,' he said without a pause, 'I shouldn't get re-elected.'

The New Labour machine did its best to make Livingstone's confident campaign quips sound totally premature. It created a complex mechanism for choosing the party's candidate, that was blatantly designed to reduce his chances. Instead of being elected purely by the party's London membership and the trade unions, both groups with whom Livingstone was known to be popular, the candidate would also be chosen by Labour's London MPs, GLA candidates and members of the European parliament: all groups where he was much less liked, and where there were plenty of inexperienced political hopefuls susceptible to pressure from the party leadership.

As an alternative to Livingstone, the leadership encouraged this elaborate electorate to vote for Frank Dobson, who had left his job as Blair's health secretary to run for mayor. An effective minister, a longstanding London MP, and a convivial and popular Labour character, Dobson was also fairly leftwing: he had voted for Benn as deputy leader in 1981. In theory, he was well suited to luring voters away from 'Red Ken', as he was being called once again.

In February 2000, the result of Labour's candidate selection was declared. From the unions, Dobson got just 28 per cent of the vote. From the party members, he only got 40 per cent. But from the MPs, MEPs and GLA candidates, he got 86.5 per cent. Thanks to New Labour's cynical voting formula, Dobson squeaked past Livingstone by 3 per cent.

For a fortnight, Livingstone stewed with anger and considered what to do next. Many journalists, who had come to share his suspicion of New Labour, agreed with him that the vote had effectively been fixed, and said so in their coverage. To exploit this mood, Simon Fletcher quickly put together a 'Stand Down, Frank' campaign on Livingstone's behalf. Dobson's candidacy was badly damaged by the controversy, but he did not stand down. If Livingstone wanted to keep running for the mayoralty, he would have to do so as an independent.

On multiple occasions, he had publicly promised never to leave the Labour party. O'Neill, Ross and other confidants warned him that if he broke that pledge and ran as an independent, without Labour's symbolic and practical support, he would lose – and then would most likely also lose his seat in parliament, probably ending his political career. As an independent, he would not just be up against Labour, in a now strongly Labour city, but also up against quite a formidable Conservative: Steve Norris, an entertainingly frank, socially liberal former transport minister, who had long supported gay rights, and was one of the few in his party who properly understood the problems of London's public transport.

Yet against these difficulties, Livingstone weighed 'the mood on the streets', which he felt was 'overwhelmingly for me to stand'. His evidence was not just anecdotal: opinion polls said the same thing. And then there was his instinctive rebelliousness, and his history of battles with the Labour leadership. He had never really been a loyal party man. In March 2000, only two months before the mayoral election, he announced he would stand.

His subsequent campaign was essentially a bigger version of his bid for the Labour candidacy. He campaigned from an open-top bus. Postal donations came in sackfuls. 'The average donation was £16,' he wrote afterwards. The broadcaster Chris Evans, then near the peak of his fame, gave £200,000, and also endorsed Livingstone on his Virgin Radio show, in breach of British broadcasting's impartiality rules. Virgin was fined £75,000, then the largest penalty ever imposed by the Radio Authority.

Despite his misgivings about the independent candidacy, Ross came back from Moscow to help. Livingstone's speeches and appearances at debates drew crowds so enthusiastic he found it hard to get away afterwards. Meanwhile Dobson addressed eerily quiet audiences. At an event of his I went to, in a cavernous converted brewery in east London, he delivered his speech in a strange, downbeat monotone, while several hundred people looked at the ceiling or their shoes, trying not to watch a decent man self-destruct.

Norris campaigned much more assertively: sometimes emphasising his liberal, London-compatible values; at other times promising to crack down on anti-capitalist protesters, who on May Day riotously took over part of central London. Most of the national press endorsed him. Even the *Guardian* considered doing so, with some of its more centrist senior staff still seeing Livingstone through a 1980s lens as a man of the 'hard left', even though he had not been that even then. Ultimately, the paper endorsed none of the candidates. Livingstone's poll lead over Norris steadily narrowed. Early on the morning after polling day, with the votes still being counted because new electronic tallying machines had broken down, the BBC reported that Norris was 'making a late surge'.

But it was a mirage – or wishful thinking. In the first round of voting, Norris only got 27 per cent. Dobson got an embarrassing 13 per cent. Livingstone got 39 per cent: no landslide, but a strong share in a race with 11 candidates. In the next round, with voters' second preferences included and all but the two leading contenders eliminated, Livingstone's share grew to 58 per cent. He had won – with by far the biggest personal mandate of any British politician. He was now the first elected mayor of Europe's largest city.

In public, and in his own mind, he initially tried to define the role as a resumption of his work at the GLC. He began his victory speech, 'As I was saying before I was so rudely interrupted 14 years ago . . .' Some of the rightwing press played along. As if Livingstone had simply repeated his internal coup from 1981, rather than convincingly won a multi-stage election, the *Daily Mail* reported that 'Left-wing extremist Ken Livingstone' had 'seized control' of the capital.

But in fact, being mayor would be very different, and he knew it. 'My powers were limited,' he acknowledged after his tenure was over. While the GLC had provided a vast range of services, from public transport to music festivals, the mayor would only oversee bodies that did so, and in a smaller number of areas: transport, policing, economic development, and fire and emergency planning. The mayor would also be closely scrutinised – in theory, at least – by an elected London Assembly with 25 members. In 2000, the Labour vote for the assembly was lower than expected, as a side effect of Livingstone's independent candidacy and Dobson's unpopularity, so the assembly ended up with only nine Labour members, nine Conservatives, four Liberal Democrats and three Greens. How this inconclusive mix of generally inexperienced politicians would get on with Livingstone, who was answerable to no party, was not clear.

Nor was it clear at first what sort of bureaucracy would carry out the mayor and the assembly's wishes. While the GLC had had tens of thousands of employees, many of them in the immense landmark of County Hall, the Greater London Authority, as the mayor and assembly were collectively known, spent its first two years in a fairly small and anonymous temporary building in Whitehall, dwarfed by surrounding government ministries. Livingstone inherited no civil servants. Many of the ex-GLC staff he might have hired 'were either dead or retired', he wrote in his memoirs. 'We were starting from scratch.'

Characteristically, he saw this as an opportunity: 'Future mayors would inherit the machine I created.' He appointed Fletcher as his chief of staff. Ross and O'Neill became senior advisors. Another was Neale Coleman, a more consensual leftist and a deft administrator whom Livingstone had worked with on and off for twenty years. Lee Jasper, a veteran black activist and fierce critic of the police, became one of the mayor's senior advisors on race relations and policing.

Meanwhile a few of Livingstone's old GLC lieutenants were again given key positions. Dave Wetzel, a chatty former bus conductor who had overseen much of the GLC's transport policy, had left politics and was helping run a Chinese restaurant. Livingstone visited him a few months before the mayoral election, officially to review the food for the *Evening Standard*, but really to persuade him to join his campaign and then his administration. In 2000 Wetzel was appointed to the board of the capital's new transport body, Transport for London (TfL). Although TfL seemed a rather corporate organisation, with slick logos and lists of priorities decorating the walls of its smart Westminster offices, a residue of leftism and unorthodox thinking lay not far below the surface. When I interviewed Wetzel in 2003 about the capital's worsening traffic problems, he spent much of our meeting trying to interest me in a scheme he had designed, outside work, for a new tax on land.

McDonnell and Diane Abbott joined a mayoral 'advisory cabinet'. It was intended to offer Livingstone some outside perspectives. In practice, the administration soon came to be dominated by him and half a dozen staff and advisors. 'I remember him saying at one meeting, "There's only one vote in this place, and it's mine,"' McDonnell told me. He 'quietly stood down' from the cabinet.

Fletcher and Coleman were the mild-mannered facilitators of the mayor's strategies. Meanwhile, O'Neill was 'the enforcer', a member of the administration told me, 'ferocious and terrifying'. And Ross was the big-picture thinker, who 'talked and talked and talked', while Livingstone and everyone else listened. 'My Monday morning meetings with my key advisors were really intense debates,' Livingstone told the writer Anna Minton in 2016, 'a really good debate by very bright people.' He liked the fact that Ross and several of his other key advisors had degrees from Oxford. During these meetings, Livingstone continued, 'Ideas were floated, a consensus would build up around something, then we could move forward . . .'

During his mayoralty, he often talked about the job in public in similarly rationalist, almost technocratic terms. In 2007, he told the centrist magazine *Prospect*:

> I can put together coalitions of interests . . . broker deals with the government or the private sector . . . There isn't a great ideological conflict any more. The business community, for example, has been almost depoliticised. One of the first people to lobby me when I became mayor was Judith Mayhew, from the City Corporation. She came and said, 'We've all changed, it won't be like the last time [when you were at the GLC], there's so much we can do together.' I didn't believe a word of it, but it turned out to be true.

Livingstone went on:

> This is not the world I would have created, but it's the world I have to live in . . . working with the most progressive forces in capitalism and [the Blair] government: to try to give Londoners the skills for the jobs that are coming, to mitigate carbon emissions, to redistribute wealth within the very limited powers that I've got, and make it a generally happier city to live in.

Along with these relatively modest ambitions, he had a larger, less often stated, more risky mayoral goal. By collaborating with business,

even with the City's ultra-capitalists, this supposedly still leftwing politician, now the most powerful in Britain, intended to make London
bigger and more important: no longer just the biggest city in Britain
and Europe but 'a world city', as pivotal as New York or Tokyo, and
potentially even more so.

Some of his motivation was personal. London, where he had lived
his whole life, and which was the only place he had represented as a
politician, fascinated him, and presented itself to him as a place in
constant need of improvement and reform – interventions which, if
successful, might enable him to join his heroes such as the pre-war
Labour city boss Herbert Morrison in the small pantheon of successful London reformers.

There was also a more political rationale for his desire to expand the
capital. With the mayor having few means to redistribute power and
wealth within it, and with capitalism victorious, for the time being at
least, in Britain as a whole, helping the capital to boom, to effectively
become a 'city state', with its own 'London nationalism', was the only
quick way, he and Ross believed, to give its millions of poor or modestly off residents a better life. That was how 21st-century socialism – or
however you thought of the state–capitalist hybrid model being pioneered by the Beijing government – was being practised in China. That
country had an added appeal, as an alternative to the American hegemony which Ross and Livingstone had long opposed. Chinese cities
were sprouting new office towers, excavating new train stations, deliberately swelling their populations. Why couldn't London do the same?

Yet before that boom could happen, the capital needed to function
better. By the time Livingstone became mayor, London was among the
six most congested cities in the world. To some authorities on the capital, such as the writer and champion of suburbia Paul Barker, this
was the natural state of a city that had started as a narrow riverside
settlement and had grown haphazardly outwards. But to Livingstone,
a non-driver who had lived in some of the city's most polluted inner
districts, and often travelled on buses that got stuck in traffic, congestion was a slow-motion social and environmental disaster. With car
usage increasing, London's population growing, and the city's roads
being dug up in an uncoordinated fashion by the country's

mismanaged privatised utilities, he and his transport advisors believed that without drastic action to cut congestion, much of the city would soon stiffen into gridlock.

A potential solution to the problem had been lying around, unused, for at least half a century. In 1951 the American free-market economist Milton Friedman, many of whose ideas had inspired Pinochet and Thatcher, co-wrote an essay titled 'How to Plan and Pay For the Safe and Adequate Highways We Need'. It argued that on crowded roads it was 'desirable to discourage traffic'; and that the best way to do that was to charge drivers 'in proportion to their use' of those roads. Since road space in city centres or affected by rush hours was especially in demand, these were the parts of the network that should be subject to 'electronic road pricing'.

Friedman's proposal sounded futuristic, but it was also an echo of the toll roads that had existed in London on and off since the 13th century. Yet from the 1950s until the late 1990s, despite the capital's worsening traffic, 'road pricing' was considered too impractical and controversial a solution. Even the GLC steered away from it. Labour considered including it in its 1981 GLC manifesto, Wetzel told me, but rejected it in favour of the more palatable option of lowering fares for public transport.

Yet Livingstone remained intrigued by Friedman's idea. On the face of it, creating a market in road use, on the advice of an infamous right-wing economist, was forbidden fruit for a leftwing politician. But as a close observer of the capital's social trends, Livingstone knew that, despite increasing car use, by the late 1990s a majority of Londoners still did not own one, and that a disproportionate number of these non-drivers were poor. Reducing congestion by charging motorists, and spending more on public transport, would effectively redistribute time and resources to the less well-off, by making the buses they predominantly used more frequent and faster. In 1999, shortly after announcing that he would run for mayor, Livingstone raised Friedman's idea in the Commons, and argued that London's traffic had got so bad that 'something like a congestion tax must be introduced'.

Less provocatively renamed as the congestion charge, it became his first major policy as mayor. For the first two and a half years of his four-year term, after which he would have to seek re-election, the pros and cons of the charge dominated coverage of the mayoralty, and absorbed much of his administration's energy. Deciding on how much of London the charge should cover; avoiding jams and anomalies at the borders of the charging zone; setting a suitable price for driving into the zone; deciding the days and hours when the scheme should operate; installing and operating the technology required to identify and charge drivers; trying to predict how the capital's economy would be affected – these and other challenges persuaded many people, outside and inside the mayoralty, that the policy was a terrible mistake. There were well-attended meetings of anti-congestion charge protesters, uniting white van drivers with car commuters from the suburbs, and wealthy and influential Londoners accustomed to private rather than public transport. Much of the press concluded from these strident gatherings, and from the car-dependency of the country as a whole, that the charge would be extremely unpopular – perhaps fatally so for Livingstone's re-election chances.

He did not discourage this speculation. He hinted that the charge could be withdrawn if it did not reduce congestion, or if 'a fundamental flaw' appeared. The head of street management at TfL, a usually understated man called Derek Turner, told me that 'Ken and I have got an understanding about what a catastrophic failure would be.' I asked him how they defined 'catastrophic'. He replied without a blink: 'Total gridlock over the whole inner ring road [the border of the charging zone] over a number of days.'

The first day of the charge finally arrived: 17 February 2003. The roads into the charging zone were so empty that morning that you could almost lie down on them. The huge stretches of barely used tarmac, not seen again until the pandemic, had an eerie grey-black beauty, like a giant artwork, or the suddenly revealed skin of a new and different city. There were no 'catastrophic failures' of the new system. Belatedly, along with other journalists, I realised that expectations had been expertly managed.

Other successes punctuated Livingstone's first years as mayor. Trafalgar Square, previously a glorified traffic island, was partly pedestrianised, and immediately took on a new identity as a place where both tourists and locals met and lingered. Londoners under 18 who were still in full-time education were given free bus travel and subsidised tube travel: a potentially life-changing new freedom for the many young people in the city without much money, who often lived isolated lives on out-of-the-way estates. With their new cargoes of not always perfectly behaved teenagers, the buses themselves moved more freely. Although traffic levels crept back up as the congestion charge became part of everyday life, TFL added new bus lanes and more buses. After decades of falling behind other European capitals, London's transport and public spaces began to catch up.

In July 2002, the mayor, his staff and the London Assembly moved out of their temporary building and into a purpose-built City Hall: a striking, stretched glass ball, with the profile of a billowing sail, sited right on the river beside Tower Bridge, where previously there had been disused wharves. The flashy modern design and location facing the City of London were strong, if unsubtle, symbols of the city's intended rebirth under Livingstone as the world's 21st-century financial capital. But he quickly humanised City Hall by referring to it as 'the glass testicle'.

His office was high up, with a view through the curving glass of the bridge and the bankers' towers, which were proliferating as his administration loosened the restrictions on high-rise building. Unlike at the GLC, he kept the papers on his desk sparse – a sign of increased administrative confidence. Sometimes, he took off his watch and laid it on the desk, near his eye line. His time mattered. He often worked in open-necked shirts, but formal ones, worn with suits and braces, looking more like a banker than the radical lecturer he used to resemble at County Hall. One of his favourite suits was a rich purple one, a gift worth £895 from Ozwald Boateng, the black British designer, born in London, who during Livingstone's mayoralty opened his first shop among the traditional tailors of Savile Row. As Livingstone moved through the city now, smartly dressed but still naughtily quotable, opening international trade fairs, attending business functions, meeting property developers, drinking good wine in elaborately decorated new restaurants, he was at ease in, and in some ways personified, the emerging new version of the capital: expansive, entrepreneurial, liberal, multicultural in its tastes, a bit pleased with itself. 'In the months that followed,' the introduction of the congestion charge, he wrote in his memoirs, 'everything seemed to come right.'

*

At a time when the Blair government was losing support and momentum, in large part because of its backing for America's reckless
confrontation with Iraq, Livingstone's success as mayor became hard
for the Labour hierarchy to ignore. The party's candidate for the 2004
mayoral election, Nicky Gavron, was an experienced London politician but not inspirational. It was hard to imagine her beating
Livingstone; and such a high-profile defeat would be another setback
for the government.

Luckily for Labour, Livingstone had a surprise for them: he was
eager to rejoin the party. His independent status as mayor had never
been completely convincing, given his continuing closeness to parts of
the Labour left, and the rather Blairite mix of business promotion and
social redistribution that made up many of his mayoral policies.
Moreover, with his usual lack of political squeamishness and nose for
power and resources, Livingstone calculated that 'by having me back
as a [mayoral] candidate,' Labour would 'have to fund a lot more of
the things I wanted,' if he was elected for a second term.

He first applied to rejoin the party in 2002, barely two years after
being elected as an independent. His Labour enemies blocked the
application for a year and a half. But Blair noticed Livingstone's
achievements and popularity as mayor, and shifted in favour of his
readmission. So did Gavron, who had served as deputy mayor to Livingstone for three years, and rather than undermine him or spy on
him, as her Labour superiors may have originally wanted, had been
impressed by his administrative ability and relative moderation. In
November 2003, she told Blair she would step aside if Livingstone
became Labour's candidate.

The same month, the aggressively rightwing US president George
W. Bush made a state visit to Britain. While he and Blair went to a
banquet at Buckingham Palace, Livingstone had a reception organised at City Hall for groups opposed to the Iraq War, and allowed
peace protesters to take over Trafalgar Square. Its pedestrianisation
had made it better for demonstrations. The protesters pulled over a
large statue they had made of the American president. Livingstone
may have moved to the right on some domestic issues, but on foreign
policy he studiedly remained a rebel of the left.

However, such radical gestures did not affect his Labour

readmission. Two months after the anti-Bush protests, he was officially welcomed back by the party. A few weeks later, he replaced Gavron as its mayoral candidate. Norris stood again for the Conservatives. His manifesto's most eye-catching promise was that he would abolish the congestion charge.

Livingstone promised to extend it instead: westwards from central London to the Tory-run borough of Kensington and Chelsea, where car ownership was higher than in most of inner London, and the traffic jams gleamed with expensive new SUVs. An opinion poll commissioned by the London Assembly showed 54 per cent support in the borough for introducing the charge, but there was also a faint whiff of hubris about the proposal. Extending the charging zone to a residential area outside central London diluted the system's original rationale, cutting commuting by car into the city centre, and implied that the zone might eventually spread a lot further. Choosing posh Kensington and Chelsea also had a touch of class warfare, or clever leftwing populism, about it. Would a re-elected Livingstone revert to being Red Ken?

Not enough Londoners were worried about that for Norris to win. While he eked out 44.6 per cent of the final vote, Livingstone got 55.4 per cent: only fractionally smaller than his first mayoral mandate. By presenting himself as a mayor who got things done, he even beat Norris in 11 of London's 20 outer boroughs, where a more suburban culture of car use and home ownership usually gave the Conservatives the upper hand. While the Tories struggled in London and in Britain as a whole, New Labour also alienated most people: the Blair government was re-elected at the 2005 general election with barely a third of the vote. In this context, Livingstone was no longer just the left's most popular politician. He was arguably the most popular politician in the country.

Much of Livingstone's second term as mayor was concerned with London's relationship with foreign states. Sometimes it felt as though the city's relationship with the rest of Britain was of secondary importance. To encourage trade and investment links, he opened offices for London, or 'Kenbassies' as they quickly became known, in Delhi, Mumbai, Beijing, Shanghai, Brussels and Caracas. The exclusion of

American cities from this list was not accidental. Ross regarded the United States as in long-term economic decline. He and Livingstone wanted London to connect itself to the surging economies of Asia instead.

Caracas was included in the list, meanwhile, because Venezuela's socialist president Hugo Chavez was exciting leftists all over the world, including Livingstone, with his populist and effective programmes to reduce poverty and illiteracy, which were funded by increasing taxes on the country's booming oil industry. South America had elected a wave of leftwing leaders during the early 21st century, but Chavez stood out, like a more hard-nosed and domineering upgrade of Salvador Allende. Although Venezuela was much poorer than London, and Britain, Chavez's programme offered tantalising hints of what Livingstone might do if he had more powers.

During the 2000s, Chavez became aware that Livingstone and others on the British left were enthusiastic and possibly useful supporters of his government. The Venezuelan embassy contacted City Hall, and suggested that their president, who was due to visit Europe in May 2006, might add a visit to London to his schedule. Livingstone's administration enthusiastically agreed, and offered to host a lunch for him at City Hall. The Blair government, which Chavez had strongly criticised over Iraq, offered no such welcome. According to Livingstone, 'Downing Street tried to stop the visit by saying . . . they wouldn't be providing [police] protection' for the president, who four years earlier had survived a violent attempted coup. But the head of the Metropolitan Police, Sir Ian Blair, a relatively liberal officer who had a good working relationship with Livingstone, provided Chavez with a police escort regardless, and the visit went ahead. For a couple of days at least, Livingstone could demonstrate to the public that he had his own foreign policy.

Before the lunch at City Hall, Chavez made a speech at the Camden Centre, a large hall owned by the north London borough's Labour council which was a traditional setting for leftwing gatherings. Livingstone chaired the event, which was broadcast live in Venezuela, and was taken aback when Chavez spoke for three hours. The centre was packed with young people, who thanks to Iraq and Blair's other rightwing mistakes were becoming more politically curious and often moving leftwards, and also with veteran radicals such as Tariq Ali. Unnoticed by most of the media, a new coalition was beginning to form.

At City Hall afterwards, a top-floor room with one of the best views of London was filled with lunch tables. Senior figures from the Labour left and the Livingstone administration arrived to meet Chavez, including Simon Fletcher, Jeremy Corbyn, Diane Abbott and Tony Benn, now 81, but as capable as ever of developing political enthusiasms. Watching Livingstone work the room, Benn forgot about their unspoken competition for the leadership of the left during the late 1980s, and instead felt admiration – though perhaps with a touch of condescension. 'He's done terribly well as Mayor of London,' he recorded in his diary afterwards. 'It's an extraordinary story really . . . He's very imaginative, is old Ken.'

The mayor introduced Benn to Chavez. 'Tony Benn – I know very well!' said Chavez, and crushed him in a hug. Benn recorded that he and Chavez had 'a wonderful talk'. Benn told the Venezuelan: 'Your vision and programme have given us hope.'

More concretely, Chavez offered to sell some of his country's huge oil reserves to the Livingstone administration at a special low price, so that the poorest Londoners could heat their homes more cheaply. After the mayor explained that few Britons used heating oil, a different deal was done. The state-owned Venezuelan oil company would give up to £16 million a year to Transport for London, to pay for half-price bus travel for up to 250,000 Londoners on benefits. Meanwhile TfL would set up an office in sometimes chaotic, congested Caracas, to advise the city government about traffic management, public transport and other urban challenges.

To Livingstone and his advisors, the arrangement was an ingenious piece of practical international socialism and pragmatic city-to-city cooperation. But to his critics in the press and parliament, who despite his successes and popularity had never fallen silent, the collaboration between the mayor of London and the leader of a poor faraway country, a foreign leader who was increasingly presented by Britain's rightwing papers as a dictator, even though he had repeatedly won elections, was an outrage and a humiliation. It was also seen by the British right, and by some in the Blair government, as a sign that the Livingstone administration was becoming reckless, extreme, even a bit mad. The 'loony left' label was taken out of storage and attached to him again.

As before, it was a caricature. Livingstone's second term continued the pro-business policies of his first. At times, he seemed to revel in being as welcoming to global capitalism as possible, as if demonstrating the infinite flexibility and heretical nature of his socialism. On a trip to China in 2006, organised by the supposed Socialist Action revolutionary John Ross and the slick PR agency Freud Communications, Livingstone told an audience of laughing businessmen in Beijing: 'I am here because I am after your money.'

In 2005, he won one of the prizes most coveted by big-city mayors, bidding successfully to host the Olympics. Being Livingstone, one of the arguments he made for this immensely risky and expensive undertaking was, to a degree, leftwing: that the Olympics would bring improvements to transport and public space and amenities to the lower Lea Valley, a large stretch of relatively poor inner east London, which would otherwise remain neglected. In the years running up to and following the eventual staging of the games in 2012, this argument would prove broadly correct. Yet it also skated over the fact that the Lea Valley actually contained quite a lot of life before the Olympics, including nightclubs, artists' studios, allotments and Europe's second-largest purpose-built housing cooperative, all of which were obliterated by the 'regeneration'. These were exactly the kind of enterprises his GLC had often protected against developers. But Livingstone, like London, had changed.

The city's selection to host the Olympics was announced at a grandiose ceremony in Singapore, which Livingstone attended. He was so tense that when the announcement was made, at first he found the news impossible to take in. He 'remained rooted to the spot', he wrote afterwards, making 'polite small talk' to the former US secretary of state Henry Kissinger, who bizarrely was also at the ceremony, 'while remembering how I had wanted him to die during the Vietnam war'. Livingstone had come a long way.

The following day, he was finally relaxing, shopping in Singapore for presents to take home to his family, when the head of his mayoral press office phoned to say that there had been an unexplained and serious power cut on the tube back in London. It soon became clear that the disruption had been caused by three bomb explosions on trains; and that there had been another on a London bus. Dozens of people had been killed. The eventual toll was 52 dead, excluding the suicide bombers, and over 700 wounded.

Livingstone rushed back to his hotel, found out as much as he could from the TV and City Hall, and was told that London's emergency services were coping. Then he went for a swim in the hotel pool, and worked out what he was going to say to all the journalists who had come to Singapore for the Olympic announcement.

In the hotel lobby, he gave an improvised press conference. He began with a statement:

> This was not a terrorist attack against the mighty and the powerful . . . It was aimed at ordinary, working-class Londoners – black and white, Muslim and Christian, Hindu and Jew . . . People from around the world . . . choose to come to London, as so many have come before . . . to live the life they choose . . . to be themselves . . .

Turning his words towards the bombers and their comrades, he continued:

> Nothing you do, however many of us you kill, will stop that flight to our cities where freedom is strong and where people can live in harmony with one another . . . You will fail.

Livingstone's emotional and well-judged speech, and others like it that he made back in London over the next few days, arguably marked the peak of his authority as mayor. Working closely with Ian Blair, who spoke publicly about the attacks in a calm, non-authoritarian tone, Livingstone helped prevent the bombings, which had been committed by Islamist terrorists, from being as divisive as was feared. The police response was not perfect. An innocent Brazilian man, Jean Charles de Menezes, was shot and deliberately killed by officers who had hastily misidentified him as one of those involved in the bombing campaign. Yet after a frightening few weeks, the capital returned to relative peace. Livingstone's advocacy of a multicultural London, which when he led the GLC had been widely regarded as fragmenting and undermining the capital, was now seen as the city's salvation.

But the praised and accomplished phase of his second term did not last that long. Much of what went wrong originated in his relationship with the press, and specifically with the *Evening Standard*. In 2002 its editor had changed: from Max Hastings, a journalist of unpredictable politics who had admired as well as attacked Livingstone since his GLC days, to Veronica Wadley, a rightwinger who had worked at the *Telegraph* and the *Mail*, and who would be made a Conservative peer by Boris Johnson in 2020.

At first, Wadley's relationship with Livingstone was cool rather than openly hostile. He invited her to lunch on the day she was made editor, but she said she was too busy. Soon afterwards, he invited her again, this time to a newsworthy-sounding lunch he was having with the mayor of New York, Rudy Giuliani. Again, she said she was too busy. According to Livingstone, they did not meet for another five years. The *Standard* did endorse him for mayor in 2004 – while at the same time criticising his 'empire-building', 'impatience with opposition', and his transport policy's creation of 'enormous debts' – but Livingstone became convinced regardless that Wadley wanted to undermine him. The *Standard*'s coverage certainly became more critical, often accusing him of bringing 'chaos' to the city, and of having 'secret plans'. It was possible that Wadley was trying to rein in a mayor who had become more powerful and entrenched than the architects of the mayoralty intended. It was also possible that the paper had simply tired of Livingstone, whose administration was no longer a novelty, and which therefore, following journalistic logic, required negative rather than positive coverage.

Yet deeper forces were also at play. In January 2005, the mayor announced that he was considering ending the monopoly enjoyed by *Metro*, the only newspaper distributed in tube stations, which was published by Associated Newspapers, the owner of both the *Standard* and the implacably anti-Livingstone *Daily Mail*. A few days later, the supposedly very busy Wadley found the time to attack him by writing an article for another publication, the rightwing *Spectator* magazine, in which she criticised his administration for 'financial recklessness' and 'clogging up the city' with underused buses. Livingstone quickly responded: accusing her within days, in the same magazine, of having a 'thin skin' when it came to the *Metro* issue, and saying that the contract governing its distribution at tube stations was 'poor value' for Londoners.

Three days after Livingstone's article, on 8 February 2005, the *Standard* sent a reporter to cover an evening event at City Hall. The event was a celebration of the 20th anniversary of Chris Smith coming out as the first gay MP. The former cabinet minister was a mild and well-liked figure, slightly to the left of New Labour, and according to the *Standard*, the paper did not intend to cover the evening critically. The era of homophobia in the rightwing press, the era in which Livingstone had grown up as a politician, was supposedly over. The *Standard* sent a relatively inexperienced reporter, Oliver Finegold, and a photographer to City Hall, and told the mayor's press office that they would simply stand outside and get brief quotes and pictures from the guests as they left.

Finegold spoke to a few departing guests, some of them Labour figures, without any problems. Then Livingstone emerged from the building. According to him, he was 'surprised' to find the two journalists waiting, since 'the *Standard* routinely ignored receptions at City Hall'. Holding a tape recorder, Finegold approached him with the photographer. The mayor refused to be photographed, saying that the press had enough pictures of him already. Finegold said he was a reporter from the *Standard*, and began asking Livingstone how the evening had gone. 'How awful for you,' Livingstone interrupted, mocking Finegold's employment at the *Standard*. 'Have you thought of having treatment?'

Finegold kept asking how the evening had gone. 'Instead of recognising that I didn't want to be interviewed, he pursued me,' Livingstone wrote in his memoirs. After Finegold had asked the question a third time, the mayor escalated his insults. He asked Finegold if he had been 'a German war criminal' before joining the *Standard*. Finegold replied: 'No, I'm Jewish . . .'

Finegold said he was 'quite offended' by Livingstone's remark.

'Well you might be,' the mayor replied, 'but actually you are just like a concentration camp guard. You're just doing it 'cause you're paid to, aren't you?'

'Great,' said Finegold, 'I've got you on the record for that. So how did tonight go?'

'It's nothing to do with you,' said Livingstone, 'because your paper is a load of scumbags ... reactionary bigots ... who supported fascism ...'

On the last point, at least, Livingstone was half-right. In 1934 the then owner of the *Daily Mail*, Viscount Rothermere, had written an article for that paper – not the *Standard* – praising the British fascist Oswald Mosley, under the headline 'Hurrah for the Blackshirts'. But in other ways Livingstone's exchange with Finegold, which ended after less than a minute, showed the mayor's least appealing sides. His outspokenness could turn into an outrageousness that was too casual about the consequences. His preoccupation with the Second World War, much of it stemming from reverence for his beloved late father's war service, could become a crass readiness to compare his enemies to the Nazis. And his defiance in the face of attacks could turn into a kind of suicidal stubbornness.

So it proved in the aftermath of his altercation with Finegold. The *Standard* did not run a story about it immediately. According to Livingstone's biographer Andrew Hosken, there was disagreement within the paper about the significance of what had happened. But Finegold was asked by his superiors to transcribe his recording of the encounter. This transcript was quickly leaked to the *Guardian*. Livingstone believed this was a calculated strategy by the *Standard*'s editors to give the story as wide an impact as possible. Hosken suggests that outrage at Livingstone's behaviour from Jewish journalists at the *Standard* may have played a part in the leaking. Either way, the *Guardian* ran a story, Radio 4's *Today* programme followed, and soon the national press and the *Standard* were full of articles about the controversy.

Livingstone was urged to apologise to Finegold, by, among others, Tony Blair, the London Assembly, and the deputy mayor Nicky Gavron, who was the daughter of a Holocaust survivor. But he refused. The Board of Deputies of British Jews, enemies of his since the early 1980s, made a formal complaint about his treatment of Finegold to the Standards Board for England, an official body responsible for ethical standards in local government. In February 2006, a full year after the confrontation outside City Hall, Livingstone was found guilty of bringing his office into disrepute. His punishment was to be a month's suspension from the mayoralty. There were whoops and high fives in the *Standard*'s offices.

But the severity of the punishment made many people uneasy, including Blair and even parts of the rightwing press. Livingstone appealed to the High Court against his suspension. There Justice Collins said that the mayor had used 'somewhat extreme language' against Finegold, 'which perhaps he would not have used if he had not been caught on the hop'. Collins continued: 'I don't want anyone to suggest Mr Livingstone is antisemitic. There has never been any indication of that ... No one can think he was making a remark like that because of antisemitism.' Collins also acknowledged that for a long time Livingstone 'had been a target' of Associated Newspapers. Generously, he judged that Livingstone had been off duty when the confrontation took place, and therefore not subject to rules governing the conduct of people in local government. Finally, Collins concluded that 'freedom of speech does extend to abuse'. In October 2006, he overturned the suspension.

For Livingstone, it was a sweet vindication. But the controversy had overshadowed more than a third of his second term. Worse, it left a lingering suspicion inside and outside London's Jewish community that he might have antisemitic attitudes, whatever Justice Collins had said on the matter.

Other controversies bogged the Livingstone administration down. Extra-long 'bendy buses', which it had introduced in 2001 to improve bus speed, capacity, and access for disabled people and prams, were increasingly regarded as a danger to cyclists and a perfect environment for fare evasion. For those hostile to or disillusioned with Livingstone's mayoralty, the giant vehicles could be seen as a sign of his hubris, as a metaphor for a mayor who wanted to go on too long.

He was determined to stand for a third term. By the next mayoral election, in 2008, he would be 62: not old for a 21st-century politician, especially not one as resilient as him. But by the latter stages of his second term, he was below his best, distracted and ground down by his feuds with the *Standard*, and perhaps slackened in his political reactions by the continuing absence in London politics of able competitors. He had recently become a father again, and one of his advisors told me in late 2007 that Livingstone was not getting enough sleep and was drinking too much. 'I'm worried about Ken,' the advisor said. 'I don't think he's going to get re-elected.'

Again, the Conservatives struggled to find a candidate who would dare stand against him. But in July 2007, Boris Johnson, bored as an MP for the soporific safe Tory seat of Henley-on-Thames, was persuaded to run. Although he had none of Livingstone's administrative ability or deep knowledge of London, Johnson could offer Londoners who had grown weary of Livingstone an even cheekier and more telegenic alternative. His campaign for mayor combined cartoonish photo opportunities, the avoidance of almost all challenging interviewers, and allegations of scandals and corruption in the Livingstone administration, which were relentlessly amplified by the *Standard*.

Labour was also in a trough of unpopularity across the country. Gordon Brown's government looked lumbering and grey compared to Blair's, and a general sense was spreading that New Labour's time was up. Livingstone campaigned hard, but it was not enough. He never managed to fight off the allegations against his administration, even though they were never proven; nor, like many Labour politicians to come, did he find a way to expose the much more ethically compromised Johnson.

When the mayoral vote came in May 2008, Livingstone performed far better than his party did in simultaneous local elections away from the capital. In the left's old strongholds of inner London, his popularity endured. But Johnson won 14 of the 20 more Conservative outer boroughs. With typical wit and smugness, he called it his 'doughnut strategy'. Livingstone lost overall, by 47 per cent to 53 per cent. The left's one powerful politician was gone.

18

'A Sealed Tomb'

On the surface, which is the part of politics to which the media pays most attention, the decade from 2005 to 2015 was barren for the left – even more so than the 20 years that preceded it. Along with Livingstone's defeat in 2008, and a second, narrower defeat when he stood for the mayoralty again in 2012, there was a steep decline in Labour's national trajectory. In 2005, the party's vote fell sharply at the general election to 35 per cent: its lowest share for 74 years. Exactly as Diane Abbott had warned Tony Blair shortly before he became prime minister, New Labour was 'losing sight of those who traditionally voted for us': the working class and leftwing Britons of all backgrounds. While New Labour's decline to an extent vindicated the left, it also seemed to make Britain a more hostile place for left-of-centre politics generally. As Labour shrank, as an electoral force and as a mass membership and parliamentary party, so the space which it contained for leftwing politics, however threatened and contested, seemed to shrink with it.

New Labour's decline had multiple causes. The Blair government's involvement in the 2003 Iraq War, collaborating closely with the particularly rightwing and aggressive Republican administration of George W. Bush, and Blair's general drift to the right in other areas, such as allowing business to provide more and more state services, made Labour increasingly seem a conservative rather than socialist or social democratic party, aligned with the interests of a corporate and foreign policy establishment from which voters felt increasingly alienated.

For a few years, the even greater unpopularity of the Conservatives, who were still searching for a post-Thatcher identity which would

appeal to a more liberal country than the Thatcherites had anticipated, helped keep Labour in power. So did the electoral system.
While 35 per cent of the vote was enough in 2005 to give Blair a solid
Commons majority, the 22 per cent attracted by the Liberal Democrats, who had opposed the Iraq War and sometimes attacked Labour
from the left, won the perennial third party only a few dozen MPs
and no breakthrough. A void was opening up in British politics where
a real leftwing alternative, fundamentally critical of the status quo,
but also properly representing in parliament the views of millions,
ought to have been.

That void opened further with the 2008 banking crisis, which in
Britain and across the West badly damaged the credibility of financial
capitalism, and of centrist governments such as Blair's which had
privileged the banks and relied on them for economic growth and tax
revenue. As wages for many people also began to stagnate and then
fall from the mid-2000s onwards, the authoritative annual British
Social Attitudes survey registered a widening disenchantment with
how the rewards of the economy were distributed. When the wage
slump became the worst since the Napoleonic wars, two centuries
before, and poverty rose, and home ownership fell, and many young
people began to realise that they would be the first generation for
decades to have less prosperous lives than their parents, the opportunity for an anti-capitalist or at least capitalism-reforming party in
Britain became glaring.

Yet the opportunity was not taken. In 2007 Gordon Brown replaced
Blair as prime minister. There were expectations, not discouraged by
Brown, who was more troubled than Blair by inequality, that he
would move Labour leftwards. But the former chancellor had too
long a history trying to persuade bankers and rightwing journalists of
his party's respectability – that it had renounced leftwing politics, in
other words – to change his habits now. Even in the aftermath of the
financial crisis, with many voters poorer as a result, and some sufficiently angry to want the reckless bankers and traders who had caused
the crisis to go to prison, the closest Brown came to rejecting the old
economic system was a highly coded passage in a London speech in
2009. 'The world of the old Washington Consensus is over,' he told a
gathering of world leaders, 'and what comes in its place is up to us.

Instead of a global free market threatening to descend into a global free for all, we must reshape our global economic system so that it respects the values we celebrate in our everyday lives.'

Few Britons knew what 'Washington Consensus' meant. It was an American think-tank term for policies such as deregulation and privatisation. Brown's generalities about what should replace it were equally opaque. He acknowledged the growing need for a new left-of-centre politics without in any way satisfying it. He lost power the following year, to a coalition between the Conservatives and the Liberal Democrats. With the latter now reinventing themselves as advocates of a drastically smaller state, Britain effectively had two rightwing major parties.

Brown's successor was Ed Miliband, the younger son of Ralph Miliband, Benn's close ally and semi-guru in the 1980s. Thoughtful, and more critical of the economic status quo than most of his peers in New Labour had been, Ed narrowly beat his more centrist older brother David to the leadership. The old tensions between the Labour right and left, which had been suppressed by the dominance of centrism during Blair and Brown's premierships, began to be felt throughout Labour again.

Miliband and his shadow ministers attacked the coalition's austerity policies. He also made some telling criticisms of how the economy worked, saying that it had too many socially malign 'predators', and that it was no longer providing a good life for 'the squeezed middle', by which he meant the less and less financially secure middle class. Yet he was not clear or consistent enough as a communicator to get his messages out effectively through a largely hostile or uninterested media. And the few reforms he proposed seemed either too abstract and technical-sounding, such as 'predistribution' – reshaping capitalism so that it required less state redistribution of wealth – or too short-term, such as a temporary price cap on energy bills, to add up to a coherent and attractive programme.

During Labour's preparations for the 2015 general election, most of Miliband's economic critique and proposals for change were stripped out of the party's manifesto by more conservative and experienced colleagues, such as the shadow chancellor Ed Balls. Unlike Miliband, they had often had key roles in the Blair government and retained many of its rightwing economic assumptions. They also out-numbered their leader and his handful of relatively leftwing supporters in the shadow cabinet. A similar situation existed in the parliamentary Labour party as a whole, where Blairites, Brownites and other factions from the right and centre of the party dwarfed the left.

In the 2015 election, Labour promoted bland or even reactionary themes, distributing party mugs printed with the words, 'controls on immigration'. When the party lost again, much of the press and many of the party's grandees concluded, regardless, that Miliband's fatal error had been to be too radical. With the Conservatives victorious, this time with a small outright majority, and therefore no need for a coalition with the Liberal Democrats, Miliband's tentative efforts to update Labour's thinking, to make it relevant to the increasingly fragile, hugely unequal Britain revealed by the financial crisis, were widely dismissed as a foolish experiment by a naive leader. Such a thing, his centrist and rightwing critics concluded, must never happen again.

Tony Benn had supported Miliband's bid for the leadership. Benn considered him 'brilliant' and as having 'very good' judgement. But sometimes Benn also found him ominously self-contained. 'When I last saw him,' Benn recorded in his diary in May 2008, 'there was a sort of glass panel between us – he looked at me in a friendly way, but I didn't think anything I could say would make any impact.'

Despite that, Miliband was one of the few Labour ministers and shadow ministers from the 1990s onwards that he had much time for. New Labour as a whole frequently appalled him. 'Blair can go to Australia as a guest of Rupert Murdoch,' Benn said in September 1995, 'who owns the *Sun*, the *News of the World* and *The Times*, which have knifed the Labour Party for years, and that's okay [according to the Blairites]. But Liz Davies [a leftwing parliamentary candidate the Blairites blocked] supports *Labour Briefing* and that's not okay ... This is what New Labour is: a party open to Liberals and Tories but not to socialists.'

Benn was also completely opposed to Blair's bellicose foreign policy and faithful support for the United States. Despite Benn's long marriage to an American, and his impression from visits that the country had plenty of 'marvellous', public-spirited, even left-leaning citizens, he increasingly regarded the United States as the centre of a web of military and economic alliances and organisations which wanted to entangle more and more of the world, and subject it to free-market policies which suited American multinational corporations. This anti-American, anti-globalisation and anti-war worldview matched that of two overlapping protest movements: an anti-capitalist one which mounted huge demonstrations in Western cities such as Seattle, Genoa and London from the late 1990s onwards; and another, perhaps even larger, against the invasions of Afghanistan and Iraq by Britain, America and other Western powers.

Benn turned 80 in 2005, but despite his age he was an enthusiastic participant in these fresh waves of street politics. For example, on 15 March 2008,

> I caught the 94 [bus] to Piccadilly Circus and walked very slowly to the Stop the War rally in Trafalgar Square, which was packed! It is the fifth anniversary of the start of the Iraq war. I sat on the platform [for the speakers] that had been erected just in front of Nelson's Column – and I spoke for four minutes and ten seconds. Two minutes was the limit, but I got away with it; they liked the phrase 'Parliament belongs to the past; the streets belong to the future.'

He had stood down as an MP before the 2001 election, 'in order to spend more time on politics', as he put it. It was a fittingly pointed way to finally reject a 51-year parliamentary role which he had found both deeply fulfilling and deeply frustrating. His Chesterfield constituency, where his majority had been solid but not enormous, fell to the Liberal Democrats at the election. But Benn did not look back, giving his party's loss of the seat only half a line in his diary. He called the volume *Free at Last!*

He used this freedom as expansively as he could. He appeared at Glastonbury, where his generally avuncular but sometimes fiery performances before tents packed with young people became a fixture of the festival. He went on speaking tours, selling out theatres from Cornwall to Norfolk. Onstage, he wore a cosy cardigan, sipped from a flask of tea, and in his soft voice made caustic remarks about the modern world, about its surfeit of managers and shortage of political principles, to eclectic audiences of veteran leftists, small-town activists, and Tory pensioners who enjoyed his criticism of Blair. He could almost have been a visiting comedian, except that his two-hour sessions of lecturing and answering audience questions were spiked with warnings about the danger to democracy from New Labour spin and globalisation. In 2008, he even addressed a group of senior servicemen at a military college in Oxfordshire – the sort of people who in such settings in the 1970s and 80s sometimes wondered whether a Benn government might need to be cut short by a coup. But this time, he recorded, 'They couldn't have been more friendly', as he laid out his alternatives to war.

Celebrities and socialites who were liberal, leftwing or simply curious became eager to spend time with him. The actress and activist Saffron Burrows became a close friend. He was invited to meet George Clooney. Benn said no, fearing that the encounter, which had been set up through the upper-class magazine *Harpers & Queen*, would be too showbiz. But he was not always quite so guarded. At a film premiere in London for *Battle for Haditha*, a 2007 drama about a massacre in Iraq committed by US marines, 'I got a kiss from a woman who told me later her name was Sabrina Guinness. I looked her up when I got home and she's the heir to the beer fortune. She's been connected with Prince Charles, Mick Jagger, Bryan Ferry, Rod Stewart . . . I must say, she was very charming to me, but I can see the danger of getting into the celebrity circuit.'

Someone as self-critical as Benn was always going to have mixed feelings about fame – especially when, with his retirement as an MP, it became detached from representing people. In 2002 he told the *Guardian* journalist Gary Younge that he was worried about being seen as 'this kindly, harmless old gentleman', rather than as a threat to the status quo. Benn's solution was to 'take the praise as sceptically as I took the abuse'. But it was only a partial solution. In the final two decades of his life, willingly or not, he became a national treasure: the personification in the eyes of many of a left which was more noble than most of today's politicians, but no longer of much significance.

He retained a great energy and disregard for rules well into old age. One summer evening in the late 2000s, I was crossing the road outside the British Library in London, woozy after a long day's research, when I almost failed to notice a Mini racing towards me down the otherwise empty street. It was Benn: impatiently hunched over the steering wheel, heading in the direction of his home in Notting Hill. He was doing at least 60 in a 40-mile-an-hour zone. I jerked to a stop, and he tore past me into the dusk.

Yet his energy ebbed in the end. His wife Caroline died in 2000, depriving him of a political soulmate at home to challenge him and urge him on. In his eighties, he found all the walking and standing around of demonstrations increasingly difficult. Corbyn often looked after him on marches, giving him sips of water on hot days.

One blazing afternoon in August 2013, when Benn was 88, both men took part in a small rally in Trafalgar Square. The protest was against a plan by the Conservative government to bomb Syria, to deter its brutal president Bashar al-Assad from using chemical weapons in his country's civil war. A similar argument had been deployed to justify the Western attack on Iraq ten years earlier. But this time the House of Commons had voted against military action, with Miliband's Labour party playing a central role. So the speakers in Trafalgar Square were in an unfamiliar, victorious mood. From the steps of Nelson's Column, they addressed the scattered crowd.

Corbyn spoke immediately before Benn. 'The vote on Thursday night was a bit of a change,' he said, slipping immediately into his plain rhetorical style, 'to something more rational, more peaceful ... We don't go and bomb people' – he spat out the word 'bomb' with contempt – 'Instead, we do solidarity. We do human rights ... You don't bomb people in order to bring about peace.' It was a decent argument, but too full of generalities to really sting.

Then the microphone was readied for Benn. He walked to it slowly, seemingly concentrating hard, one arm rigid at his side for balance. Despite the heat of the day, he was wearing a jumper and jacket. A brisk breeze was blowing across the steps, and his white hair waved wispily in the sunlight. When he began his speech, his voice was thin.

'Comrades,' he said, 'this is a very remarkable occasion, because it is an occasion when we are here to congratulate ourselves ... I've been on this platform over many years, from the time of [the British attack on] Suez onwards – over 50 years – and usually we have found that we have lost the battle. But what we must remember is that all the campaigns we've been engaged in have culminated in the decision taken by parliament this week . . .'

It was a brief speech, just a couple of minutes, yet it was a small miracle of fluency and infectious conviction. After he had finished, he was immediately interviewed by a television crew from ITN. Warmed up now, his voice was larger, and he sounded almost like the stirring Benn of his 1981 deputy leadership campaign. 'Well, I think this is a celebration of what we've achieved over years,' he said. 'But we also have to stand again, and extend our campaigns, knowing that there is a lot of support for what we're saying . . .'

The only sign that the public speaking might have drained him was a single cough at the interview's end. But he did not appear at a televised demonstration again. Six months later, on 14 March 2014, shortly before his 89th birthday, he passed away.

'The death of Tony Benn is devastating to me,' wrote Corbyn in the *Morning Star*, the socialist paper where he had taken over from his mentor as a regular columnist. Similar sentiments were expressed right across Britain's small left-of-centre press. Even in the Tory papers, which had done so much to undermine Benn's ministerial policies and to trash his personality, there were many acknowledgements that an important political life had ended. His radicalism was reinterpreted as adventurousness, his stubbornness as integrity. Death confirmed his defanged status.

Benn's passing came three days after that of Bob Crow, the general secretary of the National Union of Rail, Maritime and Transport workers (RMT), a fearsome negotiator widely regarded as one of the few remaining effective leftists in the country. And before Crow's there had been a succession of other resonant deaths on the British left: the former Labour leader Michael Foot in 2010, the former foreign secretary Robin Cook in 2005, the campaigning journalist Paul Foot in 2004. Placed alongside Livingstone's failed and final attempt to recapture the London mayoralty in 2012, the continuing dominance of the Labour party by centrists, and the resumption since 2010 of the Conservatives' traditional electoral supremacy, these deaths seemed to show that the Labour left was passing into history.

I felt as much myself. I watched Livingstone's 2012 concession speech on television. He announced his retirement from electoral politics, and spoke with wet eyes, mostly looking down at some notes, all his cheek and lizardy self-control seemingly gone. I thought that a form of politics which, for all its flaws, was the best Labour was ever going to produce, and which most closely corresponded to my own sense of how equality and freedom might fit together to make a much better Britain, was now essentially over.

Livingstone had actually only lost by 3 per cent of the vote: a much smaller margin than in his previous mayoral defeat. But the turnout had been 16 per cent lower. So his political career had ended, quite possibly, because a lot of Londoners, regular Labour supporters among them, had not bothered to vote. Apathy had trumped radicalism – or what radicalism was left in Livingstone after his decades of dodging and weaving.

Livingstone's final defeat and Benn's death left Corbyn, Abbott and McDonnell as the Labour left's three remaining major dissidents. By 2014, they were all in their sixties. Health permitting, the big majorities they had built up during their decades in parliament meant that they could probably carry on as MPs for a few more elections. In a period when many other Labour MPs clung on to their seats by increasingly small margins, the trio's enduring local popularity was a demonstration of the supposedly narrow and sectarian left's ability to create and maintain broad coalitions of voters, in London at least.

But at this stage few professional observers of British politics were interested in the left's ability to survive in parts of the capital, despite its growing wealth, its reliance on cut-throat financial services, and the competitive quality of London life in general. That the electoral successes of Abbott, Corbyn and McDonnell might suggest a way forward for their party, in a country which like London was becoming harsher and less equal, was something mainstream commentators and mainstream Labour MPs never considered.

In the vast literature written about the party between the mid-1980s and mid-2010s – all the fat, gossipy memoirs, diaries and biographies, assured overviews by journalists and historians, and detailed analyses by political scientists – Corbyn, Abbott and McDonnell rarely ever featured. The unspoken assumption, in these books as in most of the media and in parliament, was that the trio were not very important or attractive politicians: principled, yes, but also priggish, stubborn, unchanging, a bit dour, uninterested in power; more influenced by the receding egalitarian dreams of the 1960s and 70s than the modern world.

A different, in some ways contradictory, but equally common critique of the trio was that they were dangerously naive: drawn by their radicalism into dangerous alliances. A typical instance of this criticism happened in 1996. That September, a few months after the Provisional IRA had detonated huge bombs in Manchester and London, Corbyn invited the leader of Sinn Féin, Gerry Adams, to publicise his autobiography at the House of Commons. Corbyn said the event would be to promote 'dialogue' between Irish republicanism and the British government. A leading article in the *Guardian* saw the event very differently:

> Every few years the London Labour MP Jeremy Corbyn indulges his romantic support for Irish republicans by using his parliamentary privileges to give them a publicity platform. These occasions always also provide a showcase for Mr Corbyn's abiding qualities: his lack of wider political and moral judgement, his predilection for gesture politics, his insensitivity to the feelings of most Londoners and his indifference to the policies of his party ... Mr Corbyn's actions do not advance the cause of peace in Northern Ireland and are not seriously intended to do so ... Mr Corbyn is a fool, and a fool whom the Labour Party would probably be better off without.

On this occasion and several others during Blair's leadership, senior Labour figures urged Corbyn's expulsion from the parliamentary party. But Blair's fear of advertising Labour's divisions, and his simultaneous confidence that the parliamentary left was too small to make real trouble, meant that it never happened. The trio also stayed in the party for the lack, as they saw it, of a practical alternative. The centrism of Labour under Blair, Brown and, to a lesser extent, Miliband provoked the formation of a succession of new leftwing parties: the Socialist Labour Party in 1996, Respect in 2004 and Left Unity in 2013. But none of these had a lasting impact, held back by the electoral system and by their overreliance on a handful of well-known leftwingers such as Arthur Scargill and George Galloway. Corbyn, Abbott and McDonnell watched the new parties struggle and decided not to join them. 'They understood that walking away from the Labour party would just have weakened the left's position,' the former Labour MP and Corbyn ally Alan Simpson told me.

Yet the left's position inside Labour was hardly strong, and seemed to be getting worse. The Campaign Group, the left's parliamentary vehicle, had only a few dozen members during the Blair, Brown and Miliband leaderships: a small fraction of Labour's MPs. The group's meetings, at which information and gossip were exchanged, challenges for Labour party positions were initiated, and collective morale was meant to be boosted, were sometimes dispiritingly attended by barely a dozen people.

The gatherings could still be lively. Simpson remembered: 'People really talked politics. There were visiting speakers coming in. It was not like being at a meeting at Militant, where they said, "Here is the line to take." The Campaign Group was a gathering of people who wanted to question things.' When McDonnell chaired the group for a period, it took on a more purposeful quality, with some members tasked with shadowing specific government departments, such as Corbyn covering foreign affairs. McDonnell's mantra was 'Be ready. Be ready for an opportunity for a leftwing government of any sort. Make sure we're ready with the ideas.' Yet he admitted to me, 'It was tough to be ready for a long time. You needed a bit of determination to stick at it.'

Sometimes, the group meetings turned inward, looking at the future of the left, and whether it had one; and whether those MPs present – or not – were doing enough for the cause, or were too focused instead on their own careers. Benn, still involved in the group despite retiring as an MP, described one meeting in October 2007:

> McDonnell and Corbyn ... thought the moment had come [for all of us] to be quite honest with each other, and the honest truth is this: very few Labour MPs turn up at the Campaign Group, and a lot of members are not paying their subs of £30 a month ... Also, Diane Abbott, who is an officer of the group and I don't think has turned up for two years ... did turn up today and made a very angry intervention about

the extent to which the Labour Representation Committee, which John McDonnell is involved in, was taking over the group – ridiculous!

It was difficult to disentangle from this account exactly who said what about whom, but the sense of staleness was clear. Lacking fresh recruits, as new MPs were warned by the Labour hierarchy against joining it; losing some of its younger, more able members to the Blair and Brown administrations; and sometimes soured by personal, ideological and factional differences, the Campaign Group appeared to be becoming as much a trap as a refuge. Just as Blair's great manipulator Peter Mandelson had envisaged, the Labour left seemed to be in a 'sealed tomb'.

Several times between 2000 and 2015, the left's more restless spirits tried to clamber out. McDonnell was the most persistent. In 2004 he helped found the Labour Representation Committee (LRC), a socialist pressure group. It consciously revived the name of a revered earlier LRC which at the start of the 20th century had brought together leftwing bodies and unions, and had been central to the creation of the Labour party.

The aims of the new LRC were more modest, but still ambitious: to build up a network of Labour members, trade unionists and 'socialists outside the Labour Party'; to encourage the latter to join or rejoin the party; and then gradually to transform Labour from within, until it became both 'fully democratic', and committed to 'a fundamental and irreversible shift in the balance of wealth and power in favour of the working class' and 'the promotion of internationalism, peace and equality'. The echoes of what Benn and the Labour left had wanted in the 1970s and 80s were quite deliberate. With the driven McDonnell acting as chairman, rhetorician and main thinker, for its first few years the organisation was relatively dynamic and successful, at least by the standards of early 21st-century socialist start-ups. It recruited hundreds of members, held well-attended fringe meetings at Labour's annual conference, and won support from dozens of constituency Labour parties and leftwing unions, such as the RMT and the Fire Brigades Union.

In 2006, in a small leftwing newspaper called *Solidarity*, McDonnell laid out the purpose of the LRC and his other political work in Gramscian language that was both sweeping and tantalisingly cryptic: 'We're trying to win hegemony within both the party and the country. And then, use that battle of ideas to make sure that we can reflect that in the battle of organisation within the movement overall.'

The following year, he stood for the Labour leadership. He knew he had no chance of beating Brown in the contest to be Blair's successor. Instead, McDonnell's aim was to publicise his ideas, and to demonstrate that the left was taking the initiative rather than retreating. Instead of a conventional, flimsy leadership manifesto of the sort that no-hope candidates usually produced, he published a short book, *Another World Is Possible*, borrowing the bold title from the anti-globalisation movement, with which he sympathised and sometimes collaborated.

The book had a small red star on the cover, like a bashful echo of a Soviet pamphlet. But it was full of big and not always traditionally socialist ideas: a universal basic income, a land tax, renationalised industries run democratically rather than by 'remote state bodies'. The book also made far-sighted criticisms of the economic status quo, for example of 'market solutions to climate change'. The economy was beginning to lose momentum after the long Blair boom, and the book showed McDonnell thinking harder and less dogmatically about Britain's immediate and long-term problems than the New Labour figures who still regarded him as a Marxist throwback.

Yet at the leadership hustings with Brown, McDonnell seemed nervous. Suddenly a small fish in a big pond rather than the other way round, as he usually was at leftwing gatherings, McDonnell was overly deferential towards the chancellor, barely mentioned any of his alternative policies, and never suggested he had any chance of becoming leader. Meanwhile, the small group of his allies who lobbied Labour MPs to nominate him as a leadership candidate overcompensated in the opposite direction. The Labour MP Chris Mullin, a flexible leftwinger who had served both Benn and Blair, recorded in his memoirs that he received 'a long call from my old friend Jon Lansman, followed by a slightly heavier email, invoking the spirit of '81 with just a hint of betrayal should I fail to comply [with the request to nominate McDonnell]. By evening I'd had enough and went off to nominate Gordon [Brown].' Candidates for the leadership needed nominations from 45 MPs to stay in the contest to the end. McDonnell got 29.

A few months later, the 2008 financial crisis began, and started to vindicate many of his arguments against free-market capitalism and New Labour's close relationship with it. Yet when he ran again for the Labour leadership in 2010, following the party's election defeat and Brown's resignation, he only got 16 nominations. Personally and politically, he still did not have enough Commons friends.

The bureaucrat got back to work. He became a constant critic of, and organiser against, the new coalition government's austerity policies. When thoughtlessly brutal cuts in education spending brought sixth-formers, students and other protesters on to the streets in 2010, McDonnell enthusiastically supported them. At Millbank Tower in London, where Benn had once had his office at the Ministry of Technology, but which now housed Conservative party headquarters, students smashed windows and took over the roof and entrance lobby. McDonnell described what had happened as 'the students kicking the shit out of Millbank', with a relish that was just deadpan enough to keep him out of trouble.

But aggressive rhetoric and hard work could only achieve so much. 'At the LRC, we had these annual conferences,' a former member told me. 'One was at the Conway Hall in 2013. It was about half full – maybe a hundred people. Older people. Not exactly vibrant. I said to John, "This is like a funeral." And he said, "This is depressing."'

The same year, he was in the middle of a typically congested week of speeches and rallies when he got chest pains. For several days he dismissed them as indigestion. Then, shortly before he planned to drive the elderly Benn from London to Brighton, the pain got much worse. McDonnell went to A&E at his local hospital and was told that he was having a heart attack. An ambulance took him to another hospital, where he was operated on the next day.

The surgery was successful, and he insisted that the heart attack had been 'minor'. Yet the experience changed him. Once he had recovered, he went back to giving constant speeches, but they became more terse, and more softly spoken, almost muttered, as if he was conserving his energy or not wanting to get too stirred up.

A few months after the heart attack, he and his wife bought a holiday home in the Norfolk Broads. The property was a small wooden riverside bungalow not far from Great Yarmouth, where he had spent some of his childhood. 'The hut', as a spokesman for McDonnell described it to a reporter from the *Daily Mail* who was sniffing around, had two small rowing boats and an old sailing yacht which McDonnell was restoring. He began spending stretches of his summers at the bungalow, sailing, tinkering with his boats, gardening and enjoying his children and grandchildren. The bungalow could not be reached by road. Instead, he had to park on the other side of the river, arrange a water taxi to get to the property, and then use one of the rowing boats to get back to his car when the outside world required him. For the first time in a long time, he was keeping politics at a distance.

Diane Abbott seemed to be starting to do the same. Using her experience as a broadcasting professional, her polish as a communicator, and her position as one of Britain's few prominent black women, during the 2000s and early 2010s she turned herself into a television personality, as Livingstone had done a couple of decades earlier.

Her most prominent role was as a regular commentator on *This Week*, a late-night BBC2 show with a dedicated audience and an unbuttoned, only loosely party-political feel. With her distance from New Labour's increasingly worn-out orthodoxies, her pithiness, and her preference for thinking out loud rather than sticking to prepared briefs, Abbott was much more watchable than her many enemies expected. She flirted a little on the short studio sofa with her fellow commentator Michael Portillo, himself once a political rising star, but of the Conservative right. 'You couldn't watch her and think, "Here's a dogmatic, hard-left figure,"' the show's executive producer Samir Shah, nominated in 2023 by the Conservatives as chair of the BBC, told me.

She began appearing on other TV programmes, often competitive ones: *University Challenge*, *Pointless*, *Come Dine with Me*. For the latter, she hosted a raucous, boozy supper at her home in Hackney. On camera, she was unselfconscious, quite happy to talk about how untidy her home was, and good fun, shouting and laughing with everyone else. The unsmiling, fanatical Abbott of tabloid and Tory propaganda was nowhere to be seen. Potentially usefully for her political prospects, she was revealed to be a normal human being.

And yet her jolly TV appearances also had a cost. The *Come Dine with Me* episode included a brief clip of her at her Westminster office, as if to remind viewers that she still had a serious job. The desk and shelves were heavy with box files, spines clearly legible: 'Gun Crime', 'Guantanamo', 'Black Nurses Project', 'Black Socialist Society'. It felt like clever political product placement, but also poignant, and exasperating. A radical talent appeared to be being frittered away.

She had never been as austere and consistent a public figure as Corbyn or McDonnell, and that had always been part of her appeal. Her life suggested that socialists did not have to follow their beliefs 24 hours a day. She gave interviews to women's magazines about her haircut decisions, her journey up the property ladder, and her enjoyment of good clothes.

But in 2003 her very human inconsistency did lasting and nearly fatal damage to her political reputation. Shortly after the school year started, it was revealed that she had enrolled her son James at a private secondary school. When asked about her action on *This Week*, she conceded that 'Private schools prop up the class system.' She went on: 'It is inconsistent, to put it mildly, for someone who believes in a fairer and more egalitarian society to send their child to a fee-paying school.' To make her position worse, a few years earlier she had publicly criticised Blair for sending his son Euan to a selective school, even though it was a state one, on the grounds that people voted Labour because they expected the party to stand up for equality. The fees at the school which Abbott and her son had chosen, City of London, were £10,000 a year.

She justified this choice by claiming that the alternative would have been to send her son 'to a failing state school' in Hackney. There was a history of troubled schools in the borough, it was true, and black boys were the social group worst affected, both in their exam grades and their rates of suspension and exclusion. But these problems were beginning to be solved, thanks partly to a New Labour focus on improving schools across London – led by a prime minister whose personal attitude to state education Abbott had attacked – and also thanks to spiralling house prices. These meant that middle-class

residents could no longer afford to leave Hackney for pricier boroughs with supposedly better education when their children reached
school age, as had often previously happened.

Abbott's rejection of Hackney schools angered a whole range of her
constituents: the many local leftists and trade unionists who worked
in them; the majority of residents who used them, sometimes precisely
because they could not afford private schools; and even the small
minority of wealthy Hackney leftists who could afford private education but chose state schools on principle. Abbott's action also
reawakened local doubts about her dormant since the 1980s. People
said that she was an outsider with little loyalty to the area, that she
was a bit grand, even that she was not a serious leftist. The contrast
with Corbyn's response to his own school dilemma four years earlier
was not flattering.

At the next general election, in 2005, Abbott's majority fell by
almost half, to a smaller figure than she had achieved as a divisive new
parliamentary candidate in 1987. Her behaviour over her son's school
was muttered about locally years later. In fact, it still is. For some
people in Hackney, and for more people in the rest of the country, the
episode was the first thing about her they remembered.

Yet alongside this flawed, distracted, in some ways disappointing
Diane Abbott, there existed another, more impressive public version
of her, for those that cared to notice. In parliament, while at times she
could coast, making occasional, elegantly worded interventions, but
not doggedly pursuing causes as Corbyn did, or piecing together an
overarching argument, as McDonnell did, at other times she could be
inspiring and highly effective. The high hopes in her which she referred
to in her victory speech in 1987 did not seem misplaced.

One instance was in 2008, when the Brown government tried to
extend the legal limit for detaining suspected terrorists without charge
to a draconian 42 days. Abbott helped organise a parliamentary rebellion against the proposal. After receiving a phone call from Brown
himself asking her to back down, a form of pressure Labour MPs
were usually too terrified to resist, she spoke in the Commons about
the legislation. 'The proposals ... will make us less safe, not more
safe,' she argued. She said they were motivated more by Brown's

insecurity rather than by national security: 'Some people say that last year he saw an article in the *Sun* that said he was soft on terrorism . . .' Riskily, she revealed that the government was trying to push through the measure by bribing and arm-twisting MPs: 'People whom the prime minister has never spoken to in his life have been ushered into his presence . . .' She concluded that the proposals were fundamentally un-British: 'It is a test of parliament that we are willing to stand up for the civil liberties of the marginalised, the suspect . . .'

Her arguments were not watertight. It was hardly a consistent Commons tradition to stand up for civil liberties. But her words were effective. After a large Labour rebellion in the Commons, and considerably bigger opposition in the Lords, the government dropped 42-day detention from its counter-terrorism legislation, and relegated the measure to another, uncompleted bill, 'to be introduced if and when the need arises'.

The partial victory was enough to win Abbott an award for Parliamentarian Speech of the Year from the *Spectator* magazine, no defender of civil liberties, yet keen to highlight Labour divisions. The same year, Abbott was also recognised as a public figure, finally, with an appearance on *Desert Island Discs*. 'There's still a lot of things I want to change,' she told the programme. You go round my constituency . . .' But she also reinforced her reputation for preferring off-the-cuff performances to paperwork. Describing her working routine at *This Week*, she said, 'You just wander in . . . chat for an hour, have a drink, go home. Easy-peasy.'

To perform at a higher level, she needed bigger opportunities. Two years later, in 2010, Miliband's leadership win provided one. He was less hostile to the left than Brown, Blair or Kinnock had been. As Ralph Miliband's son, he had grown up around leftwing politicians and intellectuals, and he still respected them, to a degree. Like Abbott, McDonnell and Corbyn, he was sceptical about British military interventions – he had opposed the Iraq War – and he agreed with some of their critique of the modern British economy. 'On some issues, such as nationalisation, he had a bit of an open door policy towards us,' McDonnell remembered. While he and Corbyn were still too removed from the Labour mainstream, and too purist, to work formally with Miliband, Abbott was correctly seen by the Labour leader as a more flexible figure. He offered her the job of shadow minister for public health. After briefly worrying that joining the shadow cabinet would remove her ability to speak freely, as a television commentator and backbench MP, she accepted.

She used her first ever frontbench role effectively and expansively. She mobilised opposition from outside parliament against the coalition government's reckless NHS reforms, which threatened to fragment and possibly destroy the service. With well-judged bluntness, she addressed the heads of the royal medical colleges, some of whom had been drawn into helping the government refine the reforms. 'It's no good you telling me that you've been to tea at No. 10 Downing Street, and you've been promised a peerage,' she said, 'because you have to do the right thing.' In the end, 19 of the 20 colleges refused to support the reforms.

She was not afraid to argue for aggressive state intervention against business practices which damaged public health, proposing that local councils should be able to stop the clustering of fast food outlets round schools and the sale of cheap alcohol in corner shops. She also called for the removal of 'sexualised' imagery from high streets, which she said contributed to the 'pornification' of British culture. Because she had never been a consensus politician but a disruptor, and because she had never been part of New Labour's cosying up to business, she could make interventions against what she saw as the most toxic aspects of modern consumerism without seeming inauthentic or opportunistic. Meanwhile, the fact that a black woman from a poor background, who represented a constituency where many people like her lived difficult lives, was occupying a shadow cabinet position, and receiving a lot of attention for saying these relatively radical things, was a political advance in itself.

However, as Miliband's leadership became more cautious, her outspokenness became both less discriminating and more of a political risk. Straying outside her brief, she criticised him for being too anti-immigration and too influenced by the polls. In October 2013, with the next general election nearing, he sacked her. 'I think Ed wanted more message discipline,' she told the BBC, yet again unable to say the tactful thing.

PART FIVE

So Near But So Far

19

Return of the Repressed

Politics is often a game of unexpected consequences. Abbott did not realise it yet, but by the autumn of 2013 she had already made a bigger contribution to Labour's 21st-century development than her provocative interventions while in Ed Miliband's shadow cabinet.

Three years earlier, when their party had lost the 2010 election, and the contest began to replace Brown as leader, she was surprised to receive letters suggesting that she should stand as the left's candidate. The thought had not occurred to her. McDonnell had already declared his intention to run. Two leftwing candidates were even more likely to end up humiliated than one.

However, McDonnell had also persuaded Labour to extend the period for candidates to collect the required number of nominations from MPs: on the grounds that the brief five-day window originally provided was an 'establishment stitch-up' which would allow only New Labour grandees with large existing followings to participate. With New Labour having recently lost power, and many in the party consequently wanting Labour to adopt a fresh approach, McDonnell's argument was timely. But he turned out not to be its main beneficiary.

Shortly after his intervention, Abbott was approached by two well-connected Labour MPs from the right of the party, Harriet Harman and David Lammy. Harman, a strong feminist, wanted a woman to enter the contest, while Lammy, one of the growing number of black Labour politicians who had followed Abbott into parliament, felt strongly that the competition should not be all-white. With her appetite for inserting herself into alien environments reawakened, Abbott was persuaded to run.

At first, only a minority of the small number of MPs in the

Campaign Group supported her. The majority, including her close friend Corbyn, backed McDonnell. 'My view,' Corbyn told Abbott's biographers Robin Bunce and Samara Linton, 'was that John had stood before and therefore had some right to do it again.' The Labour left, supposedly so hostile to the status quo, could in reality be quite anxiously attached to precedent, especially when lacking political confidence, as now.

But Abbott refused to stand down. Since school, she had been used to people telling her that goals were beyond her capabilities, and she relished proving them wrong, for her own satisfaction and success, and sometimes for the advancement of black Britons in general. Following what Corbyn, uncomfortable with personal conflict as always, called 'some very difficult conversations' between her and McDonnell, an agreement was made that whichever of them won fewer nominations from MPs would pull out of the contest and support the other.

After almost three weeks of scrabbling around for nominations, and a day before this initial stage of the contest closed, Abbott was still behind McDonnell, and further still from receiving the relatively low minimum number of nominations required to take part in the leadership ballot, which was 33, or 12.5 per cent of Labour MPs. But then McDonnell, dispirited by his own lack of support, abruptly withdrew from the contest. Abbott won over some of his backers, and also a few MPs from outside the left of the party. They had been urged to back her by Lammy and Harman, and also by the two most centrist leadership contenders, Ed Balls and David Miliband. These two candidates were sure that Abbott had no chance of winning. They simply believed that the contest, and the inevitable centrist victory it would produce, would appear more credible if there was a proper range of candidates.

On the last day for collecting nominations, only minutes before the deadline, Abbott secured enough declarations of support to stay in the race. She and Lammy cried and hugged each other when they got the news. They believed it was a historic moment. It was – yet not quite in the way they imagined.

Abbott did well in the months of leadership hustings and televised debates that followed, cogently criticising New Labour and generally speaking her mind, which gave her a freshness compared to the other relatively guarded, sometimes overprepared, and uniformly male candidates, a freshness the media liked. Despite all this, when the ballot finally took place, she came fifth out of five. As a whole, the contest hardly raised the spirits of the Labour left. They had produced a good candidate, who was also an overdue corrective to the whiteness of senior Labour politics, and she had come last.

Almost exactly five years later, in 2015, Labour held another leadership race. Again, it took place over the summer and early autumn, a time of year when parliament is often not sitting and there is therefore more space in politics for shocks. Again, the contest happened in the restive aftermath of a Labour election defeat. And again there was a leftwing contender, who stood with low expectations, and made it on to the ballot paper at the last minute, thanks largely to the efforts of confident centrist candidates who wanted the appearance of a proper race. But this time the outcome was very different.

The 2015 contest began after Miliband resigned as leader, having been widely held responsible for that year's general election defeat. The mood at the Campaign Group was gloomy and passive. McDonnell immediately said he would not stand. A couple of other MPs with good socialist credentials but smaller followings, Ian Lavery and Jon Trickett, said the same. Abbott announced that she would seek the Labour candidacy for mayor of London instead. Meanwhile, some members of the group, including McDonnell, argued that any candidate from the left would do so badly that the left's weakness would be highlighted and the movement badly damaged. Instead, McDonnell favoured making an offer to Andy Burnham, the centre-left candidate: that the Campaign Group MPs would vote for him in return 'for a couple of people on the front bench'. McDonnell expected Burnham to win the leadership easily.

For over three weeks, leadership contenders from other parts of the party declared themselves, and started campaigning, while the parliamentary left wondered whether to take part in the contest at all. Yet the decision, it turned out, was not entirely up to them. A growing feature of politics in the 2010s was the use of social media by activists: as a way to contact, organise and encourage each other; to rapidly create waves of interest in particular causes; and to make MPs pay attention. This new, bottom-up politics was in some ways a realisation of Benn's hope in the late 1960s and early 70s that computer technology would create a less deferential and more engaged electorate. In the early summer of 2015, this new force began to push the leadership race in a direction which he would have liked.

Two frustrated Labour party members from traditionally Tory parts of the country, an aromatherapist from Worthing in West Sussex and a former train ticket collector from Orpington in outer London, launched an online petition calling for 'a suitable candidate' to 'bring ... anti-austerity ideas to the forefront of the campaign'. The two activists, Michelle Ryan and Rebecca Barnes, both women in their forties, felt that the existing leadership contenders – as well as Burnham there was Liz Kendall, Yvette Cooper and Mary Creagh – were insufficiently opposed to the government's cuts, and still stuck in the centrist mindset of the now fast-receding New Labour era. The petition achieved a modest momentum, with about 5,000 signatures, which then accelerated when Ryan, Barnes and other activists began tweeting Labour MPs about its existence. Among the quickest to respond was Jeremy Corbyn.

He had been one of the first Labour MPs to start using Twitter and other social media. They enabled him to bypass the traditional media which usually caricatured or simply ignored him. Yet in the years leading up to 2015 there had been few other signs that he was looking to raise his profile, let alone run for leader. If anything, like Abbott and McDonnell he had been retreating from non-stop politics. He had acquired an allotment in the north London suburbs, further from parliament than his constituency, which he used to grow maize and potatoes, and apples and blackberries to make jam. He got married for a third time, to Laura Alvarez, a Mexican whom he met in a very Corbyn way: while he and Tony Benn were volunteering their services and political connections to help her sister locate a missing daughter. By 2015, Corbyn was well on the way to becoming like Benn in his later years: famously kind and eccentric, almost saintly in a self-deprecating way, a radical whose refusal to sell out began to seem reassuring and grounded rather than stubborn and naive as he entered old age.

To his surprise, and the surprise of almost everyone else, these qualities proved very attractive in the shifting Britain of 2015, as the relative stability of the 1990s and 2000s gave way to more anxious times. When he first tentatively suggested that he might stand for the leadership – accounts differ as to whether the idea originated with him or with one or two desperate leftwing activists – it was met with silence at a Campaign Group meeting. Another MP who was there, Clive Lewis, speculated afterwards that a possible reason for the silence was that some of those present were 'worried about what would happen to Jeremy' if he stood. Despite his improving reputation, in his long political history lurked a lot of potential liabilities.

But as his decades as a dissident had shown, he also had a formidable ability to stick to a course once he had chosen it, and to tune out anyone who warned against it. For a few days after the meeting, he discussed his notional leadership bid with a handful of his closest staff and allies. They were increasingly positive, and his interest in the idea solidified. At the next Campaign Group meeting, in early June, with only 12 days to go before the deadline for securing MPs' nominations, the atmosphere was different from the previous gathering.

A dozen people sat round the table: Corbyn, McDonnell, Abbott and other veterans, plus a few new leftwing MPs who had become candidates during Ed Miliband's more tolerant tenure. Most of those present had come round to the idea of Corbyn running. A fear of the left declaring its irrelevance by sitting out the leadership contest had now outgrown the fear of a leftwing candidate performing disastrously, and Corbyn appeared to be the only person prepared to stand. And besides, after McDonnell's and Abbott's leadership bids, it was arguably his turn. 'Alright,' said Corbyn, after McDonnell, who was chairing the meeting, turned to him at the table. 'I'll do it.' Abbott tweeted the news from the room immediately so he could not change his mind.

Getting Corbyn enough nominations from MPs to make his decision more than a gesture, a briefly cheering footnote in histories of the left's defeats, was a task that stretched his small team of backers to its limits. Even though Abbott's leadership bid had set a precedent for centrist MPs to support a leftwing candidate – without, it seemed at the time, any harmful consequences from a centrist perspective – repeating the process for Corbyn turned out to be extremely difficult.

McDonnell became campaign manager, sometimes ticking off the names of the MPs they had won over on a clipboard. Under his command was a hurriedly assembled mixture of just-elected young MPs such as Clive Lewis and Cat Smith, much older and more experienced activists such as Lansman, and a handful of volunteer propagandists from the small world of leftwing social media, who at first almost treated the campaign as just a bit of fun – a break from the usual routine of posting Tony Benn quotes and taunting the Tories.

The range of ages involved, and the relative lack of participants in early middle age – the age group that had dominated New Labour – was an early indication of the strength and weakness of the Corbyn coalition. He and his supporters in parliament and the country were the defeated idealists of the 1970s and 80s and the discontented of the early 21st century. There were a lot of these people, it would turn out, a lot more than were assumed to exist by the conventional wisdom of British politics, which regarded other segments of the electorate such as relatively apolitical swing voters and patriotic, often pretty rightwing pensioners as being more worthy of Labour's attention. But was the Corbyn coalition big enough to capture his party – let alone the country?

During the 12 frantic days that he and his subordinates spent scraping together nominations, such questions were never asked, either by his team or by the few Westminster journalists who bothered to follow their efforts. The aim of the Corbyn campaign at this stage was simply to keep the left in the contest for as long as possible, by getting him on to the ballot paper, or at least coming respectably close to that, like a lower-division football club enjoying the publicity of a good but inevitably doomed cup run. While Corbyn was in the race, McDonnell thought, 'At least we'll be on the sofa': the left would get some rare attention from daytime television and the rest of the mainstream media.

However, just as the make-up of Corbyn's campaign team hinted at a new political alliance, so the methods they used to persuade MPs to back him began to suggest a promising new approach to leftwing electioneering. There were infectious hashtags, such as #JezWeCan, a cheeky adaptation of Barack Obama's electoral catchphrase 'Yes we can!' There was relentless lobbying of MPs by email. There was astute exploitation of Corbyn's history as a radical, for example by disseminating the photo of him being arrested at a 1980s anti-apartheid demo. And then there was the development of a new Corbyn persona. It started at the leadership hustings, where he was frank, economical in his answers, and seemingly relaxed – more appealing than the intense public speaker he had been in the past.

Three days before the deadline for nominations, a survey of readers of the website LabourList, which is independent of the party and written and read by a broad range of Labour people, produced a big surprise. For those who responded to the survey, Corbyn was overwhelmingly the preferred choice, backed by 47 per cent. The next favourite, Burnham, was on 13 per cent. And yet, it quickly became clear that this popularity did not extend to the parliamentary party. Despite the energy and freshness of Corbyn's campaign, and despite the fact that he was widely liked as a person in parliament, by the last morning for nominations, he was still a dozen short of the required 35 – itself a low bar, representing only 15 per cent of Labour MPs.

By the final minutes before the deadline, he still needed one more backer. But McDonnell had miscounted on his clipboard, and believed that Corbyn needed two. In a small room in Labour's parliamentary offices, McDonnell desperately tried to win over a group of four MPs. Characteristically, he used a mix of emotion and menace. Making his appeal, he actually knelt in front of them and cried. He also said that the Labour membership would not 'understand or forgive if Jeremy was excluded by just two votes'.

Two of the MPs yielded. Corbyn was thrilled to have made it. 'I'm on the ballot,' he told a journalist in the Commons, 'as a result of a massive campaign by Labour supporters across the country.' But mixed in with this public satisfaction were more private anxieties. Towards the end of the first stage of his campaign, when it was becoming clear that Corbyn might get enough nominations, McDonnell took an evening off, and went with his wife to the Globe theatre in London to see some Shakespeare. While he was at the theatre, he got a call from Seb Corbyn, Corbyn's middle son, who was working on the leadership campaign as well as for McDonnell. 'Seb said, "Dad's worried about running. He's worried that he might win."'

McDonnell replied with what he thought was appropriate black humour. 'Tell your dad, "Don't worry,"' he said. 'MI5 will assassinate him if he gets anywhere near No 10.'

The odds being offered on Corbyn winning were still up to 200-1. McDonnell himself did not consider it much more likely. 'I thought if we could get 30 per cent of the vote [once the contest came down to the final two candidates], that would be a huge victory', he told me. We'd be negotiating with the winner. The party wouldn't be able to ignore the left any more.'

Yet the contest opened up still greater possibilities. Its scheduling was partly responsible. Either out of conscientiousness, overconfidence, wanting a thorough contest after two election defeats, imagining that such a contest would never get out of control, or most likely a mixture of all these impulses, the Labour hierarchy had designed a long competition. It would not end for almost another three months. There was plenty of time for those choosing the leader to tire of the conventional option, Yvette Cooper, an authoritative but rather severe public performer who had been a competent minister in three different departments in the Blair and Brown governments; and also the mildly adventurous choice, Burnham, a more charming ex-minister who was associated with the left but had recently moved rightwards, rejecting what he called 'the politics of envy'. The ambition behind his shift was a little too obvious.

The summer-long contest also gave the leadership electorate time to get used to, and potentially warm to, the previously marginal Corbyn. This was made more likely to happen by two developments. First, and crucially, under Ed Miliband Labour had changed the rules of its leadership contests. Instead of MPs, party members and trade unionists all voting in the final ballot in three equally weighted categories – which gave MPs an influence disproportionate to their numbers – it was decided that individual MPs would have no more say than individual party members and trade unionists. It was also decided that there would be a new category of voter, called 'registered supporters'. Any non-member could become one, simply by paying £3.

The changes were partly intended to reduce the influence of the unions, in particular the giant Unite, which under a relatively new, assertive and leftwing general secretary, Len McCluskey, was seeking to influence the parliamentary make-up and direction of the Labour party even more than usual. The new 'registered supporters', it was widely assumed, would be more casually political people, who would dilute the power of the trade unionists and party members, and move Labour closer to mainstream – in other words, not leftwing – British values. Blair and other centrists praised the change accordingly.

But on this, as on much else over the next few years, they were wrong. The creation of the registered supporter category, when combined with the appearance of a leftwing leadership candidate, suddenly made getting involved with Labour attractive to thousands of leftwing people. Some of them were middle-aged or older Britons who had drifted away from the party during the New Labour years, disillusioned by its centrist policies. Others were young people who had not previously been involved in party politics but had been radicalised by austerity and the inhospitality towards them of the 21st-century economy. This younger group were also sometimes active in protest politics – a politics in which Corbyn was one of the few MPs to regularly take part.

Over 105,000 of these new registered supporters ultimately voted in the leadership contest. However, they made up only a quarter of those who took part. A far bigger proportion, more than half, were party members. And they, too, turned out to be much more left-leaning than expected. In 2016, nine months after the leadership contest, detailed research about the membership was published in 2016 by three political scientists, Tim Bale, Paul Webb and Monica Poletti. They found that, before the leadership contest began, there was already 'a good deal of latent dissatisfaction' among the members, 'as well as latent demand for a leader who was . . . more socially liberal and economically leftwing than Ed Miliband'. The research continued:

> When asked to rank the qualities they most valued in a leader, Labour members in May 2015 [before Corbyn declared his candidacy] put a premium on he or she having strong beliefs, while very few put the ability to unite the party top of their list . . . Members . . . weren't so much 'waiting for Jezza' in particular as longing for someone, anyone, like him . . . to come along and tell them what they wanted to hear.

*

From early June to early September 2015, the yearnings that Corbyn's candidacy was tapping into, and his equally unexpected personal appeal, became more and more apparent. In June he took part in the Pride parade in London. He had been a supporter of LGBT+ rights for decades, much longer than most MPs, yet the response to him at the parade was still a surprise. All along the route, people spontaneously chanted, 'Jeremy!'

A similar excitement grew around his rallies. Originally, he had wanted McDonnell to speak at them, too. A little diffident, and steeped in the left's collective traditions, Corbyn was not used to being the only name on the bill. But McDonnell said no: 'I didn't want to be seen as the eminence grise, and detract from the campaign.'

Instead, Corbyn's leadership team quickly realised that putting a relatively unknown, unpolished, but frank and empathetic figure in front of the public was a good strategy. Some of the older members of the team, such as Lansman, also remembered how Benn had achieved momentum in his 1981 deputy leadership campaign in a similar fashion. Corbyn could never match Benn as an orator, but unlike Benn he had an everyman quality, with his flat, faintly Shropshire accent and his anoraks, with his lack of obvious ego and slightly shy body language, with his unflashy personal habits and plain-spoken disgust at the state of the country under the Tories. Sometimes, Corbyn seemed more like an aggrieved voter than a politician: a strong asset in an increasingly populist age.

He also had an ability to make genuine-sounding promises about dramatic change. He pledged to end austerity, renationalise the railways, get rid of university tuition fees, get rid of Trident nuclear missiles, restore trade union rights, apologise for the Iraq War, introduce rent controls and a living wage, resume the building of council houses ... His promises to right past wrongs were more numerous and concrete than his pledges to enact new reforms, which could be vague. How exactly would 'passengers, rail workers and government' end up 'cooperatively running the railways'? And before that could happen, Corbyn would need to be prime minister. Even in the first, feverish summer of what surprised journalists called 'Corbynmania', that outcome felt far away.

Yet after the calculating, often compromising, ultimately disappointing governments of New Labour, it was exhilarating for leftwing Britons to hear someone from Labour speak in such an expansive way. For the first time since Benn in the 1980s, which was beyond the political memory of almost anyone under 40, a Labour politician was frenetically crisscrossing the country, telling large audiences that politics could encompass, and change, almost anything. In Liverpool, Glasgow, Birmingham, Leicester, Llandudno, Coventry, Plymouth, Sheffield, Derby, London and dozens of other places, a pattern emerged during Corbyn's leadership campaign. A venue would be booked for him. The venue would not be able to satisfy demand. A bigger one would hurriedly be found. It would fill up regardless. An overflow room would be set up. That would fill up, too. A further crowd would gather in the street. Sometimes Corbyn would end up addressing all three audiences, one after the other – on one occasion in London, from the top of a fire engine. Exactly how many people in these crowds were going to vote in the leadership election, and were not just curious onlookers, or journalists, or spies from the other candidates' camps, it was not easy to say. But the crowds gave Corbyn's campaign an energy that fed off itself.

Some of the spectacle was stage-managed. 'When we booked rooms for Jeremy,' McDonnell told me, 'I made sure that the rooms were relatively small, so that they'd look packed out, or be packed out, every time. And we would provide a limited number of chairs, so that it would be standing room only.'

But the crowds were real, and they changed Corbyn. He had never addressed so many people, so often, in a personal capacity before. This experience, together with the intoxicating effect of being a candidate, and in particular an insurgent one who was exceeding expectations, gradually broadened his ambitions: from simply trying to represent the left's point of view for as long as possible in the contest, to actually trying to win it. He half-hid this growing ambition beneath layers of self-deprecation. In late July, the midway point of the contest, the *Sunday People* newspaper – left-leaning but sceptical about his candidacy – published an interview with him under the headline, 'If I don't win Labour leadership I can always go back to my allotment.' He did not quite say that in the interview, but his actual words affected a similar modesty: 'We don't know what the result is going to be. But I shall continue being a socialist, an activist, a peace campaigner and tending my allotment where I grow my vegetables.'

Yet elsewhere in the interview he agreed to answer a question about whether he would expect loyalty from his party's MPs 'to his leadership', given all his own rebellions against Labour leaders. He replied that loyalty should not be a demand but a process: 'You get it by trying to get people working together on the same endeavour.' As well as being a sweeping criticism of past leaders, his answer suggested he was beginning to think seriously about to how to lead differently.

A few days earlier, on 21 July, the first proper poll of the campaign, by YouGov, had put him between 17 per cent and 32 per cent ahead of all the other candidates. 'The figures are disastrous for the Labour party,' said John McTernan, a former political strategist for Blair in Downing Street, on BBC2's *Newsnight*. 'There's no other way of describing it . . . And the consequence is that the other candidates . . . have to decide who is the ABC candidate – anybody but Corbyn.'

But they never did. Instead, from late July until voting closed on 10 September, the other candidates, and their many press supporters, seemed to alternate between panic and paralysis, between treating Corbynmania as a passing fad and as a profound threat to Labour and the country. As had been the case when New Labour and the press had tried to stop Ken Livingstone becoming mayor of London a decade and a half earlier, the left's opponents patronised, bored and alienated voters by telling them again and again that they should not choose an anti-status quo candidate – at a time when many voters had had enough of the status quo.

On 12 September, at the Queen Elizabeth II Centre in London, a hulking grey conference facility almost opposite parliament, where hearings had been held half a dozen years earlier into the Blair government's role in the Iraq War, the victory of Labour's anti-Blair was announced. In a four-horse race – Mary Creagh had dropped out for lack of support back in June – Corbyn won by a huge distance, with 59.5 per cent of the vote. Burnham came second with 19 per cent.

*

In the packed, hot hall where the result was read out, some people punched the air. Others chanted, 'Jez we did! Jez we did!' Corbyn, who like the beaten candidates had been told the result half an hour earlier, was almost impassive at the announcement – for a few seconds. Then, with a small, closed smile, he looked from side to side at the erupting room, and raised his eyebrows. He looked both surprised and deeply satisfied. For anyone on the left who remembered the announcement of Benn's agonisingly narrow failure to win the deputy leadership in 1981, the last time the left had made a serious bid for power in the national party, the declaration of Corbyn's win was like a dream, even though the polls had predicted it for weeks.

He had won the votes of 49.6 per cent of Labour members, more than twice as many as any other candidate. He had won 57.6 per cent of the trade union vote – again, more than twice as much as any of his rivals. And among the registered supporters, he won 83.8 per cent, over ten times as much as the next most successful candidate, Yvette Cooper.

It was an overwhelming mandate. Corbyn's overall vote share was even higher than Blair had achieved when elected leader 21 years earlier. Corbyn's mandate did not mean that his leadership was going to be harmonious, however. The expectations he had raised could not all be satisfied. And the huge support he had received in the contest from outside parliament was in total contrast to his position in the Commons, where he had struggled to get a small minority of his party's MPs even to nominate him as a candidate. This tension would be one of the central features of his leadership.

It was obvious as soon as the leadership result was announced. While clusters of Corbyn supporters jumped up from their chairs and shouted and applauded, many of the MPs present stayed seated, some in silence. They and other non-Corbynites in the hall had pensive expressions, mouths turned down or tightly shut. Some anxiously looked around. Meanwhile the Labour headquarters staff in the hall had already sent an even clearer signal that they did not plan to serve Corbyn with enthusiasm, by dressing in black, as if for a funeral.

The first few days of his tenure had a fragile air. When he and his small staff arrived at the offices for the Labour leader in the Commons, they found the doors locked. No one was there to let them in.

One of his staff shoulder-barged the door until it flew open. Once inside, they found old computers on the desks, which kept crashing when they switched them on. More modern machines which had been used during Miliband's leadership had disappeared back to party headquarters.

On his fourth day as leader, Corbyn had to address the TUC's annual conference, traditionally one of a Labour leader's most high-profile public appearances. Relations between the party and the unions, rarely as cosy as Labour's opponents claim, had often been awkward under Miliband, Brown and Blair, as the party had kept the unions at a distance, in public at least, in order to placate anti-union voters and the rightwing press. In theory, Corbyn was likely to get a warmer reception, as a lifelong union member and someone more in tune than his predecessors with the political outlook of many unions, which in recent years had shifted to the left. But fundamentally, unions are more interested in power than ideology: in the gains that they, Labour leaders and Labour governments can get for their members. As a new and completely inexperienced leader from a marginal part of the Labour party, Corbyn needed to convince the TUC conference that he was a leader with whom it was worth collaborating.

For over an hour before he arrived at the Brighton Centre, a cavernous 1970s seafront complex which the conference did not quite fill, a small crowd of chattering young Corbyn supporters waited outside for his car to pull up. They waited in the wind at the front of the building; then, when news spread that he would be arriving at another, more discreet entrance, they ran round to the back. To see a Labour leader greeted like a rock star was novel. But Corbyn quickly disappeared into the building. As was his habit, and as would remain such throughout his leadership, he was at risk of being late.

Once he was on stage, his lack of preparedness for the conventional aspects of leadership quickly became obvious. He wore a smart navy jacket, smarter than his pre-leadership clothes, but spectacles perched eccentrically on the end of his nose spoiled the effect. He spoke too quickly and then too slowly, looking down at his notes a lot and audibly taking breaths. He sometimes gripped the side of the lectern, as if for balance. He made small slips, saying 'lifes' instead of 'lives', and sometimes lost his place in his script. He often spoke in generalities.

On the government's latest anti-union legislation, which had been talked about at the conference at least as much as his leadership win, he said: 'We will try to replace this bill with something much better.' At other moments, his phrasing was so awkward that it was hard to know what he meant. 'We can look away from the policy of growing inequality,' he said.

Even his astonishing victory in the leadership contest he down-played as 'the electoral process that I've just come through'. As for his experience of leadership so far: 'I've had the very interesting task in the last few days, of a number of events and a number of challenges . . .' The applause for his speech was frequent and loud, as if the union delegates were willing him on, but the inspirational Corbyn of the leadership campaign appeared to have been quickly replaced by a greyer, more burdened figure.

Yet despite that, the sudden fact of his leadership felt dizzyingly exciting if you were on the left, as if much of the political world had been turned on its head. Earlier in the conference, I went to a fringe event in a fuggy room towards the back of the Old Ship Hotel, a warren of a venue near the pier which was traditionally favoured by leftwing delegates. After about half an hour of pretty standard speeches from union leaders and other leftists about the anti-union legislation, the event's official subject, John McDonnell slipped into the room and joined the panel.

Even though the room was warm, he was wearing a jumper in cele-bratory, socialist red. Corbyn was in the process of choosing his shadow cabinet, and McDonnell was about to be announced as shadow chancellor, despite warnings from many Labour, union and media figures that appointing such a radical would be too provocative and risky. In his red jumper, McDonnell stood up to speak. His voice was even more wheezy and intense than usual. 'Jeremy wouldn't be there if it wasn't for you,' he said, looking round the room, which was crammed with union delegates. 'Yesterday, we changed the world,' he continued. 'But they're coming at us now.'

On Corbyn's third day as leader, the newspaper headlines included: 'Labour Divisions Widen as Corbyn Takes Charge' in *The Times*; 'Corbyn Union Pals Threaten Strike Chaos' in the *Daily Mail*; 'Labour

Divide Deepens as [Chuka] Umunna Quits Over Corbyn Stance on Europe' in the *Guardian*; 'Why Labour's Jeremy Corbyn is a Danger to Britain' in the *Daily Express*; and 'Corbyn: Abolish the Army' in the *Sun* – a story spun out of a remark he had made three years earlier, that he hoped that one day no country would need an army.

Despite his huge mandate, won after a long and thorough leadership contest, there was no question of letting him do the job for a few weeks or months before judging him, as was usually the case with new leaders of the main parties. He was under constant press attack from the start, as if he were a foreign body in the bloodstream of British politics and must be expelled. The fact that large numbers of Britons, sometimes majorities, agreed with many of his policies, for example on renationalising the railways and ending austerity, and the fact that such policies suggested a return to postwar social democracy rather than full-blooded socialism, let alone something more revolutionary – these facts were rarely part of the media discussion about him. Nor did his press critics seem worried about making contradictory arguments against him: for example, that he was both a naive pacifist and a dangerous ally of terrorists. His unsuitability to be Labour leader, let alone prime minister, was considered so obvious that logic and solid evidence were often not thought necessary to make the case.

Indeed, for his critics to have been franker about why they were attacking him might well have been a risk. Corbyn's leadership was a challenge to an economic system, and a set of foreign policy orthodoxies, such as always supporting America's wars, which were becoming harder to defend on principled or pragmatic grounds, as capitalism increasingly malfunctioned during the 2010s and disorder spread from states that had recently experienced British military interventions, such as Libya and Iraq. As a lifelong anti-imperialist, Corbyn also threatened to say uncomfortable but accurate things about the British empire, which previous Labour leaders had not. For all these reasons, from the perspective of his press critics, engaging in substantive debate with him was probably best avoided. It was safer just to smear him.

His suspicion of the mainstream media, which predated his leadership, made his relations with most journalists even worse. For years, he had preferred to get his news from other sources: small leftwing websites, foreign broadcasters such as Al-Jazeera, and the *Morning Star*. With some justification, he considered most British journalists thoughtlessly pro-capitalist and pro-American, and too parochial in their focus mainly on the West. Moreover, having been a marginalised backbencher for decades, usually pursuing unfashionable causes, he had rarely developed relationships with reporters – relationships that might have shown him that not all such people are the enemy. Once he became leader, this lack of a rapport quickly showed. The day after he won, a confected media controversy began about the lack of women in senior positions in his new shadow cabinet – not a criticism made of many previous male-dominated Labour or Tory cabinets. Rather than address the issue when accosted about it in the street by reporters from Sky News, Corbyn walked away, and then silently stomped across Westminster Bridge for several minutes, his gaze determinedly averted from the journalists surrounding him, while the cameras rolled. It was not a good look for a new party leader who had promised to introduce a more accessible politics.

Nor was his refusal, a few days later, to sing the national anthem at a service in St Paul's cathedral for the 75th anniversary of the Battle of Britain. Again, he was caught on camera in stubborn mode, with a long-suffering expression on his face and his tie carelessly loose. In truth, it was probably an impossible occasion for an anti-establishment politician to get completely right. If he had gone along with the royalist ritual, he would have been accused of selling out by some of his supporters, and of insincerity by some of his enemies. But the commemoration of a national victory against the Nazis – against the far right – ought to have given Corbyn enough cover to play the traditional patriot for a few minutes, without too much reputational damage. In a country where essentially conservative national ceremonies come thick and fast, his inability to avoid the anthem trap did not augur well.

His early leadership also lacked organisation. One member of his team told the political scientists Philip Cowley and Dennis Kavanagh that at first the leader's office was 'like a hippy commune', with 'meetings randomly occurring just because the leader was interested in a topic'. As a backbencher, Corbyn had often followed his interests, and that had often been valuable, because he was interested in important things, such as the condition and exploitation of poor countries that other British politicians neglected. But for a leader of the opposition, who needs to prioritise which government weak points to attack and which alternative policies to hone and sell, and who has a limited number of chances to get much of the public's attention, an exploratory approach can be far too slow and diffuse. By the spring of 2016, only half a dozen months into Corbyn's tenure, Lansman was already so disappointed by his performance that he urged McDonnell to seize the leadership. McDonnell, loyal to Corbyn and no longer wanting the role, said no.

'Those first few months – it was horrific,' Corbyn's head of policy Andrew Fisher told me. 'I came home and cried, and said "We can't get anything done."' He was typical of one group who worked for Corbyn. A millennial in his mid-thirties, from a relatively poor, single-parent family, he had bounced impatiently between party and protest politics since an early age. He canvassed for New Labour at the 1997 election, but became totally disillusioned by the party's subsequent compromises with conservatism in both government and opposition. By the latter, most centrist phase of the Miliband leadership, in 2014, a typically furious Fisher tweet about the party read: 'The Labour frontbench is the most abject collection of absolute shite – now backing the privatisation of child protection.'

Fisher was involved with Corbyn's leadership campaign behind the scenes. After Corbyn's victory, his role became more public. His history of social media attacks on Labour was cited by some of its centrists as evidence of his total unsuitability to work for the party. The new leader was recklessly recruiting from the most thuggish parts of the hard left, the argument went. But Fisher was actually a much more cerebral figure than his press and party caricature. Softly spoken, slight and un-macho in person, he had studied politics and social policy at university, and then worked for McDonnell from 2003 to 2009 as a parliamentary researcher. Even though McDonnell was only a backbencher then, he was ambitious about the role and a demanding boss. Fisher helped him critique New Labour's policies and produce alternative ones, in a great range of areas, from the benefits system to nationalisation. Fisher also helped him produce alternative budgets, which McDonnell presented publicly at the same time as the official New Labour ones, in order to demonstrate that the economy could be managed differently, and also that the left was ready for office, in the unlikely event that the opportunity should ever arise.

As a result of all this work, Fisher was highly knowledgeable about how the economy and government worked, and wanted to help create a leftwing politics that could actually be implemented, rather than just theorised. He had been responsible for many of the eye-catching policy promises of Corbyn's leadership campaign. Now Corbyn had won, Fisher's job was to make them appealing to a wider electorate, and also to refine them, so that the promises became policies that, under a Corbyn government, could actually happen.

The other type of advisor on which the new leader relied was older and more ideological. Seumas Milne quickly became the best-known example. Corbyn hired him in his second month as leader as Labour's director of strategy and communications, recognising that so far his leadership had not had much of either. Milne was 57, almost a quarter of a century older than Fisher. Milne was also from a very different background: the son of a liberal BBC director-general, Alasdair Milne, whom Thatcher had effectively fired, and privately educated at Winchester, where in 1974 he stood in a mock election as a Maoist. His first job after Oxford University was as the business manager of *Straight Left*: a newspaper published by a faction of the Communist Party of Great Britain (CPGB) which continued to believe in the Soviet Union for longer than other groups in the party, and which also sought to form alliances with leftwing trade unionists and Labour MPs.

Milne did not join the CPGB, and left *Straight Left* for mainstream journalism, mostly for the *Guardian*. He was still there when I joined the paper decades later in 1997, a lean, urbane man in a long coat, who was respected for his cleverness, poise and charm, and almost infinite leftwing connections. For a few years, I was on a committee with him which ran the *Guardian* branch of the National Union of Journalists. We met in a worn and airless room above a pub, often at the sleepiest point of the afternoon. He was always slipping out to make and take murmured phone calls.

He was then working in the increasingly dead-end job of labour correspondent, covering Britain's shrinking unions. Shrewdly, he reinvented himself during the 2000s as a columnist and comment editor, who opposed New Labour from the left and also attacked the worldwide American hegemony, which was then at one of its peaks. At the same time, he took leftist rebellions and regimes across the world very seriously, just as Corbyn did. Soon after the Labour leader hired him, he began calling him 'The Great Milne'. It was lightly mocking, but it was also meant. Corbyn, with his thin academic record, would sometimes introduce him to people by saying, 'This is Seumas Milne. He does our thinking for us.'

Milne quickly acquired great influence over the leader's speeches and the party's media relations, with mixed results. While Milne's patrician calm and long experience as a dissenting voice at the more centrist *Guardian* equipped him to cope with hostile reporters, his habitual elusiveness made him an erratic overseer of party strategy. He sometimes drifted in and out of important meetings, or did not attend at all. Meanwhile his Communist Party associations – journalists regularly described him as a Stalinist – fed the idea that Corbynism was an extreme project. This was crucial to the process of making it seem illegitimate.

At first, Milne, Fisher and Corbyn's other appointees were hugely outnumbered by existing Labour staff. 'There were only ten of us running the office,' Fisher told me. As in the parliamentary party, much of the Labour bureaucracy was loyal not to Corbynism but to previous, less leftwing ideas of what the party should be. Corbyn was aware of this internal hostility, and feared a breakaway from Labour by centrist MPs, which he believed would ruin the party's election chances. His solution, at the parliamentary level, was to have many of his potential enemies in his shadow cabinet, such as Hilary Benn, the younger, much less leftwing son of Tony Benn, whom Corbyn retained as shadow foreign secretary, despite Benn's enthusiasm for Blair-style military interventions. Apart from McDonnell, few leftists were chosen for shadow cabinet positions. Even Corbyn's old ally Abbott, who had come a distant third in the contest to become Labour's candidate for mayor of London, was only given the relatively minor role of shadow secretary for international development. She was disappointed, but understood that Corbyn's weak position with Labour MPs gave him little choice.

Yet his attempt to be inclusive did not work for very long. Three months into his leadership, Benn made an eloquent, attention-seeking Commons speech supporting British airstrikes in Syria, directly contravening Labour's policy under Corbyn. Benn was applauded by some Labour MPs, a rare form of approval in the Commons. He was touted in the press as a potential challenger for the leadership. Corbyn did not sack him, but received no credit from the media for being so tolerant of dissenting opinions. Instead, journalists continued to describe his beleaguered leadership team as a domineering and sectarian clique.

Meanwhile, many in the Labour bureaucracy worked grudgingly for Corbyn – or actively against him. Party headquarters in London was not near the leader's office, known internally by the acronym LOTO (for leader of the opposition), but almost half a mile away, in an outwardly blank office building called Southside. There, a later independent inquiry into the party's internal battles led by a respected QC, Martin Forde, discovered 'a real antipathy towards LOTO by Labour HQ staff after Jeremy Corbyn won the Party leadership'. Corbyn, his allies and those who voted for him were routinely dismissed in face-to-face and WhatsApp conversations at headquarters as 'Trots', Labour code for leftwing extremists. Diane Abbott was described by one headquarters staffer as 'truly repulsive', a victim of racism and misogyny yet again. The report also found:

> a deliberate go-slow by certain members of staff designed to frustrate . . . efforts . . . to promote the Party's wider interests . . . factional briefing to the media . . . [and] identification of the staff with . . . the Blair years. Jeremy Corbyn's election marked the first time that the leader was seen as so out of step with the predominant political view of most of the permanent staff. This meant that the conflict reached a level of intensity not previously seen.

In their efforts to sabotage Corbyn's leadership, headquarters staff were working, directly or not, alongside former New Labour grandees such as Peter Mandelson, figures who still had significant influence in the media and parliament. In February 2017, Mandelson told an event organised by the *Jewish Chronicle*:

> Why [would] you want to just walk away and pass the title deeds of this great party over to someone like Jeremy Corbyn? I don't want to, I resent it, and I work every single day in some small way to bring forward the end of his tenure in office. Something, however small it may be – an email, a phone call or a meeting I convene – every day I try to do something to save the Labour party from his leadership.

The phrase 'title deeds' was telling. Mandelson, and the Labour right in general, believed they still owned the party. In effect, from the moment Corbyn won the leadership, and as long as he continued to hold it, Labour was split. Unlike the walkout by Labour MPs to form the SDP in the 1980s, the split was not official or fully public, but it was equally deep and permanent.

Some forces in the party opposed to Corbyn did not move against him directly, but instead built up networks and bided their time. On 9 June 2015, the day the official period began for Corbyn and that year's other leadership contenders to seek nominations from MPs, a new British company was incorporated called Common Good Labour Ltd. Its founder was John Clarke, an Irishman living in London. He had previously been involved in Blue Labour, a pressure group which during Ed Miliband's leadership had sought to make the party more socially conservative and more leftwing economically. Blue Labour had had limited impact, its rebellion against party orthodoxies not as well timed as Corbynism, and its mix of traditionalism and radicalism indigestible for many Labour MPs and party members. Common Good Labour wanted to influence the party in a less contentious, less obvious way than Blue Labour, while having a greater long-term effect.

On 1 September, a few days before Corbyn's long-since-inevitable leadership victory was officially confirmed, Common Good Labour was renamed Labour Together. In a party already bitterly divided over Corbynism, the new name had an appealingly consensual ring. Initially registered at a flat in Corbyn's constituency, as Clarke lived locally and was married to an Islington Labour councillor, Labour

Together started working with some of the more thoughtful Labour MPs from the right and centre of the party, including Jon Cruddas and Lisa Nandy. Funding was acquired from wealthy individuals including Trevor Chinn, a motoring tycoon, Labour donor, pro-Israel lobbyist and friend of Tony Blair. Labour Together then set out, as Jonathan Rutherford, an academic and associate of Cruddas, explained in the *New Statesman* in 2023, to 'win the philosophical, intellectual and policy arguments within Labour', and 'to build organisational capacity and develop a political leadership that could carry out this project'.

In layman's terms, this meant coming up with policy ideas, gathering intelligence about the party membership and how it might be won over to those ideas, attracting more donors to the cause, and ultimately identifying someone who could be leader after Corbyn. As Blue Labour had been, Labour Together was socially conservative and preoccupied with winning back the traditional white working class to the party in towns and small cities – and therefore at odds with the liberal, multicultural and urban politics of Corbynism. During his leadership, Labour Together organised meetings in parliament and at a member's club in Soho, some public and some private, where centrist and centre-left Labour MPs mingled with other politically connected guests. A well-financed and well-organised network was gradually, quietly readied for whenever Corbyn's leadership ended.

Given all this internal opposition, the press onslaught, his own limitations, the limitations of his handful of loyal staff, and the sheer difficulty of trying to transform a usually cautious centre-left party into a radical social movement rather than a traditional, Commons-dominated party, it was perhaps not surprising that Corbyn's early leadership did not produce many worked-out policies. But this lack was also damaging.

The profusion of new ideas which had helped give his leadership campaign so much freshness and energy gave way to near-silence, punctuated by occasional Labour suggestions, often directly from Corbyn, about how Britain would be different if he became prime minister. There would be four more bank holidays. There would be a prime ministerial instruction to the armed forces never to use nuclear weapons. Corbyn drafted in Livingstone, a well-known opponent of Britain's Trident nuclear missile system, to co-chair a review of Labour's defence policies.

I spoke to Livingstone soon after his appointment, and he was full of mischievous excitement about his new role, the possibilities it offered for defying and outflanking the often entitled and complacent defence establishment. I liked the sound of that. But I also wondered whether there was something a bit too cosy and predictable about his hiring, that it might be a sign that Corbyn was drawing from too small a pool of trusted old comrades, collaborating with Red Ken again, just as they had done back in the distant County Hall days.

Corbyn and McDonnell also commissioned a rethink of Labour's approach to the economy, under the guidance of a panel of leading left-of-centre economists. Like the defence review, it was a good idea: an overhaul of policies which had not been refreshed for years, and a way to envisage and argue for a less aggressive, less work-dominated country. But at least at first, neither initiative was sufficiently publicised and explained to voters, or turned into a coherent political story. 'Random comments [from Corbyn] in interviews became policy,' remembered Fisher, whose job it was to try to fit them together.

Confusingly, alongside this rather top-down approach, Corbyn sometimes also suggested that much of the job of drawing up Labour policy might be crowdsourced. In a speech in August 2016 he promised: 'We will use technology to ... devolve and open up British democracy. We will organise online and offline meetings for individuals and communities to deliberate about pressing political issues and participate in devising new legislation ... From travelling all over the UK and meeting thousands of people over the past year, I know there is a huge thirst for people to get more involved ...'

Again, the idea had appealing aspects. Britain was, and is, an unusually centralised and secretive democracy, with millions of alienated voters and non-voters. But again, Corbyn did not explain how the idea would work in practice: for example, how an electorate that was increasingly and acrimoniously divided, not least over his leadership, would manage to 'deliberate' together in a civil and constructive manner. And the concept of crowdsourcing policies was also disappointing for some of Corbyn's supporters. Had the left captured the

Labour party, at last, only to contract out the decisions about what it should do with its new power?

Despite all Corbyn's difficulties, the question was not just academic. By March 2016, six months into his tenure, the poll lead that the Conservatives had enjoyed over Labour since his leadership victory was shrinking. By June, the respected pollsters Ipsos MORI had the lead down to 1 per cent. The prime minister David Cameron still treated Corbyn with contempt. 'Put on a proper suit, do up your tie and sing the national anthem,' he told him in a typical Commons exchange in February 2016. But a large minority of voters liked the Labour leader's lack of polish and sense of principle. After six years of austerity and indifferent economic growth, Cameron's smooth, overconfident prime ministerial style grated with more and more people. A Corbyn government after the next election, by which time the Tory government would be a decade old, and probably even more stale, was not inconceivable.

But then came Brexit. The narrow vote to leave the EU on 23 June 2016 was a shock to many Britons, but particularly to centrist Labour voters and politicians, who for at least a quarter of a century had seen EU membership as a way to keep the country from straying too far to the right or the left. So when the vote to leave naturally set off a search by these remainers for scapegoats, Corbyn was quickly singled out. Already a Labour leader that centrists generally disliked, and a politician with a long history of criticising the EU, both from the Bennite perspective that membership compromised British democracy and from a more global perspective that the EU privileged Western capitalism, Corbyn was now blamed by Labour remainers for losing the referendum almost single-handed.

The evidence for this was not conclusive. Under Corbyn, Labour campaigned for Remain. Twelve days before the referendum, by which point the Leave campaign already had great momentum, Corbyn was asked on the satirical Channel 4 show *The Last Leg* to rate his enthusiasm for British EU membership. He answered: 'seven, or seven and a half out of ten'. It was not a helpful answer for the Remain campaign, and received huge publicity. Yet it reflected the view of many British leftists, who like Corbyn had switched from opposing EU membership to seeing it as the least bad option in a world otherwise increasingly shaped by authoritarian regimes and ruthless corporations. For less ideological reasons, many other Britons regarded EU membership in a similar, grudgingly approving way.

Another accusation constantly made against Corbyn after the referendum was that his campaigning for Remain had been deliberately half-hearted. He and his team kept their distance, it is true, from both the cross-party Remain campaign, which was directed by Mandelson, former ministers from the Tory–Lib Dem coalition and senior figures from the British corporate establishment; and also from the official Labour Remain campaign, which was run by the former New Labour minister Alan Johnson. But given that Mandelson and Johnson were declared enemies of Corbyn's leadership, and given that campaigning alongside the Conservatives in the 2014 Scottish referendum had effectively destroyed Labour's credibility with most left-of-centre voters in that country, Corbyn's refusal to work closely with these other Remain advocates, while damaging to the cause, was understandable. He still made 60 public appearances for Remain in the last 60 days of the referendum campaign. And in the end, two-thirds of Labour supporters voted Remain. The Scottish National Party, which presented itself as a great force for Remain, achieved a similar outcome. After the referendum, the renowned psephologist John Curtice found 'little in the pattern of the results . . . to suggest that Mr Corbyn was personally responsible for Remain's defeat'.

Yet before such nuanced conclusions could be reached and widely accepted, Corbyn's Labour enemies made their move. Two days after the referendum result, Hilary Benn phoned Labour MPs and fellow members of the shadow cabinet, and told them he was going to ask Corbyn to stand down as leader, on the basis that under his leadership Labour could not win the next election. Benn called Corbyn and asked him to resign. Corbyn sacked Benn instead. A succession of shadow cabinet resignations immediately followed. They continued for two days, evenly spaced for maximum media attention. Over two dozen shadow ministers stepped down. Then a vote of confidence in Corbyn's leadership was quickly held by the parliamentary party. Corbyn lost, by 172 votes to 40.

The crushing defeat, far worse than even that suffered by the infamously weak Tory leader Iain Duncan Smith in 2003, seemed to demonstrate that Corbyn had little remaining authority. The MPs whose reliable support he would need if he ever became prime minister had overwhelmingly and publicly rejected him less than a year into his leadership. With the next general election not expected for at least a year, the parliament had reached the mid-term stage when parties often changed their leaders, so that new ones could settle into the job before campaigning began. By all the usual Westminster measures, Corbyn's time was up.

20

Peak Corbyn

The next year and a half, from June 2016 to the end of 2017, came as a nasty and protracted shock for Corbyn's opponents. Not only did he survive as leader, despite the supposedly unstoppable weight of parliamentary and media power, public scorn and political precedent bearing down on him. He also won two fresh mandates: one from his party and one from the wider electorate. Meanwhile the Conservative party, many of whose politicians and press supporters were so contemptuous of Corbyn that they treated his early leadership as a political gift, was plunged into its own period of crisis, division and leadership turmoil. At times, it was his supposedly chaotic tenure that felt the more stable.

During these slightly calmer 18 months for Corbyn, he and his closest comrades, in particular John McDonnell, began to open up a new space in the tight world of British politics. It was a space that the left had been trying to open since the late 1960s, when Tony Benn began his long journey away from Labour orthodoxy. It was a space where, during 2017 especially, the established economic, social and political order, usually so accepted as to be almost invisible, started to be seen for what it is: a systemic bias in favour of elites and against the majority. It was a space where a different, more equal arrangement of interest groups, resources and values was sketched out, and sometimes began to be turned into practical policies, for a Corbyn government whose time was believed to be close at hand. And it was a space where, for a year and a half, British leftists had a lot more fun than usual: dreaming of power, deriding Corbyn's enemies as slow, unprincipled and too middle-aged, as 'slugs', 'melts' and 'centrist dads'. They also came up with a good, ironically laddish nickname for possibly the least laddish Labour leader in history: 'the absolute boy'.

The golden age of Corbynism had small and improbable beginnings. On 27 June 2016, the day before the parliamentary party's vote of no confidence in his leadership, dozens of the same MPs gathered in a typically claustrophobic, wood-panelled House of Commons room to berate him. 'You are not fit to be prime minister'; 'You are not a leader'; 'You are a critical threat to the Labour party': for over an hour, MPs got up from their seats and said these things, and told Corbyn to resign, often to loud applause. When the small number of pro-Corbyn MPs present tried to defend him, they were shouted down. To Corbyn's advisor Andrew Murray, the feelings at this and other meetings of the parliamentary Labour party 'sometimes seemed to teeter on the edge of physical violence directed against the Leader and his staff and supporters . . . No leader of the Labour Party in its history has been treated thus.'

Corbyn listened to his critics with the pained but unyielding expression which he had adopted when ganged up on in public ever since his school days. He defended his tenure, to the satisfaction of none of his attackers. And then he walked out of the room, out of the gloomy Palace of Westminster, and into Parliament Square.

It was a sunny summer evening, and 10,000 people were waiting for him. The hastily arranged 'Keep Corbyn' rally was a raucous mass of young and much older activists, home-made placards – 'No Jexit'; 'Shame On You PLP [Parliamentary Labour Party]' – and football-style chants: 'Cor-byn, Cor-byn'. That the protesters were trying to reawaken the fervour of his leadership campaign was made even more obvious by the presence of the fire engine he had spoken from during the 2015 contest. He climbed on to the roof of it, and made a speech which did not address the ongoing coup attempt against him, except in idealistic generalities. 'Stay together, strong and united,' he said, 'for the kind of world we want to live in.' It took an accompanying speech from McDonnell to give more concrete reasons why Corbyn should remain leader. 'Jeremy Corbyn was elected only nine months ago with the biggest mandate any elected leader has had from the rank-and-file membership of their party,' the shadow chancellor said. 'Jeremy Corbyn is not resigning.'

Rarely in recent British history had a conflict between the politics of parliament and the politics of protest been so dramatic and clear. It was a conflict that suited Corbyn. It energised him and his advisors and supporters, who mounted further supportive rallies around the country. And it reminded the wider Labour movement that he was not a struggling, leftwing but essentially conventional, Commons-focused leader, as for example Michael Foot had been during the 1980s, but a new kind of Labour leader, who drew much of his momentum and ideas from radical activists who usually worked outside the party system and regarded Labour with suspicion.

Having failed to force Corbyn to stand down through a coup, his party enemies tried to remove him through a leadership contest. It lasted for the rest of the summer and into the autumn, and included an attempt to prevent him from standing at all, despite being the incumbent, by forcing him to first secure nominations from a proportion of the parliamentary party that far exceeded his remaining Commons support. Yet the latter manoeuvre failed, rejected by Labour's national executive committee as too blatantly anti-Corbyn. The result of the leadership race then quite quickly became a foregone conclusion. Two moderately well-known Labour MPs, Owen Smith and Angela Eagle, challenged Corbyn for the leadership. But they were undermined by their association with New Labour policies. Eagle had supported the Iraq War, Smith the private-sector delivery of state services. Moreover, both of them were bland politicians compared to Corbyn. Campaigning again, he relished escaping the political intricacies of Westminster to make defiant speeches at big rallies. Eagle soon withdrew from the contest. In the final vote, Smith received a respectable 38.2 per cent. But Corbyn got 61.8 per cent. In percentage terms, and in total votes, he had done even better than when he had first won the leadership. Far from being swiftly terminated, or even weakened, his leadership was now stronger.

During the last months of 2016 and the first months of 2017, this new strength was not always obvious, however. Voters tend to dislike clearly divided parties, and in the opinion polls, a Conservative lead over Labour that had opened up during the leadership contest grew wider until by April 2017 it was 23 per cent, according to Ipsos MORI. Only a quarter of those surveyed said they would vote Labour. By winning the previous year's leadership election, Corbyn seemed to have won only the right to be removed by a wider electorate, at a time of the government's choosing.

He was now up against a fresh prime minister. After the Brexit vote in 2016 the overconfident David Cameron, who in some ways had been an opponent that suited the much more modest and principled Corbyn, had been replaced as prime minister by Theresa May, a more austere and hardworking figure than her predecessor. She was a wooden public speaker, but she had an old-fashioned English sternness which seemed suited to the disapproving side of the country that the Brexit vote had revealed. In March 2017, a long article about her for the *London Review of Books* by the revered Cambridge professor of politics David Runciman concluded that 'her domestic advantages remain formidable. She has qualities that will make her very hard to dislodge as prime minister.'

It was widely expected that she would call an early election, in 2017 or 2018, increase the small majority she had inherited from Cameron, and then use this strengthened mandate as a buffer against Tory rebellions or other difficulties during the coming Brexit negotiations. Corbyn's assumed role in this sequence of events would be to lose lots of seats to the Conservatives, lose the Labour leadership and then return to his natural position on the backbenches. In the ongoing Tory and Brexit drama he would play, in other words, a minor facilitating role.

On the morning of 18 April 2017, May made the expected announcement. A general election would take place on 8 June. The campaign would be longer than usual – over seven weeks – which meant there would be more time for unexpected events. Yet few commentators saw this possibility as significant.

Having won successive Labour leadership campaigns by big margins, as well as eight consecutive elections in his constituency, increasing his majority in all but two of them, Corbyn had the experience and the ability to make good use of the extended general election campaign, at least in theory. Yet such was the contempt for him in the Conservative party, most of the media and much of Labour that this possibility was barely considered at the beginning of the campaign – except by Corbyn himself and a few of his and McDonnell's advisors.

James Meadway was one of these optimists. A young economist who was working for McDonnell after a decade in think tanks and the Treasury, he knew in depth how badly the economy had been performing under the Conservatives since 2010, particularly for people under 40, whose wages had stagnated or fallen while rents and property prices soared. British capitalism and rightwing or centrist economic policies were more and more obviously failing the young – a situation not unconnected to their reluctance to vote, compared to their elders. If these millions of missing, discontented voters could be mobilised, Labour could greatly increase its support. And the party had the means to do it, Meadway saw, thanks to the steep increase in membership since Corbyn had first run for leader. The able and willing portion of half a million Labour members, one of the biggest party memberships in the world, was now available to invade Tory marginals and defend Labour ones, to convert or motivate voters in person.

Over the seven long weeks of the campaign, all over the country, an uneven but vigorous version of this strategy was followed. Directed by a new digital campaigning tool, My Nearest Marginal, coachloads of Labour activists were despatched to knock on doors. Meanwhile Corbyn reprised his role from the leadership elections, turning up in several towns or cities a day, almost always behind schedule, presenting himself to packed and exhilarated rallies as an ordinary citizen who could be the saviour of the nation. In the small, left-leaning town of Hebden Bridge in West Yorkshire, the crowd was so big and committed that to hear him some people stood in the town's river, as if in a scene from the Bible.

With its multiple, not always properly coordinated elements, the campaign was messy compared to the focused electoral offensives so successfully mounted by New Labour, with their carefully pared-down lists of promises. Sometimes, Corbyn and his comrades seemed to be making it up as they went along. During a walkabout in Cambridge, he was offered a salt and vinegar Pringle by someone in the watching crowd. He took it, held it up to the crowd, and then crammed it inelegantly into his mouth. Still chewing heavily, he carried on shaking hands, even speaking to someone in the crowd with his mouth half-full.

For a more normal politician, it could have been embarrassing: a clumsy and obviously inauthentic attempt to be relatable. Yet Corbyn was known for his simple tastes. His home in London, now regularly filmed, was a narrow 1960s terrace with a tiny, overgrown front garden. So he could munch a Pringle in public and seem believable. At the same time, he treated some of the episode, such as holding up the crisp to the crowd, with a droll mock-seriousness, as if to say: isn't the theatre of campaign appearances a bit ridiculous? With Corbyn, activists and voters could feel simultaneously fired up and above the usual political fray. For many students and other big social media users, both groups keen consumers of earnestness and irony, the Labour campaign's mix of seriousness and cheek was irresistible. The Pringle incident appeared in more than a million Twitter timelines.

There was also a campaign computer game, Corbyn Run, created by a leftist collective in a blocky, jerky 1980s style cleverly designed to appeal to both nostalgic middle-aged gamers and retro-obsessed millennials. The introduction to the game explained that players had to steer a harassed-looking, perpetually rushing Corbyn in 'a race against time to defeat a rigged system' – which was a very good summary of his political project – by catching bankers and other rich Britons and snatching tax revenues from them, while avoiding dangers such as May throwing champagne bottles down from a helicopter. The game was free to play, and ingeniously crammed with partisan details, such as potholes in the road Corbyn ran along, which represented all the national infrastructure which the Tory government had neglected. Corbyn Run was downloaded over 150,000 times: by more people, in other words, than were members of the Conservative party.

The Tory campaign was repetitive and uninspiring, with May stiffly working her way through a list of set-piece appearances, generally scripted and in front of vetted audiences. By contrast, Labour seemed to want to open up politics, for example by encouraging people to register to vote. Nearly 3 million did so in the first five weeks of the campaign, a large minority of them under 25. There was calculation behind Labour's renewed enthusiasm for democracy. The party knew that the unregistered, often being poor or transient or both, were more likely to vote for them than for the Tories. In this and other ways, Corbynism was an ambitious attempt to rebalance the electorate: to cancel out the advantage that the Conservatives had among those aged 65 or older, which had quadrupled from 6 per cent over Labour in 2005 to 24 per cent in 2015 thanks to the Tories' austerity policies deliberately sparing the old, and to people who had done well out of the Thatcher era entering retirement. Corbyn himself turned 68 during the 2017 campaign. But he was trying to make Britain a country where politics, state services and the distribution of assets were less dominated by the old.

Yet all the ambition, ingenuity and collective energy of Labour's campaign, and Corbyn's cosy rebel persona, too, would probably not have counted for that much if the party had not had a compelling message about what was wrong with the country, and how a Corbyn government would fix it. Often in British elections, manifestos play little lasting part: skimmed for a day or two by journalists, not even noticed by most voters. But in an election where, for the first time since 1983, actual socialists aimed to take office, a manifesto which set out the left's ideas, to a country more disillusioned with the status quo than it had been for decades, potentially had great power.

It was Andrew Fisher's job to write it. 'I wanted something accessible,' he told me. 'Something people could read and say, "Fuck yeah, I'm voting Labour." My mum left school at 15 ... I thought, I want mum to be able to read this. It wasn't meant to be a handbook for the civil service, which the cabinet secretary could read and say, "We're implementing this."'

He had plenty of experience producing policy pamphlets for unions, and had written parts of McDonnell's 2007 leadership manifesto, which seemed a more and more astute document as the problems of the British economy and Labour centrism which it had diagnosed got worse. But writing a general election manifesto, at a time of great political flux, for a Labour party that wanted to be radical, without repeating its charge-of-the-light-brigade experience in 1983 – this was a challenge on a different scale. He remembered:

> There was one point, about ten days into the election campaign, when I had about ten days left [to finish the manifesto]. I'd written virtually

nothing ... I had loads of bits of paper spread over one of the bed-rooms in my house ... I just went to myself, 'I don't know if I can do this. What if Labour doesn't end up having a manifesto?' It was a complete crisis – for about four hours. Then I told myself, 'Pull yourself together. If you don't do it, there's nobody else.' I must have worked about three 100-hour weeks. I'd wake up in the middle of the night, and think, 'I haven't put something in about this.' Type 400 words on my laptop ...

He wrote the whole manifesto to a formula. 'Every chapter started with: here in one paragraph is a positive thing [about British life]. Next, this is the problem [threatening that good thing], which is the fault of the Tory government. Then, these are the [Labour] solutions in detail.' The positive emphasis was an attempt to make politics seem worthwhile again, after two decades of low election turnouts, over-cautious or inept governments, and disillusioning scandals, for example about MPs' expenses. Being positive was also a way of trying to make leftwing policies seem fresh and active, rather than disruptive and threatening. Finally, being positive was intended to give the manifesto energy, to stop it reading like a long moan about the state of the country, however justified. Labour had tried that tack many times – the 1983 manifesto had talked about 'shattered industries' and 'ever-growing dole queues' in its second paragraph – and voters often agreed with such bleak assessments without being persuaded that Labour would govern better.

The title of the 2017 manifesto, *For the Many Not the Few*, was upbeat, too, but also frank and even aggressive in a way that, before Corbyn, Labour had rarely dared to be in its public communications. In the unequal game of British life, the party had picked a side. New Labour had rarely done so. Blair once claimed his party was 'the political wing of the British people'. But times had changed. The relatively united country of the 1990s and 2000s had been replaced by a fragmented society where opportunities were hoarded and privilege was unashamed. As Corbyn put it in a foreword to the 2017 manifesto, 'Many feel the system is rigged against them.'

Emphasising such divisions and inequalities, and converting them into mass movements which gained momentum by identifying enemies, was a hallmark of populism. Since it had revived across Europe and the US in the early 21st century, populism had been associated with the right. But some of Corbyn's advisors, particularly Milne, realised that populism's confrontational mindset could equally well be adopted by the left. He came up with the title of the 2017 manifesto, shamelessly borrowing its final five words from a slogan that New Labour had very occasionally used, in a less aggressive way, two decades earlier. The idealistic, purist politics of Corbyn's first four decades in parliament was giving way to something tougher.

With this toughness came more clarity. The document was elegantly laid out for an election manifesto, with lots of white space and slim columns of few words, in which radical thoughts were expressed in disarmingly straightforward, conversational terms. 'Britain is the fifth richest country in the world,' pointed out the foreword. 'But that means little when many people don't share in the wealth.' A central priority of a Corbyn government would be 'creating an economy that works for all', where 'the creation of wealth is a collective endeavour'. In education, Labour would 'abolish university tuition fees' and set up 'a National Education Service that is truly cradle-to-grave', on the same principles as the NHS. In housing, Labour would ensure there were 'secure homes for all'. In the benefits system, there would be 'dignity for those who cannot work'.

As with other effective manifestos, such as the Conservative one in 1979 that helped bring Margaret Thatcher to power, there were relatively few concrete proposals, but there was a distinct and appealing tone: the promise of fundamental change. As the section on Britain's housing crisis put it, 'It doesn't have to be like this.'

That the manifesto might have an unusually big impact became a certainty when it was leaked in full to the press. Instead of just a standard official launch, after which hostile journalists could have misrepresented the manifesto as a set of generic leftwing policies, and many voters might not have bothered to check whether that was the case, the document was presented to newspaper readers as an exciting revelation, and therefore received closer and more sustained attention. The result was not what most of the press expected. The *Daily Mirror* commissioned a poll on the manifesto's proposals, and found to its surprise that almost every Labour policy announcement went down well with voters . . . Renationalising the railways is backed by 52% . . . with 22% opposed . . . while nationalising the energy market is supported by 49% with 24% against . . . renationalising the Royal Mail . . . is backed by 50% of voters, with 25% opposed . . . banning zero hours contracts [has] 71% in favour and just 16% against . . . increasing income tax on those earning more than £80,000 a year . . . is backed by 65% of voters, with just 24% opposed . . .

The manifesto was so well received, for its pithiness and coherence as well as its policies, that there was speculation that it had been leaked by a crafty Corbyn advisor, perhaps Milne himself. Yet it was also widely believed that the leak had been a move which had backfired by Corbyn's enemies in the Labour bureaucracy. As in 1983, some on the right of the party saw a general election campaign not as a time to suspend hostilities with the left but to continue them by other means.

At Ergon House, the headquarters of the London Labour party, a secret organisation was set up to direct a disproportionate amount of party funds to the re-election campaigns of Labour MPs opposed to Corbyn, who were expected to take over the party when – as his enemies confidently anticipated – he resigned after a heavy Labour loss. The plotters set up a WhatsApp group called the Deck Chair Realignment Society, on the assumption that their party's campaign was sinking. Whenever Ergon House colleagues who were unaware of and not involved in the scheme came over to talk, the plotters swiftly shut their laptops. Meanwhile, some party officials based at Southside who were against Corbyn, or just highly sceptical about his project, spent the election deliberately doing as little work as possible, and exchanging satisfied private messages whenever an opinion poll showed Labour far behind the Tories.

The only problem, from an anti-Corbyn perspective, was that as the election campaign went on such polls became less common. In late April, the Conservatives' 23 per cent lead in Ipsos MORI's polls made a landslide victory look certain. By mid-May, the lead had shrunk to 15 per cent – still commanding, but no longer enough to suggest that Labour would be absolutely crushed. By the beginning of June, with the election just days away, the lead was only 5 per cent.

The Tories could no longer be sure of holding on to their Commons majority.

In its final days the campaign entered uncharted territory. On 22 May, there was a terrorist attack after a pop concert in Manchester, in which 23 people were killed and 1,017 injured, many of them teen-agers and children. Campaigning was suspended for several days. When it resumed, it was widely assumed that the campaign would be dominated by issues of national security, that this focus would suit the authoritarian May and not the civil libertarian, supposedly terrorist-sympathising Corbyn, and that Labour's momentum would drain away.

But Corbynism was about rejecting such conventional thinking. Instead of feeling intimidated by the changed context, Corbyn and Milne saw an opportunity. For decades, they had taken a highly crit-ical, often anti-Western perspective on the use of force in the world. Four days after the Manchester bombing, Corbyn restarted Labour's campaign with a speech which linked terrorism in Britain to the country's armed interventions abroad. 'Many experts, including pro-fessionals in our intelligence and security services, have pointed to the connections between wars our government has supported or fought in other countries . . . and terrorism here at home,' he said. 'That assessment in no way reduces the guilt of those who attack our children . . . But an informed understanding of the causes of terror-ism is an essential part of an effective response . . . Protecting this country requires us to be both strong against terrorism and strong against the causes of terrorism.'

It was a risky speech. At Labour headquarters, 'Everyone was on my head: "Do not make this speech!",' Corbyn told me. In places, the speech even seemed to revel in its taboo-breaking, for example by borrowing and adapting Blair's famous slogan about being 'tough on crime and tough on the causes of crime'. As with the budget leak, many journalists concluded that the Labour campaign would be ser-iously damaged. This expectation strengthened when another horrific terrorist attack followed, this time on London Bridge and at Borough Market, with eight dead and 48 injured, less than a week before poll-ing day.

Yet once again Corbyn's heresies proved surprisingly popular. A

YouGov poll after the speech found that voters concurred with his overall argument by two to one. My father, a retired soldier, and not a Labour voter, told me he agreed with every word. In person, and especially in an election campaign, even some Conservative voters found Corbyn hard to dislike. During the final week, while some polls showed the Tory lead widening again, three surveys put them ahead of Labour by only 1 per cent. Probably the most radical Labour candidate ever for prime minister was possibly on the verge of power.

In Westminster, many still did not take that possibility seriously. On polling day, I interviewed a well-informed Labour peer who told me that an MP with designs on succeeding Corbyn had already booked a battle bus, ready to start campaigning for the leadership within days of the party's inevitable defeat. I also interviewed the head of a Conservative think tank. On our way to his large office, he gestured airily at his young staff, who were hunched over keyboards at banks of desks in a less pleasant open-plan space. 'Of course, they're all voting for Corbyn,' he said. Then he let out a laugh which suggested such youthful follies did little harm.

At 10pm that evening, the usual exit poll of how people said they had voted was released. It predicted that the Conservatives would lose 16 seats and Labour would gain 34. The Tories would still be the largest party in the Commons, but they would no longer have a majority.

The forecast caused consternation and delight. Watching the TV coverage in a crowded room at Southside, Fisher shouted, 'Please be fucking right!' But plenty of other people in the room, Labour headquarters staff, looked shocked and queasy rather than thrilled. The leadership they loathed, had written off, or at best tolerated, was going to carry on.

For the next few hours, it looked like Corbyn might do even more than continue as leader. As the actual constituency results came in, slowly at first, and the Tories lost to Labour seats such as Canterbury, which had been Conservative since its creation in 1918, seats which the exit poll had not suggested Labour would win, so the prospect of a Corbyn government began to solidify in excited or panicky conversations across Westminster.

Together with Karie Murphy, Corbyn's combative, usually highly practical chief of staff, Fisher had taken part the previous day in 'access talks' with civil servants. These are a pre-election ritual in which senior opposition figures and civil servants, who otherwise never formally meet, get to know each other and their respective plans a little, in case the election leads to a change of government, a change which often happens in the early hours of the morning, when the bulk of constituency results have been declared but most of the civil service is not yet at work.

'At 1am I got an email,' Fisher told me, 'from the second person under Jeremy Heywood [the cabinet secretary], saying, "I'm just opening a channel of communications, just in case." I phoned up Karie and said, "Have you checked your email? There's been a couple of results that have shifted it [the election result] more our way ..." Karie was like, "Fuck! Shit! I'd better get somewhere where I've got a computer."' Fisher told some of his colleagues not to get too drunk, in case they had to take part in talks the following day about forming a coalition government.

After about an hour, the sense of giddy anticipation began to subside. Results from other constituencies, while still good for Labour, showed that the exit poll had been right: the Conservatives would be the largest party. 'The other results went exactly to point,' Fisher remembered, a flatness coming into his voice. 'Like Shipley [a former Labour seat in West Yorkshire which since 2005 had had a Tory majority] ... which we lost through postal votes. Though we won there on the day ...' In Shipley and across the country, it became clear, once the results were analysed, the surge to Labour had come just too late.

The morning after the election, with most of Labour's gains and the Tories' losses clear, and May reportedly in tears, McDonnell said publicly that his party was ready to serve as a minority government, and to present its popular manifesto policies to the Commons, for approval on a case-by-case basis. But as in 2010, the hung parliament was ultimately resolved in favour of the establishment party. Two and a half weeks after the election, the Conservatives formed a Commons pact with the equally rightwing Democratic Unionist Party (DUP) from Northern Ireland.

And yet, for the rest of the summer and into the autumn, the idea that Corbyn might replace May as prime minister at any moment did not go away. For one thing, he was treated as the election's moral victor. Sworn enemies appeared to have changed their minds about him. At the first post-election meeting of the parliamentary Labour party, he received a standing ovation. Peter Mandelson told the BBC: 'I was wrong [about Corbyn]. An earthquake has happened in British politics and I did not foresee it.' Even Corbyn's advisors suddenly became Westminster celebrities. Instead of the previous resentment or contempt, Fisher received handshakes and congratulations from centrist Labour MPs.

The change was vividly evident, too, in a special issue of the *New Statesman*, previously a gathering place for Corbynism's centre-left opponents. 'He has won the Labour civil war,' declared the editorial. 'Now, it is time for the party to unite behind him.' The magazine's editor, Jason Cowley, wrote that whereas beforehand he had considered Corbyn a 'holy innocent or fool', now he realised that the Labour leader had 'changed', and become 'more flexible and pragmatic than most thought possible'. In the same issue, Andrew Marr, another sceptical observer of the left, concluded that thanks to the election, 'The Labour Party's influence is greater than at any time since [it lost power in] 2010.' Two pages later, Martin Jacques, who as editor of *Marxism Today* had been a leading theorist of Labour's decay, wrote that Corbyn had led 'a brilliant election campaign'. Jacques continued: 'To be able to entertain a sense of optimism about our own country is a novel experience after 30 years of being out in the cold. No wonder so many are feeling energised again.'

A fortnight after the election, Corbyn appeared at Glastonbury. He did not perform as Benn habitually had done, as a side attraction in the Left Field, but on the main stage. The weather was unusually glorious. The immense slope in front of the stage was so thick with people that they hid the dusty grass. Corbyn was dressed with unusual elegance in cream chinos and a pale blue, open-necked shirt, like a South American leftist addressing a victory rally. Near the front of the crowd, a large homemade placard held by two young women read, 'JC HOPE' inside a red love heart.

Corbyn spoke even more expansively than he had at his most excited campaign rallies. 'Politics is actually about everyday life,' he said. 'It's about all of us: what we dream, what we want, what we achieve and what we want for everybody else.' He quoted his favourite poem by Shelley: 'Rise like lions after slumber . . . ye are many, they are few.' He was joined onstage by John McDonnell. But the audience was only really interested in the leader. As his crowds had done for much of the campaign, they chanted like football fans: 'Oh, Jer-e-my Cor-byn! Oh, Jer-e-my Cor-byn!'

Even for people too young to vote, or to know or care much about politics, he was suddenly a celebrity. A few weeks after the election, he made a little-publicised visit to my children's secondary school in Stoke Newington. It was a hot afternoon, lessons had finished for the day, and the park across the road was full of pupils larking about as usual. But on the shadeless pavement outside the school gates, a chattering crowd of about a hundred other pupils, from pre-teens to sixth-formers, built up and waited as word got around that he was coming. Eventually – he was late as usual – a couple of cars pulled up, neither of them a grand model of the kind associated with party leaders, and Corbyn got out, blinking a little in the sunshine, his slight frame encased in one of his uncharacteristically smart leader's suits. The crowd was instantly drawn to him, like magnetised iron filings. For the next quarter of an hour, he barely moved towards the gates. Instead, without any minders, he allowed himself to be slowly shifted backwards and forwards by the crowd, shaking hands, putting his arms round shoulders and posing for selfies, while a toothy grin played across his pale face that seemed part bashfulness and part pure delight. Those pupils who could not get near him in the crush craned their necks and held up their phones.

There was something thrilling but disorientating about the whole encounter. After decades of deep sourness about politicians in Britain, some of whom were actually decent and public-spirited people, to see one so welcomed felt uplifting yet somehow also too good to be true. A few dozen yards from the crowd, Diane Abbott, who was accompanying Corbyn on the visit as the local MP, received almost no attention at all. When he finally left, the pavement emptied in an instant, as if a pop star had been and gone.

Around the same time, he and McDonnell spoke at a rally in Parliament Square. Officially, it was to protest against austerity, but the event also felt celebratory, anticipatory – and impatient. The name of the rally and preceding march was Not One Day More. 'We are winning, and the battle is now on our terms,' said one of the warm-up speakers. The usual banners and balloons bobbed in the bright summer air. But the demonstration felt different from the dozens of other leftwing ones I had been to in the square since Thatcher's premiership. This time, it was possible to believe that some of the demands being made might be met; that some of the speakers might make it into the centres of power, rather than perpetually shouting outside them. McDonnell ended his speech by declaring, 'Another world is in sight!' More judiciously, Corbyn said, 'We are determined to force another election as soon as we can.'

Some observers, not just on the left, now saw him as more prime ministerial than May. Always awkward with the public, she had now lost much of her authority, and her previous reputation for sound judgement, through her disastrous election gamble. Corbyn was seen by some as shrewder as well as warmer.

Five days after the election, an enormous fire destroyed Grenfell Tower in west London, killing 72 people. Corbyn visited the area the next day, looking almost ashen with shock. Unselfconsciously, he hugged and touched the devastated people he met. May initially made a 'private visit', at which she talked to members of the emergency services rather than survivors. The fire had happened in a starkly divided borough with an inadequate Conservative council, and appeared to have been caused by cheap, combustible cladding installed by profit-maximising contractors. To many, the catastrophe was Tory Britain in microcosm; and to a growing proportion, Corbyn was the only politician with the social justice credentials and emotional intelligence to make the country right again. Fewer people called him a fool now.

During these heady weeks and months for the left, it was sometimes easy to forget that Labour had not won the election. They had ended up with 262 seats: a mediocre total by the party's post-1945 standards, and 56 fewer than the Conservatives. However, this outcome was largely a product of the electoral system. It had a strong bias against parties with intense concentrations of support, as Corbyn's Labour had in English and Welsh cities, where left-leaning electoral groups, particularly the young, increasingly congregated, drawn together by the greater job opportunities, diversity and often freedom of urban life, and by shared social values. At the 2017 election, the Conservatives received 6 per cent more votes than Labour, yet they won 21 per cent more seats. Had Britain had a system of proportional representation, a reform which a large and growing number of Labour voters wanted, yet one in which Corbyn and most of his senior advisors showed little interest, the Conservatives would almost certainly not have been able to continue in government. Support from their only parliamentary friends, the tiny DUP, would have been insufficient to form a viable coalition.

Beyond such tantalising counterfactuals, one concrete feature of the 2017 result in particular gave Corbyn's leadership a new authority. Labour's total vote had gone up by over a third. Only in 1945 and 1997, the party's two most treasured landslide victories, had Labour improved its performance so dramatically. What was more, in 2017 Corbyn had won millions more votes than Blair, supposedly the party's modern electoral genius, had done in his victories in 2001 and 2005. As May's government continued to stumble and argue with itself into the autumn, and now that discontented voters, and non-voters, could see from the 2017 election how much of a difference their participation could make, how many million more votes might Corbyn win next?

Such thoughts were still racing around the heads of many leftists when Labour held its annual conference in the autumn of 2017. The gathering was held at Brighton again: like Liverpool and Bristol, one of the places on the fringes of England where many people live apart from the mainstream, and where, probably not coincidentally, Corbynism was particularly strong.

All over the seafront there were delegates in their fifties and sixties, wearing denim jackets covered in socialist badges, exactly as they might have done during the left's expectant days in the early 1980s. 'They've all come back, the people who drifted away from the struggle,' Corbyn's old ally Valerie Veness told me contentedly. The slick young men in suits who used to flood New Labour's party conferences were still present. A rising party will always draw the ambitious. But they were no longer ubiquitous. Instead, millennial activists of all genders, often in casual, garish, cocooning outfits, excitedly rushed around: the anxious but suddenly empowered Corbyn generation made flesh. They had their own, more informal gathering right across from the main conference. It had an intoxicating name: The World Transformed.

Offstage from both events, inside the party machine, things were not quite as harmonious as advertised. The regeneration of Labour which Corbyn seemed to be leading threatened to fill the party at all levels with new, often more leftwing activists and candidates, thus reducing the power and opportunities of the incumbents. Some of the latter, working at Labour headquarters, tried to shorten the official conference slogan from For the Many Not the Few to the blander, less radical-sounding For the Many. Corbyn's team overrode the decision. But the episode made clear that Labour's conversion to Corbynism was far from complete.

On the main conference stage, Corbyn and McDonnell spent some of the gathering revelling regardless in their success and shared history. They wore identical outfits – black suit, white shirt, red tie – that combined would-be ministerial sobriety with a hint of the revolutionary. During McDonnell's speech, Corbyn, sitting on stage beside him, produced a phone and took a picture of his old comrade. During his own speech, Corbyn praised Abbott for her 'decades-long record of campaigning for social justice'. Then he announced it was her birthday. As a full minute's applause followed, Abbott, who was at the front of the hall, looked simultaneously surprised, delighted and a little unsettled. Being appreciated by the party seemed novel.

The previous year, Corbyn had promoted her to shadow home secretary. For this role to go to a champion of civil liberties, and someone from a racial group disproportionately targeted by the police and punished by the prison system, was a huge change. Usually, Labour shadow home secretaries were authoritarians, nervously echoing most of what their Tory counterparts said and did, for fear of being seen by journalists and voters as 'soft on crime'. But Abbott's approach was completely different. The first non-white person to hold the position, her priority was not placating, or feeding, the fears of socially conservative Britons about crime and immigration, but protecting the most disadvantaged against the state: for example, the detainees at Yarl's

Wood, the infamously harsh and abusive compound where young migrants were imprisoned as they waited for immigration rulings.

For more than a year, Abbott lobbied the Home Office, the almost implacable bureaucracy where she had once worked, to let her visit Yarl's Wood. When the visit finally took place, she then had to persuade the ministry and the facility's private sector operators to let her speak to detainees, some of whom were on hunger strike in protest against their treatment. So many of the migrants wanted to meet her that the camp's sports hall had to be used for the conversations. Abbott learned from one that the Home Office was sending the hunger strikers threatening letters, warning that their protest could lead to deportation processes against them being 'accelerated'. After her visit, Abbott said that Labour would close Yarl's Wood down. For the first time since the 1960s, it seemed possible that some of the British state's coercive apparatus would be dismantled rather than relentlessly expanded. If Abbott became home secretary, her desire to question and open up institutions might finally find the perfect target.

At the 2017 party conference, this sense of possibility extended to fringe events, where more honest things are often said than in the official conference. A meeting of McDonnell's socialist pressure group, the Labour Representation Committee (LRC), was held in one of the oldest centres of Brighton nonconformity, a plain but elegant Quaker meeting house which had survived in a part of the city centre otherwise given over to pubs and shops. At the gathering, McDonnell spoke with feeling about his political past and present. For much of the LRC's life, he said, 'We were . . . fighting to keep socialism alive in the Labour party.' He went on: 'They were dark days . . . If someone had told me I was going to be shadow chancellor . . .' He laughed. 'But hopefully we've left those days behind now.'

After the session, he immediately gave another speech in the pretty walled garden of the meeting house, to a small crowd who had been unable to get into the main event. It was dusk, and though it was late September, a warmth lingered, as if the summer would go on for ever. Well into his stride now, McDonnell sounded more confident, almost bullish. 'I do not want to go into government with a tiny majority,' he said. 'Or for one term.' He stood on the lawn, still trim at 66, smarter than almost all his audience in his black suit and red tie. 'We have got to become the natural party of government.'

How could Labour – especially Labour under divisive leftwing leadership – achieve this sort of dominance? Blair had managed it. But usually it was the Conservatives, with all their allies at the top of the economy and among the voters British capitalism favoured, who were the country's default rulers.

McDonnell's solution to this age-old problem, and to the equally entrenched problems of the economy – too little growth, an ever-narrower distribution of rewards and a lack of say for most employees – was for Labour to develop policies which changed fundamentally how the economy functioned, and which would appeal to a wider spectrum of voters. Just as politics had long been democratised, so economic life should be. Both assets and decision-making should be spread around more equally, and a different society would emerge.

It was easier said than done. Not least because the left in Britain, as in most other democracies, had not produced a coherent or compelling economic blueprint for decades – arguably, not since Benn's grand plans as industry minister. In their focus on how companies were owned and run, those plans had to an extent anticipated McDonnell's project. But they had been blocked and then dismantled over 40 years ago. And Benn, unlike McDonnell, had been a nationally famous politician and an exceptional communicator, operating in an era when union power was near its zenith. With less potent support from unions, McDonnell's enormously ambitious scheme to reshape the economy would have to contend with even more powerful forces than Benn did: the shareholders and business executives who ever since the Thatcher government had got used to the economy being organised on their terms.

Yet in other ways, circumstances were more favourable. By 2017, British capitalism was more dysfunctional for more people than in the 1970s, in terms of wages, inequality and working conditions. There was also ever more evidence that the free market was a major cause of the climate crisis. In Britain, as in many other countries, there was a dawning recognition that a new kind of economy was needed, not just in the left-of-centre press but also in business publications such as the *Financial Times*.

'We're in a time when people are much more open to radical economic ideas,' I was told in early 2019 by Michael Jacobs, an economist who had once been a prime ministerial advisor to Gordon Brown but was now enthused by McDonnell. 'Voters have revolted against neoliberalism, for example at the 2017 election. And the international economic institutions – the World Bank, the International Monetary Fund – are recognising the free market's downsides.' The financial crisis and the previously unthinkable government interventions that halted it had discredited two orthodoxies which had dominated transatlantic politics since Thatcherism: that capitalism could not fail, and that governments could not fundamentally alter how the economy worked. The enemies of McDonnell's plans for economic reform were still numerous and strong, but by 2017 their credibility was weaker than for decades.

Meanwhile, for first time since the 1970s, the British left was generating lots of ideas about what could replace the free-market model. In think tanks in London and elsewhere, and at more informal gatherings of activists and economists, the combination of modern capitalism's obvious difficulties and the Corbyn leadership had created a new political and intellectual network. A few of its members, such as Jacobs and McDonnell, were middle-aged. But most were much younger – young enough to have known nothing as adults but a ubiquitous yet brittle and underperforming capitalism. Thanks to the internet, their ideas for an alternative could emerge and be exchanged and refined faster than ever before.

Christine Berry, a freelance academic in her early thirties, was one of the network's central figures. 'We're stripping economics back to basics,' she told me in 2019. 'We want economics to ask: "Who owns these resources? Who has power in this company?"' The new left economists, as they became known during the late 2010s, wanted economic power to be devolved: to employees taking part-ownership of their companies; or to local politicians, so that they could reshape the economies of their towns or cities to favour local, more ethical businesses rather than outside corporations; or even to national politicians, so that they could encourage 'alternative models of ownership' such as co-operatives, and also renationalise Britain's many obviously failing public utilities.

These economists wanted, in essence, to change the relationship between capitalism and the state, between workers and employers, between the local and global economy, and between those with economic assets and those without. Yet unlike the nationalising Labour governments of the postwar years, they did not want this transformation to be wholly initiated and overseen by Whitehall. They envisaged a large role for employees, voters and consumers as well. The result, the new left economists claimed, would be an economy that suited society, rather than a society subordinated to the economy. In short, the new economics was not a purely economic creed at all. As Berry put it to me: 'It's a new view of the world'.

This worldview was promoted through social media; through new think tanks such as Common Wealth; through well-established, once Blairite but now more radical think tanks such as the Institute for Public Policy Research; and through leftwing or more broadly dissenting websites such as openDemocracy and Novara Media, the latter founded in the aftermath of the anti-austerity protests in 2011. By the time Corbyn's leadership entered a more secure phase after the 2017 election, the new left economics had become a complete and almost self-sustaining intellectual ecosystem. One of its busiest think tanks, the London-based New Economics Foundation (NEF), set up a spin-off, the New Economy Organisers Network (NEON), to run workshops for leftwing activists. There they could learn how 'to build support for a new economy', NEON's promotional literature promised, for example by telling effective 'stories' about it in the mainstream media.

Meanwhile in usually more conservative Dorset, an activist collective, Stir to Action, was publishing a quarterly magazine 'for the new economy'. The collective was also organising advice sessions across southern England, in politically active places such as Bristol and Oxford. Topics included 'Worker Co-ops: How to Get Started' and 'Community Ownership: What If We Ran It Ourselves?'

Stir to Action had also set up an annual summer festival. The 2019 edition was held outside Frome in Somerset, a nonconformist country town in an otherwise comfortably Tory constituency. In a clearing off a wooded lane, hundreds of leftists, environmentalists and people who were just curious spent several days camping, eating vegan food, and exploring the potential for transforming the economy, as if such a change were the most natural thing in the world. I took part in a panel about whether the new left economics could really expect to influence the usually cautious Labour party, a topic I had written about for the *Guardian*. The discussion was generally optimistic, but there were sceptics. Outside the open-sided discussion tent, the sleepy, sun-baked countryside waited for change to come.

As a politician with intellectual curiosity, and a shadow chancellor in urgent need of policies, McDonnell was quickly drawn to the new left economists. He often attended their speaking events, not always speaking himself, but always listening carefully from a seat near the stage, an expression of concentration and contentment on his face, educating himself as much as engaging in politics. Often, he would show support for and associate himself with what was being said, without actually committing Labour to adopting it as policy. For a politician supposed to be one of the most dogmatic on the left, he had developed an unusually deft and pragmatic touch. His long experience of, and reading about, the need for radical coalitions, from the GLC to Gramsci, had made his political thinking and tactics – if not his underlying principles – more flexible than those of most of his socialist peers.

At times as shadow chancellor, his dealings with the new left economists were disarmingly direct. The usual relationship between leftwing think tanks and Labour was reversed: instead of desperately trying to draw the party's attention to their proposals, they struggled to keep up with Labour's appetite for them. 'They're virtually asking, "Have you got anything else at the back of your cupboard?",' one delighted but slightly perplexed NEF veteran told me. 'We scrabble around, and give them anything we can come up with, as quickly as we can.'

In July 2018, NEF published a report advocating a sharp increase in the number of British co-operatives. On one of its final pages, seemingly almost as an afterthought, the report also proposed that conventionally owned companies be required to give their employees shares, to create what NEF called an 'inclusive ownership fund'. Two months later, with a few modifications, the proposal became Labour policy. 'I've never seen anything like it, from think tank idea to adoption as policy!' said Mathew Lawrence, one of the report's authors.

As with many of the new left economists' ideas, the proposal seemed modest, and not even necessarily leftwing at first. As prime minister, Thatcher had wanted more Britons to own shares, after all. But the policy was cleverly designed to gradually reshape capitalism from within. Like his comrades, Lawrence was a close student of the free-market system he wanted to replace, and he had spotted that shareholdings in British companies were becoming increasingly fragmented and short-term. So if workers owned part of a company through an ownership fund, collectively and permanently, then that shareholding, he concluded, being unusually large and long-term, would gradually exert more influence over company strategy, and would shift it in the employees' favour.

'The funds are meant to tip the balance towards a different kind of corporate culture,' Lawrence told me. Hilary Wainwright, an older socialist intellectual and activist who had worked with Benn and for the GLC, and was now enthused by McDonnell and the new left economists, described the potential of the inclusive ownership fund, and other ideas from the new left economists, more theoretically. 'Radical change,' she said, 'when it destabilises the status quo in the right way, creates further opportunities for change.'

This picture of the economy shifting incrementally but irreversibly in the workers' favour appealed to McDonnell's Gramscian mindset, to his conception of politics as a long game. Altering how capitalism functioned also appeared to offer a solution to what he saw as the deep problems of the modern state. He believed there were now limits to how far the state could increase taxes and spending. In his view, many voters were unwilling, or simply unable, to pay much more tax, since living standards had been squeezed for so long. He also believed that central government had lost authority. It was seen by the public as simultaneously too weak, short of money thanks to austerity; and too strong – too intrusive and domineering, for example in its treatment of benefits claimants. Instead of relying mainly on the state to create a better society, one of McDonnell's advisors told me, as Labour governments of both the left and centre-left had previously done, leftwing administrations, at both the national and local level, 'have to get into changing how capitalism works'.

There were a few places in Britain where, to an extent, this was already happening – where miniature versions of policies that McDonnell might follow in a Corbyn government could be seen in action. These were more modest than previous experiments in municipal socialism such as the GLC, which had taken place under a less centralised state. The most firmly established of these 21st-century experiments was in the small, ex-industrial Lancashire city of Preston. McDonnell visited it regularly, to talk to the leader of its Labour council, Matthew Brown. In a speech there in February 2018, McDonnell summed up the significance of 'the Preston model', as it was becoming known in some leftwing circles. In this and other places with innovative Labour councils, he said, 'We're seeing the early days of a better country.'

A few months later, on a soaking day in November, I went to Preston to meet Brown and look around. On its gusty hilltop, the handsome Victorian city centre was busier than I remembered from previous visits back in the 1990s and 2000s, before his tenure. In those days, the place had been slowly fading, losing business to other, bigger Lancashire cities, and waiting to be redeveloped around a new shopping centre that was never built. Now, it looked in places more like the sketches of a hipster architect come to life. There was a refurbished and bustling covered market, and artists' studios occupied former council offices. Coffee and craft beer were being sold from converted shipping containers, right behind the town hall.

All these enterprises had been facilitated by the council. Less visibly, but probably more importantly, the city's large concentration of other public sector bodies – a hospital, a university, a police headquarters – had been persuaded by the council to procure goods and services locally whenever possible. They now spent almost four times as much of their budgets in Preston as they had done in 2013.

'What we're doing in Preston is common sense, but it's also ideological,' Brown said, when we met in his sparse office, deep inside the large town hall. He was an intense, angular man in his mid-forties, shaven-headed and tall, who had been partly inspired to enter politics by seeing Benn on television as a teenager. 'We're living through a systemic crisis of capitalism,' Brown continued, 'and we've got to create alternatives.' This meant the council 'supporting local small businesses rather than big capitalists', and also using its 'leverage' as a procurer to make businesses behave more ethically: pay the living wage, recruit more diverse staff. At the same time, the council aimed to change how many commercial enterprises in Preston were owned, by making the city a place where cooperatives were mainstream rather than niche. 'My intention,' said Brown, 'is to get them to 30 per cent, 40 per cent of our economy.'

All this was happening at a time when councils were widely thought to have been weakened almost to impotence by years of Conservative cuts. As McDonnell saw it, Brown was practising radicalism on a tight budget. I asked Brown whether he had any doubts about a relatively low-profile city with a population of less than 150,000 acting as a model for reshaping the whole British economy. 'No,' he said. 'I'm quite strong-minded.'

He showed me round the city centre in the pouring rain. Walking fast and without an umbrella, he pointed out the council's many projects. We stopped in front of a half-built, generic block of student housing which it had commissioned. I asked what the rents would be like. 'Competitive,' said Brown. 'You do what you can within your socialist principles.'

In his office, I asked whether working with business could be considered socialist at all. 'We've got to be pragmatic,' he said. 'We are operating in a free-market environment, at least for now. And I don't see supporting local businesses as the same as working with big capitalists. The vast majority of small businesses employ one or two people, who are often family. There's almost no one to exploit. And shareholders are not involved . . .' Like McDonnell, he described what was happening in Preston as 'community wealth building'. When I asked again whether it was inherently socialist, for the only time in our afternoon together Brown showed a hint of impatience. 'Nationally,' he said, 'Labour is getting away from this, "are you pro-business or anti-business?" argument.'

A few hours later, I saw McDonnell speak at an evening event in London. It was in the centre of Islington, close to the Corbyn heartland, and a long queue waited in the rain, just as people did for the rock musicians the venue usually hosted. The shadow chancellor tiptoed around the issue of Labour's precise relationship with business. He talked about 'the relationship we are building up with finance capital', by which he meant an ongoing series of meetings with bankers, asset managers and other key City of London figures. 'I call it my tea offensive,' he said, 'because I won't accept a free lunch. I take them through Labour's plans. I tell them, "You won't like what we're going to do: bringing in a transaction tax [on financial trading], raising corporation tax. But you can see there's nothing up my sleeve. So you can adjust before Labour is elected."'

He presented a Corbyn premiership as better for business, because it would be more stable than a continuation of Tory rule, with its sudden changes of prime minister and policy, general administrative incompetence, and avoidant approach to the climate crisis. 'We're offering them [the City] security they're not getting from this government,' McDonnell insisted. A Corbyn government, he continued, would create an economy that was better for 'long-term investment'.

As usual, the shadow chancellor was wearing a sensible dark suit. It was the same sort of suit that he wore to his meetings every six weeks with the governor of the Bank of England, Mark Carney. The two men – the self-made socialist and the former Goldman Sachs banker – got on well. They discussed how turbulence in the markets following the election of a Corbyn government might best be managed. McDonnell anticipated that such disorder would last 'a few days', before traders realised that the new chancellor and government were serious reformers, not reckless extremists. He wanted a 'radical but stable transition' that lasted years. 'The idea was,' he told me in 2023, 'that in our first period in office we would demonstrate what we could do, all the bread-and-butter stuff. And that would give us the opportunity to move into other areas.'

Unlike Corbyn, he was a concise speaker and reliable timekeeper, and the media appetite for him rose accordingly during Corbyn's leadership, especially in 2018, the first year of Corbyn's tenure not to feature a national or Labour leadership election, events which energised Corbyn and made him more compelling. That year, McDonnell almost became the public face of the leadership, perpetually being interviewed on the *Today* programme. Corbyn usually refused to appear on it, because he considered it biased.

After McDonnell's Islington event, I was allowed just a few minutes with him. We spoke in one of the venue's stairwells. A dim blue light shone down on us, as if we were in a submarine. But McDonnell was in an upbeat, almost playful mood. 'We're beginning to reconstruct what we had in the 70s,' he said. 'A network of thinking groups. Class [a leftwing think tank] is revitalised. Michael Jacobs – he's buzzing!' He slipped into the language of leftwing revolutions: 'We're bringing forward the cadres.'

I asked how a Corbyn government would treat the 20 per cent or 30 per cent of Britons who were the free-market economy's winners. 'I think it's more like 5 per cent,' McDonnell said quickly. 'We tax them.' Trying a different ideological tack, I asked whether, as a socialist, he ever worried that if Labour did help create a more stable and sustainable economy, the party would end up helping to save British capitalism rather than replace it.

'Who incorporates who?' McDonnell said, grinning in the blue light, as if we had moved into a particularly fruitful area for discussion. 'That's the debate!' He did a quick, cartoonish impression of a leftwing Labour chancellor greeting an anxious businessman: 'Welcome into our warm embrace.'

21

'They're Coming at Us Now'

Right through 2018, and almost to the end of the following year, McDonnell continued to believe that a Corbyn government would offer a unique chance to transform Britain. In 2019, on a December morning of rare and uplifting brightness three days before the general election, I heard him speak at a Labour campaign event in London. His speech was supposed to be about what he would do in his first hundred days as chancellor, but he quickly strayed beyond his brief.

'We're setting our sights higher than any opposition party has done before,' he said, standing very upright and proud on a small temporary stage in a community centre, with the central London skyline glowing through a glass wall behind him. Labour had produced 'the most inspiring manifesto in any election I have ever stood in,' he went on. 'Another world really is possible.'

Yet in fact, 2018 and 2019 gradually became less and less about a Corbyn government's possibilities, and more and more about its impossibility. Even more than in its initial phase, his leadership was beset by crises: crises of ideology and policy, alleged prejudice and warring personalities, breakaways and dysfunctional party management; crises which overlapped, interacted and fed each other; crises which went on and on, until his tenure seemed little more than one long crisis to many inside the party, and much of the electorate beyond. Even the determinedly hopeful McDonnell sometimes felt besieged. 'There was conspiracy after conspiracy [against Corbyn],' he said later. 'Half my life was spent on just survival, and keeping the show on the road.' In the constant storms, the once-gleaming prospect of what Corbyn and McDonnell could do in Downing Street often vanished.

To try to cope with these crises, the Corbyn leadership became in some ways more conventional. It grew more closed, with less of a contribution from activists and social movements with roots outside the party, and more input from more conventional sources of leftwing talent and practices, such as the large Corbyn-supporting union Unite. In the view of Michael Chessum, a young organiser and journalist who moved from student anti-austerity activism to being a press officer and speechwriter for Corbyn as leader, the party reverted to the traditional 'modus operandi of Labourism': 'fiefdoms, loyalism, top-down decision-making, position filling, an intolerance for dissent . . . the subordination of everything to the immediate task of defeating one's internal opponents and winning elections'. Within the party and the unions, wrote Chessum, 'The opposite evolution occurred to the one promised . . . There was barely any attempt to democratise the wider Labour movement, and trade union bureaucracies were treated not just as stakeholders [in Corbynism] but as the project's key enforcers and managers.' Those democratic procedures that did exist 'were routinely shut down'.

Chessum's criticisms need to be put in context. It is hard to be a radical under siege, as Corbyn was almost constantly during 2018 and 2019; the natural impulse is to adopt a bunker mentality and bring in people with immediately useful streetfighting skills, while putting less emphasis on more principled, more long-term goals. Fighting for survival and political pluralism, one of the qualities that drew Chessum and thousands of other activists to Corbynism in the first place, rarely go together.

And unlike the left's last experience of holding office under extreme pressure, Ken Livingstone's besieged early tenure at the GLC, Corbyn's leadership lacked many of the tools which can be useful for surviving political adversity. He did not have Livingstone's ruthlessness or charisma, or his skill at building coalitions. Unlike Livingstone, he did not have colleagues from the right of the party who were prepared to work with him rather than constantly against him. And unlike the GLC leader, he was not in power. Corbyn could not placate voters or colleagues as Livingstone had done, by enacting policies, such as the GLC's pioneering grants for disadvantaged groups, that made a difference to people's lives, demonstrated the value of his ideas in practice, and created new bases of support. Without power, Corbyn's plan for the country remained abstract for most people, while his flaws and limitations seemed ever more real.

To make the situation worse, during these years of crisis some of the assets he did have became liabilities. His independence of mind sometimes became blind stubbornness. His instinctive warmth sometimes turned into conflict avoidance. His spontaneous, empathetic campaigning style sometimes degenerated into organisational chaos. And his credibility as a campaigner against racism and other prejudice sometimes became a paralysing self-righteousness. With a speed that surprised him and most of his close comrades, the brand of politics which had worked spectacularly for him in successive electoral contests in 2015, 2016 and 2017 suddenly began working much less well.

Meanwhile his enemies, who had been overconfident and inept for much of his first three years as leader, gradually worked out during 2018 and 2019 how to undermine him. These enemies also multiplied. The Conservative government's contortions over Brexit and the generally feverish state of politics meant that for most of these two years a Corbyn government remained conceivable, despite all his difficulties. A growing array of people with authority warned against it: some of them in person and some anonymously; some of them in coded language and some with newsworthy directness. Civil servants, senior soldiers, business leaders, religious leaders, MPs from across the main parties, including Labour: there had not been such a mobilisation of establishment opinion, from the hard right to the centre-left, since the relentless campaigns in the 1970s and 80s to block Tony Benn's possible routes to Number 10.

The rightwing press prophesied on its front pages that a Corbyn premiership would make Britain inhospitable, even uninhabitable, for the wealthy. During 2019, as the chances grew of an imminent general election, donations to the Conservatives surged, reaching £37 million in the final quarter: a record figure, and more than was given to all the other parties put together. Much of the money directed to the Tories came from very rich individuals, some with controversial business histories, or ongoing legal difficulties, or connections to countries increasingly seen as enemies of Britain, such as Russia, or with a combination of all these liabilities. In seeking out and accepting such donations, it was possible that the Conservatives were storing up problems for the future of both their party and the country. But in the ever more urgent effort to stop Corbyn, almost anything, it seemed, was worth the risk.

In some ways, this onslaught was political reality reasserting itself. There had been unusual, almost uncanny aspects to Corbyn's rise from 2015 to 2017, such as his apparent ability to ignore the presentational and ideological rules of mainstream 21st-century politics. He had also attracted crucial support from colleagues and voters who believed that he had no chance of winning the leadership or a general election, and that therefore backing him would be a gesture without consequences. From 2018 onwards, he operated in different conditions. No longer a novelty, no longer given the benefit of the doubt, he had to cope with the balance of political forces as it actually existed in Britain – in other words, with an environment fundamentally hostile to his kind of politics. For any leftwing Labour leader, it would have been a huge task.

Another problem for Corbyn which became clear in 2018 was that his leadership depended quite heavily on a particular kind of political drama. Elections – and the stories, scenes and themes which they create beyond Westminster – animated him and his supporters like little else. Yet after calling an unnecessary one in 2017 and losing her majority, Theresa May was in no rush to call another. She was now aware of Corbyn's electoral strengths, and her own party's fragile position in the polls, which throughout 2018 and for the first half of 2019 was never much ahead of Labour, often level, and sometimes slightly behind. Meanwhile, her government was increasingly distracted and tormented by trying to come up with a withdrawal agreement which would satisfy both the EU and the Tories' ever more polarised Brexit factions.

At times, Corbyn exploited her discomfort with some skill. He called her administration 'a zombie government', and 'a government which can no longer govern'. For a Labour leadership with big problems of its own, the May regime's brittleness, divisions and parliamentary defeats provided regular boosts to morale, and were perpetual sources of hope. The government could fall at any time, the Corbynites believed – as did many other observers – and then Labour's campaign machine would be unleashed.

Yet in fact May's weak position, and in particular the hung parliament, kept much of politics in a holding pattern: circling round and round the same Brexit and Tory dilemmas, with frequent days of Commons drama receiving huge media coverage but failing to resolve much. For someone who disliked parliament, Corbyn often performed surprisingly well in these debates. He began to create a new Commons persona, with a sterner than usual voice and a penetrating gaze over the glasses perched on the end of his nose, towards the Tory ministers sitting opposite. He seemed like a veteran school inspector, or a financial auditor, casting a disapproving and disappointed eye over shoddy work.

However, this kind of politics was still not the best use of his talents and energies. It kept him trapped in Westminster, and made him seem more like a conventional politician, playing Commons games over Brexit, rather than the straight-talking rebel that many people thought they had voted for in 2015, 2016 and 2017.

Meanwhile, with no election to mobilise for, the mass movement which had made Corbynism so powerful and fresh began to lose impetus. A big part of this movement was Momentum, a national organisation co-founded by Lansman shortly after Corbyn won the leadership in 2015. Momentum started as a loose mix of the newly politicised and veteran activists, some of them from fringe socialist parties, which aimed to promote leftwing causes in wider society as well as radicalise Labour and protect Corbyn's vulnerable leadership. Gradually, however, the organisation became more centralised, less democratic, and yet more focused on elections, both for Labour party positions and for the Commons. Momentum's flooding of marginal constituencies with activists could be highly effective. But when there was no general election to absorb its energies, the organisation could become demotivated or fractious. Many Labour MPs and some in the party hierarchy distrusted Momentum, seeing its large membership, which peaked at about 60,000 – a tenth the size of Labour's but nearly half the size of the Tories' – as potentially Lansman's or Corbyn's private army.

In June 2018, Labour put on a one-day festival of music and

politics to try to unite and re-energise a broad range of its activists –
and to raise some funds, which had been depleted by two general
election campaigns in the previous three years. Officially, the event
was given the anodyne name Labour Live, but journalists quickly
labelled it JezFest, since he would be making a speech. Despite the
leader's presence, the festival had to reduce its ticket prices to ensure
a respectable attendance. It took place in an unphotogenic north
London park under leaden skies.

McDonnell was less affected than Corbyn by the ebbing of their
movement. If anything, the shadow chancellor seemed to work even
harder. He was alarmed at Labour's multiplying difficulties and also
motivated by how close to power the party still appeared to be. Sometimes he interrupted supposedly recuperative breaks at his Norfolk
bungalow to give interviews or intervene in Labour's latest crises. Unlike
Corbyn, he was nearly always prepared to appear on hostile shows such
as the *Today* programme, and he was usually effective: composed, softly
spoken, and careful in his choice of words – disarmingly different from
the out-of-control ogre portrayed by rightwing newspaper journalists.
Yet there was strain behind this perpetually available, studiedly calm
persona. To get from Norfolk to party meetings or broadcast studios, he
had to row across the river which separated his bungalow from the
nearest car park as quickly as he could, without getting too much water
on his public clothes.

When he was in London, his schedule was even more frantic. His
home in Hayes was a handsome, Arts and Crafts-style house at the
end of a no-through road, a sign of his enthusiasm for the Victorian
socialist designer William Morris. But the road was in one of his constituency's poorest, most socially troubled wards, and was frequently
strewn with rubbish by fly-tippers. By habit, McDonnell used public
transport as much as possible, so that he could talk to and empathise
with constituents, and this meant rushing to and from a bus stop just
beyond the far end of his road. Coming home in the dark one night in
October 2018, he tripped on some of the rubbish and cut his nose and
forehead. He appeared on TV the next day and laughed off the scabs
and bruises. Yet not many politicians in their late sixties, even among
the more austere characters of the left, led lives so exposed to everyday social ills.

In the spring of 2019, all his hard work and centrality to the Corbyn project secured him a role that took him seemingly even closer to power. He became part of a Labour delegation which took part in Brexit talks in Westminster with the May government. Labour was seeking a softer Brexit deal, which it hoped would protect the economy and workers' rights, while also placating both Leave and Remain voters. The government was seeking any Brexit deal that it could get through parliament. The talks were private – though not without leaks – yet some of their stage management was highly public. Each day, with photographers and TV cameras in attendance, McDonnell, the shadow Brexit secretary Keir Starmer, and sometimes other shadow ministers and Seumas Milne would walk purposefully along Whitehall to the bone-grey cabinet office building where the negotiations were being held. The Labour delegation wore their smartest Westminster outfits and clasped neat bundles of documents. An uninformed observer could easily have thought they were ministers.

But they were not. After a few weeks, the talks ended in failure. With lethal accuracy and wit, McDonnell said the process had been like 'trying to enter a contract with a company going into administration'. But the fact that Labour could not prevail against a dying government, whether in the talks or in a broader sense, suggested that the party might struggle if a more effective Tory leader came along.

For much of 2018 and 2019, Labour made little real progress towards power. More often, the prospect receded. Without the colour and dynamism of a Corbyn-led election campaign – which even hostile journalists, being in the news business, could not completely ignore – there was more space for coverage of his setbacks and misjudgements. Given his lack of experience as a politician with a formal public role and wide responsibilities, he was likely to make mistakes when there were unexpected events. And so it proved.

In March 2018 Sergei Skripal, a former Russian military intelligence officer and MI6 informant who had settled in England, was poisoned with a lethal nerve agent, together with his daughter Yulia. They were found losing consciousness on a bench near a shopping centre in Salisbury in Wiltshire. They both survived, but only after weeks of hospital treatment. A police officer who searched Sergei's home was also poisoned and hospitalised, as were two Britons – for one of them the poisoning proved fatal – who accidentally came across and touched a perfume bottle used in the attack, in a small country town several miles from Salisbury, almost four months later.

The horror and contagion of the attack, the Middle England setting, the innocent victims, and Skripal's past as a British double agent against the Russians – all these created a charged situation in which politicians, particularly politicians who had often been smeared as pro-Russian, needed to tread carefully. Corbyn described the poisoning as 'an appalling act of violence'. He went on: 'Nerve agents are abominable if used in any war. It is utterly reckless to use them in a civilian environment.' Yet at first he also resisted linking the attack to the Russian government. He allowed Seumas Milne to brief journalists that Russian 'mafia-like groups and oligarchic interests' could have been involved, and that claims from the British government and British intelligence in this and other episodes involving alleged weapons of mass destruction were not necessarily to be trusted.

As an example of a leader of the opposition asking sceptical questions, and trying to prevent a rush to judgement in a complex and perilous situation, Corbyn's stance was justifiable. But as a piece of political positioning it was disastrous. He even asked in parliament: 'How has she [May] responded to the Russian government's request for a sample of the agent used in the Salisbury attack to run its own tests?' There was fury at this attempt to be even-handed between Britain and Russia: across the press, and on the right of the parliamentary Labour party, which made no effort to keep its feelings private. The familiar claim from Corbyn's enemies that he was 'a threat to national security' and therefore 'not fit to lead the country', a claim which had seemed too exaggerated to many voters during his leadership campaigns and the 2017 election to hurt him badly, was now presented to a more receptive public, thanks to the prospect of a new cold war with Russia. Meanwhile, a related, equally damaging anxiety about him spread even among some leftwing Britons: that if he became prime minister, he would be naive in his dealings with other countries.

Given his decades of engaging with other states and international issues, an engagement which far exceeded that of most MPs, that fear was probably not justified. But where Corbyn was naive was in expecting mainstream voters to accept his unfamiliar, unconventional and less pro-Western view of the world, without preparing them first by explaining clearly why the usual Western foreign policy perspectives were narrow and often disastrous. Having moved mainly among fellow lefties for so long, Corbyn did not always know how to communicate effectively with people who were not.

For many Britons, though, there was probably nothing he could have said or done to make himself acceptable. He was simply too leftwing. Ominously, some of these anti-Corbyn diehards worked for the British state. During 2018 and 2019, doubts in Whitehall about a Corbyn premiership were sporadically but damagingly expressed through anonymous briefings to the rightwing press. In June 2019, *The Times* ran a front-page story with the headline, 'Jeremy Corbyn too frail to be PM, fears civil service'. The paper reported that 'Senior civil servants have become increasingly concerned' that he would not be able to cope with being prime minister, 'physically or mentally'. This sense that he would be a figurehead at best was reinforced by chatter among journalists that in some Labour circles he was already known as 'Magic Grandpa', an occasional political miracle-worker disengaged from crucial daily party business and policy debates. Corbyn and Labour furiously denied the health rumours, saying that he was 'in good health' and 'running and cycling regularly'. For a man of 70, he was indeed lean and quite fit, more so than many younger politicians and journalists. But the insinuations about his literal, as well as political, fitness for office continued.

So did suggestions in the media that if he became prime minister he would not command the loyalty of the armed forces. These warnings started within days of his election as leader. In September 2015, the *Sunday Times* quoted 'a senior serving general', who said that 'feelings are running very high within the armed forces' about the possibility of a Corbyn government. 'You can't put a maverick in charge of a country's security,' the officer went on. 'You would see . . . generals directly and publicly challenging Corbyn over . . . [getting rid of] Trident, pulling out of Nato and any plans to emasculate and shrink the size of the armed forces . . . There would be mass resignations at all levels . . . which would effectively be a mutiny.' If Corbyn proved as militarily radical as promised, 'The army just wouldn't stand for it. The general staff would not allow a prime minister to jeopardise the security of this country and I think people would use whatever means possible, fair or foul, to prevent that.'

Corbyn was alarmed by the intervention. He saw it, he told me, as 'a senior serving officer saying they would not accept orders from the prime minister'. He was also not reassured by the official military response. The Ministry of Defence (MOD) merely described the general's remarks as 'not helpful'. It 'ruled out a leak inquiry', the *Independent* reported, 'on the grounds that it would be impossible to identify the culprit' – even though the *Sunday Times* article had described the general in some detail, as 'having served in Northern Ireland in the 1980s and 1990s'. Given the relative remoteness of the period, and the modest size of the British army, Corbyn was correct to think that 'there were not that many' generals who fitted the description.

A few weeks further into Corbyn's leadership, on the highly charged and militarised occasion of Remembrance Day, the head of the armed forces, General Sir Nicholas Houghton, gave a rare interview on BBC1's *The Andrew Marr Show*. When Marr asked for his views on an assertion by Corbyn that he would never authorise the use of nuclear weapons as premier, Houghton replied: 'It would worry me if that thought was translated into power.' 'So if he wins [the next election], he's a problem?' Marr asked. Houghton briefly changed the subject. Then he said: '[Nuclear] deterrence rests on the credibility of its use ... Most of the politicians I know understand that.' Again, Corbyn's politics had been placed outside the boundaries of the acceptable.

Even during the more popular periods of his leadership, he provoked extreme reactions. In June 2017, just days after Labour's unexpected near-breakthrough at the general election, a man from Cardiff with Islamophobic and far-right views, Darren Osborne, drove a rented van into pedestrians near a mosque in Corbyn's constituency. One man was killed and and nine injured. At his trial, Osborne revealed that his original plan had been to kill Corbyn. 'It would be one less terrorist [on] our streets.'

In April 2019, a video appeared on Twitter of four soldiers from the Parachute Regiment, lined up like a firing squad, using a poster of the Labour leader for target practice. The clip was titled 'Happy with that'. It had been filmed recently in Kabul in Afghanistan, a British military deployment which Corbyn had always opposed. After the soldiers ceased firing, the film showed the poster of him in close-up. There were bullet holes in his forehead, below his eyes and below his nose.

The soldiers' actions were condemned by the MOD and the government as well as by Labour, but were laughed off as minor antics by popular commentators such as Piers Morgan. Yet the whole episode, while crude, had a subtle effect. Once watched, the video was hard to forget. The image it left in your mind might be of Corbyn being mocked and symbolically attacked by members of an institution for which many Britons had unique respect – an image of his exclusion from all that was most profoundly British. Or if you were of an especially doomy persuasion, like a growing number of British socialists between 2015 and 2019, the video might be a premonition: of how a Corbyn government could end.

Less frightening forces also destabilised his leadership. During 2018 and 2019, Labour Together intensified its efforts to build a well-funded, semi-clandestine party within a party, intended to shift Labour back to the centre-left whenever Corbyn's tenure ended. In 2017, Labour Together had appointed a new director, Morgan McSweeney, a precise and relentless organiser who had worked for New Labour, and against the Labour left in local government. In the summer of 2019, with Labour politics and British politics in general increasingly dominated by Brexit, McSweeney began having conversations with the shadow Brexit secretary, Keir Starmer. Although Starmer had only been an MP for four years, his small-town, working-class background, successful legal career, high-profile and generally competent performance as Brexit secretary, and relatively unformed, ambiguous personal politics, neither Corbynite nor Blairite, made him just the kind of potential post-Corbyn leader that Labour Together was looking for. According to a *Sunday Times* investigation in November 2023 by Gabriel Pogrund and Harry Yorke, during the summer of 2019 McSweeney and Starmer 'agreed that, when the time was right, they might work together'.

Corbyn was also undermined by more blatant threats. From his very first weeks as leader, there was a stream of rumours, which never completely dried up, that MPs on the Labour right were about to break away and form a new party. The precedent of the 1981 mass defection to the SDP, during a similarly divisive leftwing ascendancy, encouraged plotting and speculation throughout Corbyn's tenure. In July 2016, a typical story appeared in the *Mail on Sunday*: 'More than 150 Labour MPs are plotting to form a breakaway party code-named Continuity Labour', if Corbyn won the second leadership ballot. He did, but this giant breakaway never materialised. The possibility of May's government collapsing, which made staying in Labour more attractive; the possibility that Corbyn's leadership might also collapse; disagreements between the anti-Corbyn plotters about precisely when and how to break away; and the fact that the SDP ultimately failed – all these factors delayed the schism.

Finally, in February 2019, almost three and a half years into his leadership, seven MPs from the Labour right and centre announced that they were leaving to form a new party, The Independent Group. Their opening press conference took place in a hired room in County Hall, the building where Livingstone had done his plotting on the Greater London Council. For a few days, the breakaway was given considerable and sometimes indulgent media attention. The new party seriously worried some senior Labour figures, including McDonnell, who remembered the harm done to their party by the SDP.

In reality, The Independent Group quickly squandered its momentum. There were gaffes from some of its MPs, including a jaw-dropping description by Angela Smith of BAME Britons as people with a 'funny tinge'. There was also a lack of eye-catching or original policies – symptomatic of the Labour right's intellectual stagnation since the later stages of Blairism. There were also failed attempts to enliven The Independent Group's bland name, which became Change UK – The Independent Group, and then The Independent Group for Change. And then, appropriately, there were splits in the party. At elections for the European Parliament in May, Change UK won 3.3 per cent of the vote, not disastrous for a new political entity, but far from historic.

Its existence did contribute, however, to the growing sense of crisis and acrimony around Corbyn's leadership. Voters dislike divided parties, when those divisions are obvious, and Labour's poll ratings fell in the month after the breakaway, and continued to fall afterwards. For the majority of people who do not follow politics closely, the fact that a group of Labour MPs had abandoned the party was a clear and memorable demonstration of dissatisfaction with Corbyn's leadership.

The breakaway also helped feed another, larger Labour crisis. One of the few memorable performers at The Independent Group's first press conference was Luciana Berger. A self-assured 37-year-old, the great-niece of a minister in the Attlee government, MP for the safe seat of Liverpool Wavertree, and a shadow minister under both Corbyn and Miliband, she had previously been identified as one of Labour's rising stars. 'I have become embarrassed and ashamed to remain in the Labour Party,' she said, appearing before the cameras despite being heavily pregnant. 'I have come to the sickening conclusion that it is institutionally antisemitic.'

Berger had been a Labour MP since 2010. A Londoner who had been privately educated and had then worked as a management consultant, her selection as the candidate for a constituency with higher than average deprivation and unemployment had divided the local party. But such tensions between activists and candidates or MPs from contrasting backgrounds existed all over the country, and often diminished with time, as both sides got to know each other. It was the response of some people to her being Jewish that poisoned her political life in Liverpool.

The abuse started at least five years before Corbyn became leader, during her effort to get selected as a parliamentary candidate. In 2014 she told the *Daily Telegraph* that 'at the height of the abuse, the police said I was the subject of 2,500 hate messages in the space of three days'. She had security measures fitted at her constituency home in Liverpool and at her home in London. That October, a member of a neo-Nazi group, National Action, which has since been banned, was imprisoned for sending her an antisemitic tweet. But the far-right campaign against her continued into Corbyn's leadership. Between 2016 and 2018, three more men were jailed for making death threats, among other offences. The threats seemed even more frightening after her fellow Labour MP Jo Cox was murdered by a member of the far right in 2016.

During Corbyn's tenure Berger was also the recipient of antisemitic abuse from people who appeared to be on the left, 'from [Twitter] accounts that use the hashtag #JC4PM in their biography', she told the radio station LBC in 2019. When the Labour party conference was held in Liverpool in 2018, her safety was considered sufficiently at risk for her to be provided with a police escort on her way to and from the secure conference zone. Whether the threat was from the left or the far right, or both, was not officially made clear.

Her own politics were nuanced. A hawk on foreign policy, strongly pro-Israel and in favour of nuclear weapons, she was a social liberal, and quite leftwing on the role of the state and business: in favour of rail nationalisation and against lowering corporation tax. That she had served in both Miliband's and Corbyn's shadow cabinets showed she was more flexible and less centrist than the many Labour MPs who kept their distance from both regimes. While disagreeing with her foreign policy views, Milne was impressed by her relative pragmatism and her hard work as a shadow minister, where she occupied a new position covering mental health, one of Corbyn's personal policy interests. She was often cited by Corbyn's advisors as a rare MP from outside the left whom they could do business with. They wished there were more like her.

But then she resigned as a shadow minister in 2016, as part of the attempted anti-Corbyn coup. By early 2018, her disillusionment with his leadership had deepened further, partly because of his failure to do anything effective, in her view, against the antisemitic attacks she was suffering. She attended secret meetings with other alienated Labour MPs, which ultimately led to the Independent Group split.

In March 2018, she came across another example of what she saw as Corbyn's negligence about antisemitism. 'Freedom for Humanity' was a long, lurid mural which had been painted on a wall in Spitalfields in east London in 2012 by Mear One, a well-known street artist from Los Angeles. The painting depicted six grotesque men in bankers' suits, two of them with what appeared to be exaggerated Jewish features, playing a game of Monopoly, with the board resting on the bent backs of a mass of naked, brown-skinned figures. Mear One insisted that he was 'most definitely not' antisemitic, and that the work was 'about class and privilege'. But many people in east London were not convinced, and the local council announced that it was going to paint over the mural. The day before the scheduled erasure, Mear One posted a complaint on Facebook about what he saw as an attack on 'freedom of expression', together with a photo of the mural. Corbyn added a comment: 'Why? You are in good company. Rockerfeller [*sic*] destroyed Diego Viera's [*sic*] mural because it includes a picture of Lenin.'

Corbyn was still a backbencher at the time, and, as ever, involved with more causes than he had proper time for. The fact that in his comment he seemed to mix up the name of the famous Mexican political muralist Diego Rivera with the name of the famous Arsenal footballer Patrick Vieira suggested that Corbyn, who is an Arsenal supporter, may not have looked at Mear One's Facebook post for very long or thought very hard about his response to it. Either way, the mural controversy, and especially Corbyn's role in it, remained relatively obscure for the next six years.

Then, 'first thing' on the morning of 23 March 2018, in Berger's words, she contacted his office 'for an explanation' of his support for the mural. When she had heard nothing by 2pm, she posted the Facebook image of the painting with Corbyn's supportive comment on Twitter. That evening, the leader's office finally issued a statement: 'In 2012, Jeremy was responding to concerns about the removal of public art on the grounds of freedom of speech. However, the mural was offensive, used antisemitic imagery which has no place in our society, and it is right it was removed.'

On Twitter, Berger described the response as 'wholly inadequate', and promised, 'I will be raising this further.' A second statement quickly emerged from the leader's office, this time from Corbyn himself. 'I sincerely regret that I did not look more closely at the image I was commenting on,' he said, 'the contents of which are deeply disturbing and antisemitic. The defence of free speech cannot be used as a justification for the promotion of antisemitism in any form. That is a view I've always held.'

Two days later, with the controversy continuing, and the way it connected, or appeared to connect, Corbyn personally to antisemitism seriously worrying some people in his office, the leader made another statement. 'Labour is an anti-racist party,' it began,

> ... which is why as leader ... I want to be clear that I will not tolerate any form of antisemitism that exists in and around our movement. We must stamp this out ... We recognise that antisemitism has occurred in pockets within the Labour Party ... I am sincerely sorry for the pain which has been caused.
>
> Our party has deep roots in the Jewish community and is actively engaged with Jewish organisations across the country. We are campaigning to increase support and confidence in Labour among Jewish people ... I know that to do so, we must demonstrate our total commitment to excising pockets of antisemitism that exist in and around our party ... I will be meeting representatives from the Jewish community over the coming days, weeks and months to rebuild that confidence in Labour as a party which gives effective voice to Jewish concerns and is implacably opposed to antisemitism in all its forms.

Corbyn's response to the mural controversy revealed more than he intended. His inconsistent tone showed that he and Labour were struggling with two related issues: their attitude to antisemitism in the party, and to those who pointed out its existence. These struggles dominated the second half of his leadership. They distracted him, they frustrated him, they upset him, they damaged him, and in some ways they destroyed him.

His statements about the mural showed his fundamental conviction that he and his party were not antisemitic: 'Labour is an anti-racist party.' On the contrary, he believed that Jewishness and socialism often went together: 'Our party has deep roots in the Jewish community.' But he also accepted that antisemitism existed 'in pockets' of the left, both 'in and around' the party – in other words, across the wider socialist diaspora through which he had always travelled. The existence of this prejudice appalled him, and yet he could not, or would not, find the words to express his feelings about antisemitism with real emotional force. Instead, he used empty-sounding formal language: 'I am sincerely sorry for the pain which has been caused.' And yet, this stiff apology sat alongside what seemed expressions of genuine determination that Labour should protect Jewish people: 'We must demonstrate our total commitment . . . to excising antisemitism,' he had said. 'We must stamp this out.'

How you interpreted these statements could depend on many things: whether you were Jewish; whether you had been a victim of antisemitism from the left; what you thought of Labour and the left in general; whether you believed that a party with a growing, quarrelsome and sometimes transient membership of half a million people was really able, or willing, to police them all for prejudice; and finally, the most divisive factor of all, how you regarded Corbyn himself. Was he one of the most dedicated anti-racists in Britain, as had previously been assumed right across the political spectrum? Or was he someone whose anti-racism was selective?

Like most people on the Labour left, he had not become deeply involved in pro-Palestinian activism and criticism of the Israeli government until the 1980s. During the earlier, formative period of his career, the 1960s and 70s, he was preoccupied by other foreign causes. But then the Israeli invasion of Lebanon in 1982, a general increase in violence and intransigence from Israel towards the Palestinians, and a long-term shift to the right by Israel's governments drew Corbyn and other British leftists into the Palestinian struggle. The movement had one of its biggest European offshoots in London, where Palestinian exiles and visitors to Britain tended to congregate, and where Ken Livingstone's GLC was sympathetic to their cause, and highly critical of Israel.

During the 1980s relations cooled drastically between much of the British left and the many Jewish Britons who were strong defenders of Israel, including the Board of Deputies of British Jews. Mutual suspicion, then open hostility, became the norm. This shift was deepened by social, economic and political trends. When many Jewish immigrants had first arrived in Britain, the exploitation and poverty they faced, and sometimes radical convictions already acquired in other countries, meant that their politics, if they had any, tended to lean left. Jewish voters, activists, councillors and ultimately MPs and ministers became an important part of the Labour movement. But then this relationship gradually weakened. 'British Jewry's "love affair" with the left lasted barely 40 years – say 1918–1959,' wrote the Jewish historian Geoffrey Alderman in the *Jewish Chronicle* in 2015. As the community 'moved upwards' economically, he continued, out of the inner city and into more prosperous suburbs, 'It's the Conservatives who have been seen as the natural friend.'

Margaret Thatcher got on well with the significant Jewish community in her suburban constituency of Finchley in north London, and appointed Jewish cabinet ministers such as Nigel Lawson, Keith Joseph and Leon Brittan. Many British Jews admired her. Others remained on the left, loyal to Labour or more radical groups. Yet some left-leaning Jewish politicians, such as the veteran London Labour MPs Reg Freeson and Neville Sandelson, were undermined in their constituencies by younger, more leftwing figures such as Livingstone and McDonnell. These internal battles were about personal ambition and differences in ideology, rather than prejudice. Essentially, one Labour generation was trying to displace another. But these battles were seen as more sinister by some Jewish voters and community leaders.

Livingstone and McDonnell also both stood unsuccessfully for parliament against the Jewish Conservative MP for Hampstead, Geoffrey Finsberg, at the 1979 and 1983 elections respectively. Again, their motives were conventionally political rather than antisemitic. But if you believed that the Labour left had a thing against Jews, these campaigns could be interpreted as further evidence.

Labour support for Palestinian rights also alienated some British Jews and community bodies. When Ed Miliband became the first Jewish Labour leader, it was widely expected that the party's Jewish support would rise. He received coverage from Conservative-supporting newspapers which had at least a whiff of antisemitism, such as a photo of him awkwardly eating a bacon sandwich, which was published repeatedly for over a year. Yet his insistence that Labour MPs support a Commons motion recognising Palestine as an independent state – a motion opposed by the Board of Deputies – proved more influential with Jewish voters than his horrible treatment by the rightwing press. According to a poll in the *Jewish Chronicle* just before the 2015 election, Jewish voters, who had been evenly divided between Labour and the Tories at the previous election, following the pro-Israel Blair and Brown governments, now preferred the Conservatives to Labour by 69 per cent to 22 per cent.

When Corbyn became leader, this earlier falling-out between Labour and many British Jews was barely ever acknowledged by his Jewish critics. Nor was there much acknowledgement that support for the Palestinians and criticism of Israel had become instinctive for many in the party, independent of Corbyn's opinions. For a potential governing party in a major Western country – a country which was usually pro-Israel – to become so pro-Palestinian made Labour under Miliband, and to a greater extent under Corbyn, an enemy of the Israeli government, at least from the Israeli government's perspective. And against such enemies it tends to act, like any assertive but anxious country which sees its reputation and leverage abroad under threat, through a longstanding network of embassy and intelligence officials, pro-Israel pressure groups, parliamentary groups, lobby groups inside political parties, sympathetic journalists, and community and activist bodies. 'Israel and its lobby have always used anti-Semitism as a political weapon,' wrote Asa Winstanley, probably the leading pro-Palestinian journalist in Britain, in 2023. 'Most people involved in campaigning for Palestinian rights in the West have stories of being falsely smeared with anti-Semitism.'

Yet instead of presenting Corbyn's leadership in the context of Israel's interests, or the evolution of the politics of British Jews, or Labour's long, complex and changing relationship with the community and with Israel, the Board of Deputies, together with other Jewish bodies and many journalists both inside and outside the community, treated Corbyn's tenure as a new and unique problem for Jews in Britain. A great deal of research was done, by everyone from academic historians to community activists to tabloid reporters, to comb his biography for evidence of antisemitism, or at least tolerance of it.

In any material that might complicate or contradict the prevailing view of Corbyn as an enemy of Jews there was much less interest. His decades of proposing and supporting Commons motions against antisemitism were rarely mentioned outside the relatively small and closed world of pro-Corbyn online media. The equally sustained importance to him of Jewish comrades, advisors and mentors such as Jon Lansman, the forthright Islington councillor Sue Lukes, and Mike

Marqusee, an American writer and activist who lived in Hackney and died in 2015, was similarly neglected. So were Corbyn's formative experiences working for the National Union of Tailors and Garment Workers, with its Jewish heritage and members. The possibility that he might be pro-Palestinian, anti-Israel and yet also greatly value some forms of Jewish politics, and be completely opposed to antisemitism, was rarely considered by his critics. Like that of many Israel–Palestine activists before and since, his relationship with the Jewish world was not assumed to have any complexity.

Instead, it was painted in relentlessly menacing colours. The process had started while he was still a leadership candidate. In August 2015, the *Jewish Chronicle* published a front-page editorial:

> We are certain that we speak for the vast majority of British Jews in expressing deep foreboding at the prospect of Mr Corbyn's election as Labour leader . . . Although there is no direct evidence that he has an issue himself with Jews, there is overwhelming evidence of his association with . . . Holocaust deniers, terrorists and some outright antisemites.

During his decades of pro-Palestinian activism, Corbyn had met people with repugnant views of Israel and Jewish history, such as the Holocaust denier Paul Eisen and members of the anti-Israel movements Hamas and Hezbollah. At a meeting in the Commons in 2009, he had advertised an upcoming parliamentary gathering to discuss the conflicts in the Middle East by saying, 'It will be my pleasure and honour to host an event in parliament where our friends from Hezbollah will be speaking . . . I've also invited our friends from Hamas to come and speak as well.'

Questioned about his use of the phrase 'our friends' by the Commons home affairs committee in 2016, he said: 'The language I used . . . was about encouraging the meeting to go ahead, encouraging there to be a discussion about the peace process.' The committee asked if he still regarded Hamas and Hezbollah as friends. 'No,' he said. 'It was inclusive language I used which with hindsight I would rather not have used.' He also insisted that he had met Eisen thinking he was purely a pro-Palestinian activist, and knowing nothing about his Holocaust denial.

In both cases, and in the mural controversy, and in a succession of other instances of association with antisemites which came to light throughout his leadership, his defence was essentially the same: that his dealings with a huge range of pro-Palestinian and other activists did not imply approval or knowledge of all their stances. It was quite a strong argument. Anyone who has ever been on a big demonstration, or attended a political meeting that involves building coalitions, will be aware that working with people you disagree with, or about whose beliefs you know – and may only want to know – a limited amount, is sometimes unavoidable. Many of Corbyn's critics had made their own questionable alliances over the years, for example the Labour right with the reckless neoconservative George W. Bush over Iraq. That these critics never acknowledged their own ethical compromises, while relentlessly calling out Corbyn for his, was another sign that he was held to different standards.

And yet his defence, while reasonable, and based on how politics often actually works, was not very reassuring or satisfying for many British Jews. In a world where antisemitism appeared to be resurgent, and spreading across the ideological spectrum, they saw a Labour leader who was more critical of Israel than any before him, and who according to many commentators, from the *Daily Mail* to the *Guardian*, often held extreme views and mixed with unacceptable people. He was also a leader who seemed to act against antisemitism in his party only when he was forced to.

On 26 March 2018 a rally was held in Parliament Square to protest against Labour antisemitism and Corbyn's approach to it. Berger took part and made a speech, as did the centrist Labour MPs Wes Streeting and John Mann, neither of whom was Jewish, but who were both constant critics of Corbyn and of his handling of antisemitism in particular.

It was the day after he had promised to 'stamp out' the prejudice in the party. It was also less than an hour since he had sent an apologetic letter – his fourth such statement in four days since the start of the mural controversy – to the Board of Deputies and the Jewish Leadership Council (JLC), a coordinating body for the community's charities and lobby groups. In the letter, he said that Labour antisemitism 'has too often been dismissed as simply a matter of a few bad apples'. Only the previous day, he had said that the prejudice 'has occurred in pockets in the Labour party'. One of the most stubborn people in British politics appeared to be shifting his position.

Yet the demonstrators in Parliament Square were not convinced. The chairman of the JLC, Jonathan Goldstein, told the crowd: 'We are here to say to Jeremy Corbyn: "Enough is enough. The time for talking is over, the time for words is over, and the time for action has begun."'

The previous year, only one Labour party member had been expelled for antisemitism. In 2018, ten were expelled. In 2019, the figure was 45. Larger numbers of people either left the party while under investigation or were suspended: in 2019, the totals were 104 and 296 respectively.

What exactly did these numbers reveal? For Corbyn and his defenders, the upward trend showed that his leadership was taking the problem more seriously. Starting in 2018, a new, pro-Corbyn Labour general secretary, Jennie Formby, oversaw the implementation of a quicker but more thorough system for recording complaints and then investigating, including monthly panels advised by a barrister to hear cases, more sophisticated searches of suspects' social media posts, and the involvement of the national party, with its greater resources, in examining all antisemitism allegations.

The fact that despite this greater rigour the number of antisemites discovered remained tiny compared to the size of the party could be interpreted in two ways. One possible explanation was that Labour was not willing or able to investigate the problem properly. Despite the appearance of an improved investigative process, a leader who for many months had been reluctant to admit the problem existed was instructing his subordinates not to look too hard, or even to cover the issue up. This interpretation had some of the circularity of a conspiracy theory: the fewer antisemites Labour found and expelled, the more guilty the party was; the more it found and expelled, the more guilty it was. Yet the circularity did not stop this mindset being adopted by most of the mainstream media and many of Corbyn's Jewish critics. In turn, this certainty that Labour had a huge problem affected public perceptions. In 2019, the leftwing media analysts Greg

Philo and Mike Berry published the findings of polling and focus groups they had commissioned to measure how the public saw Labour antisemitism. 'On average, those surveyed believed that 34 per cent of Labour Party members had had complaints for anti-Semitism made against them,' Philo and Berry wrote. The actual figure was 0.1 per cent.

That this low figure might mean that antisemitism was not widespread in the Labour party, after all, was a possibility barely considered by Corbyn's critics. Yet there was quite a lot of evidence from authoritative sources that this was the case. In 2017 a report by the Institute for Jewish Policy Research, 'Antisemitism in Contemporary Great Britain', found that although 'all parts' of the left 'exhibit higher levels of anti-Israelism than average', 'Levels of antisemitism among those on the left-wing of the political spectrum, including the far-left, are indistinguishable from those found in the general population . . . The prevalence of antisemitism on the far-right is considerably higher than on the left . . .'

Also in 2017, the Campaign Against Antisemitism's annual Antisemitism Barometer found that the proportion of Labour voters – not members – who 'endorsed at least one antisemitic statement', was 32 per cent, compared to 40 per cent of Conservative voters. The report also found antisemitic attitudes rarest among the young, who made up much of Corbyn's most loyal support. Since 2015, the year he had become leader, the report added, 'Antisemitic prejudice among British adults has declined.' His tenure had not led to an explosion of bigotry.

In October 2016, just over a year into Corbyn's leadership, a report on 'Antisemitism in the UK' by the Commons home affairs committee concluded: 'Despite significant press and public attention on the Labour Party . . . there exists no reliable, empirical evidence to support the notion that there is a higher prevalence of antisemitic attitudes within the Labour Party than any other political party.'

It was possible to argue that Corbyn and the party he led should be held to higher standards than other politicians and parties, since he and his circle had long emphasised their anti-racist credentials. It was also true that the anti-racist milieu in which their attitudes to prejudice had largely been formed, during the 1970s and 80s, had often prioritised minorities who were poorer and darker-skinned than most Jewish

Britons. They were seen by many on the left as relatively safe from everyday racism such as workplace discrimination and police harassment.

However, as Corbyn's history of supporting Commons motions against antisemitism showed, he and socialists like him had hardly forgotten that the prejudice existed. And was it really plausible that a party which under him had become much more focused on identity politics was still a safe space for antisemites? Finally, even if his record as a defender of Jews did not match his record as a defender of Palestinians, the charge of inconsistency or hypocrisy was rarely the one laid against him. Instead his critics made much larger claims.

In July 2018, Margaret Hodge cornered him behind the speaker's chair in the Commons and shouted, 'You're a fucking anti-Semite and a racist!' He replied, 'I'm sorry you feel like that.'

The immediate trigger for her fury was Labour's adoption of a new code of conduct on antisemitism, which controversially did not incorporate all the examples of the prejudice included in a definition of antisemitism produced by the International Holocaust Remembrance Alliance. The definition had been widely adopted, but also criticised for repeatedly mentioning opposition to Israel in its examples of antisemitism.

Hodge was also one of the strongest Labour opponents of Corbyn's leadership in general. She had sponsored the motion of no confidence which started the attempted coup against him in 2016. The fact that only a few years before her Commons outburst against him he had helped her beat the antisemitic British National Party in her constituency seemed to be of no relevance to her. For critics of Corbyn over antisemitism, his long record of opposing it appeared not to exist.

In September 2018, the former chief rabbi Jonathan Sacks went even further than Hodge. He told *The Andrew Marr Show*:

Jews have been in Britain since 1656. I know of no other occasion . . . when . . . the majority of our community are asking 'Is this country safe to bring up our children?' There is danger that Jeremy Corbyn may one day be prime minister . . . and I'm afraid that until he expresses clear remorse for what he has said and what his party has done to its Jewish sympathisers as well as its Jewish MPs, then he is as great a danger as Enoch Powell was.

The comparison to the most infamous racist in British politics since the Second World War – a man whose socially conservative, free-market worldview was utterly different to Corbyn's – showed how terrible things had become between the Labour leader and many British Jews. Despite his repeated public apologies; despite the party's better procedures for expelling antisemites; despite endless efforts by Lansman and other senior Labour figures to liaise between Corbyn and his Jewish critics; despite attempts by McDonnell, both privately in meetings with Corbyn and publicly in the media, to come up with a language about Labour and antisemitism that would resonate with the Jewish community, and which would stop the political bleeding; and despite the lack of solid evidence that Labour had a widespread antisemitism problem – despite all this, by 2019 Corbyn's entanglement in the issue was much worse than it had been when he was elected leader in 2015.

He hated confrontations and being disliked. He was horrified, and sometimes paralysed, by the fact that something so central to his sense of self – his anti-racism – was being so relentlessly questioned, or simply dismissed. To some of his oldest allies, this feeling of bewilderment, not always at the top of his mind but constantly distracting him, prevented Corbyn from focusing properly on the antisemitism crisis and how he could fight back against those allegations against him which were not justified. 'I think he could have defended himself better,' Abbott told me.

Often, he retreated to his constituency, as he had done during the 1980s and 90s, and sought advice from a small circle of mostly Jewish leftists whom he had known and trusted for decades. It included Sue Lukes and David Rosenberg, founder of the Jewish Socialists Group and a strong critic of Israel. Their views were so important to Corbyn that even when he was not with them he still sought their approval. Before agreeing to Labour initiatives on antisemitism, he would sometimes ask his aides: 'What does Sue Lukes think?'

To his confidants in Islington, the Board of Deputies was a right-wing lobby group which was unrepresentative of Jewish opinion. They also believed that Labour MPs such as Berger were using their campaign against antisemitism in the party to pursue a broader anti-Corbyn and pro-Israel agenda. Just as significantly, the Labour leader's confidants told him that giving ground to any of these critics would make the antisemitism row worse, as it would give allegations credibility, and his critics would never really be satisfied until his leadership ended.

There was more than a grain of truth in these statements. Many of the fiercest critics of his leadership, such as Hodge, Berger, Louise Ellman and Joan Ryan, were members of the parliamentary lobby group Labour Friends of Israel. And when Corbyn did act against antisemitism, or even against perceived antisemitism, in the party, these MPs did not moderate their criticisms of him, let alone halt them. While they were right that Corbyn sometimes moved too slowly on the issue, for example over the mural, on other occasions his approach to Labour figures accused of antisemitism, even close allies of his, was very different.

In April 2016, Ken Livingstone had been interviewed by Vanessa Feltz on BBC Radio London. She had asked him about a controversy involving Naz Shah, a Labour MP and aide to John McDonnell. The rightwing website Guido Fawkes had discovered that shortly before Shah became an MP she had shared on Facebook a post suggesting that one 'Solution for the Israel-Palestine conflict' would be to 'Relocate Israel to the United States'. As a result, Shah had recently been suspended from the party, despite claims from Livingstone and others that her intention in sharing the post had been satirical rather than antisemitic.

On the radio show, Feltz suggested to Livingstone that the shared post and other Facebook posts by Shah about Jews and Israel, including, as Feltz put it, a reference to 'what Hitler did', did constitute antisemitism. Livingstone replied that Shah's behaviour had been 'completely over the top'. 'But it's not antisemitic,' he continued. 'Let's remember that when Hitler won his election in 1932 his policy then was that Jews should be moved to Israel. He was supporting Zionism before he went mad and ended up killing 6 million Jews.'

Feltz, who is Jewish, did not respond directly to Livingstone's hugely provocative statement. Instead, she said that 'some people' believed that in the Labour party 'a deeply embedded systemic antisemitism is hidden behind a mask of anti-Zionism or criticism of Israel'. Livingstone dismissed the allegation. 'I've been in the Labour

Party for 47 years,' he said. 'I've never heard anyone say anything antisemitic.' Later in the interview he added, 'There's been a very well-orchestrated campaign by the Israel lobby to smear anybody who criticises Israeli policy as antisemitic.'

Livingstone's claims about Hitler and Zionism were not totally accurate. In 1932 Israel did not exist: it was still Palestine. And the Nazi party did not win a majority at that year's two sets of parliamentary elections. But it was true that from the early 1930s until the Holocaust began in 1941, part of Nazi policy towards German Jews was to drive them out of the country and into Palestine. It was also true that this policy involved cooperation between Hitler's government and some German Zionists, through the intensely controversial 1933 Haavara (Transfer) Agreement, which arranged for fleeing Jews to sell their assets in Germany, and then use the money to buy exported German goods useful for their new lives in Palestine.

However, Livingstone had summarised this highly complex and unsettling story, which was still argued about by historians and not widely known by the public, with such brevity and insensitivity that there was an immediate uproar in Westminster and far beyond. The same day, Corbyn suspended him from the Labour party, and sacked him as co-chair of the review of its defence policies. Livingstone remained suspended for two years, before finally resigning from the party in 2018. 'I do not accept the allegation that . . . I am in any way guilty of antisemitism,' he said on quitting. 'I abhor antisemitism, I have fought it all my life and will continue to do so.' Then he remembered to add an apology: 'I also recognise that the way I made a historical argument has caused offence and upset in the Jewish community. I am truly sorry for that.'

The month before Livingstone left the party, finally, for a retirement from politics that seemed to promise little more than lingering semi-disgrace, the leftwing American magazine *Jacobin* published a long article about Corbyn and antisemitism. 'The question "does Labour have a problem with antisemitism?",' wrote Daniel Finn, *Jacobin*'s features editor, 'should be seen for what it is: a rhetorical trap with a built-in conclusion.' You did not have to share Finn's broader politics, or his pro-Corbynism, to see what he meant. As leader, Corbyn did not handle the issue of Labour antisemitism well. But it was hard to see how handling it better would have ended the controversy, so convinced were many of his critics of his fundamental hostility to Jews and Israel.

It was also hard not to see another motivation at work among some, but not all, of those who attacked his approach to antisemitism. During his campaign for the leadership and the first two years of his tenure, his disorientated enemies had searched hard among what they saw as his endless flaws, looking for the one which could be used to undermine, immobilise and terminally damage his radical project. Corbyn's contentious political beliefs, lack of traditional leadership skills or charisma, lack of leadership experience, and excess of contro-versial personal political history – none of these weaknesses had proven fatal, however tirelessly his enemies tried to exploit them. But in his alleged tolerance of antisemitism they had finally found an attack line that worked.

22

'We Are Building to Reach
the Stars'

As Corbyn's leadership struggled through 2018 and 2019, spinning its wheels in the mire of the antisemitism controversy, and in ever more tangled parliamentary arguments about Brexit, there remained a hope on the left that somehow politics would become simpler and more dramatic again. That it would return to the streets: to where Corbyn and the movement around him had been so effective in the 2017 election and his leadership campaigns.

On 28 August 2019, the chance seemed to come. That morning the Conservative leader of the Commons, Jacob Rees-Mogg, secretly flew with the Tory leader of the Lords, Baroness Evans, and their party's chief whip in the Commons, Mark Spencer, to the Queen's summer residence at Balmoral in Scotland. There the Conservative delegation asked the monarch to suspend, or prorogue, parliament, and she agreed. For five weeks from 9 September to 14 October, the Commons and Lords would be closed.

Britain is a stop-start democracy, where parliament's operation is frequently paused for prorogations and recesses, often to the advantage of ailing or secretive governments. But there had not been a prorogation of this length in the previous 40 years, nor one with such a blatantly party-political motivation. Boris Johnson had replaced Theresa May as prime minister a month earlier. Having avoided being held accountable wherever possible throughout his political career, he now wanted to minimise the time available for MPs to examine his sketchy plans for withdrawing from the European Union.

The whole prorogation manoeuvre could not have been better designed to outrage and alarm anyone who believed that British democracy was vulnerable to a prime minister with an authoritarian streak and no scruples. The secret flight to Balmoral; the involvement of the supercilious Rees-Mogg, one of the left's hate figures; the fact the prorogation had been granted by royal prerogative, a power that Tony Benn and generations of other republicans had warned against; and the attempt by the Johnson administration to pretend that suspending parliament was something that 'all new governments do' – all this enraged a lot of Britons, and the left in particular. By the afternoon, the opponents of prorogation had a slogan: 'Stop the Coup!'

I could hear it being chanted as soon as I came out of Westminster tube station. There were thousands of protesters, blocking the pavements, spilling on to the roads, filling all the green spaces outside parliament, not sure exactly where their spontaneous action should be focused. One of the last warm afternoons of the summer was cooling and fading into a pale evening, but some of the demonstrators were still in shorts and T-shirts. Others had come straight from work. A very tall, middle-aged man in a grey suit stood chanting loudly outside the gates of Downing Street, a briefcase between his feet. He was joined by a woman I recognised: my children's previous secondary school headteacher. The range of ages and dress styles, the chants, and the air of excitement and mild rebelliousness made it feel like a Corbyn gathering, except that some people were waving EU flags.

The Labour leader did not appear. But Diane Abbott did, walking determinedly through the crowd towards parliament. Unusually, her hair was in a ponytail, and for several minutes no one seemed to recognise her. Then they started to. 'That's Jeremy Corbyn's sidekick,' said one demonstrator. 'That's Diane Abbott, my favourite MP,' said another. People began to touch her elbow affectionately as she passed, or pat her on the shoulder, or approach her to have a few words. She ignored them all, looking straight ahead, not stopping. The kind of random chats with voters that Corbyn enjoyed so much, as an affable white man with middle-class confidence, were not for her.

A while later, as dusk was coming, she made a short speech to the protesters in front of parliament. Suddenly, she was transformed. She stood on a patch of grass, and a space in the crowd opened up deferentially in front of her. With no amplification except for a small hand microphone, she had to shout. 'If we were a Latin American country, this prorogation would be called a coup,' she said, 'complete with an

American president supporting it!' Her head bobbed emphatically as she made each point. 'Boris does not represent the British people ... This is an attack on democracy! What do we want?' She paused. The crowd chanted back: 'Stop the coup!' John McDonnell also spoke at the protest. 'I warn Boris Johnson this,' he said gravely, shaking his head. 'You've unleashed a force that you do not understand ... the power of the British people.'

Twelve days later, on 9 September, as anti-prorogation demonstrations continued, Corbyn spoke in the Commons a few hours before it was due to be suspended. 'This is a parliamentary democracy,' he said, with a reverence he rarely showed towards Westminster. 'We don't have an executive president who can overrule us.' The possibility that a disruptive leftist who was supposedly 'a danger to national security' might end up as a guardian of the British constitution, to his great political benefit, hung tantalisingly in the air that afternoon, and for several weeks afterwards. But more radical signals were also sent by the left during the prorogation crisis. In the minutes after parliament was suspended, some Labour MPs including McDonnell refused to leave the Commons chamber. Instead they stayed in their seats and sang 'The Red Flag'.

Some of these heightened feelings carried over to the Labour party conference a fortnight later. As at Corbynism's most hopeful moments in 2015 and 2017, the conference was held in Brighton. This time, the speeches were even more ambitious, in the main hall as well as on the fringe. McDonnell promised that a Corbyn government would 'build a million new homes that our people need', introduce 'self-management by workers' and 'reduce the working week to 32 hours within the next decade – with no loss of pay'.

In her address as shadow home secretary, Abbott said things which probably no home secretary, Labour or Conservative, ever had before, such as: 'Labour thanks all the migrants who come here.' Meanwhile Corbyn pledged to oversee 'investment on a scale our country has never seen'. In order to make that happen, he said, at the next general election Labour would mount 'the biggest people-powered campaign this country has ever seen!' The repetitive language of the promises which he and other shadow ministers were making suggested hasty policy-making, if you were a sceptic; or, if you believed, a transformation of the country which ordinary political language struggled to convey.

A few hours before Corbyn's conference speech, the prorogation was ruled illegal by the supreme court. Parliament was to resume its activities the next day. The authority of the Johnson government, both moral and political, seemed seriously damaged, perhaps even fatally. Leftwing politicians such as Corbyn who had opposed the proroga- tion were vindicated, and seemed to have acquired a new respectability. After his speech, he left the conference to return to Westminster, a day ahead of schedule, as if he was ready to save the nation.

That evening, I stayed in Brighton and went to a rally a few minutes away from the main conference venue, at a fringe site occupied by the latest iteration of The World Transformed. The site was a small park, its windblown trees surrounded by busy roads. It felt precarious, even beleaguered: an appropriate gathering place for defenders of Corbyn's leadership.

The rally took place in a large marquee. A dozen Campaign Group MPs addressed a boisterous, mostly young crowd. No longer was the parliamentary group made up mostly of white men of a certain age, as it had been in the 1990s and 2000s. Instead, many of the speakers were youthful, and often from other ethnicities: Dawn Butler, Zarah Sultana, Bell Rebeiro-Addy. Fired up by the prorogation decision and the manic mood of the conference, they all made fierce, short speeches, one after another, with barely a pause in between. The tent shook with cheers, chants and applause. The Labour left seemed to be regen- erating at last. Inside the tent at least, it was still possible to believe that the left was also carrying the party towards government.

The most confident speaker of all was Richard Burgon, a former lawyer from Leeds with a very loud voice. Still in his thirties, he had been appointed by Corbyn as shadow lord chancellor and shadow justice secretary. In the next general election, which was expected at any moment, the party would be coming for 'Alexander Boris de Pfef- fel Johnson', Burgon vowed theatrically. He said the prime minister's full, privileged name with taunting relish. Finally, and not before time, I thought, the party of nice Jeremy Corbyn was turning nastier.

Contrary to tradition, parliament kept sitting during the following week's Conservative party conference. Having tried illegally to sus- pend democracy, Johnson now had to face more parliamentary scrutiny than usual, from enraged and emboldened MPs. But in one way he still managed, characteristically, to evade it. His conference speech was scheduled for the same day as prime minister's questions. This meant that, according to another of the Commons' endless and elastic conventions, he was allowed to choose a senior minister, in this case the foreign secretary Dominic Raab, to stand in for him. Labour, in turn, could select a shadow minister to stand in for Corbyn. The Labour leader announced his choice on Twitter:

> This #BlackHistoryMonth we're inspired by the struggles of black campaigners, including the first black MPs elected in 1987. Tomorrow one of those pioneering MPs, a child of the Windrush Generation, Diane Abbott, will be the first black person to represent their party at #PMQs.

For the occasion she wore a black jacket with sharp lapels and a draped white blouse, an outfit that made her look even more like a lawyer than usual. But in the Commons she seemed a little nervous at first. Most of the faces in front of her and behind her, and above her in the press gallery, were white, as usual. During the long minutes before she was due to ask her first question, she alternated between staring at a sheaf of papers on her lap and staring across the room at Raab and the other Tories, over the despatch box. When he answered the traditional preliminary question from a Tory MP, she leaned right forward, as if about to stand up prematurely.

When it was finally her turn, she started with a mention of Black History Month. It had first been marked in Britain the same year that she had first been elected as an MP, and that initiative had originated in Livingstone's 'loony' GLC. But now, three decades later, when Abbott referred to Black History Month reverently at the despatch box, there were no disapproving mutters. A victory had gradually been won.

She was about to move on to her first question when Raab, who also looked nervous, and seemed to think she had already asked one, abruptly stood up. In response, she sat down. Realising his mistake, he sat down too. She stood up again. Laughter echoed round the chamber. But it sounded more supportive than mocking:

sympathy for two understudies to the party leaders who had misunderstood unfamiliar protocol. Abbott caught the suddenly lighter mood. 'If I may continue,' she said, in a now louder, wittier voice, 'uninterrupted . . .'

From then on, she was more confident and fluent. She was also strikingly severe towards Raab and the government. She asked him about the onslaught of abusive and violent messages against female MPs who challenged the government, a subject she knew plenty about. She asked about the increase in women in poverty under the Tories; the increasingly confrontational tactics of anti-abortion campaigners; and the 'abhorrent' official requirement that mothers who had been raped and were seeking state financial support to fill out a form 'to prove' how their child had been conceived. All her questions were about women. She seemed determined to make her brief tenure at prime minister's questions as radical as possible.

Between dodging her questions, Raab awkwardly paid her a tribute. 'She has blazed a trail and made it easier for others to follow in her footsteps,' he said, apparently reading from a prepared text. 'That is something in which I and every honourable member in this House can take pride . . .' She listened unsmilingly, then asked her next question.

Leaning on the dispatch box, she began to look down at her papers less and at the Tories more, glaring at them over the top of her glasses. Her questions were punctuated with emphatic nods, chopping gestures, and pointing fingers. Her language became precise and withering: 'Will the foreign secretary take the opportunity to apologise . . . ?'; 'So, we can take it there is no apology . . .'; 'How much more dismissive can the foreign secretary be . . . ?'

Unusually for prime minister's questions, there was little barracking from Conservative MPs, disarmed perhaps by Raab's praise for Abbott, or by the surprisingly steely quality, to them at least, of her despatch box performance. By the end of the session, she seemed to be relishing the experience so much that she tried to ask an extra question. The speaker intervened: 'I believe the shadow home secretary has had her six questions.' There were shouts from the Labour benches: 'More! More! More!'

*

461

Yet at this moment, and at many others, the autumn of 2019 was a time of illusions for Corbynism. The movement had become weaker than many of its participants and enemies appreciated. It was no longer advancing but retreating. Instead of exploiting the vulnerabilities of Johnson's inexperienced, often chaotic government, which was repeatedly defeated in parliament over Brexit and forced to postpone the country's exit from the EU, Labour turned inward, agonising over its own Brexit policy and preoccupied by personal and factional disputes.

Some leading party figures, Abbott and McDonnell among them, wanted the party to have a 'remain and reform' stance on the EU. Like many people on the British left, they had gradually come to see the UK's membership as an imperfect but necessary protection against increasingly rapacious global capitalism and rightwing populism, as exemplified by Donald Trump's administration in the United States. Abbott had originally shared Tony Benn's hostility to the EU, but being an MP during Margaret Thatcher's attacks on the organisation as an obstacle to free-market capitalism had gradually changed her view. As London MPs, she and McDonnell were also conscious that the majority of Corbynism's urban supporters were strongly pro-EU. For Labour to accept Brexit instead, a policy backed by socially conservative nationalists such as Jacob Rees-Mogg, would be a betrayal of the party's new cosmopolitan heartlands, Abbott and McDonnell argued.

Yet they were opposed by an influential pro-Leave group, which included Seumas Milne, Corbyn's chief of staff Karie Murphy and the general secretary of Unite, Len McCluskey, Corbyn's most powerful union backer. These leavers did not believe that the EU could be reformed. They saw it as Benn had done, as a fundamentally undemocratic, free-market body which would restrict any leftwing British government, for example by its rules limiting state aid to companies. And they saw Labour's heartlands less as the pro-EU big cities and more as the smaller cities and towns, often ex-industrial places in the north of England and the Midlands, where an older, whiter electorate had generally voted Leave and was intrigued by Johnson's promises to rescue their neglected localities once Britain left the EU. McCluskey and his allies argued that a pro-Remain Labour party could lose dozens of seats in these regions; whereas if Labour just accepted the Brexit referendum result and concentrated on other, more obviously left–right issues, as it had at the 2017 election, then it would hold on to these traditional working-class voters, which it needed at least as much as its more diverse urban ones.

During 2019 these competing visions of Labour's electoral and EU strategies, and in some ways of the party's whole identity, were fought over in formal and informal internal meetings, media briefings and counter-briefings, drawn-out party conference debates, and laboriously written and rewritten policy statements. To make things worse, Corbyn found the process both extremely difficult to manage and also not that interesting. Averse to personal conflict, he preferred to think and talk about more large-scale, more abstract clashes: between classes, or between independence movements and imperialists.

While he had voted Leave in the first referendum on the issue, in 1975, and for many years afterwards had echoed Benn's hostility to British membership, for Corbyn the EU was not a fixation. It was just one international bogeyman of many. When he became leader, remainers on the Labour right, and in other parties and the media, insisted that his view of the EU was still unyieldingly hostile. As supposedly conclusive evidence, they cited his failure to campaign for Remain as wholeheartedly as they wanted during the 2016 referendum. Yet to believe that Corbyn was still an unreconstructed leaver also required you to believe that he was happy to ignore the views of the hundreds of thousands of new, overwhelmingly pro-EU Labour members who had made his leadership possible, and who remained some of his most loyal supporters.

Also, his leadership actually saw a big change in his party's position on EU membership: from 'Labour accepts the [2016] referendum result', in its 2017 manifesto, to a very different undertaking in 2019. 'Within three months of coming to power,' that year's election manifesto pledged, 'a Labour government will secure a sensible [Brexit] deal. And within six months, we will put that deal to a public vote alongside the option to remain.' The pro-EU faction in the Labour hierarchy ultimately won.

However, the fact that this victory took so long to achieve, and that Corbyn seemed so ambivalent about it, and that the party's anti-EU faction seemed so reluctant to accept it, meant that in terms of polit-ical presentation, if not actual policy, by the autumn of 2019 Labour ended up left awkwardly and vulnerably stranded between Remain and Leave. Many pro-EU voters did not trust the party with the deli-cate task of essentially re-running the Brexit referendum. Meanwhile many anti-EU voters did not trust the party with the equally tricky task of renegotiating the Brexit deal. Other voters simply did not believe that a single government, especially one led by a diplomatic novice such as Corbyn, was capable of performing two such seem-ingly contradictory tasks in quick succession.

No such complexities dulled the appeal of the Conservative policy on Brexit when it finally crystallised in October 2019. Seemingly unfazed by all the delays, policy conundrums and government defeats in the Commons which had hampered Brexit since the referendum three years earlier, Johnson negotiated a new withdrawal agreement with the EU which simply glossed over difficult issues such as how to operate the border between the EU and Northern Ireland without undermining the Irish peace process. He then set about persuading the Commons to vote for an immediate general election – shamelessly dropping his own par-ty's commitment since 2011 to 'fixed-term' parliaments – so that he could win a Commons majority and 'get Brexit done'.

Three times he failed to convince enough MPs to vote for an elec-tion so obviously timed to help his party. But then in late October, the Scottish National Party and the Liberal Democrats, both now believ-ing that their strongly anti-Brexit stances would win them seats from the Tories and Labour, since millions of people who usually voted for the main parties were remainers, switched from opposing to support-ing a snap election. Anxiety in the Commons, amplified by the media, about the effect that parliament's paralysis by Brexit since September – in reality, only a few weeks – was having on a public supposedly already disillusioned by politics did the rest. On 29 October, Johnson introduced a bill for an early election, and it passed easily. The contest would be held on 12 December.

General elections are rarely held in winter. The short, cold, often wet days are terrible for campaigning, and discourage people from voting. The grey light and sense of entropy and tiredness can be particularly unhelpful for political parties which are trying to sell hope. While a few people in the Labour hierarchy, such as Karie Murphy, the party chairman Ian Lavery, and sometimes Corbyn, welcomed the election, arguing that the spirit of 2017 would be reawakened, many more people in the party regarded the coming contest with foreboding. McDonnell was one of them. He thought the election had come two years too early, depriving Labour of the time it needed to refine its radical policies, explain them to the public, and make them seem rational and necessary rather than reckless.

But now matters had been taken out of Labour's hands. In early November 2019, in incessant drizzle, the party unveiled its campaign bus in Liverpool. It was parked near the waterfront, beyond the city centre, outside a co-working building which was also a music venue: the sort of lively, community-orientated place that suits the making of political promises. Corbyn and McDonnell both gave speeches, and lots of journalists had come from London. Yet the event lacked spark. The slogan on the bus, which was also the title of the manifesto, was strained and unmemorable: 'It's Time for Real Change'. The bus was a cheering bright red, accentuated by the dim weather, but if you looked past it a flat, empty expanse of debris-scattered dockside stretched into the distance, still awaiting redevelopment after decades of dereliction. It was not the most encouraging setting in which to claim you could change the country.

As in 2017, Labour began the campaign well behind the Conservatives in the polls. As in 2017, Corbyn believed that part of the solution was for him to visit and make speeches in as many places as possible. Meanwhile other party figures who were almost as headstrong, such as McDonnell and Lavery, a former miner from the north-east of England, also toured the country according to their own, largely independent schedules. Labour did not have one carefully coordinated campaign so much as several semi-improvised ones. From the start, there was too much going on for its overworked campaign staff – and for many voters – to take in.

Meanwhile the Conservatives did the opposite: minimal public appearances by Johnson, a relentless focus on Labour seats in northern England and the Midlands, and few policy messages except 'Get Brexit done'. For an electorate which over the past five years had had to process the EU and Scottish independence referendums, three general elections and the seemingly endless Brexit dramas in parliament, the Conservative offer to make politics less central to national life again was timely and tempting.

Andrew Fisher felt uneasy for most of the campaign. Again he had written the Labour manifesto. As in 2017, it was conversational in tone and refreshingly radical in content. Its whole first section was about 'a green industrial revolution', the first time that a major British party had taken the environment and climate crisis so seriously. Yet unlike in 2017, the manifesto often sounded like someone trying to tell you too much, too fast. 'Some people say this is the Brexit election,' began a typical passage, in the foreword. 'But it's also the climate election, the investment election, the NHS election, the living standards election, the education election, the poverty election, the fair taxes election ...' The urgency of Labour's diagnosis of Britain's problems, and the profusion of policies that followed, was exhausting to read. Although the manifesto was almost 20 pages shorter than the 2017 one, it did not feel like it. As well as more policies, there were more words on each page.

'The reason there were so many policies,' Fisher told me, 'was because every day there was a message from the comms team: "What are we doing today? What's the policy drop?" In most campaigns you don't drop a policy every day, because you've also got a clear narrative and strategy. But in 2019 a lot of those bits of the operation, like choosing the right seats to campaign in, just weren't there.' McDonnell agreed. 'We didn't develop our narrative, or sustain it coherently. I was throwing policy after policy into the campaign, to distract from Brexit.'

His appetite for new ideas, such a strength outside elections, also contributed to the overload. As a keen attender of community meetings, he had been struck for years by how people all over the country told him that their family, social and economic lives were hindered by a lack of decent broadband. Two weeks into the election, with his strong backing, Labour announced that it would create 'British Broadband', a state-owned company to 'connect communities across Britain by delivering free full-fibre broadband for all' by 2030. The plan would partly be paid for by properly 'taxing multinational corporations such as Amazon, Facebook and Google', and would 'save the average person £30.30 a month'.

In many ways, it was a great policy: modern, much-needed, inclusive, and funded with clever populist symbolism by a contribution from many people's favourite economic ogres, the tech giants. 'The polling on it was excellent,' McDonnell told me. Back in the early, most creative days of New Labour, Tony Blair had announced something similar: an agreement with British Telecom in 1995 that the company would connect schools, colleges, universities and libraries to the internet for free. Yet in 2019 the idea of British Broadband was unveiled so suddenly, with even Labour's press office only told about it the day before, that many voters did not understand the proposal, or thought it was too good to be true. The rightwing newspapers were able to present it as an impractical gimmick. 'We hadn't laid the groundwork,' said Fisher. And for those voters who did like the idea, British Broadband only got a day or two as the focus of the Labour campaign. Then other new policies took its place. The thousands of activists who were knocking on doors for the party, many of them new to campaigning, as in 2017, often did not know which of these policies they were supposed to be mentioning to voters.

Labour did make some progress during the campaign. The Tory lead in Ipsos MORI's polls shrank from 16 per cent in mid-November to 12 per cent in early December, as support for Labour grew. But then Labour's improvement seemed too slow. Meanwhile support for the Conservatives remained steady, or even grew. After nine years of divisive, often divided Tory government, 'Get Brexit Done' was a slogan which all Britain's warring rightwing tribes could unite behind. Most crucially, the Brexit Party, which had planned to contest every seat in the country, announced a fortnight into the campaign that it would not put up candidates in the 317 constituencies that the Conservatives had won at the last election.

Labour had not anticipated this manoeuvre. Like many press commentators, it had assumed that the often vicious competition between the Brexit Party, and its forerunner UKIP, and the Tories for the anti-EU vote over the previous few years would continue. But Labour should have been more thorough and flexible in its election planning. Once the party had changed its policy on EU membership to re-running the 2016 referendum, there was always a chance that the Leave parties would form an alliance, to close off the possibility of a vote to Remain. Again, Labour had not fully thought through the implications of its Brexit policy – probably because the whole party hierarchy did not believe in it. The looseness of Corbynism had once been a strength, an ability to get fractious leftwingers to work together while holding on to their different beliefs and identities. Yet in a less expansive and more bad-tempered election than 2017, this looseness was a weakness.

With support for the Tories staying above the 40 per cent which they needed to win, throughout the campaign, Corbyn's rallies took on a valedictory quality. They became a chance to see him not on his way to victory, but performing on a big stage for a final time.

One lunchtime in the last week of the campaign, he was scheduled to appear in Bristol, a place where the kind of environmentally conscious leftwing policies Labour was offering were particularly popular. The rally was on College Green, a large grassy space in the city centre. For once, the sun was out. It lit the huge crowd that waited for him, a multicoloured sea of schoolkids, students, millennials and middle-aged activists, fashionable streetwear and old leather jackets, as if everyone was waiting for a legendary act at a special winter edition of Glastonbury.

Corbyn was over half an hour late, as he usually was during the campaign, but the crowd was cheerful, almost festive. Then someone near me said, 'Oh my god, there he is!' A forest of phones shot up in the air.

He made a short speech, fuzzily amplified, which was heard at first in reverent silence. He spoke mostly in generalities. 'It's time to bring their regime to an end,' he said of the Tories, as if the government was a Latin American dictatorship. He said he wanted 'to start the process of changing things around' in Britain. When he reached his peroration, people began cheering so loudly and continuously that it was hard for much of the crowd to hear his words. But people did not seem to mind. 'Cute man,' said a young guy next to me. As Corbyn walked to his campaign bus to leave, people ran after him to grab selfies. There were shouts of 'Go on Jez!' He gave a toothy grin. His eyes – often tired and dull during 2019 – were alive again.

He was less animated by the televised debates with Johnson. While the prime minister did his aristocratic rogue act in the cold studio light, periodically breaking character to accuse Corbyn of being a ditherer on Brexit and a tool of the Russians, the Labour leader mostly looked away. Whether it was out of woundedness, or distaste at Johnson, or at the gimmicky debate format, it was hard to say. Johnson had his own vulnerabilities on Russia and Brexit. His party was heavily reliant on Russian donors, and during the referendum campaign he had famously written newspaper columns both for and against Brexit, before deciding at the last minute to publish the former. Yet Corbyn did not mention these damning facts. To the intense frustration of some of his campaign staff, like Benn he almost never made personal attacks. The closest he came in the debates was to say pointedly: 'I do not ever use racist language in any form.' Those familiar with Johnson's journalism would have known that he could not credibly make the same denial. But many viewers probably thought Corbyn was talking about Labour antisemitism.

That issue hung like a toxic cloud over the party's campaign, sometimes obscuring its better features altogether. In late November, Labour published a special 'race and faith' manifesto, about the work a Corbyn government would do to protect and recognise the value of religious and other minorities. The document was 19 pages long, carefully written and comprehensive. 'We will . . . amend the law to include attacks on places of worship (synagogues, temples, mosques and churches) as a specific aggravated offence,' it pledged. 'We will defend the right to wear religious and other dress . . . [for] Muslims, Jews, Hindus, Christians, Sikhs and many others. We will protect . . . the production of kosher and halal meat.'

The manifesto was launched at an arts centre in Tottenham, one of the most multiracial parts of north London. Outside, in full view of the arriving journalists, someone had parked two vans with long, built-in billboards. In huge black capital letters on a red, Labour-style background, the billboards read: 'A Vote for Labour Is a Vote for Racism' and 'Keep Antisemitism Out of Downing Street'. Beneath both messages was the hashtag #NeverCorbyn.

A few protesters against Labour antisemitism were handing out material near the billboards. I got talking to one of them, a friendly middle-aged woman in a denim jacket. 'A Jeremy Corbyn government will stop kosher and circumcision,' she told me. But the Labour manifesto did not actually say that, I responded. 'Lots of people do things in power that they say they're not going to,' she said. I asked if she was sure that Johnson, with his history of racist journalism, would be a better protector of minorities. 'Oh yes,' she said.

The antisemitism issue gave journalists across the political spectrum, from the *Daily Mail* to the *Guardian*, a respectable-seeming reason to cover Labour with suspicion and hostility – as a political party that was uniquely nasty, and not fully legitimate. During the campaign, a real-time study of the election's print and TV coverage by six academics at Loughborough university found that 'The overall high level of negativity towards the Labour Party has remained constant throughout the election campaign, increasing week by week.'

The coverage of Corbyn, and to a lesser extent Abbott and McDonnell, had been equally negative at the 2017 election. But then the attacks had not been that effective, and had sometimes even backfired. A veteran Tory organiser in Kent told me that some rightwing voters had complained to him on the doorstep that Corbyn was a decent, if misguided man who was being 'bullied' by the tabloids.

Yet in 2019 the attacks worked much better. Two more years of anti-Corbyn stories had chipped away at his righteous image and lodged in voters' minds. The themes of these stories were often helpfully echoed by former MPs from the right of his own party, such as John Woodcock and Ian Austin. The Loughborough study found that these two men received more coverage during the 2019 campaign than many Tory and Labour ministers and shadow ministers. From the Labour right, from the Liberal Democrats and from Conservatives of every type came the same insistent message: Corbyn 'was not fit to be prime minister'.

Meanwhile, the argument that allowing the notoriously lazy, chaotic and mendacious Johnson to carry on in Downing Street was a much bigger risk – an argument which subsequent events, such as Johnson's handling of the pandemic, would prove horribly correct – was barely made by Labour. Nor was the argument that Conservatism in general had become reckless, given all the careless Tory experiments since 2010 with slashing the state and redrawing the country's trading relationships. McDonnell believed that if risk became a theme of the election, Labour would be damaged more than the Conservatives, whose incautious ideas were indulged much more often by voters and the establishment. It was a pessimistic, but quite possibly shrewd assessment. And yet, given the state of the polls, it was also possible to wonder: if Labour did turn the campaign into a referendum on two competing radicalisms, what exactly did it have to lose?

It never happened. Instead, by the last couple of days before the election, while still campaigning hard, he and Corbyn seemed to have retreated into their political comfort zones. In Carlisle, Corbyn told a pub crammed with wet people, who had been waiting for him out in the rain for hours, that he had been 'on a tour round the whole country, to Wales, the south of England and the north . . .' Like Benn, he believed that meeting the people was an end in itself. And in some ways, it was. Political energy and information were exchanged. Formative experiences took place. 'If he wins, I was there,' a 22-year-old woman at the pub told me, drinking in her second ever general election, seemingly oblivious to her soaked hoodie.

McDonnell, meanwhile, kept on promoting his grand schemes, right to the end. In London on the last Monday morning of the campaign, he told a room full of activists, think tank staff and economists – but tellingly, almost empty of journalists – that he had drawn up 'draft plans to hand to civil servants on Friday'. He continued calmly: 'We'll set up our National Transformation Unit before Christmas . . . My first budget will be given on 5 February – the day on which almost ten years of cuts will come to an end . . .' With Labour's small rise in the polls now tapering off, well short of what might be needed to produce an election shock, his determination to keep describing what could be Britain's first truly socialist government felt painfully deluded, yet also heroic somehow, and poignant.

The evening before polling day I went to the final rally of the Labour campaign. The atmosphere outside the east London venue, a converted old canalside building, was strange. Anti-Labour protesters unfurled a banner reading 'Racist Corbyn', and were booed and obstructed. Activists from an unnamed leftwing group handed out leaflets about 'the fightback' and 'carrying on the struggle afterwards', as if Labour had already lost. Pupils from a nearby school, mostly too young to vote, milled around excitedly in their blazers. Millennials walked past in Corbyn-printed leggings and Christmas jumpers embroidered with his face.

Inside, the venue was too small for the occasion. Beyond a crush of people, mostly in their twenties, still in coats and slowly overheating, the shadow cabinet sat squeezed together on a low stage. Abbott was the first to speak. 'It's been a long road,' she said, 'to stand here on the brink of power.' Her voice was strong, and the rhythm of her oratory echoed her first, intoxicating victory address as an MP, 32 years earlier. But from well back in the audience I could see that this time her hands were shaking.

Corbyn spoke next. Under the lights, he seemed pale and thin. But he reminded the room that he was resilient: this was his tenth consecutive election, he said, as a parliamentary candidate or an MP. Speaking without notes, he then meandered in his usual way between earnest, angry passages and a few sharp and well-timed jokes. 'Billionaires are quite mean,' one of them started. 'Only 50 out of the 150 in this country have contributed to the Tories.'

As he neared the end of the speech, his voice suddenly and unexpectedly began to crack a little. 'Many people have inspired me in my life,' he said. 'One such person is the Chilean poet and folk singer Victor Jara. He worked endlessly to get the Popular Unity government elected. Then, when the coup came, he was arrested and taken to the stadium. They shot him, and cut his fingers off.'

Corbyn continued: 'One of the last songs he wrote was called "My Guitar", and I'm going to read a few lines from it.' The room was silent for a few moments, no world visible beyond its fogged-up windows. In his quiet, not very lyrical voice, the leader of the Labour party said:

> My guitar is not for the rich no,
> nothing like that.
> My song is of the ladder
> we are building to reach the stars.

Epilogue: A Future Unclaimed

On another winter evening, three years later, the American politician Bernie Sanders appeared at the Festival Hall in London. The tickets to hear him speak and be interviewed cost up to £25: quite a lot in the middle of a recession, on a cold Thursday, to listen to an 81-year-old senator from a very different political system. But the large auditorium was almost full. The response when Sanders loped onstage was deafening. People whooped and cheered, as if they were celebrating a political victory, rather than living through the fourteenth year of a Tory government.

Sanders made a speech and answered questions in the way he had done for decades, in a stop-start, earnest monologue without rhetorical flourishes, but with a cumulative power. He laid out the ills of the Western world: the growth of inequality, the inability of modern capitalism to provide most people with a decent living, and the gaming of the economy and destruction of the planet by 'oligarchs'. But he also gave reasons for hope: the revival of trade unions, the ongoing radicalisation of young people, the opportunities that new technologies could provide for lives to become less dominated by work. And he suggested how people could make political change happen. Get involved in local politics, he said. Set up a worker-owned business. Use identity politics to build broad coalitions, rather than to divide the liberal majority into factions.

After talking almost non-stop for nearly two hours, he loped off the stage to a standing ovation. When the lights of the auditorium came back up, many people in the audience looked elated, stirred and reinvigorated.

Yet there was also something less uplifting about the occasion. Much of what Sanders had said had already been said, for decades, by British

473

politicians on the left. Sanders did mention one of them, Nye Bevan, who as health secretary in Clement Attlee's government in the 1940s had overseen the creation of the NHS. But Sanders said nothing about the Labour left more recently. Most glaringly, he said nothing about a Labour politician who in age, ideology, history, durability, late-career success, late-career failure, popularity with the young, adherence to personal principles, stubbornness, speaking style, unkempt appearance, and ability to connect with audiences exactly like the one in the Festival Hall was surely his British equivalent. Nor was this politician mentioned in any of the dozens of questions Sanders answered at the event. For the purposes of the evening, and indeed for the purposes of mainstream British politics, Jeremy Corbyn no longer existed.

The process of erasing him, and the Labour left in general, began on election night in 2019, before most of the votes had even been counted. 'Go back to your student politics!' said the former New Labour minister Alan Johnson, once a Marxist himself, to a grim-faced Jon Lansman. They were in the ITV studios, absorbing the results of a national exit poll which had just predicted Labour's worst result – in terms of seats if not total votes – for 84 years.

'Corbyn,' said Johnson, almost spitting out the word, 'couldn't lead the working class out of a paper bag.' Momentum, an organisation then with about 40,000 members, which Lansman had co-founded, was 'a little cult', Johnson continued. 'I want them out of the party.'

When the votes were finally counted, Labour was found to have just over ten million: a fifth fewer than in 2017, but considerably more than in its narrow defeats under Ed Miliband in 2015 and Gordon Brown in 2010. More counter-intuitively still, given the instant consensus that Labour had performed disastrously at the 2019 election, Corbyn had actually attracted almost three-quarters of a million more votes than Tony Blair in 2005, when Labour had last won a general election; and only half a million votes fewer than Blair in his landslide victory in 2001. The large crowds at Corbyn's rallies right up to the bitter end of the 2019 campaign had not lied.

As long as you avoided considering the much greater, almost unprecedented size of the Tory vote in 2019 – nearly 14 million: a measure of the extraordinary hostility Corbyn had provoked – it was possible to interpret the election result, Tony Benn-style, as something less bleak for the left than a totally crushing defeat.

To the intense frustration of Alan Johnson and many others in the political and media establishment, Corbyn did not resign the Labour leadership immediately after losing the election as expected. Instead, he stayed on as leader for almost another four months, until April 2020. He spent much of this strange, almost posthumous leadership period insisting publicly that his policies and political approach had not been discredited by the election defeat, and in fact were being vindicated by the statist turn the Conservative government's approach suddenly took during the pandemic. To the last as Labour leader, Corbyn seemed determined to make the most of the rare opportunity for the left which his tenure represented – and not to play the standard political game. There was something awesome, as well as infuriating, about his capacity for stubbornness.

But once his leadership was over, his Labour status swiftly diminished. In October 2020, Corbyn was suspended from the party. The following month, he lost the Labour whip in the Commons. In February 2023, his successor as leader Keir Starmer declared: 'Let me be very clear, Jeremy Corbyn will not stand at the next general election as a Labour party candidate . . . The party [is] changing . . . and we are not going back, and that is why Jeremy Corbyn will not stand.'

For a former leader of a major party to be marginalised and then excluded so quickly and completely is very unusual in British politics. Yet so have been some of the circumstances of Corbyn's ostracism. His suspension in October 2020 came after the publication of a report by the Equality and Human Rights Commission [EHRC] on antisemitism in the Labour party. It found 'serious failings in leadership and an inadequate process for handling antisemitism complaints across the Labour Party . . . a culture within the Party which, at best, did not do enough to prevent antisemitism and, at worst, could be seen to accept it.'

The report also said that 'the comments made by Naz Shah' about Israel 'went beyond legitimate criticism of the Israeli government', as did 'Ken Livingstone's support for those comments'. His statements, the EHRC said, 'caused shock and anger among Jewish Labour party members' and breached the 2010 Equality Act. The report concluded: 'It is hard not to conclude that antisemitism within the Labour Party could have been tackled more effectively if the leadership had chosen to do so.'

Corbyn responded with a written statement on Facebook:

Antisemitism is absolutely abhorrent ... and responsible for some of humanity's greatest crimes. As Leader of the Labour Party I was always determined to eliminate all forms of racism and root out the cancer of antisemitism. I have campaigned in support of Jewish people and communities my entire life and I will continue to do so.

The EHRC's report shows that when I became Labour leader in 2015, the Party's processes for handling complaints were not fit for purpose. Reform was then stalled by an obstructive party bureaucracy. But from 2018, Jennie Formby ... made substantial improvements, making it much easier and swifter to remove antisemites ...

Anyone claiming there is no antisemitism in the Labour Party is wrong. Of course there is, as there is throughout society ... Jewish members of our party and the wider community were right to expect us to deal with it, and I regret that it took longer to deliver that change than it should.

One antisemite is one too many, but the scale of the problem was also dramatically overstated for political reasons by our opponents inside and outside the party, as well as by much of the media ...

My sincere hope is that relations with Jewish communities can be rebuilt and [their] fears overcome. While I do not accept all of [the report's] findings, I trust its recommendations will be swiftly implemented to help move on ...

A few hours after this statement was posted, Corbyn lost the Labour whip. At a press conference the same day, Starmer said that those who 'deny there is a problem' with Labour antisemitism 'are part of the problem', particularly 'those who pretend [the problem] is exaggerated or factional'.

This effort by Starmer and his allies to present Corbyn's downfall as almost entirely the result of his behaviour over antisemitism was undermined, however, by Starmer's own approach to party management, which was much less tolerant than his predecessor's. In February 2022, 11 leftwing MPs including Abbott and McDonnell were told that they, too, would lose the Labour whip unless they removed their names from a letter written by the Stop the War coalition criticising NATO for its history of aggression in countries such as Afghanistan, and its 'eastward expansion' in the years leading up to the Russian invasion of Ukraine. After the MPs complied, a Labour spokesperson told the *Independent*: 'This shows Labour is under new management.'

As leader, Starmer dropped most Corbyn-era policies, such as nationalization, despite the fact that as a leadership candidate he had promised to retain them. Under him, for constituencies requiring new candidates, Labour chose dozens of figures from the centre and right of the party, and almost none from the left – a level of ideological control not even achieved by New Labour at its most intolerant, as McDonnell's selection in 1997 demonstrated. Meanwhile, for party political broadcasts and leader's speeches, Starmer surrounded himself with Union flags and adopted a conservative-sounding language of 'opportunity, family and security'. In a typical speech in February 2023, he also addressed what remained of the Labour left. 'If you don't like the changes we have made,' he said, 'the door is open and you can leave.' He added: 'The Labour Party is unrecognisable from 2019 and it will never go back.'

As a party built out of disparate, sometimes warring elements, from radical socialists to incremental reformers, metropolitan liberals to small-town social conservatives, centralisers to semi-anarchists, Labour has always had a fear of purges. Whenever the left has significant influence over the party, which has not been often – Corbyn's contested leadership and Benn's brief heyday are the past half century's only examples – political journalists and Labour centrists warn that a 'Stalinist' cleansing of the party by the left is coming. It never really does. Attempts by the left to deselect MPs have been rare, and successful ones rarer still, as McDonnell discovered as a young activist in the 1970s, when he spent years trying and failing to unseat his local MP, Neville Sandelson, a man so limited in his loyalty to Labour that he defected to the SDP.

Instead of the left, it is much more often the Labour right that carries out purges, vetoes policies, micromanages the parliamentary party, runs the Labour machine, and decides what the Labour party means. A psychoanalyst might even say that the Labour right's preoccupation with the left's supposed dogmatism, intolerance and aggression is actually a form of projection, an inadvertent display of its own vices.

In these and other ways, the Starmer leadership, though often portrayed by his press supporters as a series of brave reforms, was really a reversion to the political mean. As Benn once said, 'The Labour party has never been a socialist party, although there have always been socialists in it.'

How, then, should these outnumbered, derided, often defeated socialists lead useful political lives? And are such lives possible outside Labour, without these people becoming hopelessly marginalised? After losing the party whip, Corbyn tried to find out, by doing what he had always done as an activist and politician: campaigning for causes he believed in, without worrying too much about the wider implications.

In March 2022, a few days after the Russian invasion, he was scheduled to speak at a Stop the War rally in London, under the slogan 'No to War in Ukraine'. The venue was the austere old Conway Hall, a plain, theatre-like 1920s auditorium which for almost a century had been one of the best-known public gathering places in Britain for political dissidents, free thinkers and sometimes doomed causes. At first, McDonnell was also on the bill. Yet threatened with also losing the Labour whip, at the last moment Corbyn's oldest friend in politics pulled out.

There was no sign of Corbyn, either, when the long evening rally began. Onstage, between the other speakers, a chair stood conspicuously empty for the first three-quarters of an hour. Then Corbyn suddenly appeared from backstage to loud cheers. For a supposedly disgraced former leader, he looked well. He was wearing a suit: there had been no lapsing back to his pre-leadership jumpers. And his eyes were brighter, his tread lighter than during the later, besieged phases of his Labour tenure. He gave an unusually pithy speech, about the Russian attacks on Ukrainian civilians: 'there can be no justification whatsoever'; about Vladimir Putin's government: 'a regime run and financed by, and for the benefit of . . . robber barons'; and about the ways in which the invasion both revealed and obscured the true nature of international power. 'The real issues,' said Corbyn, 'are global inequality, global poverty. It's the poor what pays for the rich man's game of fighting these wars.' He paused. 'Speak up for peace!'

Almost a year and a half later, in the summer of 2023, I interviewed him at his constituency office. The war in Ukraine continued. Israel had just invaded the Palestinian city of Jenin. The Labour leadership's attitude to Corbyn remained unforgiving. The possibility of him standing against the party as an independent at the next general election, despite his 57 years of Labour membership, seemed to be becoming a certainty.

The interview was in a bare meeting room without external windows, towards the back of the bunker-like office building. Characteristically, Corbyn arrived late. For the first few minutes of our conversation, one of the legs in his dapper stone-grey chinos jiggled impatiently under the table. But then he relaxed into expansive anecdotes about his endless political life, from anti-Vietnam activism – 'I've still got the posters' – to talking to soldiers and ex-soldiers during his leadership: 'I would meet them at Armistice Day parades. They were very interesting, not horrible to me at all ...' About all the attacks during his leadership, he tried to sound philosophical. 'I knew we were in for a bumpy ride,' he said quietly. 'I always knew that.'

Because he was an internationalist, he went on, brightening again, he saw politics as multilayered and global. Setbacks for the left in the Commons or in Britain as a whole were often offset by gains somewhere else. 'There's always other stuff going on,' he said, a classic Corbyn formulation, low-key but utterly determined, for the international anti-imperialist struggle.

He ended with a story about having lunch with Tony Benn at the Commons in 2001, when Benn was 76 and had recently retired as an MP. 'John [McDonnell] and I are having egg and beans on toast in the members' tea room,' said Corbyn, 'occupying the SNP's [habitual] table, just to wind them up. Tony comes bustling in with a tray and his disgusting food, which is a mug of tea, a Mars bar and a banana. His eating habits were appalling. He sits down, and I say to him, "You're looking very happy, Tony. Are you OK?" And he says, "Ah yes, yes. You know what? I've just had a death threat! It proves I'm relevant!"'

Corbyn chuckled for quite a few seconds. Then he got up to leave. 'Sorry I kept you waiting earlier,' he said, his manner as placatory as ever. 'I had to be with my friends at the RMT. And now I've got a community event.'

Livingstone appeared to handle life after the Labour party less well. I met him at his house in London in early 2020, four years after his suspension and two years after his resignation from the party. His energy levels seemed low, like a lizard in cold weather. 'I haven't been at a Labour party meeting for nearly four years,' he said. 'From the moment I was suspended . . . it was like a wall came down. With the exception of one event in Istanbul and one event in Moscow, all my work abroad was cancelled.'

We were sitting in his narrow kitchen. Slouching in a chair in old skinny jeans and an untucked plaid shirt, he looked faintly like a retired rock musician. On the back of the door hung an apron with 'Keep Left' printed on it. A portly labrador wandered in and out. 'I've just been sitting here as a househusband,' Livingstone said. He returned to the subject of his suspension: '[The Labour general secretary Iain] McNichol suspended me without bothering to pick up the phone to find out what I'd said . . . For McNichol to suspend me legitimised the idea that I was an antisemite . . . that was the big lie that was going around . . . Recently it was in the bloody *Guardian*, and the *Observer* . . . I had to send a letter . . .'

He became more animated. 'In my eight years as mayor, antisemitic incidents in which the police were called halved. When Boris Johnson was mayor, they doubled.' He began to speak more freely, his urge to say surprising, quotable things kicking in. 'When I did my tour of Israel in 1986, I loved it . . . If someone said, you've got to spend the rest of your life living in the Middle East, the only place you'd go would be Israel.' He laughed. 'I want to have a drink every night! Israel is a genuinely progressive regime. It's got a bit worse under Netanyahu, but the culture is progressive . . . Can you think of any Arab regime that isn't pretty appalling? Has any Arab leader ever come out in favour of gay rights?' It was hard to imagine Corbyn talking about allies of the Palestinians in this way. Livingstone continued: '. . . And if I was antisemitic, how do you explain my two relationships with Jewish women? They might have noticed if I was an antisemite . . .'

I asked if he ever saw Corbyn. 'I bump into him. We were at a Cuban embassy event a couple of weeks ago. We had a nice long chat. I never thought I'd see anyone subject to more lies and smears than I was. But . . . he's survived quite well.' Livingstone suddenly became more serious. 'If me or Jeremy had been politicians in Argentina, or Chile, or Brazil, we would've been murdered.'

McDonnell might have been even more of a target. He had Corbyn's doggedness, and Livingstone's ability to build coalitions, but also an intensity and a questing quality that made him an unusual and potent politician. Two days after the 2019 defeat, he said on *The Andrew Marr Show* that the result had been 'catastrophic'. With a voice even raspier and smaller than usual, McDonnell continued: 'It's on me. I own this disaster. So I apologise . . .' Yet within a few minutes, he was rallying. 'I'm not going away,' he told Marr. 'I'll be back on picket lines and demonstrations. Politics is not a career. It's more of a vocation.'

Nine months after the election, in the middle of the pandemic, he launched Claim the Future, a new online think tank and hub for leftwing activists. Ambitiously, it aimed 'to ask and answer some of the questions that the pandemic has raised about the economy and society', 'to link new [political] thinking with campaigning and action on the ground', and even to examine 'what future there should be for our planet'. According to its plain but intriguing website, Claim the Future would employ a 'small team', including Andrew Fisher, McDonnell's and Corbyn's former advisor, to draft 'policy position papers' and hold public web meetings.

That at least some of this work would be more free-ranging than the usual leftwing gatherings of the like-minded soon became clear. In September 2020, McDonnell spent an hour online with his old enemy Gordon Brown, discussing how to get rid of tax havens and create a fairer global economy. Both men, born in the same year, the formidable but too careful former chancellor and the radical chancellor that never was, wore red ties and white shirts, and treated each other with a respect that felt novel. Indirectly, McDonnell acknowledged that New Labour had done some good things, and Brown acknowledged that Corbyn's leadership had been more than an idealistic dead end. The encounter was refreshing, and hopeful. Perhaps the Labour left and centre-left could find a way to talk to each other, and even work together, after all.

Yet the meeting was also frustrating. Why had such constructive public conversations never happened before? With the Conservatives then seemingly entrenched in power, ahead in the polls despite their often catastrophic handling of the pandemic, and Brown and McDonnell both about to enter their seventies, unlikely to ever hold office again, their rapprochement felt too late.

McDonnell, however, does not think in the same timespans as most MPs and journalists. His hero Gramsci is the great theorist of gradual, almost unnoticed leftwing victories – or, you could say, the great rationaliser of leftwing defeats. In his own life, McDonnell has also replaced one faith, Catholicism, with another, socialism. He is prepared to endure a lot of setbacks and delays on the journey to what he thinks would be a better society – a society that in his mind has no permanent form, anyway.

In the giddy aftermath of the 2017 election, when there seemed a real possibility that he would soon become chancellor, I asked him to sum up how he would change the economy if that happened. We were standing in the middle of an excited anti-government march, but he answered soberly. For several minutes, he talked about Labour's plans to 'learn from Germany' about how to create a more high-tech, more long-term economy. With his neat silver hair, and wearing a striped shirt with a bright summer jumper slung over his shoulders, he even looked a bit like an off-duty German industrialist.

But, I asked, didn't he want to replace the current economic system rather than reform it? For years, he had listed one of his interests in *Who's Who* as 'fermenting the overthrow of capitalism'. He gave me a big, knowing smile. His aim now, he said, was 'a staged transformation of our economic system'. What the end point of that would be, he did not say.

Under Starmer, despite all the moves against the left, there were also sometimes signals that the party is still drawing on the thinking which went on during McDonnell's shadow chancellorship. At the 2022 party conference, Starmer announced that a Labour government would establish Great British Energy, a new, publicly owned company 'that takes advantage of the opportunities' emerging in energy generation from renewable sources. He also promised to 'make work pay for the people who create this country's wealth'; and to 'transform the state so the decisions which drive growth in communities are made by local people'. Repeatedly as opposition leader, he also emphasised that he will lead 'a Labour government that creates an economy that works for working people'.

The pledges lacked specifics. But in his willingness to make systemic criticisms, and to at least sketch out fundamental reforms, Starmer seemed to be leaving behind the economic approach followed by Brown and Blair, which was far more accepting of the status quo, and to be tentatively moving into territory mapped out by McDonnell and his advisors and associated intellectuals during the Corbyn leadership.

In Starmer's youth during the 1980s, he was part of a radical collective that produced *Socialist Alternatives*, a short-lived magazine for which he once reverently interviewed Tony Benn, and also wrote articles in favour of GLC-style coalitions between Labour and social movements such as feminism and environmentalism. After becoming leader, he disowned this phase of his political life. 'We were out to change the world,' he said on *Desert Island Discs* in 2020. 'I said some things that were daft.'

During 2023 and 2024, he and Labour scaled back most of the relatively radical policy pledges he had made as leader, such as substantially increasing state investment in a climate-compatible economy. With the general election nearing, Starmer appeared to be conducting the standard Labour leader's manoeuvre, followed by all except Corbyn in recent memory, of positioning the party further and further to the right, in an almost self-flagellating way, in order to reassure swing voters, the rightwing media and the country's numerous other conservative interest groups and institutions that Labour would be 'responsible' in power.

And yet, Britain's dramatic economic decline relative to other rich countries since 2010, and the worsening material conditions of many voters' lives and of the state itself – a deterioration which in recent years has accelerated alarmingly, with schools and other public buildings literally crumbling – mean that changing the structure and operation of the British economy will probably have to be a priority for any Starmer government, whether he likes it or not. And since the right and centre of his party have produced few fresh ideas since the Blair and Brown governments, paralysed by the loss of office and by the financial crisis which they failed to see coming, Starmer will probably have to take some economic ideas from the left, however much he waters them down or disguises them. The 'security' he promises voters will almost certainly require him to confront at least parts of British capitalism's great insecurity-producing machine.

At the 2022 edition of The World Transformed, which took place in a converted chapel half a mile away from the Labour party conference in Liverpool, the mood of people I spoke to was strikingly mixed. Anger and despondency at the left's treatment by Starmer sat alongside tentative satisfaction and surprise at how many leftwing policies, or traces of leftwing policies, had appeared in his speech.

By the following year's Labour conference, the gap between it and The World Transformed seemed to have widened again. Though they were held in the same Liverpool venues as before, few people attended, or even paid much attention to, both events. A leftwing activist I talked to at a café midway between them spoke about Starmer's party with cool contempt, as if centrism was Labour's natural state. And yet, many of the speeches at the party conference, while proposing few bold policies, were blunter, more class-conscious and more egalitarian in their rhetoric than New Labour ever dared. A feeling remained that, in response to the country's deep inequality and many crises, a Starmer premiership might have no choice but to take British centrism into unfamiliar, more leftwing territory. As Benn and Livingstone liked to say, and as Corbyn, Abbott and McDonnell still believe, in politics there is no such thing as total victory or total defeat.

There may also be no such thing as a Labour approach to Israel and Palestine which satisfies all parts of the party. During 2023 and early 2024, as violence in Israel and Gaza escalated to levels not seen for decades, with over a thousand Israeli civilians and far greater numbers of Palestinian civilians killed, Labour again saw splits, resignations, and malfunctions in its electoral machine. As Corbyn had done as leader, Starmer struggled to find a stance and a language simultaneously acceptable to British Jews, Zionist and otherwise; to British Muslims, who usually make up a large and vital part of the Labour electorate; and to supporters and critics of Israel in other British communities. For some pro-Palestinians inside and outside the party, Starmer's moral authority as leader was badly compromised, or completely discredited, just as Corbyn's had been in the eyes of some supporters of Israel. At a chaotic by-election in the substantially Muslim town of Rochdale, Labour abandoned its candidate after he promoted an anti-Israel conspiracy theory, and the Labour seat fell to the pro-Palestinian George Galloway. Like his predecessor, on the Israel–Palestine issue Starmer was now variously seen by his critics as weak, out of his depth, malign or simply not to be trusted. No one dared say it yet – Labour's antisemitism crisis was still too live – but Corbyn's handling of Israel–Palestine, and all the other huge issues connected to it, began to look less uniquely disastrous.

Diane Abbott's reputation also remained unsettled. During her four decades in parliament, she has received more hate mail than any other female MP. In the six months leading up to the 2017 election, a period in which she was particularly prominent as a key Corbyn ally and shadow minister, she received almost a third of all abusive tweets directed at female MPs, according to research commissioned by Amnesty International. A week after the election, Abbott revealed that she had recently been diagnosed with type-2 diabetes, symptoms of which include blurred vision and constant tiredness – debilitating for anyone, but particularly so for a politician, with their need to absorb information quickly and get through days of public engagements. More often than most MPs, Abbott was regularly accused of not knowing essential facts and of being lazy.

In her constituency I was often told by people, usually Labour voters and sometimes members of the local party, that she was prickly, vain, self-absorbed, unreliable, disorganised and difficult to work with. Yet her majority grew at almost every election, until even in Labour's 2019 defeat it was one of the biggest in the country. After that election, there were 66 MPs from minority ethnic backgrounds: still a disproportionately low number but a 16-fold increase on when she was first elected.

After losing her chance to be a pioneering home secretary, Abbott just carried on: calling out racism and threats to civil liberties, making lawyerly interventions in the Commons and blunter ones on social media, criticising Starmer much as she used to criticise Blair, for being too intolerant of dissent and not paying enough attention, as she piously but accurately put it, 'to ordinary Labour supporters and ordinary trade unionists'. In Hackney, she was still a distinctive presence, nearly always dressed up, a little remote, plodding along some streets that had gentrified almost beyond recognition since 1987, and others which were as full as ever of desperate situations awaiting her intervention. Despite all the threats and abuse against her, she rarely used a security escort. As well as her value as a role model, her political survival alone was a kind of success, as all the rage against her from racists and other reactionaries inadvertently acknowledged.

In 2023, her political life became that much harder. In April, research was published about the experience of racism in Britain during the pandemic. The *Observer* published an article about the research, highlighting a finding that a greater or similar proportion of Britons who identified as Jewish, Traveller or Irish said they had experienced racism compared to most groups of Black or Asian heritage, among them people identifying as Black Caribbean. In a letter to the paper, Abbott responded to the research and its coverage. 'Irish, Jewish and Traveller people all . . . undoubtedly experience prejudice,' she wrote.

> This is similar to racism and the two words are often used as if they are interchangeable. It is true that many types of white people with points of difference, such as redheads, can experience this prejudice. But they are not all their lives subject to racism. In pre-civil rights America, Irish people, Jewish people and Travellers were not required to sit at the back of the bus. In apartheid South Africa, these groups were allowed to vote. And at the height of slavery, there were no white-seeming people manacled on the slave ships.

In some ways, the letter was typical Abbott: provocative, addressing a hugely important subject, persuasive and precisely expressed in places, clumsily so in others. But with there being great sensitivity still about Labour and antisemitism, her comments were widely seen as offensive. The party withdrew the whip from her, as it had from Corbyn, and began an investigation into the episode. Abbott apologised for the letter, saying that it had contained 'errors [which] arose in an initial draft being sent'. Her future as an MP was now uncertain.

Six months later, in October 2023, I met her at her Westminster office. Officially, the investigation into her letter was still ongoing, despite the fact that the document was only two paragraphs long. 'I'm under no illusions about what's going to happen to me,' she said, with a level voice and a neutral expression. She was sitting at her small desk in one of the more remote corners of the parliamentary annex Portcullis House, far from the offices which housed Starmer and his entourage. With the coolness she often showed in public, at first she kept her chair facing the desk, and turned to look at me slightly side on.

'Even before the letter,' she continued, 'there were rumours going round my constituency that I wasn't going to be allowed to stand again.' Since the letter, she believed that Keir Starmer had 'pre-judged' the investigation. The day after the letter's publication, and the day after the party had announced its inquiry, he had publicly commented: 'In my view what she said was to be condemned, it was antisemitic.' From that moment, Abbott told me she had doubted that the investigation would recommend anything other than the most severe punishment. 'No one's readmitting me, or Jeremy, to the party.' And then, 'They' – she meant the party – 'will wait until the very last moment before the election, and then impose somebody as their candidate in Hackney.'

Did she have any regrets about the letter? 'Maybe I could have worded it better.' She said her Jewish constituents were still 'fine' with her being their MP. 'I've spent 36 years fighting antisemitism.'

Her modestly sized office was as crammed with papers and files in purposeful piles as Corbyn's or McDonnell's. It did not look the office of a lazy MP, as she was sometimes said to be. Nor did it look like the office of a politician who had given up.

'People are saying, "You should run as an independent,"' she said. But then she quickly added: 'I wouldn't want to do that. And I'm not sure that Jeremy wants to do that, either. He's torn . . . He's a Labour person. He's always been a Labour person . . . I'm a bit like that.' As for Benn before them, the party was both a vehicle and an obstacle, hostile environment and home.

I asked what her plans were. 'I'll stay an MP for as long as I possibly can.' She was sitting facing me properly now, and her manner was warmer, more expansive. Through a window behind her, an autumn sun flared and faded over the jagged Westminster rooftops, and we talked for a while about how all political careers were finite; and about

487

how conventional politicians and political journalists underestimated the importance of dissidents simply being there, in parliament, representing and inspiring people that conventional politics usually did not care much about – and sometimes also changing society itself.

Then she went quiet, and nodded at a faded set of photos on a windowsill across the room. 'Look, there's the four of us,' she said. The pictures were from a few weeks after the 1987 election: small portraits of her, Bernie Grant, Keith Vaz and Paul Boateng, the quartet of pioneering MPs.

Grant had died in 2000. Vaz had stood down as an MP in 2019, after a sex and drugs scandal. Boateng had become a lord in 2010, after moving rightwards and enjoying a substantial ministerial career in the Blair government, including becoming the first ever black cabinet minister. Yet Abbott gave me no sense that she envied Boateng. Instead she said with satisfaction: 'I'm the last one left standing.'

After the next election, it may be McDonnell, the last after Benn, Corbyn, Livingstone and Abbott to make it into parliament, who has that status. As a white working-class man from the north of England, who rose by hard work, canniness and talent, and who knows, most of the time, when to keep his mouth shut, he is the kind of socialist that the British political and media systems can just about tolerate.

Yet by the autumn of 2023 even he sensed the precariousness of his position in parliament. 'I've been re-selected by my constituency,' he told me. 'I'm careful of what language I use. But anything we [leftwing MPs] say or do is being trawled . . . If they [the Labour hierarchy] see the opportunity of taking me out, they will.' He paused. 'If they are going to come for me, I'll choose the ground on which they take me out. It will be a concrete issue.'

Whether he was to survive or not, he was sure that the left's time would come again. If Starmer got into government, he said, as ever picturing scenarios and planning strategies, 'The opportunity will come after the first 12–18 months. When they look around and think, "Christ, what do we do now? Things have got to change, or we're sunk."'

It is possible that the terrible damage done to Britain by David Cameron and George Osborne, by Theresa May and Boris Johnson, by Liz

Truss and Rishi Sunak, and by the all-consuming capitalism which they all support, will weaken or even end this country's anti-left bias. Yet even if that never happens, politics is about much more than elections. It is about social movements, social mores, ways of seeing and thinking, global causes, global emergencies, contests over resources and over how power is exercised, from inside personal relationships to across multinational corporations. Amid this deeper flux, the new left that Benn, Livingstone, Corbyn, Abbott and McDonnell helped form has been much more of a force. Today, pamphlets issued by Livingstone's 'loony' GLC, about the importance of diversity in recruitment, for example, read like standard memos from human resources. In this and other areas of everyday life, the left has won so many battles that its victory has become invisible.

When these gains are contested, still, as in the right's 'war on woke', there is often a note of panic in the newspaper and Westminster assaults. The small number of Conservatives who currently pay attention to demographics, social trends, and the voting habits of different age groups know that this counter-revolution is probably on borrowed time. Even the Tory victory in 2019, their first convincing one for 32 years, contained an ominous detail for the party, and for other British social conservatives. Among voters aged under 35, across all classes, the Tories lost to Corbyn's socially liberal, supposedly hopeless party by more than two to one.

At the Festival Hall three years later, the most striking thing about the audience to hear Bernie Sanders, apart from its size and enthusiasm, was its age. Everyone was so much younger than he was. There were couples in their twenties, groups of millennials, and middle-aged parents with teenage children. The audience was multiracial, male and female in roughly equal proportions, and mostly dressed in the casual but sometimes prestigious fashions of the modern middle- and working class. I had seen the same mix at Corbyn events, throughout his tumultuous leadership. It did not look like a Britain whose political time had gone for good.

Select Bibliography

A NOTE ON SOURCES

Politicians who have spent a lot of their lives outside the mainstream do not feature as much in traditional histories, official documents and national media coverage as their more orthodox colleagues. Those who work with, or against, such nonconformists often understandably prefer not to be identified. Many of the people I spoke to are not listed here. Nor are all the fragments of video footage, fleeting appearances on news programmes, and brief mentions in political pamphlets, newspapers and online, which together helped form a picture of these rebel lives. What follows is a list of the more conventional and classifiable sources that I found useful. Those that contributed to more than one chapter are listed by their first relevance.

INTRODUCTION

Benn, Tony, *Free At Last!: Diaries 1991–2001*, London: Arrow, 2003

Blair, Cherie, *Speaking for Myself: The Autobiography*, London: Sphere, 2008

Blair, Tony, *A Journey*, London: Hutchinson, 2010

Financial Times, 9 February 2024, 'Why are young people deserting conservatism in Britain but nowhere else?'

McDougall, Linda, *Cherie: The Perfect Life of Mrs Blair*, London: Politico's, 2001

Rentoul, John, *Tony Blair*, London: Warner Books, 1996

Sopel, Jon, *Tony Blair: The Moderniser*, London: Bantam Books, 1995

1. Benn's Epiphany

Adams, Jad, *Tony Benn: A Biography*, London: Biteback, 2011

Ali, Tariq and Susan Watkins, *1968: Marching in the Streets*, London: Bloomsbury, 1998

Barnett, Anthony, author interview, 10 March 2020

Benn, Tony, *Office Without Power: Diaries 1968–1972*, London: Hutchinson, 1988

Benn, Tony, *Out of the Wilderness: Diaries 1963–1967*, London: Hutchinson, 1987

Benn, Tony, *Years of Hope: Diaries, Letters and Papers 1940–1962*, London: Hutchinson, 1994

Black Dwarf, 1 June 1968

Boltanski, Luc, and Eve Chiapello, *The New Spirit of Capitalism*, London: Verso, 2005

Bristol Post, 14 August 2018, 'Looking Back at the Fantastic Year that was 1968', https://www.pressreader.com/uk/bristol-post/20180814/282449939858630

Caute, David, *The Year of the Barricades: A Journey through 1968*, New York: Harper & Row, 1988

Howard, Anthony (editor), *The Crossman Diaries: Selections from the Diaries of a Cabinet Minister, 1964–1970*, London: Cape, 1970

The International Times, 12 July 1968

Livingstone, Ken, *Livingstone's London: A Celebration of People and Places*, London: Muswell Press, 2019

Livingstone, Ken, 'Why Labour Lost', *New Left Review*, July/August 1983, https://newleftreview.org/issues/i140/articles/ken-livingstone-why-labour-lost.pdf

Livingstone, Ken, *You Can't Say That: Memoirs*, London: Faber, 2011

Nelson, Elizabeth, *The British Counter-culture 1966–73: A Study of the Underground Press*, Basingstoke: Macmillan, 1989

Powell, David, *Tony Benn: A Political Life*, London: Continuum, 2002

Quattrocchi, Angelo, and Tom Nairn, *The Beginning of the End: France, May 1968*, London: Verso, 1998

Rowbotham, Sheila, *Promise of a Dream: A Memoir of the Sixties*, London: Allen Lane, 2000

The Times, 24 May 1968

Tony Benn: Will & Testament, Praslin Pictures, 2014

Travers, Tony, *London's Boroughs at 50*, London: Biteback, 2015

Vinen, Richard, *The Long '68: Radical Protest and its Enemies*, London: Penguin, 2018

Widgery, David, *Against Miserabilism: Writings 1968–1992*, Glasgow: Vagabond Voices, 2017

Widgery, David, *The Left in Britain 1956–68*, London: Penguin, 1976

Winstone, Ruth (editor), *The Best of Benn*, London: Hutchinson, 2014

2. Jamaican Imports

Achebe, Chinua, *Things Fall Apart*, London: Heinemann, 1958

A Good Read: Diane Abbott and Bill Nighy, BBC Radio 4, July 1997

Aidoo, Ama Ata, *Our Sister Killjoy, or Reflections from a Black-eyed Squint*, London: Longman, 1977

Bunce, Robin and Samara Linton, *Diane Abbott: The Authorised Biography*, London: Biteback, 2020

Bower, Tom, *Dangerous Hero: Corbyn's Ruthless Plot for Power*, London: Collins, 2019

BuzzFeed News, 25 October 2015, 'John McDonnell: The Socialist Firebrand Who Wants to Be Chancellor', https://www.buzzfeed.com/emilyashton/who-is-john-mcdonnell

Corbyn, Jeremy, author interview, 6 July 2023

Jeremy Corbyn and Ben Okri: in conversation, Festival Hall, 15 July 2016

Diane Abbott in conversation with Tobi Kyeremateng, Black Girl Festival, May 2019, https://www.youtube.com/watch?vKXsaGAJQXow

Eastern Daily Press, 18 December 2016, 'Shadow Chancellor Shares Memories of Growing Up in Great Yarmouth', https://www.edp24.co.uk/news/20854841.shadow-chancellor-shares-memories-growing-great-yarmouth/

Guardian, 26 September 2006, 'Honest John', https://www.theguardian.com/politics/2006/sep/26/labourleadership.labour

Corbyn, Jeremy, foreword to *Imperialism: A Study* by J. A. Hobson, Nottingham: Spokesman Books, 2011

McGuire, Scarlett (editor), *Transforming Moments*, London: Virago, 1989

Mullin, Chris, *Hinterland: A Memoir*, London: Profile Books, 2016

New Statesman, 5 September 2018, 'Who Is the Real John McDonnell?' https://www.newstatesman.com/long-reads/2018/09/who-real-john-mcdonnell

Pope John XXIII, *Pacem in Terris*, 1963

Prospect, 18 September 2018, 'John McDonnell, the Self-made Socialist', https://www.prospectmagazine.co.uk/politics/41715/john-mcdonnell-the-self-made-socialist

Rodney, Walter, *How Europe Underdeveloped Africa*, London: Bogle-L'Ouverture Publications, 1972

Rodney, Walter, *The Groundings with My Brothers*, London: Bogle-L'Ouverture Publications, 1975

Sheppard, David, *On Some Faraway Beach: The Life and Times of Brian Eno*, London: Orion, 2008

Taylor, David and Ruth, *Mr Adams' Free Grammar School*, Chichester: Phillimore, 2002

Thackeray, William Makepiece, *Vanity Fair*, 1847–8

Wilde, Oscar, *De Profundis*, 1905

Woodham-Smith, Cecil, *The Great Hunger: Ireland 1845–9*, London: Hamilton, 1962

3. Politics for a New Society

Benn, Anthony Wedgwood, *The New Politics: A Socialist Reconnaissance*, London: Fabian Society, 1970

Cole, G. D. H., *Guild Socialism Restated*, London: Transaction Books, 1920

Fleet, Ken, author interview, 11 March 2020

Foot, Michael, *Loyalists and Loners*, London: Collins, 1986

Galeano, Eduardo, *Open Veins of Latin America: Five Centuries of the Pillage of a Continent*, London: Monthly Review Press, 1973

Marxism Today, Arthur Scargill interview, April 1981

Polanyi, Karl, *The Great Transformation*, New York: Octagon Books, 1944

Scargill, Arthur, Audrey Wise and Mike Cooley, *A Debate on Workers' Control*, Nottingham: Institute for Workers' Control, 1978

Tawney, R. H., *The Acquisitive Society*, London: G. Bell and Sons Ltd, 1921

Taylor, Richard, *English Radicalism in the Twentieth Century: A Distinctive Politics?* Manchester: Manchester University Press, 2020

Wainwright, Hilary, author interview, 12 February 2020

Wainwright, Hilary, author interview, 26 February 2020

4. The Young Turks

Beckett, Andy, *Pinochet in Piccadilly: Britain and Chile's Hidden History*, London: Faber, 2002

Corbyn, Jeremy, speech to Sussex LRC on Chilean coup's 40th anniversary, https://www.youtube.com/watch?v=p8tn6Mh6mo4

Lansley, Stewart, Sue Goss and Christian Wolmar, *Councils in Conflict: The Rise and Fall of the Municipal Left*, Basingstoke: Macmillan 1989

New Statesman, 16 July 1971

Prince, Rosa, *Comrade Corbyn: A Very Unlikely Coup – How Jeremy Corbyn Stormed to the Labour Leadership*, London: Biteback, 2016
Seyd, Patrick, *The Rise and Fall of the Labour Left*, London: Macmillan, 1987
Wainwright, Hilary, *Labour: A Tale of Two Parties*, London: Hogarth, 1987

5. Workers' Control

Benn, Tony, Frances Morrell and Francis Cripps, A Ten-Year Industrial Strategy for Britain, Nottingham: Institute for Workers' Control, 1975
Benn, Tony, *Against the Tide: Diaries 1973–1976*, London: Hutchinson, 1989
Black, Lawrence, Hugh Pemberton and Pat Thane, *Reassessing 1970s Britain*, Manchester: Manchester University Press, 2013
Coates, Ken (editor), *The New Worker Cooperatives*, Nottingham: Spokesman Books, 1976
Cooley, Mike, *Architect or Bee? The Human Price of Technology*, London: Hogarth, 1987
Holland, Stuart, *The Socialist Challenge*, London: Quartet, 1975
Holland, Stuart (editor), *The State as Entrepreneur: New Dimensions for Public Enterprise – The IRI State Shareholding Formula*, London: Weidenfeld & Nicolson, 1972
Holland, Stuart, *Strategy for Socialism: The Challenge of Labour's Programme*, Nottingham: Bertrand Russell Peace Foundation for Spokesman Books, 1975
Let Us Work Together, London: The Labour Party, 1974
Part, Antony, *The Making of a Mandarin*, London: Deutsch, 1990
State Intervention in Industry: A Workers' Inquiry, Coventry, Liverpool, Newcastle and North Tyneside trades councils, 1980
Tony Benn: Labour's Lost Leader, BBC2, 14 March 2014
Wainwright, Hilary and Dave Elliott, *The Lucas Plan: A New Trade Unionism in the Making?*, London: Allison & Busby, 1982

6. Stop Benn!

Benn, Caroline, *Keir Hardie*, London: Hutchinson, 1992
Benn, Tony, *Dare to Be a Daniel: Then and Now*, London: Hutchinson, 2004
Castle, Barbara, *The Castle Diaries 1964–1976*, London: Papermac, 1990
Coates, Ken (editor), *What Went Wrong: Explaining the Fall of the Labour Government*, Nottingham: Spokesman Books for the Institute of Workers' Control, 1979

Foot, Paul, *Who Framed Colin Wallace?*, London: Macmillan, 1989

Guardian, 16 April 2019, 'European Spies Sought Lessons from Dictators' Brutal "Operation Condor"', https://www.theguardian.com/world/2019/apr/15/operation-condor-european-spies-dictators-cia-documents#:~:text=The%20European%20intelligence%20services%20wanted,groups%20in%20each%20other%27s%20territories.

Haines, Joe, *Glimmers of Twilight: Harold Wilson in Decline*, London: Politico's, 2003

Haines, Joe, *The Politics of Power*, London: Jonathan Cape, 1977

Heffer, Eric, *Never a Yes Man: The Life and Politics of an Adopted Liverpudlian*, London: Verso, 1991

McIntosh, Ronald, *Challenge to Democracy: Politics, Trade Union Power and Economic Failure in the 1970s*, London: Politico's, 2006

Medhurst, John, *That Option No Longer Exists: Britain 1974–76*, Alresford: Zero Books, 2014

Nineham, Chris, *The British State: A Warning*, Alresford: Zero Books, 2019

Observer, 2 February 1975

Saunders, Robert, *Yes to Europe! The 1975 Referendum and Seventies Britain*, Cambridge: Cambridge University Press, 2018

Sunday Telegraph, 12 June 1975

Wilson, Harold, *Final Term: The Labour Government 1974–1976*, London: Weidenfeld & Nicolson, 1979

Wright, Peter, *Spycatcher*, New York: Viking, 1987

7. Seeding the Capital

Abbott, Diane, author interview, 16 October 2023

Abbott, Diane, In Conversation at the Mile End Institute, March 2017, https://soundcloud.com/qmulofficial/diane-abbott-at-the-mile-end-institute

Forgacs, David (editor), *A Gramsci Reader*, London: Lawrence & Wishart, 1988

Hoare, Quintin and Geoffrey Nowell-Smith, *Selections from the Prison Notebooks of Antonio Gramsci*, London: Lawrence & Wishart, 1971

McDonnell, John, author interview, 4 September 2023

New Statesman, 15 March 2016, 'Exclusive: John McDonnell Named Lenin and Trotsky as his Biggest Influences in 2006', https://www.newstatesman.com/politics/2016/03/exclusive-john-mcdonnell-named-lenin-and-trotsky-his-biggest-influences-2006

Observer, 23 January 1977

Observer, 11 November 1979

Shukra, Kalbir, *The Changing Pattern of Black Politics in Britain*, London: Pluto Press, 1998

The Times, 27 November 1976

The Times, 21 January 1977

8. Fine Margins

Benn's Bandwagon, Thames Television, 1981

Benn, Tony, *Arguments for Socialism*, London: Cape, 1979

Benn, Tony, *The End of an Era: Diaries 1980–1990*, London: Hutchinson, 1992

Cromwell, Irving Allen Productions, 1970

Curran, James, Ivor Gaber and Julian Petley, *Culture Wars: The Media and the British Left*, London: Routledge, 2018

Faligot, Roger, *Britain's Military Strategy in Ireland: The Kitson Experiment, 1983*, London: Zed Books, 1983

Foot, Paul, *Three Letters to a Bennite*, London: Socialist Workers Party, 1982

Hill, Christopher, *God's Englishman: Oliver Cromwell and the English Revolution*, London: Weidenfeld & Nicholson, 1970

Hill, Christopher, *The World Turned Upside Down: Radical Ideas During the English Revolution*, London: Penguin, 1975

Lansman, Jon, author interview, 1 July 2020

Marx, Karl and Friedrich Engels, *The Communist Manifesto*, London: Lawrence & Wishart, 1948

New Statesman, 10 June 1977

New Statesman, 20 February 1981, 'What did a Tory MP say in the Cumberland Hotel?'

Panorama, BBC1, 23 February 1981

Routledge, Paul, *Public Servant, Secret Agent: The Elusive Life and Violent Death of Airey Neave*, London: Fourth Estate, 2002

Winstanley, Brownlow Mollo, 1975

Winstanley, Gerrard, *The mysterie of God, concerning the whole creation, mankinde. To be made known to every man and woman, after seaven dispensations and seasons of time are passed over. According to the councell of God, revealed to his servants*, London, 1649

9. 'Take the Power!'

Ali, Tariq, author interview, 11 September 2019

Bash, Graham, author interview, 8 September 2017

Beckett, Andy, *Promised You a Miracle: UK80–82*, London: Allen Lane, 2015

Beer, Samuel H., *Britain Against Itself: The Political Contradictions of Collectivism*, London: Faber, 1982

Benn, Tony, *Parliament, People and Power: Agenda for a Free Society: Interviews with New Left Review*, London: Verso, 1982

The Campaign, BBC2, 22 January 1983

Carvel, John, *Citizen Ken*, London: Chatto & Windus, 1987

Forsyth, Frederick, *The Fourth Protocol*, London: Hutchinson, 1984

Freeman, Alan, *The Benn Heresy*, London: Pluto Press, 1982

Hatherley, Owen, *Red Metropolis: Socialism and the Government of London*, London: Repeater, 2020

Jaggi, Max, Roger Muller and Sil Schmid, *Red Bologna*, London: Writers and Readers Publishing Cooperative, 1977

Knight, Chris, author interview, 8 September 2017

Livingstone, Ken, author interview 11 March 2013

London Edinburgh Weekend Return Group, *In and Against the State*, London: Pluto, 1979

London Evening Standard, 8 May 1981

London Labour Briefing, February 1980

London Labour Briefing, August 1980

London Labour Briefing, June 1981

New Statesman, 15 January 2018, 'Jon Lansman's Long March to Labour's Top Table', https://www.newstatesman.com/politics/uk-politics/2018/01/jon-lansman-s-long-march-labour-s-top-table

Sunday Times, 12 April 1981

The Times, 9 December 1981

Veness, Keith, author interview, 8 September 2017

Veness, Valerie, author interview, 8 September 2017

Vote Labour in London: A Summary of Labour's GLC Election Proposals, London: Labour Party, 1981

10. A Beginning and an Ending

Beckett, Andy, *When the Lights Went Out: Britain in the Seventies*, London: Faber, 2009

Golding, John, *Hammer of the Left: The Battle for the Soul of the Labour Party*, London: Biteback, 2016

Hayter, Dianne, *Fightback!: Labour's Traditional Right in the 1970s and 1980s*, Manchester: Manchester University Press, 2005

Jones, Trevor, Brian MacLean and Jock Young, *The Islington Crime Survey: Crime, Victimization and Policing in Inner City London*, Aldershot: Gower, 1986

The New Hope for Britain, London: Labour Party, 1983

11. Man of the People

Clay, Bob, author interview, 8 September 2017

Hannah, Simon, *A Party with Socialists In It: A History of the Labour Left*, London: Pluto Press, 2018

Miliband, Ralph, *Parliamentary Socialism*, London: George Allen & Unwin, 1961

Newsnight, BBC2, February 1984

Simpson, Alan, author interview, 15 September 2017

12. Socialism in One City

Ali, Tariq and Ken Livingstone, *Who's Afraid of Margaret Thatcher?: Tariq Ali in Conversation with Ken Livingstone*, London: Verso, 1984

Denselow, Robin, *When the Music's Over: The Story of Political Pop*, London: Faber, 1989

Hollingsworth, Mark, author interview, 27 March 2013

Hollingsworth, Mark, *The Press and Political Dissent: A Question of Censorship*, London: Pluto Books, 1986

Islington Tribune, 'Livingstone Is Not Anti-Semitic – But His Poor Judgment Invites Notoriety', 18 April 2017, https://www.islingtontribune.co.uk/article/livingstone-is-not-anti-semitic-but-his-poor-judgment-invites-notoriety

Livingstone, Ken, *If Voting Changed Anything, They'd Abolish It*, London: Collins, 1987

Mackintosh, Maureen and Hilary Wainwright (editors), *A Taste of Power: The Politics of Local Economics*, London: Verso, 1987

Marxism Today, April 1986

Rich, Dave, *The Left's Jewish Problem: Jeremy Corbyn, Israel and Anti-Semitism*, London: Biteback, 2018

Rowbotham, Sheila, Lynne Segal and Hilary Wainwright, *Beyond the Fragments: Feminism and the Making of Socialism*, London: Merlin, 1980

Sunday Times, 19 July 1981

Waller, Robert, *Moulding Political Opinion*, London: Croom Helm, 1988

Whitehouse, Wes, *GLC – The Inside Story*, Sunbury-on-Thames: James Lester, 2000

13. 'A Lot of Hope Rides on Our Victory Tonight'

Abbott, Diane, 1987 election victory speech, https://www.youtube.com/watch?app=desktop&v=3g7mgTQL70U

Butler, Tim, *Gentrification and the Middle Classes*, Aldershot: Ashgate, 1997

Donington, Katie, Ryan Hanley and Jessica Moody (editors), *Britain's History and Memory of Transatlantic Slavery: Local Nuances of a 'National Sin'*, Liverpool: Liverpool University Press, 2016

Grant, Eric A., *Dawn to Dusk: A Biography of Bernie Grant*, London: ITUNI Books, 2006

Harrison, Paul, *Inside the Inner City: Life Under the Cutting Edge*, London: Penguin, 1983

MacWilliam, Rab, *Dramas and Dissent: Twelve Hectic Years in Stoke Newington as Seen Through the Pages of its Local Magazine*, London: Clissold Books, 2013

Observer, 15 December 1985

The Times, 18 May 1987

The Times, 22 May 1987

The Times, 12 June 1987

Wright, Patrick, *A Journey Through Ruins: The Last Days of London*, London: Radius, 1991

14. Exile at the Westdale Hotel

Blade, John, author interview, 15 October 2019

'Derbyshire Coalfield – Chesterfield Area', Northern Mine Research Society, https://www.nmrs.org.uk/mines-map/coal-mining-in-the-british-isles/derbynotts/chesterfield/

15. A Desk in the Corridor

Ali, Tariq, author interview, 11 September 2017

Costello, Nicholas, Jonathan Michie and Seumas Milne, *Beyond the Casino Economy: Planning for the 1990s*, London: Verso, 1989

Hefferman, Richard and Mike Marqusee, *Defeat from the Jaws of Victory: Inside Kinnock's Labour Party*, London: Verso, 1992

Jacques, Martin, author interview, 8 March 2018

Kogan, David, *Protest and Power: The Battle for the Labour Party*, London: Bloomsbury, 2019

Livingstone, Ken, *Livingstone's Labour: A Programme for the Nineties*, London: Unwin Hyman, 1989

Mullin, Chris, *A Walk-on Part: Diaries 1994–1999*, London: Profile, 2012

Panitch, Leo and Colin Leys, *The End of Parliamentary Socialism: From New Left to New Labour*, London: Verso, 2001

Question Time, BBC1, June 1987

The Wilderness Years, BBC2, 1995

16. 'A Wasted Resource'

Benn, Tony and Andrew Hood, *Common Sense: A New Constitution for Britain*, London: Hutchinson, 1993

Benn, Tony, *More Time for Politics: Diaries 2001–2007*, London: Hutchinson, 2010

Cowley, Philip, *Revolts and Rebellions: Parliamentary Voting Under Blair*, London: Politico's, 2002

Desert Island Discs: Tony Benn, BBC Radio 4, January 1989

Finlayson, Alan, *Making Sense of New Labour*, London: Lawrence & Wishart, 2003

The Islington Cook Book, London: NSPCC, 1993

Sinclair, Ian, *The March that Shook Blair: An Oral History of 15 February 2003*, London: Peace News Press, 2013

'Sixty Times Jeremy Corbyn Stood with Jewish People', in Jamie Stern-Weiner, (editor), *Antisemitism and the Labour Party*, London: Verso, 2019

Stewart, John, author interview, 6 September 2017

Winstone, Ruth, author interview, 17 September 2019

17. The Limits of Leftism

Carvel, John, *Turn Again Livingstone*, London: Profile Books, 1999

Hosken, Andrew, *Ken: The Ups and Downs of Ken Livingstone*, London: Arcadia, 2008

Ken Livingstone's Manifesto for London: Ken 4 London, London: Livingstone for London, 2000

Minton, Anna (editor) and Ken Livingstone, *Being Red: A Politics for the Future*, London: Pluto Press, 2016

Prospect, 28 April 2007, 'Interview: Ken Livingstone', https://www.prospect-magazine.co.uk/essays/57745/interview-ken-livingstone

Ross, John, *Thatcher and Friends: The Anatomy of the Tory Party*, London: Pluto, 1983

Socialist Economic Bulletin, June 1994

Socialist Economic Bulletin, February 1996

Socialist Economic Bulletin, March 1998

Travers, Tony, *The Politics of London: Governing an Ungovernable City*, Basingstoke: Palgrave Macmillan, 2004

18. 'A Sealed Tomb'

Benn, Tony, *A Blaze of Autumn Sunshine: The Last Diaries*, London: Arrow, 2014

Come Dine with Me, ITV Studios Entertainment, 10 January 2011

Desert Island Discs: Diane Abbott, BBC Radio 4, 23 May 2008

Financial Times, 30 March 2015, 'UK election 2015: Labour strains', https://www.ft.com/content/f8bacb60-d640-11e4-b3e7-00144feab7de

Fisher, Mark, *Capitalist Realism: Is There No Alternative?*, Ropley: O Books, 2009

Gollentz, Marie, *Stop the War: A Graphic History*, London: Francis Boutle, 2011

McDonnell, John, *Another World Is Possible: A Manifesto for 21st Century Socialism*, London: Labour Representation Committee, 2007

Minkin, Lewis, *The Blair Supremacy: A Study in the Politics of Labour's Party Management*, Manchester: Manchester University Press, 2014

Mullin, Chris, *Decline and Fall: Diaries 2005–2010*, London: Profile, 2011

Murray, Andrew and Lindsey German, *Stop the War: The Story of Britain's Biggest Mass Movement*, London: Bookmarks, 2005

Murray, Andrew, *The Fall and Rise of the British Left*, London: Verso, 2019

Murray, Andrew, *Stop the War and its Critics*, London: Manifesto Press, 2016

Shah, Samir, author interview, 7 September 2017

19. Return of the Repressed

Corbyn, Jeremy, *2015 Leadership Manifesto: The Economy in 2020*

Corbyn's Cabinet Chaos: The Inside Story, Sky News, 14 September 2015

Jeremy Corbyn the Musical: The Motorcycle Diaries, Rupert Myers and Bobby Friedman, 2016

Fisher, Andrew, author interview, 11 February 2020

Fisher, Andrew, *The Failed Experiment: And How to Build an Economy that Works*, London: Comerford and Miller, 2014

Forde, Martin, *The Forde Report*, 2022, https://labour.org.uk/wp-content/uploads/2023/01/The-Forde-Report.pdf

'Jeremy Corbyn: The Outsider', Vice News, 1 June 2016

Livingstone, Ken, author interview, 12 September 2017

Milne, Seumas, *The Revenge of History: The Battle for the 21st Century*, London: Verso, 2012

New Statesman, 'The Thin Controller', 16 April 2016

Nunns, Alex, *The Candidate: Jeremy Corbyn's Improbable Path to Power*, New York: OR Books, 2018

O'Neill, Martin and Joe Guinan, *The Institutional Turn: Labour's New Political Economy*, Renewal, 2018

Pogrund, Gabriel and Yorke, Harry, 'The secretive guru who plotted Keir Starmer's path to power with undeclared cash', *Sunday Times*, 12 November 2023

Puppet Masters: The Men Who Really Run Britain, Channel 4, 4 November 2019

Rutherford, Jonathan, 'What Is Labour Together?', *New Statesman*, 15 November 2023

Seymour, Richard, *Corbyn: The Strange Rebirth of Radical Politics*, London: Verso, 2017

20. Peak Corbyn

Alternative Models of Ownership, Labour party, 2017

Barbrook, Richard, author interview, 6 June 2019

Bastani, Aaron, *Fully Automated Luxury Communism: A Manifesto*, London: Verso, 2019

Berry, Christine, author interview, 20 November 2018

Berry, Christine and Joe Guinan, *People Get Ready!: Preparing for a Corbyn Government*, New York: OR Books, 2019

Bolton, Matt and Frederick Harry Pitts, *Corbynism: A Critical Approach*, Bingley: Emerald, 2018

Brown, Matthew, author interview, 27 November 2018

Co-operatives Unleashed, New Economics Foundation, 2018

Corbyn Run, Rosa Carbo-Mascarell and Richard Barbrook, 2017

Cowley, Philip and Dennis Kavanagh, *The British General Election of 2017*, Basingstoke: Palgrave Macmillan, 2018

Economist, 19 October 2017, 'Preston, Jeremy Corbyn's Model Town', https://www.economist.com/britain/2017/10/19/preston-jeremy-corbyns-model-town

Economist, 17 May 2018, 'Corbynomics Would Change Britain – But Not in the Way Most People Think', https://www.economist.com/britain/2018/05/17/corbynomics-would-change-britain-but-not-in-the-way-most-people-think

Financial Times, 2 March 2018, 'John McDonnell Interview: Is Britain Ready for a Socialist Chancellor?', https://www.ft.com/mcdonnell

Financial Times, 31 August 2019, 'Jeremy Corbyn's Plan to Rewrite the Rules of the UK Economy', https://www.ft.com/content/e1028dda-ca49-11e9-a1f4-366940iba76f

For the Many Not the Few: The Labour Party Manifesto 2017, London: Labour Party, 2017

Goodwin, Adam G., Dicken Goodwin and Jonathan Parkyn, *Jeremy Corbyn Annual 2019*, London: Portico, 2018

Guinan, Joe, author interview, 14 November 2018

Howell, Steve, *Game Changer: Eight Weeks that Transformed British Politics*, Abercynon: AccentPress, 2018

Jacobs, Michael, author interview, 8 November 2018

Kelly, Marjorie and Ted Howard, *The Making of a Democratic Economy: Building Prosperity for the Many, Not Just the Few*, Oakland: Berrett-Koehler, 2019

Lawrence, Mathew, author interview, 19 November 2018

McDonnell, John, author interview, 1 July 2017

McDonnell, John, author interview, 27 November 2018

McDonnell, John (editor), *Economics for the Many*, London: Verso, 2018

New Statesman, 16–22 June 2017

'Our Town', Labour party political broadcast, September 2018

Perryman, Mark (editor), *The Corbyn Effect*, London: Lawrence & Wishart, 2017

Standing, Guy, 'Basic Income as Common Dividends: A Report for the Shadow Chancellor of the Exchequer', London: Progressive Economy Forum, 2019

21. 'They're Coming at Us Now'

'Antisemitism Barometer 2017', Campaign Against Antisemitism

'Antisemitism in the UK', House of Commons Home Affairs committee, 2016

Chessum, Michael, *This Is Only the Beginning: The Making of a New Left, from Anti-Austerity to the Fall of Corbyn*, London: Bloomsbury, 2022

'General Election 2019', Loughborough University, https://www.lboro.ac.uk/news-events/general-election/

Jacobin, 9 April 2018

Jones, Owen, *This Land: The Story of a Movement*, London: Allen Lane, 2020

Marqusee, Mike, *If I Am Not for Myself: Journey of an Anti-Zionist Jew*, London: Verso, 2011

Murray, Andrew, *Is Socialism Possible in Britain? Reflections on the Corbyn Years*, London: Verso, 2022

New Statesman, 13 November 2018, 'How John McDonnell Plans to Transform the State from Within', https://www.newstatesman.com/politics/2018/11/how-john-mcdonnell-plans-transform-state-within

Panorama, BBC1, 10 July 2019, 'Is Labour Anti-Semitic'?

Philo, Greg, Mike Berry, Justin Schlosberg, Antony Lerman and David Miller, *Bad News for Labour: Antisemitism, the Party and Public Belief*, London: Pluto Press, 2019

Pogrund, Gabriel and Patrick Maguire, *Left Out: The Inside Story of Labour Under Corbyn*, London: Bodley Head, 2020

Staetsky, Daniel L., *Antisemitism in contemporary Great Britain: A Study of attitudes towards Jews and Israel*, London: Institute for Jewish Policy Research, 2017

Winstanley, Asa, *Weaponising Anti-Semitism: How the Israel Lobby Brought Down Jeremy Corbyn*, New York: OR Books, 2023

22. 'We Are Building to Reach the Stars'

'Election Review 2019', Labour Together, https://electionreview.labourtogether.uk

'Funding Real Change', Labour party 2019, https://labour.org.uk/wp-content/uploads/2019/11/Funding-Real-Change.pdf

Gilbert, Jeremy, openDemocracy, 13 January 2020, 'It Was the Centrist Dads Who Lost It', https://www.opendemocracy.net/en/opendemocracyuk/it-was-centrist-dads-who-lost-it/

Gilbert, Jeremy, openDemocracy, 14 January 2020, 'Corbyn Was Intensely Moral, But Never a Working Class Hero', https://www.opendemocracy.net/en/opendemocracyuk/corbyn-was-intensely-moral-never-working-class-hero/

Gilbert, Jeremy, openDemocracy, 15 January 2020, 'Labour Should Have Argued Against the Last 40 Years, Not Just the Last Ten', https://www.opendemocracy.net/en/opendemocracyuk/labour-should-have-argued-against-last-40-years-not-just-last-ten/

Gilbert, Jeremy, openDemocracy, 16 January 2020, 'Labour Let the Right Shape Both Sides of the Brexit Debate', https://www.opendemocracy.net/en/opendemocracyuk/labour-let-right-shape-both-sides-brexit-debate/

It's Time for Real Change: The Labour Party Manifesto 2019, London: Labour Party, 2019

Jara, Joan, *Victor: An Unfinished Song*, London: Jonathan Cape, 1983

Labour Party Race & Faith Manifesto, London: Labour Party, 2019

Leaders' Debate, BBC1, 6 December 2019

Leaders' Debate, ITV, 19 November 2019

Mattinson, Deborah, *Beyond the Red Wall: Why Labour Lost, How the Conservatives Won and What Will Happen Next?*, London: Biteback, 2020

Rayson, Steve, *The Fall of the Red Wall*, independently published, 2020

'Tory Landslide, Progressive Split: A Datapraxis Analysis of the UK General Election', Datapraxis, 2019

Epilogue

Claim the Future, John McDonnell in conversation with Gordon Brown, 22 September 2020, https://www.google.com/search?client=safari&rls=en&q=%22john+mcdonnell+in+conversation+with+Gordon+Brown%22&ie=UTF-8&oe=UTF-8

Gilbert, Jeremy, *Twenty-First Century Socialism*, Cambridge: Polity Press, 2020

Livingstone, Ken, author interview, 4 February 2020

Milburn, Keir, *Generation Left*, Cambridge: Polity Press, 2019

Sanders, Bernie, *It's OK to Be Angry About Capitalism*, London: Penguin, 2023

Wainwright, Hilary, *A New Politics from the Left*, Cambridge: Polity Press, 2018

Acknowledgments

First, I would like to thank Diane Abbott, John McDonnell, Jeremy Corbyn and Ken Livingstone for talking to me during the formal research period for this book, and Tony Benn for talking to me when this book was forming without my quite knowing it yet. I would also like to thank these other interviewees: Tariq Ali, Richard Barbrook, Anthony Barnett, Graham Bash, Christine Berry, Matthew Brown, Bob Clay, Andrew Fisher, the late Ken Fleet, Joe Guinan, Mark Hollingsworth, Martin Jacques, Michael Jacobs, Chris Knight, Jon Lansman, Mat Lawrence, James Meadway, Samir Shah, Alan Simpson, John Stewart, Keith Veness, Valerie Veness, Hilary Wainwright and Ruth Winstone. Tony Simpson of the Bertrand Russell Peace Foundation took great care to arrange my conversation with Ken Fleet, a few weeks before Ken died. Thank you, too, to the many other interviewees who asked not to be named. Speaking up for the left in Britain – and sometimes simply providing accurate facts about them – is not always without risks.

Partly for that reason, there are far fewer books about the left than about the Labour party's other factions, or other parts of the British political spectrum. I would particularly like to thank these authors, whose revelatory books (detailed in the bibliography) did much to help to make this one possible: Jad Adams, Robin Bunce and Samara Linton, John Carvel, Owen Jones, Alex Nunns, Gabriel Pogrund and Patrick Maguire, Rosa Prince, and Richard Seymour. Tony Benn's diaries were also invaluable.

At the *Guardian*, many colleagues provided ideas, commissions and conversations which, intentionally or otherwise, contributed to this book, especially Rob Evans, Joseph Harker, Simon Hattenstone,

Charlotte Higgins, Yohann Koshy, Paul Laity, Clare Longrigg, Kirsty Major, Hugh Muir, Jonathan Shainin, Barbara Speed, Jenny Stevens and David Wolf. Uki Goni provided me with valuable evidence of how far some South American governments were prepared to go to suppress the left, and about how some in the British state were interested in their methods. Other people outside the *Guardian* listened patiently to my theories and stories about the left, and sometimes made me think again, particularly Andrew Bagley, Henny Beaumont, Tom Campbell, Daniel Cohen, Adam Curtis, Will Davies, Chandrika Deshpande, Steve Epstein, Anna Funder, Jeremy Gilbert, Dan Hillman, Stuart Kerr, Conrad Leach and Paul Myerscough.

At the British Library, the staff of the Social Sciences reading room helped provide me with so many forgotten but vital books, journals, political newspapers and pamphlets, and the staff of Origin Coffee made me enough macchiatos to have the energy to read them. At lunchtimes, the Gazelle Dates café made me delicious sandwiches and reminded me that there was an outside world. Sometimes, trade unionists involved in the waves of strikes during 2022 and 2023 would come into the café from their nearby London offices and picket lines. Throughout the time I worked on this book, the British left was busier than for years, protesting, organising, thinking – and sometimes even winning elections. All this was a regular and very useful reminder that leftwing politics is rarely the dead end its enemies would love it to be.

My editors at Penguin, Tom Penn and Eva Hodgkin, were always enthusiastic and perceptive. They appreciated that this book was meant to be full of possibility as well as melancholy. And the revisions and additions they suggested made the book richer. Robert Sharman copyedited the manuscript with great precision, but also sensitivity and flexibility.

My agent Sarah Chalfant and her colleagues at The Wiley Agency, Jessica Bullock and Alba Ziegler-Bailey, understood the book, and how it related to other books and journalism I had written, from the very beginning. And they were always resourceful about how its stories and ideas might best be disseminated.

My parents, who both passed away during the research and writing of this book, were fascinated by, rather than supporters of, their near-contemporary Tony Benn. They brought me up, as a child in the 1970s and a teenager in the 1980s, to see Benn as a maverick, which helped get me thinking that he was someone whom it might be worth learning more about. They were excited by what they knew of this book. Richard Holloway and Jean Holloway, and Elizabeth Beckett and Robert Milnes were also always interested in how I was getting on, without asking too many questions about deadlines.

At home, Lorna and Gillen let me earnestly explain Benn and his political descendants to them without too much Gen Z mockery, and with occasional expressions of concern that I might never experience a radical socialist government. Meanwhile Sara, still the best ex-editor in the country, discussed the book with me for hours, read the manuscript, and pointed out where its themes and punctuation became too ambitious. All radical projects require a little discipline.

Index

Abbott, Diane (DA): personality of, 6, 35–6, 110, 177, 298–9, 485; constituency life in Hackney North, 7–8, 296–9; as absent from political histories, 8, 360–1; background of/early life (to 1973), 34–8; early experiences of racism, 35, 37; dress-style/physical appearance, 36, 110, 112, 247, 257, 460; at Newnham College, 38, 109–10; as graduate trainee at Home Office, 110–11; clear diction of, 110, 112, 254; vulnerability of as public figure, 110, 295–7, 299, 485; as race relations officer at NCCL, 111–12, 176; joins Labour Party (1978), 112–13; friendship with JC, 113, 115, 185, 248, 249–50, 256, 295, 374; meets JC (1978), 113; as civil libertarian, 115, 138, 368–9, 417, 485–6; personal life, 115, 185, 243, 367; relationship with JC, 115, 185; helps KL in Hampstead, 117; TB as a political hero of, 138, 261; at *Briefing*'s editorial meetings, 160; media career, 176–8, 242–3, 249, 250; tone in public settings, 177, 246–7, 254, 257, 298–9; as local councillor in Westminster, 243–4, 250; pragmatism of, 243, 244, 369–70; trade union jobs, 243, 250; and Black Sections movement, 245–7, 252, 255; party conference speech (1984), 246–7; defeated by KL in Brent East selection, 247–50; KL and forged document incident, 248–9, 256; not selected in Westminster North, 250; and Hackney North's candidacy selection, 252–5; 1987 election in Hackney North, 255–6, 257, 261; media attacks on/harassment of, 255, 296, 470; *New York Times* interview (1987), 256–7; inhospitality faced by at Westminster, 287–8, 294–5; marginalized by Labour leadership in Commons, 287–8, 294; special branch files on, 290; *Question Time* appearance (June 1987), 296; and New Labour, 299–300, 317, 352, 368–9, 374–5; in *The Islington Cookbook*, 303; and KL's 'Right to Stand' campaign, 331;